AF834944

Advanced Praise for *Queering EMDR Therapy*

"The *Queering EMDR Therapy* collection is a must-read for EMDR Therapists seeking to practice with authenticity, inclusivity, and anti-oppressive intention. This book is a groundbreaking anthology that brings voice, visibility, and validation to LGBTQIAA2S+ experiences in trauma treatment. With unflinching vulnerability and liberatory vision, Roshni Chabra and 26 contributors weave essays, narratives, and art into a resource that is both profoundly human and professionally transformative."

–Nedra Glover Tawwab, LCSW
New York Times Best-Selling Author

"*Queering EMDR Therapy* distills what I have witnessed in clients, colleagues, and myself: the moment where healing requires not just clinical skill, but truth-telling. It captures the exhaustion of internal division and the urgency of becoming whole. There was a time in my professional life when I stood aligned with frameworks that excluded and patholigized identities now rightfully centred in this volume. Through study, reflection, and the labour of unlearning, my understanding has changed. What has emerged is a more compassionate, inclusive vision of EMDR Therapy and the people it serves. This anthology, edited by Roshni Chabra and shaped by the voices of 27 remarkable contributors, is a bold reclamation. It expands EMDR's ethical and conceptual boundaries and invites us to practise trauma therapy not only with competence, but with courage."

–Professor Paul W. Miller, MD, MB, BCh, BAO, DMH, MRCPsych, FRSA
Author of *EMDR Therapy for Schizophrenia and Other Psychoses*

"*Queering EMDR Therapy* is a necessary, bold, and soul-stirring disruption of the status quo. This collection reclaims EMDR as a tool for liberation—centering voices, bodies, and truths too often sidelined in clinical spaces. It's not just a book; it's a call to practice with integrity, creativity, and fierce inclusivity."

–Rebecca Kase, LCSW, EMDR Trainer & CEO of Trauma Therapist Institute
Author of *Polyvagal-Informed EMDR and The Polyvagal Solution*

"Get ready to widen the discourse in EMDR to include more diverse perspectives and practices. *Queering EMDR* explores complex and often difficult themes with courage, honesty, and clinical expertise. One of the most essential tasks of allyship is to listen, and it was a true honor to read the diverse firsthand experiences of the authors who illuminate intersections of Queer identity, race, neurodivergence, sexual expression, attachment, oppression, discrimination, and grief. This book challenges the cisnormative and heteronormative frameworks that have long shaped clinical research and practice. As a therapist committed to providing Queer-affirming trauma therapy, often in contexts where Queer identities are criminalized or heavily stigmatized, I have found *Queering EMDR Therapy* to be an illuminating resource on how to be more affirming of my clients' lived realities. The authors offer innovative skills and guidance on adapting EMDR to be more inclusive of sexual and gender diversity, helping clients heal from the pain of stigma and discrimination and move toward liberation in their lives. *Queering EMDR Therapy* is a timely and urgent resource for all clinicians who strive for justice, equality, and truly affirming care."

–Jennifer Marchand, MA, CCC, RCAT, EMDRIA-Approved Consultant
Author of *Ecotherapy-Informed EMDR: A Holistic and Creative Approach to Providing Culturally Responsive Trauma Treatment*

"This collection of essays is exceptional; this will lead to the creation of a new Frontier. It is a celebration of breaking the chains of Social Structure through the "Queer Lens." This body of work will provide EMDR clinicians guidance in working and understanding the uniqueness of true diversity within the Queer population."

–Diane DesPlantes, LCSW, S.U.R.G.E., EMDRIA-Approved Trainer

"Powerful and liberating, this book is both a call to action and a compassionate guide informed by lived experience, communal wisdom and clinical insight. *Queering EMDR Therapy* challenges us to rethink trauma not just as an individual experience, but as something deeply shaped by social context, systemic harm, and marginalisation. It invites readers to critically deconstruct EMDR through a neurodiversity, queer, and gender-affirming lens."

–Monique Mitchelson
Autistic, ADHD'er and Queer Clinical Psychologist, M. Psych
Co-Director of Divergent Futures Training, Co-Host of The Neurodivergent Woman Podcast, Co-Author of *The Neurodivergence Skills Workbook for Autism* and *ADHD: Cultivate Self-Compassion, Live Authentically, and Be Your Own Advocate*

"*Queering EMDR Therapy* captures the essence of healing layered systemic trauma specific to the queer identity. The stories on the pages reflected back to me threads of my own narrative and those of my clients in a deeply touching and inspiring way. I'm in awe of the beautiful process work the authors shared in their personal narratives, their brave clients' stories and the compassionate lens the practitioners bring to healing queer trauma. I recommend this book to anyone wishing to learn more about post-traumatic growth within intersections of gender, sexuality, and self expression using EMDR standard protocol. For clinicians wanting to expand their frameworks for working with non-heteronormative clients this book is a must read."

–Gail Neves, LMHC, EMDRIA-Approved Consultant
Integrative Psychedelic Therapist & Educator

"Reading *Queering EMDR Therapy* feels like being welcomed into a space of profound vulnerability and unwavering trust. This book is not just a guide—it is a deeply personal journey through each author's own childhoods, struggles, and triumphs, woven seamlessly with clinical expertise. This book is a powerful tool for anyone seeking to provide genuine, empathetic support to queer communities. The contributors remind us that healing is not just a process of theory, but of humanity. This is a remarkable piece of work that will undoubtedly resonate with anyone in the EMDR community."

–Suzanne Rutti, MSW, LISW-S
EMDRIA-Approved Trainer and Consultant
Author of the forthcoming, *STARS: Secondary Traumatic Stress, Awareness, Resilience, and Support*

QUEERING EMDR THERAPY

Creative Mindfulness Media, the publishing home of The Institute for Creative Mindfulness, is committed to publishing exceptional materials addressing topics in the areas of trauma recovery, addiction recovery, and the use of embodied expressive arts approaches to create healing and wellness.

For more information, visit www.instituteforcreativemindfulness.com

© 2025 by Roshni Chabra (Editor) and Jamie Marich (Production Editor)
All rights reserved. Published 2025. Printed in the United States of America.

No part of this publication may be reproduced, stored in a retrieval system, or transmitted in any form or by any means, electronic, mechanical, photocopying, recording, or otherwise, without the written permission of the publisher.

Publisher: Creative Mindfulness Media
123 S. Miller Rd. #101A
Fairlawn, OH 44333
Editor: Roshni Chabra
Production Editor: Jamie Marich

25 24 23 22 21 20   1 2 3 4 5

Library of Congress Control Number: 2025910624
Print ISBN: 979-8-218-66075-8

Second Printing 2026

Every attempt has been made to contact copyright holders. If copyright holders have not been properly acknowledged please contact us. Creative Mindfulness Media will be happy to rectify the omission in future printings of this book.

Publisher's Note: This book contains general information about trauma, addiction, recovery, and wellness. The information is not medical advice. This book is not an alternative to medical advice from your doctor or other professional healthcare provider.

Our books represent the experiences and opinions of their authors only. Every effort has been made to ensure that events, institutions, and statistics presented in our books are accurate and up-to-date. To protect their privacy, the names of some of the people, places, and institutions in this book may have been changed.

Cover art by Irene Rodriguez
Cover design and interior design by Chris Berge, Berge Design

To see full color versions of the artwork in this book, please visit:
www.queeringemdr.com

QUEERING EMDR THERAPY

CREATIVE MINDFULNESS MEDIA

Creative Mindfulness Media, the publishing home of The Institute for Creative Mindfulness, is committed to publishing exceptional materials addressing topics in the areas of trauma recovery, addiction recovery, and the use of embodied expressive arts approaches to create healing and wellness.

For more information, visit www.instituteforcreativemindfulness.com

© 2025 by Roshni Chabra (Editor) and Jamie Marich (Production Editor)
All rights reserved. Published 2025. Printed in the United States of America.

No part of this publication may be reproduced, stored in a retrieval system, or transmitted in any form or by any means, electronic, mechanical, photocopying, recording, or otherwise, without the written permission of the publisher.

Publisher: Creative Mindfulness Media
123 S. Miller Rd. #101A
Fairlawn, OH 44333
Editor: Roshni Chabra
Production Editor: Jamie Marich

25 24 23 22 21 20 1 2 3 4 5

Library of Congress Control Number: 2025910624
Print ISBN: 979-8-218-66075-8

Second Printing 2026

Every attempt has been made to contact copyright holders. If copyright holders have not been properly acknowledged please contact us. Creative Mindfulness Media will be happy to rectify the omission in future printings of this book.

Publisher's Note: This book contains general information about trauma, addiction, recovery, and wellness. The information is not medical advice. This book is not an alternative to medical advice from your doctor or other professional healthcare provider.

Our books represent the experiences and opinions of their authors only. Every effort has been made to ensure that events, institutions, and statistics presented in our books are accurate and up-to-date. To protect their privacy, the names of some of the people, places, and institutions in this book may have been changed.

Cover art by Irene Rodriguez
Cover design and interior design by Chris Berge, Berge Design

To see full color versions of the artwork in this book, please visit:
www.queeringemdr.com

QUEERING EMDR THERAPY

Edited by **Roshni Chabra, LMFT**
Foreword by **Dr. Jamie Marich**

We want to dedicate this book to all who will read and benefit from knowing you are not alone.

To Angela, Baba and our Queer Elders, thank you for paving the way. We will keep on fighting!

Production Team

Editor

Roshni Chabra, LMFT (she/her) holds bachelor's degrees in Women's Studies and Psychology, and a Master's in Feminist Clinical Psychology. Chabra is Co-Owner, Chief Clinical Officer, and MET(T)A (Mindfulness and EMDR Treatment Template for Agencies) Protocol Agency Director at Roots Training Group, LLC (formerly StartAgain Associates, Inc.) Chabra is also the Founder and President of Lavender Healing Collective, a psychotherapy practice dedicated to supporting BIPOC LGBTQ+ communities. Chabra is an EMDR International Association Certified Therapist, Approved Consultant, and EMDR Trainer. With over 20 years in the mental health field, she has supported diverse populations and specializes in working with LGBTQ+ individuals, couples, families, people struggling with chronic pain and chronic illness, sexual violence and addiction. Her background includes five years in the Rape Crisis Movement, providing direct services and holding leadership roles. Chabra has extensive experience in nonprofit management, having served as Program Manager and Director in Wraparound services for families in challenging systems. Chabra additionally acts as a Clinical Advisor to HapTech Holdings Inc., which holds 16 patents for innovative 360-degree haptic feedback technology. Chabra is passionate about healing through mindfulness, EMDR Therapy and technology.

Production Editor and Foreword Writer

Dr. Jamie Marich (she/they/we) began her career as a humanitarian aid worker in Bosnia-Hercegovina from 2000-2003. Marich is the founder of the Institute for Creative Mindfulness (soon to become the Creative Mindfulness Network). Marich is the author of over a dozen books and manuals in the field of trauma recovery, most notably *Trauma and the 12 Steps: An Inclusive Guide to Recovery Enhancement* (2012/2020) and *Dissociation Made Simple: A Stigma-Free Guide to Embracing Your Dissociative Mind and Navigating Life* (2023). Her personal memoir about surviving spiritual abuse called You Lied to Me About God came out in October 2024, and she is also the author or co-author of three EMDR Therapy books. NALGAP: The Association of Lesbian, Gay, Bisexual, Transgender Addiction Professionals and Their Allies awarded Jamie with their esteemed President's Award in 2015 for her work as an LGBT advocate. The EMDR International Association (EMDRIA) granted Jamie the 2019 Advocacy in EMDR Award for her using her public platform in media and in the addiction field to advance awareness about EMDR therapy and to reduce stigma around mental health.

Cover Artist

Irene M. Rodriguez, LMHC, REAT, (she/her) is a bilingual expressive arts artist, trauma therapist, and EMDRIA-Approved EMDR Trainer whose creative work reflects a deep commitment to healing and self-expression. Irene uses mixed media to tell stories as she feels them. She founded Mindful Journey Center that offers therapy, retreats, consultations, EMDR Therapy, and Expressive Arts Therapy training. She has an innate and practical way of making learning environments welcoming, compassionate, and inclusive. In every thing that she does, Irene brings both depth and humor. She believes art is not only a form of expression, but a pathway to healing, connection, and reclaiming joy. Irene currently lives in her home island of Puerto Rico with her rescued dog, Lucky Bones, and four beloved lovebirds.

Contents

Foreword

When my friend and colleague Roshni Chabra approached me with her idea to do a book on *Queering EMDR Therapy*, my body, mind, and soul said YES! With the idea of queering psychotherapy entering into the lexicon of more progressive and justice-oriented therapists following Julie Beth Tilsen's 2021 book *Queering Your Therapy Practice*, it seemed like there was more than enough material within the EMDR Therapy community to offer something unique to EMDR.

In deciding to support Roshni with her vision, my company Creative Mindfulness Media (part of the Institute for Creative Mindfulness, soon to be Creative Mindfulness network) jumped at the chance to produce it. Having a good deal of experience working with publishers ourselves as an established author and knowing how certain capitalistic and institutional rules and restrictions can keep authors stifled, we truly wanted to *queer* every aspect of this book. Many of our contributors cite the work of Dr. Nick Walker, an autistic, transgender scholar, in their chapters. Walker asserts that "intentionally liberating oneself from the culturally ingrained and enforced performance of heteronormativity is sometimes referred to as *queering*, intentionally liberating oneself from the culturally ingrained and enforced performance of neuronormativity can be thought of as *neuroqueering*" (Walker, 2021, p. 155).

The heart and soul of the *Queering EMDR Therapy* project are our 26 contributors–all EMDR therapists–who share some aspect of how their queerness and their commitment to EMDR therapy intersect. The contributors are diverse in terms of background and identities on the LGBTQIAA2S+[1] spectrums. I am just as excited by the collection of work that they submitted and that we are offering

1 *This abbreviation is commonly understood as Lesbian, Gay, Bisexual, Transgender, Queer or Questioning, Intersex, Asexual, Aromatic or Agender, 2 Spirit, and + acknowledges the spectrum of other identities that exist outside of expressions of sexuality, gender, and identity that are considered "mainstream" by dominant culture. In this book we allow individual contributors to use the version of the abbreviation that they prefer in their chapters, as many variations of it are in use.*

to you in the pages of this book. You will take in some chapters that are more traditionally academic (yet with a queer twist), others that share more deeply from lived experience, some that combine the two, and other chapters and contributions that are more artistic: poetry, graphic novels, artwork. As the production editor, it was a privilege to read and help authors refine these chapters knowing that these words, this level of authentic boldness will be a gamechanger in how we approach EMDR Therapy.

I am proud of Roshni, for her vision in bringing this book together, and for calling out things that need to be said in her boldly written introduction to this book of boldly written truths. While many of the truths spoken here might make you, the reader, uncomfortable or unsettled in a variety of ways, I encourage you to *just notice* what is coming up for you as you read. Put the book aside if you need. Embrace that discomfort, in a way that we ask the people that we serve to do, and then *go with it*. Do the work. Our hope is that the contributions that follow will give you gentle yet bold guidance around looking at your own stuff. In my view, doing that is the heart and soul of being a solid EMDR therapist. As the world seems to be falling down around us, may we hold space for *everybody*'s pain.

Being an EMDR therapist has gifted me with scores of opportunities to grow. When I attended my first EMDR International Association (EMDRIA) conference in 2007, I did not get the sense that I was fully safe to be myself in that space. The cliquiness and reservedness of the members intimidated me, and I felt that I had to perform. And not just because of my queerness, which I was not yet public about in professional settings. My discomfort with the overt emphasis on protocols, procedures, and empirical research, which I now understand EMDR Therapy needed to be seen as credible by the larger psychological and medical community, was significant. I felt like, in many ways, EMDR Therapy was a cult because of the blind devotion to founder Dr. Francine Shapiro that I witnessed from many and her standard protocol was spoken about as something from which we could not deviate. As a qualitative thinker, researcher, and someone with my own lived experience of mental health and addiction struggles, it all seemed so pretentious. Yet as much as I struggled, I found pockets of hope as well. My first consultants, namely Dr. Sara Gilman and Dr. Howard Lipke, embraced and appreciated my rebel mind and worked with me to become the best possible EMDR Therapist. I clearly remember coming out as bisexual to Robin Shapiro at the 2010 EMDRIA Conference in Minneapolis when she disclosed her queerness to me, the first time I ever shared that with someone in professional circles.

Then as I grew and evolved as an EMDR therapist, qualitative research, writer, and trainer, I had the distinct pleasure and privilege of meeting other folks like me–rebellious, queer, fabulous, and committed to bringing about deep healing to our communities that need it so desperately. Growing up LGBTQIAA2S+ (regardless of the specific letter or letters that apply to you) means that in one way or another, you will encounter people who are afraid of you and committed to misunderstanding you. Some of us are raised by such people. Many of us were churched with such people, and being told that we are going to hell for who we love and how we show up in the world is a regular occurrence. This was certainly my story. So when I've encountered what are generally called microaggressions (which is really just a dressed up word for discrimination) from EMDR Therapists towards queer and trans people, I am troubled. And I realize that as far as we've come, we still have a very long way to go.

My hope is that our collection that we offer you as *Queering EMDR Therapy* is that bold testament to how far we have come. I further hope that you respond to our contributors' calls to action on how we can level up and queer up our EMDR Therapy in our quest to trudge on in our fight for justice, recognition, and freedom.

I edited the final versions of these chapters in the Spring and early Summer of 2025 as my own mentor, "Baba" Dharl Chintan (1942-2025) was dying of cancer. It was the great privilege of my life to help take care of him during his last months on this earth. As a man who was out in the 1960s in our home state of Ohio, along with his husband Mike who died in 2024, Baba taught me that authenticity is a Higher Power. As a clinical social worker who received training in EMDR Therapy in its early days, he believed in the power of this modality and supported all of my efforts in spreading the good word about how healing it can be for people like us. As the man who loved me like the father I needed in the last 10 years of his life, I hope this book would have made you proud, Baba. Thank you for showing your queer kids how it's done, and may all of us draw from your example now as we become the elders.

–Dr. Jamie Marich
Akron, Ohio (Erie Nation Land)

Introduction

Roshni Chabra, LMFT

When I first started this project, I could not have imagined how it would take on a life of its own, bringing together 27 incredible people who are talented, bright lights in this very dark world. To write is to bear your soul and this community of writers, friends, and therapists have endured so much in this life to be brave enough to put their words here for you to read. When I first started this project, my working title for my chapter was *I'm fucking afraid all the time* and I was, and I am. I'm just not alone anymore. I called in my Queerdos and they came!

I truly love and admire each of you for your courage to speak your truth in a time when truth no longer matters to some. This is real courage and I see each and every one of you. Meeting with you, formulating directions for your chapter, reading, editing and working with each of you on feedback has been beyond the Queerest joy to me. It has brought me the courage and strength I needed to keep going. Thank you does not feel adequate enough for what you have brought to this book and to my life. The world and especially Los Angeles has been on fire, both literally and figuratively as 200,000 people descended on the streets of Los Angeles to say - DON'T FUCK WITH US! So I say that again, don't fucken fuck with us! Our Queerific and Transtastic (to quote the good Rev. Karla Fleshman) folks are not afraid of you. We have had everything taken away over and over and we have fought tooth and nail for every inch of equality with all of our lives. We will not stop. We cannot be destroyed no matter how hard you try, we will always rise again!

Many of us understand so deeply, what it is like to know that everyone who loves you will walk away just because you are true to who you are. We put up barriers to protect ourselves and we find our family of choice; it impacts us differently, it shows up in our attachments, our relationships and in the work we do in therapy. This is why we are *Queering EMDR* and Trans-ing EMDR and

Nonbinary-ing EMDR and Intersex-ing EMDR (and every identity in the Queer alphabet soup of LGBTQIAA2S+) and maybe even others that we don't even know about yet. Please join us in Queering EMDR because to Queer something is inherently political. It is about fucking shit up, especially systems, oppressive, broken systems. We wrote this for me and you and all of you are included and if you are not in this book, I want you to know that you do belong here. If you don't see yourself anywhere else, you likely belong here.

Read on and see...

I thought about calling this chapter or introduction *Queering Roshni*. However Roshni didn't have to be queered, she came that way and if there were other ways to be even more of a Queerdo, she would find them in the years to come. You might find yourself dividing up your identities to belong and yet you still don't feel like you belong. Even at the age of 45, I still feel I can either be Indian or be Queer, I cannot be both. That is the rub. Walking around Cerritos/Artesia, California known as "Little India" the looks I get are puzzled, discerning and then arriving at their own uncomfortable conclusion, never looking within at the discomfort. We have a long way to go.

I thought of doing a land acknowledgement here and it felt a bit performative. How can we acknowledge that the land under our feet was stolen?

> We say stolen but what are we actually saying–
> *Genocide*
> Wiping out an entire culture
> Like nothing happened
> disappeared
> Now we have a holiday, Indigenous People's Day
> So that makes it better
> The only thing we can do to make this right
> Is to give this
> LAND BACK!
> And while you're at it
> GOVERNMENT BACK!
> As my best friend, Toivo, says

And it is true that someone else should give this a try
This experiment has failed
Greed has won
Greed
Is god.

It is not enough to do land acknowledgments and stop there, it is not enough to be anti-oppressive; we must be liberation focused. We will never be free if we are not free together. True liberation is not negotiable. Even as I write this, I hold my breath, afraid to speak my truth knowing that fragility will place me into a box but there's never been a box I have been put in that I belong in so far. I am reminded of Audre Lorde's words - YOUR SILENCE WILL NOT PROTECT YOU. So I will take heed of Audre's words and I invite you to as well. I still hesitate to speak and I am reminded that silence did not protect my people from their colonizers, especially those 1,500+ who were trapped and gunned down where they stood. Being at the memorial of the Jallianwala Bagh massacre years ago in Amritsar, India and seeing the amount of bullet holes in the walls was unreal. Literally, it felt unreal. That 1,500+ people stood there and their lives were taken for no reason other than existing.

This is why liberation is the only way.

While doom scrolling and struggling with how open I should be for my support of Palestine in all areas of my public life, including in this book, I came across this post on Instagram and it gave me clarity. I felt called to share this with you:

> Please remember that your soul signed up for this very important time in humanity. Know in your bones that your soul is equipped for these times.
>
> Come back to this as many times as you need: If we do not learn to transmute the pain, we do the colonizers' work to ourselves.

> Everyone in the western world is complicit in this gEnocid€ & it is our sacred responsibility to speak up & take a stand in every way we are able.
>
> Please use your voice & all your spheres of influence to call for an end to gEnocides. This is true leadership.
>
> We ARE NOT powerless. This is a colonial narrative. We are far more powerful than what we have been led to believe.
>
> Please remember this: They are coming at us full force because they know their end is near. They SEE OUR power and THEY ARE THE ONES IN FEAR.
>
> Despite what we physically see, please remember there is more available to us in the unseen. We are here to dismantle the oppressive system and co-create a new ancient world.
>
> Collective liberation starts with DECOLONIZING & LIBERATING YOUR OWN MIND. If you do not do the inner work needed to dismantle the internalized oppressor, you will continue to cause harm to others, our Earth Mother, and YOURSELF.
>
> There is medicine and wisdom in your blood & bones. May you do the spiritual healing work to be able to activate your DNA (Meza, 2025).

This post really struck me on a deep level and felt like a clear answer for me. As a leader it makes sense to me that I must lead us toward liberation otherwise what integrity can my leadership have? I sometimes joke about heading to another planet where folx are nicer than humans. When we feel like running or exiting this world, Dr. Meza reminds us that our souls have chosen this time. If we are the ones being targeted right now, then we are the ones on the frontlines, pushing back against forces of harm. This is our purpose. If you feel called to what I am saying then this applies to you. We become complicit in harm if we do not actively use our voice when we have it to stand against harm. It is time for us to find that wisdom and medicine in our blood and bones. I appreciate how Dr. Meza invites us back as many times as needed to transmute our pain, reminding us that we have the knowledge within. Transmuting our pain is what has brought together the authors, artists and poets in this book from a shared belief in the healing power of EMDR Therapy. EMDR helps us to deprogram our colonized mind so we are able to access wisdom meant for us. I am truly guilty of doing the colonizers' work and I feel called in to do the work of decolonizing my mind. I hope you will join me to be more compassionate with our thoughts and ourselves. May this book inspire you as it has me to decolonize and Queer the fuck out of everything!

Lately I have been in a suspended state, frozen yet furious, heartbroken yet shocked. In Los Angeles at the moment of this writing, ICE (U.S. Immigration and Customs Enforcement) is ripping children out of their homes and schools and abducting people off the street, leaving fruit carts and taco stands unclaimed. The law is meaningless or only applies to some. There are reports that ICE agents are given free reign to abuse, rape, pillage, and kill whoever they want. This is not new, this has literally happened over and over in history.

Genocide seems to be the state of our world
Did you know that Germany had a trial genocide in Africa?
The Nazis learned tactics from slavery in America and the genocide of Native Americans in their attempt to wipe out Jewish people, the Romani, the disabled, dissenters and those of us who are the focus of this book in which you now read.
Pink triangles, yellow stars, alligators
Marked for death
Many antisemitic Americans supported the Third Reich and did not want to join the war
No one talks about the Armenian genocide
Or the current genocide in America against Black folx
Trans folx
Women
Immigrants
Indigenous folx

Poor folx
Unhoused folx
Anyone else they feel like
America has a dark history and a dark present
I could throw a dart at a map and there is likely a genocide or war taking place now
Nowhere is safe
Systems of oppression are no longer attempting
To bother with brainwashing, neuro-linguistic programming and propaganda
They are emboldened.

Last year when we were seeing a lot of live videos from Palestine on social media (if you dared to look), I was having an understandable reaction to genocide: fear, panic, depression, overwhelm but I did not receive the support and community care I needed to be able to come back to baseline and do something that would make an impact. I did not realize I needed community care and I didn't know how to ask for it. Twenty years ago I was working at an organization that took a stand in support of Palestine and as a direct result had a significant amount of their funding pulled. The organization was almost shut down and had to start over. Folx who understand the power of shutting down anything that threatens the status quo know what this means. The consequences of not getting in line and going with the approved narrative are clear.

Oppression may always exist but that doesn't mean I need to tolerate it. Neurodivergent folx have a strong sense of justice, especially restorative justice. Oppression trauma is a distinct kind of complex and ongoing trauma that often involves unconscious responses including fawning, downplaying oppressive comments, freezing and allowing yourself whatever is needed to cope. It can be difficult to recognize oppression trauma as we normalize it. It can feel overwhelming and insurmountable when you begin to pull at that thread so take it slow, listen to your intuition. Start there. When I get overwhelmed, I will say (and sometimes chant) - one thing at a time, one foot in front of the other.

For white allies who want to do the work, start with any areas that you feel defensive about and look within, journal, write, think about it on a walk or talk to another white person about it (be careful not to exploit the labor of folx of color). The other important work for allies is to begin to understand and work against these systems that may seem to benefit them in the short term but ultimately harm all of us. The harm is layered, shows up in many ways and one of the most disturbing ways to me is syntax, language and the blatant manipulation of words in a game of power. Let's start with the word White: it is meaningless, it is the absence of color. Manipulating which groups of people have access and which do not through inception is insidious. Various groups that are now considered white or caucasian were long discriminated against. The category and therefore privilege is a moving target, it is not real. It is crazymaking and it is akin to the phrase: because I said so!

When my parents first came here in 1973 after their arranged marriage, they were expected to check off caucasian on forms. India had been a British colony and the absolute insane thinking is that this made my people white?! What the actual fuck! My mom would even say she was a British citizen because that is what my people were told to believe. The British nuns who taught my mother, left an imprint that sometimes shows up in even my language. The way in which I say *again* is pronounced weird, they would say, but I couldn't even hear it. The legacy of colonized oppression feels neverending. It seems that each day a new racist truth comes to light. It feels like there are land mines everywhere. It is overwhelming and necessary, all at once. To see the true nature of people is horrifying, literal terror.

How can we have any hope seeing
They have no soul
Lynching
Feeding babies
To
Alligators
Watching
Just beneath the surface

Always there
You sense it
It never stops
Just when you are ready to
Let that wall down
You remember or hear
Something
Devastating
Soulless people should wear their true alligator skin
So we see them coming.

White is the color of a wall, not a description of a person's culture. We don't have to go with these arbitrary categories. Let's lean into the cultures that have been erased by not just stopping the conversation at *yeah, I'm white*. I don't know what that means. I don't know what that says about your ancestors, which is way more important to me than anyone feeling guilty around the things they may be responsible for because you won the lottery of being chosen to be in a box that represents nothing and everything depending on what we are told to believe. We are beginning to wake up and remember our ancient ways, inherited resilience and learning to stand in our own power, all things that we were conditioned to forget through colonialism. All of us are waking up. So tell me the stories of your ancestors.

While you are at it, check off *Other* and tell me where your ancestors are really from! Let's all be *Other* because there is not a checkbox that can handle all that I am and all that you are! Oh what will they do with so many *Others*!! When I ask about your ethnicity, I am really asking, I want to know where your people came from and what they did to survive, I want to hear all the legends and stories. Just like when I ask how you are doing, I am really asking! I don't want to hear the teenager answer, even from my nephew, who just says, "Good." I want real answers and real information! Let's not let these cultures get lost into the default.

I felt disconnected from my ancestors a few months back and in a meeting with one of the authors, Mish. I asked them, how do you communicate with your ancestors? Their response was *one step at a time*. It gave me chills and I recalled that feeling immediately and turned that channel up. The way I receive the guidance is that it comes through as my own thought although it feels dropped into my head as opposed to a thought originating from me. This is how I personally experience my ancestors through claircognizance (clear knowing). How do you experience your ancestors? We need them now more than ever. We need our ancestors because this work, anti-oppressive work, is exhausting and we need them to guide us, recharge us and share their wisdom. The exhaustion of having to deal with incorrigible people who have it all wrong. Once you have seen behind the curtain, you can't unsee it. It's time to wake up and get to work!

The transformative words in this book of these beyond FABULOUS authors, artists and poets turned friends has inspired me and given me life at a time when wanting to be alive does not come easy. There are a lot of things that are making many of us want to run, get out of here or even end it all and complete suicide. I understand and I'm still asking you to stay and fight as long as you can and do whatever you have to in order to stay alive because you matter, you are important and you are truly here to help humanity - and gurrrl, do we need help! Queers, Trans folx, Neuroqueers, outcasts and all other trouble makers are here to change these systems that hurt all of us, even those that they benefit. We are here to fucken Queer the world!!

On May 12, 2007, my mentor, Dr. Angela Bowen addressed the graduates in her keynote speech at the first Lavender Graduation at California State University, Long Beach. She said:

> And of course, you organizers will pass along to the next group which follows in your footsteps all the information you have gathered in producing this praise-worthy event. How far, how very far we have come. And, let's face it, how far we have yet to go. And, as my mother used to say, we, as black folks, could only change things by helping to move the line forward.

> Who knows where you'll put your energies? You'll keep your eyes and hearts and brains open to all possibilities; and whatever you do, if your goals of equality are not attained at the end of your time, you'll pass the baton, as crusaders have always done. And at some point in time, although our goals might be achieved, it is likely that some of us will not be here to celebrate it. But that's fine because we will have moved that line forward, just as some previous somebodies did for us.

Dr. Bowen was a Women's Studies Professor at CSULB where we first crossed paths when she was the Professor of my Black Women in America class. Angela really saw me, she mentored me, she loved me unconditionally and she became family. She taught me to always document everything, every meeting and every event in order to leave behind a manual for the next organizers because first and foremost she was an activist. She taught me how to write, gave me confidence in my words and encouraged me to be the best I could be. She would push my chin dimple whenever we parted for good luck but I think I'm the one who got all the luck knowing you, Angela. You are the reason I am writing this today. Here it is, Angie, I'm moving that line forward.

Now join me.

References

Bowen, A. (2007, May 12). Move the line forward: Lavender Graduation speech. In The passionate pursuits of Angela Bowen [Speech transcript]. Jennifer Abod. http://www.jenniferabod.com/films/the-passionate-pursuits-of-angela-bowen.html Transcript: bit.ly/45OcJOY

Meza, R. [@drrosalesmeza]. (2025, May 14). [Instagram post]. Instagram. Available: bit.ly/4erqOUR

Lorde, A. (1984). The transformation of silence into language and action. In *Sister outsider: Essays and speeches* (pp. 40-44). Trumansburg, NY: Crossing Press.

When Our Powers Combine

Autism, ADHD, Gender Identity, and EMDR with Adolescents and Teens

Dr. Lanza, LCSW, M.Ed., CST

Yes, this chapter is about working with adolescents and teens; but please don't run away! If you don't work with kids, that is okay! There will still be something here for your practice.

Phew, thought I lost you there for a moment!

This chapter focuses on the intersection of specific populations in the Neurodivergent community - Autistic, ADHD, and AuDHD (Autistic and ADHD) - and areas of gender development. This chapter offers information on ways to approach the EMDR process with adolescent and teen clients in order to help their healing and growth journeys. This chapter includes strategies to:

- Minimize fears around working with adolescents and teens
- Find creativity and flow in EMDR to meet an array of brains
- Enhance the clinical dance with each client

So much of our clinical work is focused around adult brains and behaviors. Clinicians tend to pull from adult brain research when working with adolescents and teens. Developmentally, that doesn't work. What does work, however, is utilizing strategies that are geared towards adolescents and teens for use with adults. Why? Adults come with adolescent and teen experiences, parts, and traumas. Adolescents and teens don't come with adult experiences, parts, or trauma - yet. The coolest part, helping young humans heal their traumas - while empowering their identities - helps them become big humans without reactivity from their past. Now, *that* is what I call a super power!

Language

Language is the foundation of understanding concepts and identities. Having a conceptualization of the words and phrases used in this chapter will help with processing and absorbing the information. As language is constantly evolving, words and phrases used in this chapter are specific to the time in which it was written. The language used in this chapter is most often used by those with lived experience and advocacy movements. The framework is identity-first language as compared with the previously assumed person-first language. For example, instead of saying a person with Autism, we would say an Autistic person. This language may not fit for all individuals, making it important to always ask what language framework works for an individual when interacting with them. Identity-first language is preferred for use in wider forums and generalized communication in contemporary settings.

The list below is not exhaustive; language is a beautiful and expansive experience. The definitions below support how these concepts are operationalized in the chapter. However, they may be slightly different from other settings and writings. The goal is not to memorize these concepts; the goal is to have a reference when working with specific areas of focus and identities.

Concepts

Sexuality: Dr. Dennis Dailey (1981) defines human sexuality as a "core aspect of being human which encompasses biological, psychological, sociocultural, and ethical dimensions." Dailey breaks sexuality down into five circles or categories: sensuality, sexual identity, intimacy, sexual health and reproduction, and sexualization (1981).

Gender identity: This is an internal sense of self; how one lives, breathes, expresses, and understands their gender. Gender identity is separate from, and does not define, one's sexual orientation.

Gender binary: A societal construction (meaning people within a society created this concept) that there are only two genders (different than sexes) man and woman. Gender binary assumes that all humans fall within two opposing genders with no variation.

Sex assigned at birth: Specific to sex - male, female, intersex, etc. - that a medical professional (doctor, midwife) uses to describe a child at birth based on their external anatomy (HRC, 2023), specifically their visible genitalia.

Transgender (Trans): An umbrella term for those whose gender identity and/or expression is different from the cultural expectations of the sex assigned at birth (HRC, 2023).

Non-binary (Enby): An identity outside of the binary (meaning two) conceptualization of gender. A person can identify as being both man and woman, being inbetween these binary concepts, or being completely beyond the binary (HRC, 2023). Some people in this community identify as part of the transgender community or under the trans umbrella.

Gender expansive: A human with a wide and flexible range of gender identity and expression than generally associated with the binary gender system. This can also be a space for those kiddos or young folx who are still exploring the vast possibilities of their gender identity and expression.

Cisgender (Cis): Someone whose experience of gender identity aligns with the sex the medical professionals assigned them at birth.

Sexual orientation/Orientation: Inherent enduring emotional, romantic, or sexual attraction to other people (HRC, 2023). Every single human has a sexual orientation or orientation. This is how you would identify your way of connecting with others around you based on all forms of attraction (not just sexual attraction). One's sexual orientation or orientation is not the same as one's gender identity.

Cisherteronormative: A term to describe the pervasive systems of belief that centers the binary system of assigned sex matching gender identity (cisgender) and heterosexuality with distinct rigidity in its way of being. The systems that believe that cisgender and heterosexuality is the primary, normal, or only experience.

Masking: A conscious or unconscious strategy that Neurodivergent folx use to blend into a neurotypical society. This is done in an attempt to hide their Neurodivergent traits to avoid harm, bullying, and other negative responses.

Neurotype: A general term to denote the differences in variations of one's brain. A way to describe how your brain and systems operate. A neurotype feels like a fingerprint, everyone's is different! Your neurotype can be neurotypical, neuroconforming, or neurodivergent.

Neurotypical: One's neurotype that falls within the dominant standards and norms of a society of thinking, feeling, communicating, behaving, etc. (Wise, 2024).

Neuroconforming: A term used to describe someone who appears to have a societally expected form of a neurotype. Many individuals do not have the privilege of diagnosis or assessment, leading to neurodivergent people going through life not knowing their neurotype and assuming their experience conforms to that of the majority of society.

Neurodivergent: Word developed during the Neurodiversity movement referring to the atypical (as per societal typicality) neurological development of one's brain (Mendes & Maroney, 2019). Neurodivergent is an umbrella term encompassing the various neurotypes that fall outside of dominant social norms

(Wise, 2024). Neurodivergent includes innate, genetic, acquired, or developed conditions (Wise, 2024).

Neuroqueer: A word created as both a verb and identity (Walker, 2021). In verb form, this is an intentional subversion of dominant culture norms to neurotypicality and heteronormativity by rejecting the pressures to mask - act neurotypical - and embracing all forms of gender identity and expression (Walker, 2021). For an identity, it describes the intersection of neurodivergence and queerness as they intertwine for a person and challenge the normative structures (Walker, 2021).

Autism or Autistic: A natural variation in human cognition and sensory experience (Price, 2022). This definition was written in such a way to move away from disordered language and definition to highlight that there are different neurotypes, rather than a series of deficits. Neuroaffirming movements have focused on updating language and levels around Autism. Much of the language comes from harmful history and from neurotypical professionals. Additionally, putting a level to one's Autism can dismiss their needs based on how the level is defined and assessed.

- Autism Spectrum Disorder or ASD: Autistic advocates are working to shift the perception of Autism away from a disorder and moving towards neurotype.
- Spectrum: The concept of spectrum implies a linear conceptualization which limits how Autistic individuals can define their experience when it is much more expansive than having less or more of limited traits.
- Asperger's: This diagnosis has a harmful history going back to WWII; specifically Hans Asperger and "race hygiene." The difficulty of differentiating between Asperger's and Autism has been discussed as another reason it is no longer used. Diagnostically, this was removed from the Diagnostic and Statistical Manual (DSM) by merging with Autism Spectrum Disorder.

It is important to note that although the larger Autistic self-advocate communities are moving away from the above language, some individuals may still connect with one or more to refer to themselves. So much of these changes have come as a result of the dedicated Autistic self-advocates and the expansion of diagnosis. With more AFAB (assigned female at birth) individuals getting Autism diagnosis and adults being late-diagnosed, we are dismantling the stereotypes originally documented by neurotypicals observing a subset of Autistics by embracing the true expansiveness of this neurotype. In summary, Autism is just Autism. Each individual has their own experience of Autism and that cannot be captured in various levels or abbreviations.

Attention deficit hyperactivity disorder (ADHD): Typically classified as a developmental disorder; this is a neurotype that can experience higher levels of inattentive, hyperactive, and impulsive experiences.

- Similar to the Autistic movement of language, ADD has been dropped from language. Inattentive, predominantly hyperactive/impulsive, and combined are ways that assessors identify the form of ADHD one has, making ADD obsolete.
- The original stereotype of a child running around the classroom defining hyperactivity no longer fits as the only form of hyperactivity. Many ADHDers experience hyperactivity of their thoughts.

AuDHD: An abbreviation to describe a neurotype that is both Autistic and ADHD to create another unique neurotype. AuDHD is described as the experience of the overlap of Autism and ADHD, not just having both Autism and ADHD. Individuals can experience not just the overlap and interaction of Autism and ADHD, it is also about how that can contradict one another. For example, seeking and avoiding sensory input, hyperfocus and forgetfulness, and craving routine while struggling to keep it.

All shifts in language start with a movement within the community that is then backed by the most up to date research and understanding of experiences. These shifts are imperative to unlearning disordered language that has long been harmful to marginalized communities. The focus is normalizing the variation in human experience without differences being a disorder.

Learning new terms and keeping up with identities and communities forced into marginalization can feel like a never-ending process. It is. We are consistently evolving as humans which makes us more aware, educated, and brings clarity to our individual and collective experiences. It is important to make the effort to understand neurodivergent and gender-expansive identities as an integral part of trauma-focused care. If we are not seeing the whole person and honoring the most beautiful parts of them, we are doing a disservice to our clients and their healing journey.

Sexual Development

Our academic institutions and professional training typically lack education around sexual development. There is a strong emphasis on general human development but it is not complete without including sexual development. Having even a foundational understanding of sexual development can positively impact one's professional and clinical skills. Sexual development is a central part of human development (WHO, 2006) and understanding it will provide the necessary context to clinical work with youth and adults.

Sexual development is often oversimplified and dwindled down to solely the physical aspects of interacting with another human; such as kissing or first intercourse (van der Doef & Reinders, 2018). Sexual development is a life-long process; from womb to tomb. Each stage includes developmentally appropriate sexual development; from an infant's awareness of the sensation of touch or adolescents experiencing the stressors of reproductive capacity all the way to elder adulthood reintroduction to physical pleasure as a body ages and movement changes.

The World Health Organization (WHO) defines sexuality as the central aspect of being human throughout life (WHO, 2006). Sexuality includes experiences of sensuality, intimacy, sexual identity, sexual health and reproduction, and sexualization (Dailey, 1981). This information was created by Dr. Dennis Dailey within his model of The Circles of Sexuality. Each one of the above circle topics include subcategories to further describe the experience of each sexuality topic (Dailey, 1981). Every human being experiences sexual development and aspects of sexuality throughout their life.

Sexual Development Models

There have been a number of variations of sexual development models. This next section will briefly describe specific sexual development models from traditional to contemporary. A large portion of sexual development for all humans is influenced heavily by the society in which they are raised. Beginning at birth, children are already starting to differentiate the world; in this case through a gendered lens. By two years old, children are identifying physical differences between what it means to be a boy or girl (Martin & Ruble, 2010). As early as three years old, children have a grasp on their gender stability, which can also be when children begin to question their gender identity (Martin & Ruble, 2010). Gender understanding and learning occurs at a variety of paces. There are many factors that can influence when a gender journey is revealed by the individual.

Sigmund Freud's Psychosexual stages (Freud, 1905/1953) included five proposed stages of development. Those five stages are oral, anal, phallic, latency, and genital (Freud, 1905/1953). Freud's model of psychosexual development is limited. There is a lack of empirical support, gender bias is pervasive, it is binary in its gender descriptions, it has a cisheteronormative focus, and the impact of hyperfocusing on early childhood experiences of development leaves a gap in the majority of the human lifespan. There is no application or adaptation for Neurodivergent individuals as developmental stages align with rigid age-based assumptions that leave no room for alternative interpretation.

Erik Erikson's stages of psychosocial development focused on eight stages of development, only a couple of which focused on gender and sexuality. These stages include identity versus confusion (adolescence) and intimacy versus isolation (young adulthood). In adolescence, Erikson posits that the identity versus confusion stage the development of sexual and gender identity occurs. In young adulthood, the focus is exploring relationships, intimacy, and self-expression. Erikson's model assumes linear and age-based progression which is not a universal experience. This model does not account for later life discovered gender or sexual identities, which can be common in Neurodivergent individuals especially. Additionally, Erikson does not consider the expansiveness of sexuality throughout the model.

Attachment theories, like those developed by John Bowlby and Mary Ainsworth, also have a part to play in sexual development models. Bowlby and Aimsworth focus on early attachment styles labeled secure, anxious, avoidant, and disorganized. These attachment styles are said to influence or shape future sexual and romantic relationships. A major limitation within traditional attachment model development is that Autistic individuals, for example, have different attachment styles influenced by sensory and social processing differences. Another limiting factor is that attachment styles can be heavily impacted by the trauma of rejection, lack of affirmation, and/or minority stress often experienced by the LGBTQIA+ community.

Another traditional development model - often touted for its inclusivity at the time - is Alfred Kinsey's scale and sexual continuum (1948). Kinsey's work emphasized sexuality as a fluid continuum rather than a binary specific to heterosexual or homosexual experiences. Kinsey's work was expanded upon by Storms (1990) and then Klein (1993) where attraction was broadened across the lifespan. Storms expanded through a two-dimensional model versus Kinsey's linear scale, which ultimately made space for bisexuality and asexuality to be more meaningfully represented. Similarly, Klein expanded dimensions to orientation, including emotional preferences, lifestyle, self-identification, and time; all of which was expansive and intersectional for the time. This model was more applicable to gender expansive and Queer identities than any of those mentioned above. The concern when using the original Kinsey model or subsequent additions by Storms is that the focus is on attraction as a pivotal point rather than identity formation reaffirming that self is defined by others rather than by self (Kinsey, 1948; Storms, 1990).

More contemporary models attempted to rectify the limits and forgotten elements of their predecessors. D'Augelli's lifespan model of lesbian, gay, and bisexual (LGB) identity development (1994) looks at the phases that LGB individuals encounter as they understand their orientation. There is a recognition that sexual orientation evolves over time. Stages include:

- Exiting a heterosexual identity
- Developing a personal lesbian, gay, or bisexual identity status
- Developing a lesbian, gay, or bisexual social identity
- Becoming a lesbian, gay, or bisexual offspring
- Developing lesbian, gay, or bisexual intimacy status
- Entering a lesbian, gay, or bisexual community

D'Augelli's model attempted to focus on inclusion in sexual development research. This model recognizes orientation fluidity and the social influence on one's orientation development. This allows for more applicability to the Neurodivergent community who may experience delayed or non-linear orientation realization. Like other models, however, there are limitations. In an attempt to create a universal model for LGB orientation development, D'Augelli fell into the binary model of gender that only acknowledges men and women. There is no discussion of non-binary people being LGB and no discussion of LGB people being attracted to those outside the gender binary. Similar to other contemporary models, there is an emphasis on coming out, community, and engaging in romantic and sexual relationships, all of which can enhance or impede reaching full LGB identity. This model does include elements of the importance of community for queer identity formation (Galbraith, 2022). However, access to these communities can be a deterrent to Neurodivergent youth and adult sexual development.

Other contemporary models attempted to incorporate elements of inclusivity and nuanced experience through their interpretations of sexual development. Meyer (2003) created the Gender and Sexual Minority Stress Model, which focuses on the impact of stigma, discrimination, and minority stress on one's gender and sexual identity development. This model discusses how external stressors like harassment and rejection coupled with internalized stigma can affect one's ability to move through stages. Meyer looks at the coping and resilience of the individual as a factor. Additionally, Meyer's model helps explain the higher rates of trauma among trans and Neurodivergent individuals. Meyer's model does this by highlighting the impact of chronic stressors like discrimination, stigma, and social rejection this community experiences. They experience higher levels of external stressors such as harassment, violence, and systemic barriers. In addition, they experience higher levels of internalized stressors such as shame, hypervigilance, and identity concealment that are compounded over time. The differences in neurodivergent trans individuals' difficulties with social communication and sensory processing can further increase their vulnerability to mistreatment and trauma. This model shows the importance of incorporating minority stress into the EMDR work with these populations.

Having models that allow for understanding or extrapolation of information to specific communities can positively impact one's healing journey. In the 1990s, Dr. John Bancroft and Dr. Erick Janssen developed a model during their work at the Kinsey Institute called The Dual Control Model of Sexual Response (Bancroft & Janssen, 2000). This model focuses on excitatory and inhibitory factors that influence one's sexual development. This model can help support Neurodivergent community members who have differences in excitation and inhibition responses due to sensory processing differences. EMDR can support these clients by helping to reduce the inhibitory responses caused by trauma. The issue with this model - like many others - is that the underlying research focused on experiences for cisgender men, who are often treated as the default.

Sexual Development - Neurodivergent Experience

There is no model developed to describe the path neurodivergent individuals experience with sexual development. Sexual rights, education, and support for those with a disability have been denied, ignored, and suppressed for decades (Gougeon, 2010). Publications like Tony Attwood's *The Autism Spectrum, Sexuality, and the Law* (2014) recognizes the unique expressions of attraction, sensory driven preferences, and differences in social and romantic navigation of relationships for Autistic individuals. It traverses the same path many authors do discussing problematic sexual behaviors or relationship vulnerability (Attwood, 2014).

Author Hannah Belcher (2022) provided research around late self-diagnosis of Autism or ADHD with delayed-life experience of gender and orientation identity development as a result of masking and the learned social expectations. An Autistic or ADHD individual has so much more to process, retain, learn, and understand in their day-to-day life than a neurotypical individual. This inherently creates distance for the individual to prioritize learning about themselves. They quickly learn their place in society as a neurodivergent individual and do all they can to assimilate to the world around them to avoid punishment, ridicule, isolation, hate, and violence. In Attwood and Belcher's work, the emphasis is on relationship building and connection more so than gender identity development (Attwood, 2014; Belcher, 2022).

Much of the research and lived experience information that is available, focuses on the struggles or pathology of sexual development for Autistic and ADHD individuals. Many of the struggles these individuals face in their development are due to the incongruence of socializing and social communication between the neurotypical and the neurodivergent worlds. This is one of the factors that creates increased vulnerability for Autistic and ADHD individuals in regards to abusive relationships and assault. For those who are also going through a gender journey, this can exacerbate that vulnerability. For example, an Autistic individual, assigned female at birth who identifies as a man, can experience higher levels of sexual assault due to the social limitations of boundaries, consent, and communication.

A few aspects of the Autistic experience are difficulty recognizing and asserting boundaries, interpreting social cues, and navigating complex interpersonal dynamics. An unfortunate response to these aspects is that they can make it harder for an Autistic trans individual to detect coercion or manipulation, particularly in a society that often disregards the autonomy of both Autistic and trans individuals. Trans women face a heightened risk of violence and exploitation due to systemic transphobia, social marginalization, and economic vulnerabilities. This leaves Autistic trans women disproportionately exposed to predatory behaviors from others along with a lack of an accessible and affirming support system.

For many Autistic and ADHD children and teens, their brains are wired to not accept or understand societal rules, such as binaries. This can create a freedom when it comes to their gender identity as they do not see gender as a rule that society deems it necessary to follow. They see their gender in its most authentic form, that it just is, no matter what others are expecting it to be. In many cases, the positive and affirming impact of living their gender identity and expression does not meet or exceed the intense negative impact of masking or living in a neurotypical-focused world. The bigger impacts may be encountered when seeking gender-affirming and neuro-affirming care and being believed and respected about their gender identity by loved ones and acquaintances.

Most of the sexual development models focus on linear, age-driven experiences of development, whereas most neurodivergent adolescents and teens experience nonlinear sexual development. This can include later life recognition of attraction as a result of sensory differences and/or social masking. This may also include exploration into non-traditional orientations like asexuality or fluctuating sexual interests based on sensory regulation. There is also a propensity for nontraditional relationship structures, such as polyamory or Ethical Non-Monogamy (ENM) that help the individual affirm their autonomy and safety. Sexual development for neurodivergent children and teens is about breaking the mold of societal expectations and carving a path that creates a sense of spacious exploration at a pace that feels authentic to that person. This journey, if supported and affirmed, could evolve throughout their lifetime.

Unique Experiences

This section cannot be fully understood without making an explicit statement about the struggles that transgender Autistic and ADHD individuals face. These struggles are not a result of one's neurotype or gender identity. They are a result of the limitation created by a society that refuses to reconstruct its limited assumptions based on cisnormative and neurotypical experiences. Creating a society in this way inherently excludes certain humans and does not provide accessible care to those in need.

Those who have not yet started the work to decolonize our society are more likely to assume the issues these communities face are a direct result of their neurotype or gender identity rather than historical oppressive systems. For example, the increased statistics for mental health struggles in the transgender community would be seen as a result of being trans rather than the result of the discrimination, hatred, and violence trans folx experience. The struggles in accessing gender-affirming care for Autistic individuals would be seen as a deficit in their communication skills versus a lack of understanding of what is needed to create accessibility for Autistic patients. An ADHDer who consistently misses their appointment for their gender affirming care could be seen as lazy and not setting up a process such as putting it on a calendar, versus seeing the medical offices not providing reminders in their apps and online portals or only offering appointments at times that are inaccessible to the client. We need to move beyond this way of thinking about the individual as the problem and move into understanding that American society was built purposefully to exclude certain groups from accessing needed resources and support.

Gender Identity, Autism, and ADHD

Autistic individuals are more likely to be transgender (Cooper, Mandy, Butler, & Russell; 2022; Van der Miesen et al., 2018; Walsh et al., 2018; Warrier et al., 2020), creating a multi-marginalization experience. Similarly, ADHD individuals are more likely to have transgender identities or gender expansive identities (Cooper et al., 2022). In communities that experience societal violence and discrimination (such as the trans community), individuals within those communities carry the burden of the oppression in mind and body (Gratton, 2020). One way to conceptualize this experience is through minority stress theory (Frost & Meyer, 2023) which informs how stress that originates in prejudice and stigma has an incredible impact on a community and its individuals (Frost & Meyer, 2023).

A common stressor for Autistic and ADHDers is believing in their capacity to understand themselves and the world around them. As a result of these neurotypes, the stereotype is that they are immature, child-like, or infantilized due to their ADHD and/or Autism. Then an Autistic adolescent or teen coming out as transgender is more likely to be met with dismissive comments, disbelief, or thoughts of this being a phase rather than being respected and honored for their identity journey. A neurodivergent individual seeking therapy to explore gender identity is often met with therapists assuming they are coming to therapy to heal from trauma related to questioning their gender. Similarly in medical settings, their gender identity is less likely to be respected because professionals do not see them as capable of understanding these concepts.

Contrary to the ableist transphobic assumptions, Autistic and ADHD individuals tend to hyper-focus or do hours of research and reading on their gender identity before they share their thoughts about their gender with another person. Then it only stands to reason that being dismissed feels mind boggling after the extent of in-depth self-analysis that occurred. This is also incredibly harmful and traumatic for the individual because it becomes its own form of gaslighting and invisibility.

Adapting EMDR for Neurodivergent and Gender-Expansive Clients

Traditional trauma frameworks often operate within cisheteronormative and neurotypical paradigms, which reinforces binary understandings of healing. By queering your EMDR practices, therapists embrace a nonlinear, creative, and embodied processing method that honors the fluidity of neurodivergent cognition and queer identities.

To truly queer EMDR for Autistic and ADHD adolescents and teens, we turn to Queer Theory as our foundation. Queer Theory came about around the 1990s from the influences of Feminist Theory, Poststructuralism, and LGBTQIA+ activism (DeLauretis, 1991). Amazing advocates such as Gloria Anzaldua (inspired by Michel Foucault's work), Gayle Rubin, Eve Kosofky Sedgwick, and Judith Butler, all gave voice to Queer Theory and its pivot away from gender essentialism and focus on the entire experience of human sexuality as a discursive social construct that is fluid and continually negotiated. It is not fixed or stagnant; it's constantly evolving. Based on Queer Theory's expansive conceptualization through discussion of identities, we make radical inclusivity possible. Queer Theory brings you into affirming therapy by challenging the pathologizing frameworks and rigid identity categories. It does this by decentering normativity, affirming fluidity, critiquing power structures, centering lived experience, and embracing the intersectionalities within humanity like neurodiversity and queerness. Queer inclusion in EMDR will not always seem as blatant during the process if conditions prior to the beginning of formal EMDR Therapy sessions establish queer-inclusive rhetoric and practice.

Beginning With Queer Theory Based Affirming Care

Even before child, adolescent, or young adult clients enter your space, your affirming care begins decolonizing your work. The Adaptive Information Processing (AIP) model focuses on the distress resulting from maladaptively storing memories. For trans Autistic and ADHD clients, distress is often due to chronic minority stress, societal oppression, and medical pathologization. This is not from an internal dysfunction. EMDR work should focus not just on integrating past traumas, but on helping clients resist oppressive narratives that have influenced or shaped a client's sense of self. As clients are continuing to develop their language and identities, we must be in a consistent space of affirming the fluidity of identity.

There are numerous points of identity invalidation for the folx addressed in this chapter that create core wounds in their systems. Some therapists would use the EMDR approach to see this as a cognitive distortion. Instead, Queer Theory would encourage the therapist to validate the non-normative experience of identity invalidation instead of a distortion that needs correcting. Most importantly, the power is in affirming cognitions. Having a list or graphic of affirming cognitions can really benefit clients. Instead of statements like "I have to be normal to be safe," we want these clients to believe "I am worthy exactly as I am." No critique, no fixing, no deficits; they are worthy exactly as they are!

Recognizing where this group of humans experiences microaggressions and identity invalidation is crucial to being an ally. Healthcare and its gatekeeping is one of the biggest culprits. Gender-affirming care for this group is crucial. The majority of gender-affirming care consists of using the person's name, pronouns, along with acceptance and celebration of them as a human. Use EMDR to help them process their medical traumas - like forced medical interventions (i.e., hospitalization) and denial of gender-affirming care (due to state laws) - by validating their trauma responses to the systemic oppression they are experiencing. It's not a client problem, it's a system problem.

Preparation and Resourcing

Many Autistic and ADHD individuals are incredibly concrete in their thinking and processing. Avoid abstract language and metaphors. Be direct, concrete, and clear in all of your verbal interactions. Don't be afraid to ask if what you said made sense to them if it feels like it didn't land. The best strategy I have found while working with neuroqueer adolescents and teens is consistency, predictability, and repetition in everything that I do. Even if they roll their eyes or giggle at me saying the same thing for the millionth time, it helps their sensory system regulate while building trust and comfort during our time.

Many neuroqueer individuals crave co-regulation and building trust can take longer. Connecting over the individual's passions (i.e., video games, anime, reading, or Broadway) can help build rapport, co-regulation, trust, and provide vital information for the next section of BLS. This is also the start to learning the client's sensory system. Finding regulation techniques can be difficult, especially if all of this is new to your client. Engaging both the client and caregiver(s) at this stage could be beneficial. What you are focused on is looking for what sensory stimulation helps the individual's system regulate (weighted objects, fidgets, movement, pacing, etc.).

Resourcing for a neuroqueer individual can be incredibly difficult in terms of visualization. Having concrete, known, and familiar resources will be more successful and effective for your neuroqueer clients. This is where finding the joy and pride in their identities can be a valuable resource, as some individuals may not be there at the time they start working with you. Clients may have a photo taken of them where they feel euphoric in their gender; having that with them during sessions for a resource to refer to can be a powerful tool in their therapy process. Clients who do various forms of art can engage that talent to create a visual for themselves in their resourcing.

Bilateral Stimulation

Autistic and ADHD individuals have a heightened sensory experience. Their brains and bodies process sensory input at incredible speeds and with undeniable intensity. This can be both a benefit and an overload in attempting bilateral stimulation. Don't let this scare you away, we have so many options to support BLS with neuroqueer clients! The best part, is when we lean into the creativity mentioned above, there are an extraordinary amount of options to achieve BLS within EMDR. Outside of healing one's trauma reactivity, BLS can be used specifically for this population as a way to process dysphoria, address erasure of their community or identities, and reinforce self-determined narratives of gender and orientation.

Identifying BLS

Let's begin with adjusting our way of thinking about BLS. Having the right BLS for your client parallels having the right medication. Each sensory system is different and should be cared for as such. We are seeking a therapeutic dose when looking for the right BLS for our clients, just as a doctor would in prescribing a medication, brand, dosage, etc. Many of us were trained strictly on eye movements as the only form of BLS. Eye movements can be difficult to track an object, distracting, uncomfortable, painful, and quite annoying for many people. This is outside of the potential contraindications such as one who has a medical eye condition or chronic migraines. This is specific to the processing and sensory system of an individual. I have found that my clients, over the years, have rarely requested eye movements as their form of BLS. It is also rare that my clients request the use of tappers as the sensation of the tappers can be incredibly overwhelming to one's system especially as a neurodivergent person. The majority of my clients will choose music and/or movement as their form of BLS.

One of my favorite things about working with adolescents and teens is learning about what brings them joy. By the end of an intake, I have a list of those items that I can easily turn into resourcing and also BLS. Getting to know a client during intake should be so much more than building rapport; it is truly the most direct way to collect data. This approach can be important for clients who have sensory aversions or sensitivities that should be honored throughout the process. Music is an easy and accessible option for most individuals and can be used for both virtual and in-person sessions. Most music platforms now have specific BLS music where clients can choose which they like most. Movement or fidgeting can be a comfortable and familiar form of BLS. Have you ever seen a teen use a gaming controller or texting? Their fingers can go a mile a minute! Imagine having the teen use/bring in a gaming controller and practicing only using their thumbs on the two joysticks going left, right, left, right. How about that teen who loves sports and uses a ball, throwing it to either hand left, right, left, right. Even more fun - combining the BLS music with their movement of choice! Are you noticing your creative neurons firing yet? The possibilities are endless!

Once you identify options for BLS, communicating those ideas to the client is important so that they can have a sense of control over their therapeutic work. In general, I give clients no more than three options. This can minimize decision fatigue or paralysis for those who struggle to be definitive in their wants and needs which many neurodivergent individuals experience. Those three options can then move you into the next step, practice!

Using the three options of types of BLS, you can practice with the client through the next steps of their EMDR journey: their peaceful place and container. As most adolescents and teens would be new to EMDR, they have no schema on this experience to draw from which can cause stress and anxiety. By practicing new things on low stakes items, this helps the individual truly see what may or may not work for them. Explain the peaceful place and container concepts to the individual, then ask if using those names for each element works for them. As many of us are trained that it is a safe space versus a peaceful place, it is important to note that language can make an impact on the client. Our neuroqueer youth rarely have a sense of safety - in themselves or in the world around them. The word safe should be used with purpose and caution. Now, you are taking the BLS options that they have identified and using them as practice while creating the container and peaceful place with the individual. The individual is now creating a resource for themselves and has the option to provide feedback on their choice of BLS before going into target reprocessing.

Adjusting BLS

As the client is learning and reprocessing, it is important to keep their sensory system at the forefront of the work. As trauma is reprocessed through the correct channels, their sensory systems may shift; just as their sensory systems may be on high alert at first starting out with BLS. We are taught that there are specific speeds to attune to during BLS: faster for processing, slower for containing or resourcing. This does not provide an affirming space for one's sensory system. Each individual should have space to find their therapeutic dose of BLS in speed and intensity. Some individuals may need slower or rhythmic stimulation where others may want faster, more intense BLS.

Knowing your client and their system and being able to ask the client what they are noticing to communicate what they need are huge benefits to this process. One of the biggest flexibilities or accommodations to have here is recognizing that picking one long-term option will not suffice. There are times that I have clients shifting their BLS intensity or speed set to set as they need throughout the duration of the session. This is an invitation for the individual to be themselves, potentially for the first time, without the pressure of having to follow directions which can be difficult for many neurodivergent people. What is coming up for clients can dictate the needs they have with BLS. If they are having a more intense set in their thoughts, body, images, or emotions, they may need a slower option for their BLS. This is where rocking or swaying may be incredibly impactful for the client to stay in their window of distress tolerance and not go into sensory overload causing the processing to pause or have to stop altogether.

Processing Strategies

As individuals move into processing, you may find a few things that are different for neuroqueer individuals, including prompting needs, check-ins, and breaks. Have a discussion pre-processing about how they want to set up their space virtually or in-person; this can help them create a sense of stability. Let the client know that EMDR Therapy can be hard work, so it can help to have comfort items during the process. Comfort items should be up to the client and- if they need suggestions- those suggestions should come from the intake session where you learned about your client. Does the client want a weighted lap pad or blanket, warm beverage, fidgets, stuffed animal, favorite hoodie or comfy clothes, or a specific spot to sit for their BLS time? Creating a routine around BLS sessions can help mitigate the anticipation of what is to come.

As processing goes on, it can be incredibly overstimulating. Clients may need a movement break between sets to readjust their sensory system. These breaks can look like briefly pacing in the space, flapping their limbs, and/or jumping up and down. Such breaks are also an incredible skill development for the client as they might be learning system regulation. As the clients are processing or even when taking their breaks, they are continuing to make connections. You may find that these clients easily circle back to past targets as their understanding of themselves evolves. This does not indicate an uncleared target that needs attention. Often neuroqueers will draw connections quickly integrating their healing to prior sessions at different rates.

It is fascinating to see the connections the client can make and where their beautiful brains take them in their journey. Being open to whatever the client is experiencing is the most neuroaffirming approach. As mentioned above, this community can be literal thinkers. They can also be incredibly versed in tangents and long-winded responses. Let it happen! This is their way of processing, understanding, and learning. On the contrary, if words are not coming easily or minimally, let it happen. Check the client's comfort in what they can share and if they need support in any way. Taking notes (literally or in your mind) of themes or pieces that the client brings up can be a great way to then have something ready to provide to the client when returning to a BLS set.

Many Autistic and ADHD clients struggle to transition from sharing what came up in a set then go into another set and shift their focus. Using the notes you took, provide the client with one or two suggestions then ask "What are you feeling pulled to use for this next set?" This can help them decide between options you provided or inspiration for their own idea. Additionally, reframing cognitive interweaves for these clients can make a world of difference in their processing. Many clients will repeat stereotypes and what they have been told about their identities, like "I am broken." We might be inclined to jump to the neurotypical and cisheteronormative positive belief instead, being "I am normal." However, to a neuroqueer teenager, this may never feel true. Many have lived their life being told directly and indirectly that they are not normal, and some have embraced this as a positive part of their identity. Instead, use expansive language such as, "I am whole in my own way" or encourage your client to come up with their own.

Structuring sessions based on the client's needs is imperative to all forms of affirming therapy. This could include shorter, more frequent sessions or longer sessions bookended by clients sharing their passions or general talk therapy. It is important that this may ebb and flow for the client. It also may not be something they can identify until after they have already started the process. Lean into flexibility and find a rhythm together. Oftentimes family members will make grandiose statements about what is possible for a young client only to find that once given the flexibility to find their own way, they can accomplish more in one hour than they do in a whole school day.

Other EMDR Strategies

The majority of neuroqueer individuals are going to have more than single-event traumas. In most cases, they won't have events they can identify. The reason being many experiences are more insidious or not in one's ability to process as a trauma. These can include sensory overload, social rejections, rejection sensitivity, justice sensitivity, masking, and so much more.

It can be incredibly ableist to assume that all clients feel and think in the same way. For many neuroqueer individuals, they may have more non-linear ways of thinking, little to no introspection (body awareness), or not be able to identify emotions with sensation (identifying when they feel happy). In fact, many adults, regardless of neurodivergent neurotype, struggle with identifying and connecting their emotions to the body sensations they experience. This can be a significant challenge for neuroqueer individuals due to their unique cognitive and sensory processing patterns. It is important to allow the client to move, breathe, and experience the world in the way that they know and continue to assess the intersection of their neurotype on the therapeutic work. It is also ableist to use EMDR as a way to help someone stop masking completely. In our current society, complete unmasking can be impossible and dangerous. Being realistic with your clients on where, when, and how to unmask along with when masking is necessary and part of their safety is vital.

Similarly, it is important to be open and ready for various levels of what an emotional response can look like for a neuroqueer client. We are programmed to look for emotional expressions of anger or tears. For a neuroqueer individual, their form of tears could be to shut down. Their anger could include eliminating the use of spoken words. We are also programmed to focus on the body sensations and emotions, but many neuroqueer individuals find more benefit from connecting the dots, logical analysis, and verbal processing between sets.

Summary and Conclusions

EMDR can do amazing magic around processing the negative experiences one has had in life. It can also empower one's identities and their sense of self. Watching a client's face during BLS turn from a frown to a big beautiful smile as they see or feel themselves as their true identity is the greatest gift and astounding to witness. By taking your foundational skills of EMDR and amplifying them through neuroaffirming work and Queer Theory, your therapeutic practice moves beyond symptom reduction and into identity affirmation and healing. Healing isn't just about surviving one's past; it's about how these young humans can reclaim their agency, authenticity, and - most importantly - their Queer joy. As my trans AuDHDer clients would say: now that's bussin'!

Dr. Lanza (they/them) is a dedicated LCSW practicing in Pennsylvania and New Jersey, with a Ph.D. in human sexuality. With a deep commitment to fostering healing and empowerment, they specialize in working with LGBTQIA+ individuals, disabled and neurodivergent communities, people of the global majority, and those living with chronic illness. Dr. Lanza provides gender-affirming care and trauma-focused therapy, particularly supporting survivors of child sexual abuse and sexual assault. As their primary modality, EMDR is woven into sessions with accessibility and creativity, ensuring that each person's healing journey is both personalized and deeply affirming.

References

Attwood, T. (2014). *The autism spectrum and sexuality: Public policy, legal, and ethical issues.* In D. E. H. L. Brown (Ed.), *Autism and sexuality: Public policy and legal perspectives* (pp. 87-104). Jessica Kingsley Publishers.

Bancroft, J. & Janssen, E. (2000). The dual control model: The role of sexual inhibition & excitation in sexual arousal and behavior. *Journal of Sex Research, 37*(2), 105-114. https://doi.org/10.1080/00224490009552003

Belcher, H. L. (2022). *Taking off the mask: Practical exercises to help understand and minimise the effects of Autistic camouflaging*. Philadelphia, PA: Jessica Kingsley Publishers.

Cacciatore, R., Korteniemi-Poikela, E., & Kaltiala, R. (2019). The steps of sexuality – A developmental, emotion-focused, child-centered model of sexual development and sexuality education from birth to adulthood. *International Journal of Sexual Health, 31*(3), 319-338. https://doi.org/10.1080/19317611.2019.1645783

Cooper, K., Mandy, W., Butler, C., & Russell, A. (2021). The lived experience of gender dysphoria in autistic adults: An interpretative phenomenological analysis. *Autism 26*(4), 963-974. https://doi.org/10.1177/13623613211039113

D'Augelli, A. R. (1994). Lesbian and gay male development: Steps toward an analysis of lesbian and gay life span development. In B. Greene & G. M. Herek (Eds.), *Lesbian and gay psychology: Theory, research, and clinical applications* (pp.118-132). Thousand Oaks, CA: Sage.

Dailey, D. (1981). Sexual expression and ageing. In: Berghorn D and Schafer D (eds.) *The Dynamics of Ageing: Original Essays on the Processes and Experiences of Growing Old*. Boulder, CO: Westview Press, pp. 311-330.

Dailey, D. (1981). The five circles of human sexuality. *SIECUS Report, 9*(4), 1-5.

De Lauretis, T. (1991). Queer Theory: Lesbian and Gay Sexualities. *A Journal of Feminist Cultural Studies.*

Freud, S. (1905/1953). *Three essays on the theory of sexuality* (J. Strachey, Trans.). In J. Strachey (Ed.), *The standard edition of the complete psychological works of Sigmund Freud* (Vol. 7, pp. 123-243. London: Hogarth Press. (Original work published 1905)

Frost, D. & Meyer, I. H. (2023). Minority stress theory: Application, critique, and continued relevance. *Current Opinion in Psychology, 51*, 1-6.

Galbraith, M. C. (2022). The need for liberatory understandings of Queer and Trans identify development: A critical review of identity development models. *The Vermont Connection, 43* (17), 167-183.

Gougen, N. A. (2010). Sexuality and Autism: A critical review of selected literature using a social-relational model of disability. *American Journal of Sexuality Education, 5*, 328-361. htttps://doi.org/10.1080/15546128.2010.527237

Gratton, F. (2020). *Supporting Transgender Autistic youth and adults*. Philadelphia, PA: Jessica Kingsley Publishers.

Human Rights Campaign (HRC). (2023, May 31). Glossary of terms. *Resources. https://www.hrc.org/resources/glossary-of-terms*

Kinsey, A., Pomeroy, W. B., & Martin, C. E. (1948). *Sexual behavior in the human male*. W. B. Sunders.

Klein, F. (1993). *The bisexual option* (2nd ed.). Binghamton, NY: Haworth Press.

Martin, C. L. & Ruble, D. N. (2010). Patterns of gender development. *Annual Review of Psychology, 61*, 353-381. https://doi.org/10.1146/annurev.psych.093008.100511

Mendes. E. A. & Maroney, M. R. (2019). *Gender Identity, Sexuality, and Autism: Voices from across the Spectrum*. Philadelphia, PA: Jessica Kingsley Publishers.

Meyer, I. H. (2003). Prejudice, social stress, and mental health in lesbian, gay, and bisexual populations: Conceptual issues and research evidence. *Psychological Bulletin, 129*(5), 674-697. https://doi.org/10.1037/0033-2909.129.5.674

Price, D. (2022). *Unmasking Autism: Discovering the new faces of neurodiversity*. New York: Harmony Books.

Storms, M. D. (1990). Theories of sexual orientation. *Journal of Personality and Social Psychology, 60*(1), 164-172. http://doi.org/10.1037/0022-3514.60.1.164

van der Doef, S. & Reinders, J. (2018). Stepwise sexual development of adolescents: The Dutch approach to sexuality education. *Nature Reviews Urology, 15*(3). https://doi.org/10.1038/nrurol.2018.3

Van Der Miesen, A. I. R., Hurley, H., Bal, A. M., & de Vries, A. L. C. (2018) Prevalence of the wish to be of the opposite gender in adolescents and adults with autism spectrum disorder. *Archives of Sexual Behavior,* 47, 2307-2317. https://doi.org/10.1007/s10508-018-1218-3

Walker, N. (2021). *Neuroquuer Heresies.* Autonomous Press, LLC.

Walsh, R. J., Krabbendam, L., Dewinter, J., & Begeer, S. (2018). Brief report: Gender identity differences in autistic adults: Associations with perceptual and socio-cognitive profiles. *Journal of Autism and Developmental Disorders, 48*(12), 4070-4078.

Warrier, V., Greenber, D. M., Weir, F., Buckingham, C., Smith, P., Lai, M. C., Allison, C., & Baron-Choen, S. (2020). Elevated rates of autism, other neurodevelopmental and psychiatric diagnoses, and autistic traits in transgender and gender-diverse individuals. *Nature Communications, 11*(1), 1-12.

WHO (2006.) *Defining Sexual Health—Report of a Technical Consultation on Sexual Health 28-31 January 2002, Geneva. Sexual Health Document Series,* World Health Organization, Geneva.

Wise. S. J. (2024). *We're all neurodiverse.* Philadelphia, PA: Jessica Kingsley Publishers.

Healing Relationships

Queer Trauma and the Power of Love

Steven Halady, PhD, LCSW

Shortly after 4am on Saturday, September 14th, 2019, my father died after a sixteen-month long battle with brain cancer. We buried him on Wednesday. The following Saturday, I was alone on a plane over the Atlantic Ocean flying to Tallinn, Estonia, for a week of training and professional conference where I would become a member of the Motivational Interviewing Network of Trainers (MINT), an international organization of trainers, researchers, and practitioners of motivational interviewing.

As a little gay kid coming of age in Buffalo, New York in the 1990s, my relationship with my dad was complex. Given what I now know, I can see now how aspects of that relationship were traumatic, specifically around issues of attachment in the context of a parent who did not have the tools to meet the emotional needs of a queer kid. Now in my forties, I am still unpacking it all in my own EMDR therapy, and I am grateful to have a skilled and compassionate guide through that labyrinth.

Old Town Tallinn (Courtesy of the Author)

I do not mean any of this to be a slight against my father, or to suggest that those words encapsulate all that our relationship was. Dad was a good man. As a rehabilitation counselor, he worked tirelessly toward improving the lives of people struggling with physical and intellectual disabilities. As a military veteran, he dedicated his life in the service of our country. He worked hard and made an effort to be physically present in the lives of his three sons, coaching our sports teams, attending my choir concerts, sitting through more than one cringe-worthy high school musical theater production, and once I got to college, taking an active interest in my academic work in philosophy. He did his best to raise me and my brothers, and largely succeeded. Whatever success I have achieved in my life I owe in large part to the foundations laid by him and my mother.

And, as so many queer folk know, even his best wasn't everything I needed. This gap between what we need as queer folk and what our parents, families, and communities can provide is one central piece of what I am calling 'queer trauma'.

What is Queer Trauma?

If we are going to consider EMDR and trauma healing in the context of the experiences of queer people, it is important to have a clear sense of what is unique about those kinds of trauma and where they intersect with other forms of trauma. It is important to note that the conception of *queer trauma* that I explore here comes primarily from my own lived context as a white, cisgender middle-class and able-bodied male in the United States, and may not translate to other contexts, communities, or experiences. I also use the word *queer* in a very broad and inclusive sense to encompass the whole range of identities, experiences, expressions, and behaviors that are not sanctioned as "normal" in a patriarchal, cisnormative, and heteronormative society. However, I do not wish to suggest that all queer people experience or respond to queer trauma in the same ways. What I share is a more general picture that, in my experience, is common enough to explore more deeply. Take what is helpful for you and leave the rest.

With that said, what do I mean by *queer trauma*?

Growing up as a star in the queer constellation, our society too often denies us the opportunity to shine. Simply existing in a society dominated by homophobia, transphobia, and patriarchy is traumatic. Gay therapist and writer Joe Kort has suggested that all queer people experience covert cultural sexual assault just by living under these systems of oppression. He describes this form of sexual assault as the "chronic verbal, emotional, psychological, and sometimes sexual assaults against an individual's gender expression, sexual feelings, and behaviors" (Kort, 2018; p. 54). The idea is, if sexual violence is the use of sex or sexuality as a tool to exercise domination over another, then those of us who exist outside of heteronormativity and cisnormativity are constantly barraged by the violence of these power structures due to our sex, sexuality, and gender.

In using gender and sex as tools to exercise domination over others, this kind of covert violence operates in ways that bear notable parallels to more overt sexual violence and both the physical and emotional forms it can take. As a survivor of sexual abuse, recognizing these parallels has been a powerful part of my own trauma healing.

My experience is that systemic violence rooted in sex, sexuality, and gender is an important contributor to queer trauma. As with more overt forms of sex and gender-based violence, the violence of queer trauma can alienate us from our own bodies, tainting our thoughts and emotions as embodied, sexual, and gendered persons. It can drive a wedge between our sense of self and what otherwise would be a more spontaneous and joyful experience of our self in relationship with others. Oppressive domination of a person through sex and gender, whether overt or covert, sends a message: you are the wrong kind of person, and what is wrong in you must be violently negated. The resulting shame can be compounded by the fear of further harm. The steps we take to protect ourselves can also alienate us from ourselves and from others who want to know and love us.

So, while not identical, there are parallels between how overt sex and gender-based violence can operate, as well as in the destructive effect it has on those who experience it. However, unlike more overt instances of sex and gender-based violence, which are often enacted upon queer people for being queer, the covert violence experienced by queer people goes beyond the experiences of more direct acts of violence. Similar to complex-PTSD, experiences of queer trauma can be hard to define as traumatic because they cannot all be broken down into discrete, identifiable events. In addition to overt acts of violence and hate crimes, queer people can experience a kind of "death by 1,000 papercuts." The covert and systemic nature of much of queer trauma makes it insidious. It is difficult to recognize, and its impacts can be subtle.

Many repeated and incremental traumas, slights, aggressions, invalidations, and threats create an eroding effect on many queer people, reinforcing and complicating deep-seated experiences of shame, fear, and guardedness. In queer trauma, both the trauma and emotional experiences are often directed toward our selves, leading to complex layers of self-hatred. When the effects of queer trauma are present, they can be treated as just further evidence that there is something wrong with us, rather than recognized as reasonable responses to unreasonable circumstances.

The impacts of queer trauma are not simply a direct response to the accumulation of the anti-queer experiences a person has encountered. While each of those experiences does take its toll, they also contribute to a larger and more comprehensive impact. In this way, what I am calling *queer trauma* bears similarities to complex and attachment traumas.

Complex trauma is the result of ongoing traumatic events. Attachment trauma is experienced most often in our early developmental years when relationships with primary caregivers, often our biological parents, are repeatedly disrupted without adequate repair. Given common family and economic structures in the United States, individuals often experience significant overlap between complex and attachment trauma. However, this overlap is not necessary. One can exist without the other. Complex trauma may develop at any point in our lives, outside of our developmental years or relationships with caregivers. Attachment trauma may result from single large events that lead to a break in our attachment relationships, rather than ongoing abuse or neglect.

In queer trauma, we experience similar overlaps. The constant exposure to anti-queer violence in its myriad forms is ongoing and often inescapable, leading to complex trauma. Growing up queer in the context of an otherwise cisgender and heteronormative family structure can result in our emotional needs as queer people being overlooked. This can be in addition to more active abuse, or being forced by parents, caregivers, teachers, and others to conform to lives and identities that they wish for us but are not our own. While queer trauma can be caught up with both complex trauma and attachment trauma, this connection isn't necessary.

Trauma and Identity

One parallel that does exist among complex, attachment, and queer traumas is that they are often rooted not only in the bad things we did experience, but also in the good things that we needed but lacked. In this, queer trauma and the damage done to our sense of self is suffered through deprivation. We often lack family who are knowledgeable and attuned to the experiences and needs of queer folk. Queer community must often be carved out, creating spaces that are separate from more dangerous and oppressive areas of our society. We lack healthy role models and healthy representation in culture and media. While many of these barriers to a healthy sense of self have improved over the years, there are still long ways to go. These experiences of deprivation can deny us the social resources needed to develop healthy senses of our self and of our place in the world. They also can be barriers to recognizing our worth both as persons in general and queer people specifically. This damage and denial of healthy and empowering queer identities is another central aspect of queer trauma.

The damage that trauma can do to our sense of self and of self-worth is not unique to queer experiences. Psychiatrist Judith Herman describes the various paths by which trauma undermines our sense of self, including developing shame and guilt as core emotional experiences, fostering a sense of helplessness and undermining belief in our own competence, overriding bodily autonomy, violation of human connection and ability to trust, and shaking beliefs in a meaningful world governed by justice (Herman, 2022). These destructive impacts are often present in queer trauma.

Philosopher Susan Brison explores the ways that trauma can disrupt our sense of identity though examining her own experiences in the aftermath of a brutal sexual assault (Brison, 2002). She discusses three aspects of our sense of self often shattered by trauma: our embodied self, our ability to make autonomous choices, and the narrative story of our lives.

Trauma alienates us from our own bodies, especially when that trauma involves physical or sexual violence. As Herman describes it, "Traumatic events violate the autonomy of the person at the level of basic bodily integrity. The body is invaded, injured, defiled. Control over bodily functions is often lost; in the folklore of combat and rape, this loss of control is often recounted as the most humiliating aspect of trauma," (Herman, 2022; p. 76). The somatic experiences of traumatic recall, the ways that traumatic memories are encoded as implicit memories, the disruption of our awareness by sensory flashbacks, dissociation, the ways that our fight-flight-freeze responses can physically immobilize us or hijack our behavior, the physiological felt experiences of anxiety, depression, and hypervigilance – all contribute to the severing of our sense of connection and wholeness with our bodies. It is common for people to change their appearance in response to sexual violence, including through how they dress or by changing their body through disordered eating. Thus, our relationships with our own bodies and how we present them can be disrupted.

Though I reject the idea that sexual orientation and expressions of gender identity are biological, aspects of these parts of our identity are embodied, connected to the lived experiences of our bodies. Notable parts of queer identities are tied to our bodies. The kinds of bodies that we are attracted to, how we carry our bodies and use them as ways to express ourselves, and the relationships our bodies have to social norms and scripts are all factors that can be important to queer identities. Alienation and dysphoria in relation to our bodies, as well as social expectations of what our bodies are supposed to do and be, take on additional weight in queer trauma.

As trauma undermines our relationship with our body, our reactions, and behaviors, it also undermines our sense of ourselves as autonomous agents able to make conscious and intentional decisions that we then act upon. Symptoms of activated trauma can render involuntary many of our behaviors and responses, causing us to think, feel, and behave in ways that are incongruent with our goals and values, which can then cause further damage across our lives. The function of substance use, disordered eating, and other compulsive behaviors to numb and dissociate from our traumatized selves are prime examples of the ways our capacity to act autonomously can be hijacked by trauma.

Trauma survivors can also experience a loss of control over their environments. Brison gives her own example of being unable to take a walk outside without fear after having been assaulted while on a walk. She notes, "If a rape victim is unable to walk outside without the fear of being assaulted again, she quickly loses the desire to go for a walk [. . .] Some reactions that once were under the will's command become involuntary and some desires that once were motivating can no longer be felt, let alone acted upon," (Brison, 2002; p. 60).

In queer trauma, we can see this loss of autonomy played out in many ways. Many of us experience things like adopting a "straight voice" or different ways of dress in certain contexts, being out in some spaces and not in others, engaging in queer relationships *on the down low*, being selective about pronoun use when meeting new people, or avoiding places that are not safe to be queer. My own EMDR uncovered ways that I silenced my own pain to accommodate other people's bad behavior. This pattern was rooted in my protective responses to my dad's anger when I first came out. These practices can help to keep us safe in potentially hostile environments, and they also require bracketing off aspects of ourselves for fear of that safety.

In terms of the narrative story of our lives, acute experiences of violence often bring about a distinct break between before-trauma and after-trauma. There is a sense that who we are is not the same across this divide. In the case of the more complex forms that queer trauma can take, there is not as clear a sense of before and after, though these patterns place a real limitation on our conceptions of the kinds of stories that are possible for us. For example, queer kids are often not born to queer parents, and spend our developmental years surrounded by cisgender heteronormativity. Even if well-meaning and relatively queer-informed parents are aware enough to introduce and open possibilities for connecting with queerness during their kids' developmental years, there is only so much that can be done to stave off the ill effects of larger oppressive social structures. There will also be things that cisgender heterosexual parents simply will not know about lived queer experiences. Their limitations can lead to blind spots in their parenting of queer children, even in a best-case scenario.

My own experiences in school illustrate the ways that cis-normative and hetero-normative societies can limit the possibilities for the stories that we can tell about ourselves. Growing up, my family was at least nominally Catholic, not particularly religious, but religious enough that I attended local Catholic schools from pre-kindergarten until I graduated from college. We attended Mass regularly, and I even served as an altar server through middle school. In high school, I joined my school's choir, and we regularly sang Mass both at the school and at churches throughout the community. We also had weekly religion classes that included Catholic theology and ethics, Biblical study, and an introduction to world religions as a part of the standard curriculum.

Starting in fifth grade, students at my school took "human growth and development," the school's Sex Education class, and health class became a regular part of the curriculum. I honestly couldn't tell you much about these classes, but I can say with certainty that there was absolutely nothing presented in them that even obliquely acknowledged the existence of people who were not cisgender and heterosexual. At no point in either my middle school curriculum or family life was the idea of gayness introduced as even a concept.

The possibilities for understanding my sense of self were limited. I was deprived of the language that might help me to recognize or understand my own experiences around my identity and my place in the world. I started my first year at an all-male Catholic high school by joining the freshman soccer team. One afternoon, the coach decided that one of my (straight) teammates should have the nickname "Flamer." At the time, I lacked the words and concepts to know what it meant, or that it was an anti-gay slur. It didn't bother me at the time because I had never been given the opportunity to know that I should be bothered by it. Even decades later, I think back on this moment, still able to see the image of it in my mind, and a heavy sadness comes over me. Not because of what happened, but because of my own socially imposed ignorance. I look back on my fourteen-year-old self and try to hold him with compassion. He was never even given the opportunity to know he was being slapped across the face. This is only one prominent example of the casual homophobia that I faced every day.

It was just over two years after the "Flamer" moment that I was able to connect the dots about my own identity. While I had a general sense of being more attracted to other men, I had gone on a few dates with girls because that is just what guys did. I still did not have the language or concepts to consider that there were possibilities beyond *just what guys did.*

Language is powerful in creating opportunities and possibilities. I didn't learn the word *gay* until I was sixteen, a junior in high school. I was on the patio at a local café talking with some classmates before we went to one of their houses to work on a group project. The conversation turned to another classmate who was struggling with his parents after coming out as gay. I was quiet and listened as my two classmates talked, integrating the idea that something existed outside of the world I was allowed to inhabit. The rest fell into place, his story and experience giving me words that I could then apply to my own experiences. I don't recall if I contributed much to the class project afterward, but I do recall spending hours on the couch in my classmate's basement after we finished working, integrating the new concepts into my worldview and using them to make new sense of my own experiences. Knowing what I know now, I was laying there dissociating until around two or three in the morning. My classmates didn't know what was going on in my head, but they were kind enough to just give me the space before driving me home. It took being taught the words and concepts for experiences outside of cis- and heteronormativity to figure out that I am gay. Later in my life, it took digging into the concept of queerness to figure out that "queer" also describes some aspects of my experiences.

These examples illustrate ways that queer trauma is rooted not just in specific acts of violence and deprivation, but also systemic structures. A fundamental aspect of queer trauma is that it is often systemic oppression that plays the role of gatekeeper for what kinds of lives are possible. Growing up middle class and Catholic, I grew up in a context where gayness and queerness were not talked about. There were no gay characters on TV. It would take three years from the beginning of my own coming out process for *Dawson's Creek* to air the first romantic gay male kiss on Primetime TV. Oppressive systems denied me the words, concepts, and role models that would have allowed me to live with a broader sense of self-awareness and integrity while growing up.

At the same time, systems of oppression also shape the kinds of lives we think we could have. Coming out while the AIDS epidemic was a major defining factor for gay male queer experiences, I distinctly recall the nonchalance with which I told a friend at the high school lunch table that there was a very good chance that I would die young from AIDS. I remember the shock on his face. That idea did not make sense to him. For me, whose only knowledge of gayness and queer history at the time was deeply entwined with the AIDS epidemic, that possible future was simple fact.

Social structures beyond the words and concepts that we are taught also contribute to the kinds of lives that we can imagine. Having spent much of my adult life watching the fight for marriage equality in the United States unfold, I can look back and see distinct changes in what is possible, as changes in laws and social structures shifted from "the best I can hope for is to find a partner and just be left alone," to "maybe marriage equality might actually happen" and then to actually saying "I do" with my husband in front of our family and friends. Time will tell what other possibilities will be opened or closed by changing social structures.

As queer people, the kinds of narratives that we can conceive of as part of our lives are shaped by the larger social, economic, political, legal, and family structures that exist around us. These examples highlight an important aspect to queer trauma that distinguishes it from some other forms of trauma: queer trauma ties to larger-scale systems that perpetuate traumatic violence against queer people as queer people. These macro-level factors are structural and systemic, meaning they are not reducible to the actions, beliefs, or values of specific individuals. They are rooted in societal patterns around how certain lives, identities, and bodies are valued, as well as the concrete ways that material resources and opportunities are arranged and made accessible with respect to those lives, identities, and bodies.

Social work researchers David Avruch and Wendy Shaia provide a helpful framework for understanding this systemic aspect of anti-queer violence and oppression: socially-engineered trauma, or SET. They define *socially-engineered trauma* as "traumatic events rooted in the forces of oppression and inequality" (Avruch & Shaia, 2022; p.178-179). SET is distinct from other forms of trauma in that it occurs non-randomly. Marginalized individuals and communities are more likely to be exposed to both overt and covert traumatic experiences. This group-level vulnerability to trauma causes those at the intersections of marginalized social identities to bear a much greater and oftentimes more insidious traumatic load. SET is not limited to oppression on the basis of sex, gender, or sexual orientation, but also includes many other aspects of an individual's identity, including race, ethnicity or national background, religious affiliation or lack thereof, physical or mental ability, economic class, etc.

To summarize, some essential aspects of queer trauma are that it involves the insidious, constant, and incremental erosion of our senses of self and self-worth. It limits access to a queer community. Queer trauma is inescapably linked to our relationships with ourselves, other people, our communities, and broader society. Insofar as the systemic and acute trauma we experience as queer people involves violence aimed at damaging these relationships, queer trauma is fundamentally relational. This is part of why recognizing the parallels between queer trauma and other forms of sexual violence is important. Both are interpersonal, direct, and intentional violations of a person's embodied self. Both queer and other forms of sexual trauma can shatter our ability to trust and be our genuine selves with those around us. Queering EMDR needs to take these aspects of queer trauma into account when supporting queer healing.

Queer Trauma Requires Queer Healing

The centrality of relationships and community to queer identity is a big part of why my father could not be who I needed him to be as a burgeoning queer kid. As a heterosexual, cisgender male, he never needed to find, create, or travel in any kind of queer community. To my knowledge, I am the first openly queer person in the family, so my dad had the privilege of not needing to think about connecting with queer community for himself or his sons. Until I came along, queerness really did not loom large in my family's world.

My family was only the first instance of *being the only one*, an experience that would crop up repeatedly throughout my life. I was one of only three or four "out" teens in my high school, and as a result was typically the token gay in my social groups. Being the only one came with a lurking loneliness that was unspeakable because I never knew any other way of being. Things became better as an adult, where there were other queer people present in work environments. However, there still were few opportunities to connect with other queer people, and when there were, it was often centered around survival and the work we needed to do to challenge the homophobic and cis-normative systems we were in. Loneliness persisted, the kind of disconnection where I didn't know what I was missing until I found community beyond individuals.

The harm of my queer trauma goes beyond simply not having a community. Trauma can damage, even fracture, our sense of self, resulting in a loss of a coherent sense of who and what we are as people in the world. I avoid defining the *self* as an individual because not everybody experiences themselves as the kind of atomistic, unified individual that is often assumed in Western European and Anglo-American societies. Notably, people who experience a significant degree of dissociation as an expression of trauma may identify as a team, a system, an internal family, or some other variety of internal multiplicity. Identifying as a system of multiple parts can be just as coherent a sense of self as identifying as a more atomistic individual. In addition, many identify as members of families or communities first, and as individuals second. Whether we understand ourselves as an individual, a multiplicity, a member of a larger community, or some combination of these, our relationships with our larger communities are essential components for building our *selves*.

There is an immediate sense in which the material conditions of our environments, communities, and larger social systems shape the possibilities of who and what we can be. For example, it is impossible to be or to identify as a professional social worker in a time and place where there is no system that creates a profession of social work. The same point applies to environments where concepts such as *gay* or *queer* are not a part of the vocabulary.

In addition, there is a deeper sense in which our social environments shape us as people through *moral recognition*. Moral recognition is about acknowledging both the facts and moral value of another person and their identity. Recognition in this sense can affirm and uplift, creating the interpersonal context to be and thrive as your authentic self. As philosopher Charles Taylor, describes it, "Our identity is partly shaped by recognition or its absence, often by the *misrecognition* of others, and so a person or group of people can suffer real damage, real distortion, if the people or society around them mirror back to them a confining or demeaning or contemptible picture of themselves. Nonrecognition or misrecognition can inflict harm, can be a form of oppression, imprisoning someone in a false, distorted, and reduced mode of being," (Taylor, 1994; p. 25). Invisibility, denial, and devaluation of who people are can cause real psychological wounds.

In offering or denying moral recognition for queer people, the character traits of our communities play a central role in both the creation of queer trauma and in its healing. However, this aspect of moral recognition at the level of community is not a part of EMDR, traditionally conceived. The EMDR Standard Protocol laid out by Shapiro is developed from a paradigm of individual clients sitting with individual therapists to resolve traumas from specific bad events (Shapiro, 2018). EMDR Basic Training is aimed at establishing a basic competency of the Standard Protocol, which is then adapted for working effectively with more complex, chronic, and deprivation-based traumas. For example, while writers such as Laurell Parnell and Shirley Jean Schmidt provide helpful strategies for preparing people who have experienced significant attachment trauma for EMDR, the EMDR Standard Protocol remains the same (Parnell, 2013; Schmidt, 2020).

EMDR, built to work with individuals who have experienced discrete traumatic events, tracks the history of thinking about trauma in mainstream mental health treatment. Judith Herman points out that we learned about trauma through two paradigm cases: soldiers returning from war and intimate partner and sexual violence against women (Herman, 2022). In both cases, you have relatively discrete events that lead to trauma and its expressions. Though the diagnostic criteria for PTSD have evolved over time, the assumption that PTSD symptoms are a response to discrete events remains central to understanding of trauma and its treatment. EMDR works squarely in this paradigm.

It is interesting to consider that EMDR has within it the tools for a more robust conception of trauma beyond the "specific big bad thing that happened" paradigm. The foundational theoretical explanation of how EMDR works is the Adaptive Information Processing (AIP) model (Shapiro, 2018). According to the AIP model, information about traumatic experiences is stored in the memory in a maladaptive state. A simplified explanation of how EMDR works is by breaking down the maladaptive information and building up more adaptive information regarding a traumatic event. According to this model, EMDR should work on any kind of experience that leads the brain to store information about an event in a maladaptive format. These kinds of experiences will include not only the large bad things that happened, but also the buildup of impacts from chronic small events and the experience of missing out on good things that we needed.

It is unclear whether EMDR is capable of evolving into a modality that can incorporate all of the community-level aspects of queer trauma into its standard paradigm, or if that is even a desirable goal. No single therapy can - or should - be all things to all people in all contexts. To try to make it so is not only unrealistic, it's dangerous. A one-size-fits-all therapy would reduce the beautiful complexity of human experiences to fit it into a single unified theory, and in so doing reproduce the oppressive structures that bring too many people to therapy to begin with.

Consequently, queering EMDR cannot mean changing the Standard Protocol to address systemic oppression itself. I do not know what such a trauma resolution would look like, or if what remains would still be EMDR. What I think queering EMDR does mean is that EMDR can only be one aspect of a more comprehensive approach to healing trauma. While reprocessing traumatic experiences can be a powerful and important component to trauma healing, it is not and cannot be the whole story. For queer healing, EMDR is neither necessary nor sufficient. Healing trauma requires healing communities as well.

This perspective moves us outside of the conception of healing as the removal of negative signs and symptoms of distress that is a common assumption in the Western medical model of healing. It requires EMDR providers to rethink our professional structures, practices, assumptions, history, education, and relationship with oppressive structures like the State through licensing (Mullan, 2023). Such a re-thinking is beyond the scope of this essay but is necessary if we truly want to queer EMDR.

To support the healing of queer trauma, we need to incorporate the community into our healing journeys, both for those we serve and for ourselves. Community may look like many things to many different people. Imagining and building such communities is essential for healing what is queer in our trauma. While EMDR itself may not be able to expand to be a community-level intervention, we can queer EMDR by bringing community building into how we do EMDR and where we see EMDR in the context of a larger healing experience.

What's MI Got to Do with It?

It was rainy and overcast when I arrived in Tallinn, Estonia, three days after my father's funeral. I had spent the better part of the previous twenty-four hours traveling through multiple airports and countries only to arrive at my destination to find that one of the wheels on my luggage had been smashed in transit. Not knowing the city or the native language, I got off the public transport at the wrong stop. What I thought would be a short walk to my hotel turned into a few miles hike through the city with my broken suitcase in tow.

Alexander Nevsky Cathedral, Tallinn

As uncomfortable as it was to half-drag a heavy suitcase with only one good wheel through the strange streets, it was at the same time oddly refreshing walking in the rain. Following the map on my phone while managing a large suitcase after a series of flights was physically tiring, but it had a known endpoint. Unlike dad's brain cancer and the drawn-out physical and cognitive decline it inflicted upon him, I knew how to navigate a map and lift with my legs. I arrived safely, checked in, and had that night and all the next day to explore the city before the start of the events I had traveled for.

After a sixteen-month ordeal from dad's diagnosis to his death, being alone on another continent in a city where I knew no one was freeing. I remember the day I spent exploring as one of the best of my life. I wandered aimlessly through Old Town, walked out into the Gulf of Finland, discovered a Soviet era prison turned into a museum, and happened upon a hundred other small wonders throughout Tallinn. But most of all, I let myself forget the past year, my dad's illness, and death. Yes, when I happened upon the Naval Park, I thought about how dad would have wanted to drive the boats. Though I had long ago left the religion I was raised in, I made a small offering and lit a candle in the Alexander Nevsky Cathedral in Old Town in memory of my father. There were plenty of moments where he was still present with me. Mostly, I let myself be in a completely different world.

The next day, I began a three-day train-the-trainer event. Membership in the Motivational Interviewing Network of Trainers (MINT) officially begins when you complete a Training of New Trainers (TNT). This is an active, intense, and highly experiential training that covers many aspects of how to effectively train motivational interviewing. Each full day is immersive and collaborative, and evenings were spent with the new friends I was making in my training cohort, getting to know each other and exploring more of the city. It was a great way to not have to think about dad's death for a few days.

Motivational interviewing is founded on the capacity to build empathetic relationships with others, and this was evident in how quickly the group members became comfortable with one another. By the end of the third day, what started as a few dozen strangers from all around the world had begun to transform into a community of colleagues. The closing experience of my TNT involved the whole cohort sitting in one large circle, going around with the opportunity to share about what the experience over the past three days had meant to them. There was joy, there was laughter, there were stories shared, there were moments of personal pain and worry, and of hope and connection. As I sat in the circle waiting for my turn and trying to figure out something meaningful to share, I realized that I was at the end of the line. I would be the last person in the group to have a chance to share. And it hit me; I knew what I needed to say.

I felt myself starting to shake, holding back tears, and struggling to keep my attention in the room as my mind tried to scramble away and be anywhere else. I don't remember what exactly I said when it came to my turn. I wasn't completely in the room. But after three days of not telling a soul about what I had been holding on to alone, I shared about my father's illness and recent death, how proud he was of me, and how I knew I had to come to the TNT despite everything because he would have been so disappointed if I had let this opportunity pass by because of him. I was only a little bit in the room, and that moment was a blur. There were tears, mine and others. And there were hugs. So many hugs. People from all over the world who had been complete strangers seventy-two hours before were holding me, physically and emotionally, as sixteen months of trying to keep my shit together all broke down and broke free. And for all of my dissociation, there was no doubt in my mind or body that I was completely safe to do so.

Physically and emotionally, I was held by a room full of people I barely knew. That moment did more to help me heal from the trauma of dad's brain cancer than anything else before or since.

How I was able to experience such powerful healing in this moment has a lot to do with what brought this group of strangers together: motivational interviewing (MI). MI is a way of engaging with people to help them to change and grow. It was created by psychologist Bill Miller in the 1980s in the context of supporting people with problematic alcohol use by applying the wisdom of Carl Rogers to substance use treatment. With the core text now in its fourth edition, MI has grown from a tool to help people change their problematic alcohol use to a comprehensive way of working with others, or, as Miller and co-author Stephen Rollnick call it, "a way of being." Over the decades, over 2,000 controlled trials, many other outcome studies, and over 200 systematic reviews and meta-analyses have established MI as effective for supporting change and growth in a wide range of areas, including mental and behavioral health, physical health, education, social work, and athletic coaching (Miller & Rollnick, 2023).

MI combines a range of skills and techniques common across many counseling, helping, and service professions, and adds to them an emphasis on recognizing and resolving ambivalence about change, as well as a framework and set of skills for drawing out and strengthening a person's own reasons for making desired changes.

MI is helpful for recognizing and avoiding *the fixing reflex*, an often well-intentioned tendency to want to step in, problem-solve, and help others when they have a problem. The fixing reflex can be problematic in many ways, especially when supporting people in healing from trauma. It can invalidate their experiences by communicating that those experiences need to be fixed by someone else. It can weaken relationships by communicating that a person's struggle is more than you can handle. The fixing reflex focuses attention on cognitive problem-solving, which can raise a barrier to encountering and working through the emotional and somatic components of trauma. Given the damage that trauma has on our sense of self, the fixing reflex can convey the message that we are a problem to be solved, adding to shame.

The skills of MI also focus on establishing deep *accurate empathy*, the ability to both accurately understand another person's own experiences and effectively communicate that understanding. Accurate empathy has been found to be one of the strongest predictors of positive outcomes in therapy independent of the modality used (Miller & Moyers, 2021).

MI was developed from the ground up. It was found to work, and then examined to determine how it works. There are many psychological theories that have been proposed to explain MI's effectiveness. Two of these are particularly relevant to understanding how MI can contribute to EMDR: Self-Perception Theory and Social Dominance Theory.

Self-Perception Theory was developed by Darryl Bem in the 1960s (Bem, 1967). Bem's research points to at least two interesting aspects of how humans develop our sense of self. First, people often don't know what they believe until they hear themselves say it. Second, we are inclined to trust our own voices more than others' voices. Part of what makes MI effective is that the skills are aimed at getting people to make their own argument for change so that they hear their reasons for change in their own voices.

Social Dominance Theory draws on evolutionary psychology (de Almeida Neto, 2017). As social animals, humans are keenly tuned in to social dynamics, though this is often unconscious. Having a sense of power or control in a social situation is also often important for getting the resources needed to survive. When a person tells or suggests that we should do something, they are subtly putting themselves in a position above us, which puts us in a lower position. This power dynamics can trigger a response to re-assert ourselves through doing something other than what we are being told to do, even if our rational minds agree that what they suggest will be good for us. MI approaches conversations about change from a position of equal partners or by taking a one-down position, focusing on evoking a person's own reasons for change rather than providing them.

Consequently, a large part of why MI is effective is that it works with the ways our brains function to help guide people toward reducing barriers and creating opportunities for change and growth. The ways that MI engages psychological processes fit well with what is known about what can be helpful for supporting trauma healing (Bennett, 2017). Avoiding the fixing reflex and building accurate empathy in an accepting relationship creates a powerful experience of moral recognition.

A central aspect of MI that makes it particularly powerful is its *Spirit*. There are four character traits that a person must embody in order to be doing MI: partnership, acceptance, compassion and empowerment. No matter how technically adept a person may be in the core skills, strategies, and tasks of MI, if they are not also embodying the Spirit, they are not doing MI.

The Spirit of MI is central to its healing power. It was the spirit of MI, embodied by my colleagues, that made it possible for me to have such a powerful healing experience in Tallinn. A community of people both personally and professionally dedicated to the Spirit of MI created the space where I could say out loud what I was carrying and have it recognized by caring *others*. I had been alone in bearing my traumatic experiences for over a year; a community was necessary for this to be a healing experience. As Brison puts it, "In order to construct self-narratives we need not only the words with which to tell our stories, but also an audience able and willing to hear us and to understand our words as we intend them," (Brison, 2002; p. 51). A story told without anyone to hear it is just words.

Direct Applications to the Phases of EMDR

I don't know what community EMDR would be or what it would look like. If such a thing is possible, it would need to be more than individuals working through the standard protocol in the same room at the same time. I also don't know if community-level EMDR is even desirable. EMDR is a tool, and all tools have their uses and their limitations. Asking it to be all things for healing all aspects of trauma is unreasonable.

However, based on the understanding of queer trauma and informed by motivational interviewing, I propose some direct applications for queering EMDR, that is, making it more attuned and responses to the experiences of trauma that queer people are more likely to have experienced.

The first suggestion is to remember that, no matter how powerful a tool EMDR is, it is still one tool among many. Given the complex forms that queer trauma can take, healing may require forms of individual and social action across multiple systems that go beyond the scope of EMDR. A broad social and cultural history-taking that includes experiences around community, identity, anti-queer oppression, and resistance to oppression during Phase 1 is essential for recognizing where EMDR reprocessing may be helpful and what aspects of healing might require different tools.

Second, MI teaches us that engagement and motivational work are not just steps we take to get someone to the healing work. Engagement *is* the work. Queer trauma is deeply social and rooted in misrecognition. Having a secure relationship with a strong foundation in accurate empathy and a space where your authentic self can be recognized is itself healing. A community of two in a therapy room is still a community, and by building the experience of compassionate acceptance, we are resisting anti-queer oppression and facilitating a healing experience. If all you do in a meeting with a client is to show up with accurate empathy, you have already done more than most people in their lives. That power cannot be understated. So, slow down and do not rush Phase 2 to try to get to reprocessing. Engagement is trauma healing.

Third, we are more likely to believe something when we hear ourselves say it out loud, so be strategic about what you ask a client to say. Minimize inviting clients to speak negative cognitions out loud, and maximize opportunities for them to say their positive cognitions. During Phase 5, invite your client to repeat their positive cognition over and again during eye movements.

Similarly, use clients' own language for positive cognitions and interweaves. They are likely to use language that resonates with them, and so using that language conveys accurate empathy. It can also be helpful to evoke interweaves as much as possible and minimize offering them yourself. Use Socratic questioning or reflect back interweaves that a client shared at an earlier point. The adaptive information that is installed during EMDR should come from clients as much as possible.

In developing interweaves, positive cognitions, and safer/calmer place imagery, think at the community level. What are their positive thoughts and experiences around queerness? Who are their queer role models and icons? Explore if there are queer spaces that resonate with them. The Stonewall Inn may not be a serene place for calming imagery, however imagining themself at the riot could connect a queer client with a sense of power or self-worth, connect them with a larger community, as well as honor righteous anger in response to oppressive forces.

Graffiti on a building in Tallinn

For this goal, educate yourself as much as possible on queer history, and draw on it as much as possible to connect clients with their queer ancestors. Queer history is full of strengths, creativity, resistance, community, and celebration, as well as stories of individuals who lived, loved, and fought for their dignity, recognition, and healing. All these important and adaptive resources that can bolster every step of the journey to queer healing. One place to start is the podcast *Making Gay History*, which includes recordings of interviews with pioneers in queer liberation movements. You learn about the work of queer champions like Marsha P. Johnson and Sylvia Rivera in their own voices (Marcus, 2016).

Finally, do your own deep work. What are your own experiences around queerness and queer trauma? What beliefs about queer people and communities have you internalized? How might these beliefs be coming forward and shaping the healing space you hope to create? Are you aware of your righting reflex and how it comes forward? Is there something in you that is pushing toward your goals for your clients rather than their own? Excavating and exploring these questions and their answers can help to open your capacity to be fully present with those you serve.

The Queer Spirit of EMDR?

Something analogous to MI's Spirit would be powerful in creating a sense of community in the context of EMDR. Though there are discussions of the ethics of doing EMDR well, there is no analogous sense of spirit. What might a Spirit of EMDR look like? I propose four candidates for consideration as a part of a Spirit of EMDR. They are: *evocation*, *genuineness*, *courage*, and *love*.

Evoking

In his classic work on liberatory education, Paulo Freire discussed what he calls *the banking model* of education. In this model, "Education becomes an act of depositing, in which the students are the depositories and the teacher is the depositor. Instead of communicating, the teacher issues communiqués and makes deposits which the students patiently receive, memorize, and repeat," (Freire, 2003; p. 72). This model treats the receivers of the teacher's knowledge as passive and lacking, in need of what the teacher gives them. Moreover, in the banking model, education becomes an "exercise of domination [that] stimulates the credulity of students, with the ideological intent (often not perceived by educators) of indoctrinating them to adapt to the world of oppression," (p. 78). Freire describes this kind of education as itself an oppressive act of violence.

Freire contrasts the banking model with a *problem-posing model*, where it is not the teacher's job to provide information (though that can be a part of it), but to engage students in a shared, collaborative process of co-creating meaning and a shared understanding of the world. This process occurs through critical reflection on our lived experiences. It rejects the hierarchy of authority and subordinate, replacing it with critically-minded co-investigators in dialogue with each other. Freire describes this as "education as the practice of freedom," (p. 81).

This liberatory, co-creative stance toward working with others is a core part of MI and provides an important framework for EMDR. In EMDR, all else being equal, it is better if adaptive information and internal resources come from the client in their own words.

This evocative orientation not only promotes both congruence and accurate empathy, but also operates from an empowering perspective. Those we serve through EMDR are not lacking in what they need, and our job is to help them recognize and draw out their own resources rather than provide them.

We cannot heal by reproducing the circumstances that led to our being harmed in the first place. To heal, we need a new and different experience. Neuroscience shows that creating a new and different kind of experience around our traumatic memories is the essential part of healing them (Ecker, et al., 2012). The experience of working with someone who takes a stance of evocation can itself be transformative, especially for queer folk. Lack of control and a sense of helplessness are core aspects of trauma. These can be especially impactful when control is denied us through systemic oppression, as in queer trauma. Moreover, cis- and heteronormativity actively cultivate the idea that queer people are less-than, lacking, and deficient. Working with people who have experienced trauma from a stance of evocation, seeing people as already having what they need, contributes to an anti-oppressive healing experience of being competent and powerful.

This evocative stance is already a part of standard EMDR. The directives we give during Phases 4-6 to guide clients through free association - "go with that," "notice that," "just think of it," etc. - are in themselves evocative, provided we follow Shapiro's guidance and offer them "in a suggestive, not directive, tone of voice," (Shapiro, 2018; p. 268). The main strategies that Shapiro describes as ways of getting cognitive interweaves are evocative (pp. 270-273). In addition, being a grounded, affirming, and empathetic presence as a person reprocesses their trauma – having good engagement – is itself adaptive information. We often don't need to add anything, only be our best selves.

While there are times where it is appropriate or necessary in EMDR to provide adaptive information more directly, an overall stance of evocation is already built into EMDR. Making this more explicit in EMDR training and consultation to actively cultivate it as a character trait for EMDR practitioners will only strengthen our work.

Genuineness

Trauma drives disconnection from ourselves, our loved ones, and our communities. Healing from trauma involves re-learning how to embrace each of these. In order to embrace what we have disconnected from, we must do so with openness and honesty. That is, we must do so with genuineness.

Disingenuousness is often protective. We hide parts of ourselves away from the world to keep them safe from judgment. This is often true of those of us providing EMDR and other therapeutic services. As Miller and Moyers put it, "Disingenuousness involves hiding yourself in some way. Without an authentic presence, helpers may cling to a role, often as an expert or a detached observer. Partly for self-protection, they may appear to be reserved, detached, or wholly objective. In short, they keep far too much of themselves out of their professional interactions," (Miller & Moyers, 2021; p. 54). They go on to note that the empirical data shows that therapists who are more genuine in their work tend to see better outcomes and better working alliances.

Bringing our humanity into our work can be especially powerful in the context of queer trauma. Much of queer trauma is rooted in oppressive structures that mandate disingenuousness across many areas of life. Miller and Moyers's comment about hiding yourself is likely familiar to any of us who have needed to utilize closets to protect ourselves.

To build genuineness is to bring congruence among the different parts of ourselves internally, as well as congruence between those internal experiences and our external behaviors and relationships. Genuineness is not only felt through self-knowledge; it must also be acted in relationship with others. In building congruence and bringing it into our healing work, EMDR providers can model genuineness and create the relational experience of being congruent with another. In this way, it is not just what we do but also who we are that fosters healing.

There is an important balance to be struck. Bringing too much of ourselves into EMDR work can be damaging. We don't want to hold our humanity back or present ourselves as a detached inhuman professional. We want to avoid dishonesty and defensiveness, and be attuned and honest about our responses to what happens in our work. At the same time, we do want to hold back negative thoughts or emotions that arise about our clients and the people in their lives. We do not want to be "working through our own stuff" with our clients in the therapy room. While self-disclosure is an important part of genuineness, we must be intentional in it, making sure that it is appropriate, boundaried, and always in the service of what would likely be helpful for those we serve.

Courage

Facilitating EMDR requires us to be calm, grounded, and present as we guide another through re-experiencing the most horrific moments of their lives. For a client to be willing to go along with EMDR and face their worst experiences requires tremendous courage. It also requires tremendous courage on the part of those of us facilitating EMDR. To be courageous in the face of another's trauma allows us to model what courage can look like, as well as communicate that the fear, though terrible, can be faced. Vicarious and secondary trauma are real, and I suspect that I am not the only EMDR therapist who will never quite forget certain details of their clients' trauma stories, even after engaging in our own healing work around these vicarious traumas.

Though by no means the same as the experience of those doing the reprocessing, sitting in the therapist's seat as you support and guide others through such immense suffering is frightening. This is especially the case when we care about the well-being of those we serve and respectfully recognize therapists' power to cause harm. We have good reasons to fear what will come up, and if we will be adequate to the task. In this context, what might it mean to embody courage?

In his works on ethics, Aristotle said that all virtues, including courage, are a mean that falls between two extremes. This does not translate to virtue always being moderate. It means that, in trying to live by any virtue, we can go wrong in two ways: deficiency and excess. A deficiency of courage is cowardice, too great an avoidance of scary things. An excess of courage is recklessness, rushing into dangerous situations when it is unwise to do so. For Aristotle, a courageous person knows both when to engage fear and when to step back. Practical wisdom requires us to consider both possible errors.

On this view, courage is not the absence of fear but how we choose to respond to fear. This understanding of courage provides some practical guidance. "When is someone ready to move from preparation into the more active reprocessing phases?," is one of the most asked questions in EMDR Therapy. Courage guides us to adjust our pace, to weigh the wisdom of pushing forward against the wisdom of pausing until we are ready.

MI also provides some guidance here. It reminds us that our work with others is a partnership, and that we as therapists are an essential part of that partnership. Courage requires us to look at ourselves and ask, what traumas am I able to face? Is there something in me that is pushing me to engage the fearful thing too quickly and rush into reprocessing? Is there something in me that is leading me to pull away from engaging the trauma? Are there certain kinds of trauma where I am better or worse suited to facilitate EMDR, and might a referral to another provider be prudent?

There are no set answers to these questions. The target we aim for is always moving, and we must be constantly awake to the question of what the properly courageous course will be for the person in front of us on a given day. Recognizing the risk of both deficiency and excess provides us with important questions to reflect upon in deciding when to step forward and when to step back from engaging trauma. Courage requires us to learn to be comfortable navigating grey areas with no clear answers, to be willing to take wise risks, and that the safe option can sometimes be the brave one as well.

Love

Compassion is a core component of the spirit of MI. Though closely related to empathy, Miller and Rollnick note that compassion is not a feeling and describe it as "an *intention* to give top priority to the health and well-being of the one you are serving. It is a commitment to benevolence, an intent to alleviate suffering and support positive growth," (Miller & Rollnick 2023, p. 8). In the therapeutic context, compassion is not a sense of caring, rather, an intentional way of acting toward another motivated by an unselfish desire for their well-being. Compassion is about *being with* another in a particular way that involves both feeling for and acting to benefit them.

Compassionate engagement is rooted in our biological evolution. It fosters healthy relationships and secure attachment, promotes prosocial behavior, and is closely associated with empathy (Gilbert, 2020, Solomon, 2007). Whether directed toward ourselves or others, compassion can engender hope while counteracting shame and self-doubt (Neff, 2011). Cultivating compassion builds resilience and connection, and meeting another with compassion when they are deep in the reprocessing of a trauma can be a powerful tool to reconsolidate that memory. For these reasons, cultivating compassion for self and others is a clear candidate for incorporating into a spirit of EMDR.

However, given what queer trauma teaches us about the effects of trauma on ourselves and our connection with community, compassion alone is not sufficient. I propose that *love* is the last ingredient to a Spirit of EMDR. In this, it is helpful to consider that, for the Ancient Greeks, what we call 'love' was covered by three different words. *Eros* is romantic or sexual love, *agape* is universal love, and *philia* is family and friendship love.

In the context of EMDR, *eros* is the least directly relevant sense of *love*. Erotic love for clients can cause serious harm if not carefully addressed. However, our general human capacity to fall in *eros* can still teach us much about the role of love for the healing of trauma.

All emotions direct us toward seeing the world in certain ways, highlighting aspects of it as salient. Anger tells us that the world is unjust, and fear that the world is dangerous. Guilt and shame highlight the perceived badness of what I did or who I am, respectively. *Eros* draws out those aspects of the world that are sources of delight. To see another through the lens of *eros* is to see them as beautiful. In his dialogue *Symposium*, Plato writes that the first step toward learning moral goodness is to fall in *eros* with another. Seeing beauty and goodness in a beloved individual expands our minds to be able to experience them more generally. Nothing is better than *eros* at helping us see past human shortcomings to recognize the beauty in imperfect people, nor does so with more force or passion. *Eros* also has its wild irrational side. Through this aspect, *eros* connects us with the pain and confusion that comes with the human condition, and the vulnerability in us at the prospect of that love going unrequited.

When properly cultivated, *eros* provides us with a nuanced blending of what is wonderful and what is reckless in ourselves and each other. *Eros* can teach us to be in the presence of the worst in a person and still seek what is best in them. We do this first with our beloved, and then generalize this capacity to others. Through this process of generalization, we move toward a more universal form of love. While we must be careful about not directing our erotic capacity toward clients, the capacity for *eros* itself has much to teach us about being open and vulnerable to the breadth of human experience. This capacity is especially important when a person's trauma is rooted in how others' have responded to their erotic attachments, as in queer trauma.

Though *agape* is the sense of *love* that is most in-line with unconditional positive regard, a staple of all good therapy, it is inadequate as the sense of love needed in EMDR. *Agape* is universal love, the sense of 'love' that underlies the idea of "human moral dignity" at the heart of human rights. Medieval Christian theologians held that *agape* was so universal and pure, only God could actually embody it. As such, *agape* is impersonal. It is shared equally among all people.

Like *agape*, compassion can be impersonal (though it need not be). We can care for others without a personal connection with them. I can be equally compassionate for an individual I know as for the billions of others who I will never meet. While I can hold *agape* for the world's population, this sense is insufficient for the kind of care needed in the healing of trauma, especially in queer trauma which is rooted in our personal self and relationships. Given the roles of systemic oppression, misrecognition, and relationships in trauma, healing requires a more personal connection. This is not to deny that compassion cannot come with a felt sense of concern for another. It is to say that the necessary sense of love is personal in ways that compassion need not be.

Of the three senses of love, *philia* seems to be the most closely connected to the kind of love we should cultivate in EMDR, especially in the context of queer trauma. Family love is personal, and involves a sense of belonging to one another in ways that go deeper than unconditional positive regard. In philia, the beloved is seen and known as the unique, messy, glorious person they are. *Philia* is when another is at home in your heart, which is fundamentally different from the love of all people being held in a universal heart. Consequently, *philia* involves the self in ways that *agape* does not. While *agape* extends to all regardless of who they are, *philia* is essentially connected to who we are as individuals, and the care for others that it involves connects to what is uniquely good in them.

In healthy families, love is mutually shared but not identical in practice. Our roles within a family shape what concrete forms the love takes. Parents care for children in ways that it is harmful for children to reciprocate, just as therapists provide care for clients in ways it is harmful for them to reciprocate. The universality of *agape* separates it from the specifics of role and so misses this element of relationship among individuals.

In all three senses of the word, love stands apart from compassion. It focuses us on what is delightful in another, cultivates healing recognition of what is imperfect in them, and leads us to seek their good. Moreover, while compassion flows in one direction, love is bilateral. We are as much affected by a loving relationship as the people we love are. As philosopher Robert Solomon eloquently puts it, "Love is not selfless, as we so often hear, but essentially involved with the self. But love isn't selfish either [. . .] The self in love is an enlarged or expanded self that includes or embraces the other," (Solomon, 2007; pp. 61-62). This transformative power of love not only seeks the good in those we love, it draws out and enriches what is good within us, forging a bond of community grounded in care for people just as they are. This is exactly the kind of power needed to heal trauma.

In sum, love is about the personal experience of a relationship that draws out the good in one another. Through love, we seek and recognize another's beauty as people even when, or perhaps especially when, they are at their worst. Thus, while compassion is care for a person, love is *transformative* care for that person through a unique human relationship. Especially for queer folk whose trauma is driven by disconnection from self and others because of who we are, love captures the way of being with another necessary to repair the wounds of trauma.

In Memoriam

I dedicate this essay to my father, in full recognition of the fact that he would likely be horrified by some of the things I shared about him and my experiences as his son. But that's the thing about fathers and sons, about queerness, trauma, grief, and healing. We don't always get to choose how things go. And the trauma I experienced growing up gay in a family that didn't know how to love that part of me (though they tried!) is as much a part of his legacy as the wisdom or lessons I also acquired along the way.

And that's the thing that my journeys through my queerness, philosophy, trauma, and healing have taught me about love: it isn't love if it doesn't include the ugly bits, the warts and scars and broken pieces that we shame away from the world. Love requires the courage to put aside our fixing reflex so we can draw out and embrace what is most painful in those we love - including ourselves. We do this not to lessen the pain, but to experience it just as it is, accepting it with no agenda for it or against it.

EMDR asks us to love ourselves and our trauma in this way. Living genuinely, free and queer requires no less.

This is a lesson that I needed my father to have learned before my teenage self came out as gay. I don't think he ever did learn it.

My hope is that whatever nuggets of wisdom that can be found in this story can help other queer kids and their families to take a step toward embracing those pieces of ourselves and each other that we have been taught to fear or hate.

I love you, dad.

Steven W. Halady, PhD, LCSW (he/him) earned his doctorate in philosophy and worked as a professor for a few years before taking a swan dive off the academic ship and into the sea of clinical social work. He is a member of the Motivational Interviewing Network of Trainers since 2019, and has facilitated workshops on working effectively with queer folks for international audiences. He is an EMDRIA-Certified EMDR provider and consultant-in-training. He currently maintains a small clinical private practice outside of Buffalo, NY, where he lives with his husband and cats (Beemo and Casper). He is eternally grateful to all the friends, colleagues, teachers, trainers, consultants, mentors, elders, editors, and ne'er-do-wells who have contributed so much to his life and work. He would say that this is a debt of gratitude that could never be repaid, except gratitude isn't an accounting book to be balanced. Gratitude is a garden where our hopes and dreams bloom. Thank you to everyone who has planted seeds.

References

Avruch, D.O. & Shaia, W.E. (2022). Macro MI: Using motivational interviewing to address socially-engineered trauma. *Journal of Progressive Human Services*, 33(2), 176-204.

Bem, D. J. (1967). Self-perception: An alternative interpretation of cognitive dissonance phenomena. *Psychological review*, 74(3), 183.

Bennett, M.S. (2017). *Connecting paradigms: A trauma-informed & neurobiological framework for motivational interviewing implementation.* Bennett Innovation Group, L3C.

Brison, S.J. (2002). *Aftermath: Violence and the remaking of self.* Princeton, NJ: Princeton University Press.

de Almeida Neto, A.C. (2017). Understanding motivational interviewing: An evolutionary perspective. *Evolutionary Psychological Science 3*, 379–389.

Ecker, B., Ticic, R., & Hulley, L. (2012). *Unlocking the emotional brain: Eliminating symptoms at their roots using memory reconsolidation.* New York: Routledge.

Freire, P. (2003). *Pedagogy of the oppressed.* (M.B. Ramos, Trans.) Continuum. (Original work published 1970).

Gilbert, P. (2020). Compassion: From its evolution to a psychotherapy. *Frontiers in psychology, December*(11), 1-31. doi: 10.3389/fpsyg.2020.586161

Herman, J. (2022). *Trauma and recovery: The aftermath of political violence - from domestic abuse to political terror 2nd Ed.* New York: Basic Books.

Kort, J. (2018). *LGBTQ clients in therapy: Clinical issues and treatment strategies.* W.W. Norton & Company, Inc.

Marcus, E. (2016). *Making gay history.*[Podcast] https://makinggayhistory.org/

Miller, W.R. & Moyers, T.B. (2021). *Effective psychotherapists: Clinical skills that improve client outcomes.* New York: The Guilford Press.

Miller, W.R. & Rollnick, S. (2023). *Motivational interviewing: Helping people change and grow, 4th Ed.* New York: The Guilford Press.

Mullen, J. (2023). *Decolonizing therapy: Oppression, historical trauma, and politicizing your practice.* New York: W.W. Norton & Co.

Neff, K. (2011). *Self-compassion: The proven power of being kind to yourself.* New York: William Morrow.

Parnell, L. (2013). *Attachment-focused EMDR: Healing relational trauma.* New York: W.W. Norton & Co.

Schmidt, S.J. (2020). *Ego-state therapy interventions to prepare attachment-wounded adults for EMDR.* DNMS Institute, LLC.

Shapiro, F. (2018). *Eye movement desensitization and reprocessing (EMDR) therapy: Basic principles, protocols, and procedures 3rd Ed.* New York: The Guilford Press.

Solomon, R.C. (2007). *True to our feelings: What our emotions are really telling us.* Oxford, UK: Oxford University Press.

Taylor, C. (1994). The politics of recognition. In: A. Gutmann (Ed.), *Multiculturalism: Examining the politics of recognition.* Princeton, NJ: Princeton University Press.

Rainbow Walking Into The World

Queer Trauma and the Power of Love

Mishma Kumar-Jonson, AMHSW

The old adage goes
a person walks into a doctor's office and says,
"Doctor, it hurts when I move my arm like this"
and the doctor goes
"So don't move your arm like that."

1.
A queer person walks into a therapists' office and says,
"Hey therapist, it hurts when I move through the world as a queer person"
and the therapists says,
"Have you tried breathing?"
"Have you tried, you know, catching your negative thoughts and changing them to positive mantras?"
"Have you tried dressing a bit more, you know, normal?"
"Have you tried asking yourself how *you* contribute to the problem?"
"Sometimes we have to take responsibility for the choices we make, you know?"

2.
A trans woman walks into a therapist's office for family violence trauma and the therapist is surprised that she is not there for gender dysphoria
Insists they spend the session exploring how her gender plays a role in her life,
Exclaiming disbelief when the trans woman expresses love for her authentic self
Says,

"I've never met anyone who chooses this and is not traumatised by their gender"
Asks
"How are you dealing with the news?
Must be hard seeing a supreme court say you don't exist,
Surely, in these circumstances it's better to be missed"

The horror and bruise of family violence a tombstone in her body,
The session, a heavy weight of remembering there is no safety,
only the certainty of
"Your identity is up for debate when I choose it to be so"

Never seen as woman enough to deserve care
Transphobia never the problem.
often being told she is experiencing hate because of her gender
never being told you are experiencing hate because the world
fucking hates you.

Therapist exclaiming,
"I could never be 'brave enough' to live the way you do"
Being told
"You know, it's better to be a man, you'll have far more rights if you do"
Being charged $250 an hour just to hear that if she wasn't her, the world wouldn't be so cruel
Told
if only she didn't defy the accepted order she wouldn't have to grovel for a morsel of life

The tombstone from her body now 6 feet above her head
She is no longer proof of a living trans life

3.
The queer person walks into the therapist's office and asks
Hey therapist
How do you support the queer community?

The therapist says,
I'm not here to talk about me
Let's focus on all the things that happened that shouldn't have
And all the things that didn't happen that should have
Community joy and belonging forgotten
in the long litany of trauma-informed therapy

4.
The queer person stops walking into the therapist's office
and starts working into the world saying
"World, it hurts to live like this"
And the world says
"*So stop living*"

Like this is somehow not already the baseline for those of us
whose pride never quite stacked up to the high that belonging
brings
Somehow always too square for the "I want you around"
Too round for the sharp corners of safety that straightness brings
Always seeking the pot of gold
Never quite arriving to the end of *that* rainbow

5.
The queer person walks into a healer's space and says
Healer, I am tired of being this and the healer says
So, stop existing like this
and start living the way your queer heroes did.
Says,
Your shine cannot be found in people who spread darkness
Says,
Your worth cannot be measured in their straightjackets
Says,
Take my hand, I will be with you on this journey
Says,
I will hold the faith till you can see there's more to life than their
purgatory

Says,
There is strength in your community
There is joy in your belonging
There is hope in your softness
There is love in your existence

But most of all,
Here is space for your grief,
Here is room for your rage
Come in the knowing that your experience doesn't have to be brief
It is yours whenever you need
I am with you
in the organising of your resistance
Remember,
Your very existence, a fuck you to their mission.
Says,
Healing is messy,
I'll be here for the entirety.

6.
The queer person walks into community
And says,
I want to find joy in walking through the world as me
And the community says
"Finally,
thank you for living like this"
"For it allows all of us to be seen."

Mish Kumar-Jonson (they/them), a plural system that is non-binary, queer, disabled, neurodivergent and a social worker of colour on land that always was and always will be Aboriginal Land, is an EMDR consultant and Practitioner. Mish is the Chair of The Iceberg Foundation and principal practitioner at Niram EMDR where they bring an anti-oppressive and anti-colonial lens to their practice with the LGBTIQAP+ and Neurodivergent communities across so called Australia.

Loving Yourself And Community

With The Help Of EMDR Parts Work, Psychedelics, and Dance

Cash Waller MA, LPC

Hey y'all, I'm Cash (they/them pronouns). I am a transgender nonbinary person. I am white, able-bodied, neurodivergent, in my 30s, and have chronic pain. I am a licensed counselor in the state of Michigan, and I practice trauma informed Eye Movement Desensitization and Reprocessing (EMDR) with my queer/transgender caseload. I am also a psychedelic integration coach. I have many critiques of the counseling system, and I disagree with reliance on the medical model for understanding mental health. This chapter explores how EMDR, parts, psychedelic medicines, and dance work can help people illuminate what is in their subconscious mind. To engage with EMDR is a dedication to oneself and this healing can be seen in and out of the therapeutic session. Over my lifespan I have been exploring my subconscious mind to better understand myself and my healing.

The subconscious is like the ocean, it is under-researched, unknown, most people fear it, and there are cool intergalactic beings down there just waiting to be discovered. Many people remain closed to the depth of their subconscious because what is in their innermost self is intimidating. If you truly know all of yourself, will you like everything that you find? The answer is no, and that means that once you find things you don't like, you must work on them in a new type of way to heal them and get in right relationship with yourself. It is easy to ignore the subconscious, some people do it for their entire lives. Often it feels like monsters live in the subconscious and it can be intimidating to shine a light on them. When these monsters stay un-witnessed, they show up in a person as pain: emotional, physical, or psychological. No matter how hard a person tries to lock the monsters out, they will end up having keys to all the doors you attempt to use to keep them locked away. They will not settle down until they are pulled in for healing. This chapter is about going towards the unknown, not only shining a light on what is dark, rather, learning how to adapt to and be comfortable with what is in the dark. When we explore our subconscious, we liberate ourselves from the toxic norms of this culture, the pain of intergenerational trauma, and the cage our mind has been put in by negative self-concepts.

I have found this life to be awfully confusing and I am going to explain how I have used EMDR to make any sense at all of what is going on here in this strange place called Earth and existence. There is something that feels very anti-human about the oppressive systems that we live under: People have lost their connection with nature and plants. Read *Braiding Sweetgrass* by Robin Wall Kimmerer if you want to learn how to cultivate this relationship. We are experiencing a climate crisis at an ever-increasing rate. We have to pay for health insurance that doesn't cover anything. Racism remains pervasive. Capitalism has us all working so fast and hard that we have no energy to put into our own desires. People are being detained without just cause. We live in isolation without a consistent connection to community. We can't be the gender we know ourselves to be without being persecuted. Immigrants are being tortured. Our Westernized individualistic society is ringing in the wrong tune here. I picked up on it when I was a kid because I was trans in a cis world, and I have forever since been trying to figure out what the heck is going on. I've been asking myself, how can I attempt to liberate myself from the toxic socialization that has been non-consensually forced onto all of us? EMDR has been a big part of finding my truth and finding a way through trauma symptoms.

Currently, I am writing this at the beginning of 2025 as America falls further into fascism. Donald J. Trump and his loyalists are on a tirade to destroy people's mental wellness by destabilizing the systems that American citizens have to participate in and this fear is impacting the entire country. Which means I am dissociated, my clients are dissociated, my friends are dissociated, my family is dissociated, and hell, the plants and animals are probably dissociated too. Transgender people being dehumanized by the government sends a collective shudder through the queer community. It zaps all your energy and makes it feel like there are sandbags attached to your soul. You try your best to take care of yourself and keep up with your normal life, and its responsibilities. And yet these responsibilities just don't feel as important when your rights are being stripped away. We all desperately want to check out, and no amount of television series binging is going to suffice.

Humans. Want. Liberation.

Writing a chapter in this revolutionary book about queering EMDR is amazing *and* also a bit of a challenge because my mind keeps looking for ways to drone out the constant attack on folx of color, immigrants, transgender folx, disabled folx, and queer folx. This is a micro level metaphor for what this country is trying to do on the macro level: make us all so dysregulated and dissociated that we can't see straight, and we won't have any bandwidth left to band together to tell these abusive systems to fuck right off. So, I will be writing this chapter even if it hurts, because it is a resistive act against these oppressive systems to be in community with other queer people and humans who support us. The systems that oppress us don't want us to communicate in this way because if we are in close community, we will brainstorm ways out of the patriarchal, capitalistic, white supremacist hellscape they have us locked in. Thanks for taking the time to read my words and be in community with me.

Trauma and Systems of Oppression

Systems of oppression start impacting us from childhood, so that is where I will begin to describe how trauma initially gets its claws into people. My childhood was traumatic, and many people I see around me also had trauma baked into their upbringing. We have not yet lived in a society that has gentle, calm, loving parenting incorporated into its overall social fabric. Our parents grew up in trauma and many of our children still grow up in trauma. Our caregivers had children because America socialized them into thinking that it would make them happy and give their life meaning. Turns out, most caregivers have a shit ton of trauma, and they unknowingly (sometimes knowingly) take that out on their kids, which is one way that intergenerational trauma gets passed down. Many parents are emotionally immature, and due to this, children end up raising their adult parents, siblings, or themselves (or all three). We are living through an epidemic of trauma. It is my experience that just about everyone I have ever met has endured trauma that has led to poor health outcomes (both mental and physical). The adverse childhood experiences (ACEs) study done in the 1990s gave us a clear, researched understanding that there is widespread trauma among children. Yet, it is very peculiar that our culture doesn't help people understand that they have trauma and give no education on how to reprocess trauma. We could have classes when we are young that would help teach us techniques to regulate our nervous systems and how to support one another in a co-regulating way. Some children are getting this information, but not enough to create a culture that understands trauma and how to handle its effects.

Many people deny having trauma or will say, "well it isn't as bad as other people's trauma." The reality is that we all have trauma. It is all bad and it is prevalent. I think trauma varies and because of this it is easy to say "look over there at that person living through worse trauma than me." This serves as a way to discredit one's own trauma, so they don't have to look at the pain behind it. If we look at the pain behind the trauma then we can heal it and lead a healthier life. If we all, as a community, discredit our trauma and don't heal our wounds, who does that serve? It serves the systems that want to keep us held down in negative cognitions and self-limiting beliefs, so we are too preoccupied with our self-hatred to hate the systems controlling us. Every friend, family member, client, and human I have ever met dislikes, or hates, something about themselves. Isn't that curious? If we hate ourselves enough, we will continue to take whatever shit our oppressors feed us: lack of health care, bad water quality, incarcerate loads of human beings and convince people it isn't slavery, frack the planet to death, deport people, turn the ocean (and our bodies) into plastic, condone genocide, socially erase transgender people, let transgender children kill themselves. There is an equation going on here and it equals us hating ourselves for a greater purpose.

I disliked many aspects of myself from a young age due to internalized transphobia and trauma. When I was a kid, shit was toxic in my family dynamic. My mom and dad had many kids and were not able to stay regulated due to their own mental health issues. There was a lot of violent communication, alcoholism, other addictions, and dissociation - all around a difficult time. A confusing time. Little me, trans as hell, did not know what was going on. I made myself small and tried to be a shadow so that I could escape the constantly scary environment. I learned how to dissociate and that helped me survive. Everything became more confusing because I grew up in a rural town in Michigan where things were very heteronormative, segregated, cisgender, white, and religious. I was assigned female at birth, but my family and I quickly figured out something was different in me than what society had deemed normal for gender. If I would have known what I know now about gender I would have identified as transgender nonbinary from birth, but those labels weren't easily discovered at that time. I still grieve for my own little 5-year-old self who could have benefitted from the identity term, transgender. My entire outlook on myself could have been more aligned.

I grew up knowing I was different: servers called me a boy, my grandma disagreed with my mom letting me wear male clothing, and people made fun of me for my short hair. This feeling of difference seeps into your bones and creates a toxic understanding of self, a.k.a. internalized transphobia. Society has a way of making a plan for people. I didn't fit that mold. On some level I knew that, and it formed negative cognitions about myself. All of this happened in the subconscious. That is the worst part, you learn to hate yourself without even realizing that something, outside of yourself, made you hate yourself. Trauma also makes people hate themselves. My little self convinced themselves that if my parents loved me, they wouldn't choose their addictions over me. That rejection was the birth of so many negative cognitions that grew like mold in my subconscious. These trauma nodes from my childhood were only getting bigger as I aged, and life was a swirl of toxic cultural norms and traumatic experiences.

High school continued this theme of confusion in my life. I could tell there were a bunch of social rules I should be following but at that time I didn't understand what socialization was. Was I supposed to look like a girl? What did a girl look like? Was I supposed to date boys? I didn't feel like a girl, I liked looking like a boy, and yet I didn't want to act like a boy or a girl. Socialization forces people into heteronormative, gender normative, white, able-bodied, Christian stereotypes. That process causes so much internalized queer phobia. We don't fit in, so we wonder, "What is wrong with me? Why am I different?" And those questions subconsciously eat away at us queer folx. A queer person must try hard to love themselves because the world wants them to hate themselves so much.

I didn't like myself, even though I didn't recognize that and everyone around me didn't really like themselves, which I also hadn't noticed yet. I felt in my heart something was funky with this place, this social world full of hate, for ourselves and each other. Now looking back, I realize I was dissociating all the time to survive. Suicidal ideation started to come in because of my lack of understanding of why the fuck was I even on this miserable planet that just came with loss, illusion, inauthentic people, violence, and hate. Suicide is a way for a person to have control when they feel a complete lack of control otherwise. When you struggle from internalized hate for yourself, suicide can draw you in as it seems like an end to the pain. Our beautiful queer community often struggles with suicidal ideation. This is a result of the hate towards our population wearing away at the fabric of our wanting to live. It is an extra complex layer in the battle that it takes to survive this world and its discrimination. When dissociation and suicide cloud a person's reality, they have a lower chance of being in alignment with themselves and the world around them. I was fighting to stay alive in a world that hated me, and it wasn't until college that I was able to unlock the doors to creating a habitable life for myself.

Two things helped me start to have the first understanding of who I really was: My Women, Gender, and Sexuality (WGS) studies degree in undergrad, and beginning EMDR. WGS showed me that there were toxic systems that were working against human beings' safety in this world and it opened my consciousness up to gender diversity and expression. This aided in the beginning of the decolonization of my mind. I had my first experience with EMDR when I was about 19-years-old. The therapist who showed me the modality ended up being an extremely abusive person (because not all therapists are good, y'all). And yet the EMDR worked anyway because it was a process I was doing inside of myself. EMDR reprocessing was the first time I had entered my subconscious in an intentional way, and it expanded my understanding of myself. I started metabolizing my trauma and had a reduction in anxiety, depression, and anger. I started to make sense to myself. I started to fall in love with myself. I started to see all the ways I had been controlled by society, by my trauma, by the heartbreak of this world. I was evolving into a new being with more capacity to love, appreciate, and grow. In this way I was achieving a liberation inside of myself. The theme song to this personal liberation is "Get Free" by Mereba, from my favorite album "The Jungle is the Only Way Out." To be in love with myself now, as a transgender person in recovery from internalized transphobia, is the single most freeing experience I have ever lived through.

EMDR as a Self-Love Tool

Let's dissect why EMDR has the capacity to help someone see themselves clearly and learn a liking relationship with oneself. As I mentioned earlier, people dislike aspects of themselves because of the trauma they experienced programming self-limiting beliefs into their subconscious. The reprocessing phases of EMDR help to find the trauma locked inside of the mind, go towards it, and come out having more positive cognitions. It is a seriously romantic thing to do with yourself: face your own fear, hold yourself, and walk through to a more adaptive place. We live in this society where the cultural norms decide that everything is supposed to be done with a primary partner, best friend, or family member. We seldom get chances to have long journeys falling in love with ourselves in this lifetime. This is such a shame since we are essentially inside of our own mind by ourselves until we die. You would think that we would want to foster a loving relationship inside the container of our own consciousness? In honor of loving oneself in this way, I have dedicated EMDR to be my own lifelong self-love journey. I believe it can be used in this way: a tool to create a loving relationship with yourself and to liberate yourself from the trauma that was unfairly placed inside of you by society and family.

Individually we are trapped, controlled, and influenced by our trauma, both intergenerationally and socially. It takes an exponential amount of energy to get free from that weight and the process can be quite intimidating. So much so that many folx decide to not tackle their trauma and instead learn to live with the symptoms of it. People can be in counseling for over a decade and still suffer from debilitating mental anguish. EMDR is one way that can aid an individual in speeding up their process of getting free from the symptoms that trauma causes. It is a special way to go about individual liberation because it is an experience you essentially do with yourself, inside of yourself. Yes, it is helpful for the facilitator to be there to witness you as you journey with yourself and the therapeutic relationship can make all the difference when bravely facing your darkness. Yet essentially, EMDR is a big ole journey with the self.

Each phase of EMDR is a step towards self-love, self-worth, and self-liberation:

Phase 1 (Client History): You remember the things that have happened to you, you get real with yourself, and validate that unfortunate things occurred that need to be looked at.

Phase 2 (Preparation): You learn how to mindfully reassure yourself and tap into techniques that help you ground your own body and mind.

Phase 3 (Assessment): You look at some of the ickiest shit that you have gone through and attach it with these negative cognitions that have haunted you.

Phase 4 (Desensitization): You face that shit! You take your metaphorical sword and armor (and tissues for crying) and you look at the uncomfortable monsters that are locked in the depths of your subconscious. It is a beautiful, brave, romantic thing to do for yourself.

Phase 5 (Installation)*:* You take the positive cognition that you chose to replace, the preexisting negative cognition, and develop the new healthy belief into your consciousness. You now have real access to that positive cognition and surprisingly, you believe it! I have noticed that after my positive cognitions are installed, I think of them days and weeks after like a new shiny discovered gem.

Phase 6 (Body Scan): You say, "Hey body, I see you, I am listening, are there any other disturbances still here, still present"? In this way, you show your mind-body connection love and validate that you are paying the utmost attention to its needs. Western cultural norms keep folx from formulating a relationship with their body. The mindfulness part of EMDR helps people discover a connection to their body. EMDR is like a positive Trojan horse delivering a body-mind connection to folks in our sinister Westernized culture.

Phase 7 (Closure): You double check the process. You show yourself care to come back to the present moment. One honors themselves and what they just experienced inside of their subconscious.

Phase 8 (Reevaluation): You check in on yourself and give yourself even more opportunity to make sure you were heard, and everything feels clear and adaptive. The structure of EMDR allows the individual to metabolize their trauma to a point where falling in love with the self is a possible outcome, one that is easier when the trauma is out of the limbic system, where it once caused disturbance.

I believe that our society is set up to love others, to focus on people outside of ourselves, and to bend over backwards to get people to love us. In America, the prescribed goal is to find a partner, get married, have children, and become wealthy. All of which are compromised by the increasingly frightening threat of climate crisis, late-stage capitalism, and unhinged governing systems. The feeling of decreased negative mental health symptoms from trauma and the keen ability to focus on the love of the self is endlessly rewarding. When you go inside of your subconscious, carve out trauma nodes, and become your truest self, you begin to have respect for your person. There is pride in the work that you have accomplished right at home inside of your mind and consciousness. EMDR helps a person hone in on the most important relationship that you will have in this lifetime, the one with yourself. Ironically it is this relationship that we forget to tend to most often. It is so important for queer people to love themselves! Internalized homophobia and transphobia are real insidious diseases. Society declares what is "normal" and if you live outside of that you are deemed "abnormal," and that then seeps into how you feel about yourself. Reprocessing these unfortunate byproducts of a queerphobic world ends in queer people liking themselves more and in turn being able to participate in community at higher rates.

EMDR as a Community Builder

Community is when a group of people organize with a common goal, whether that be to create something or share human energy with each other. Many people may have community already, but the experience I have gathered while being a counselor is that there are large swaths of the populous who do not have friends, do not have groups to hang out with, and are suffering greatly due to the lack of access to stable consistent connections. The United States is an individualistic society that claims people can work hard to get ahead and that we should be taking care of our own wellness. This pins us against each other instead of making life a collaborative project where we support each other through our unique contributions. If we continue to not have most of the culture invested in the creation of community then we cannot work towards collective liberation. We will be too disconnected to galvanize change. These conditions are traumatic, people are not hardwired to live in such separate environments.

White folx have privilege and this means they have had an easier time living outside of community. They may have accumulated wealth due to their privilege that has helped them buy necessities of life so that they don't need help from others. I am a white person who, because of my privilege, was able to navigate the academic world with more comfort because the system was made for white folx. Therefore, I had a leg up at graduating from higher education and entering into a career where I could sustain myself financially. There are a myriad of ways the oppressive systems work well for white people so they must decolonize their privilege to start to help balance out the power of the world. This privilege has made it so many white people are not skilled at navigating community. People of color have built communities to endure systematic racism. White people should not steal or appropriate cultures; instead, we should learn from folx of color on how to organize, participate in community, and honor a more collectivist way of gathering. We will not reach our highest capacity for healing until we intentionally pull the majority of our country into the social fabric of liberation.

As mentioned, many people in the States are suffering from isolation. Counselors see this often. Sometimes we are the only people that clients get to speak to in a vulnerable way in a week or a month. Anxiety, depression, dissociation and more keep people from being able to go out and navigate spaces that could bring community into their life. Anxiety can be a huge barrier to trying to leave the house, go to a new location, park at an establishment, meet new people, understand new social scripts, and navigate new places. Y'all know what it feels like to leave the house and do something when in a depressive episode? The worst type of experience! It sucks when you try to go to an event but are out of your window of tolerance and so you dissociate through the whole experience, not comprehending what others are saying and wishing you were home.

In many places there aren't enough people who can take a break from their capitalistic work week and plan consistent events that would get people out and connected to each other. The blame for this isolation should not be put on individuals: our society does not have community built into it. Therefore, the blame deserves to be placed on toxic societal norms of individualism and the capitalistic system that keeps us working until death. Where in our forty-plus hour work week do we have the motivation to get out? It takes a lot of energy, passion, and commitment to formulate and sustain community. Energy most people do not have. If the governing systems can keep us separated and not communicating, then we can continue to be a cog in their capitalistic war machine. By keeping us mentally and physically isolated, oppressive systems can prey upon us more effectively. This pushes us to buy items for happiness instead of engaging with others to create joy. The good news is that society is waking up to wanting to be in community with each other. Now, more than ever, people are looking for friends and groups where they feel loved, supported, and a sense of connection.

EMDR helps with this process because if a person gains self-love and agency they can start to interact with others with less fog, tension, and negativity. I saw this in my own life. Before starting EMDR, my depression, anger, trauma, dissociation, and anxiety made it difficult to be in relationship with other people. I always say life is two things: conflict management and decision making. Both are difficult entities that trigger the shit out of people. Side note: conflict management is inherent in all relationships, and it is imperative to learn how to do it so that conflict doesn't rip relationships apart. Conflict management is healthy and aids in relationships becoming stronger as you work through disputes together. You know what two things you cannot do if you are riddled with negative cognitions, anxiety flare ups, obsessions, ruminations, traumatic flashbacks and dissociative episodes? Manage conflicts and make decisions. If people are engaging in toxic relationships and unable to make decisions, then people are not going to have the skills and tools it takes to navigate community.

I developed my EMDR practice with myself and I started to see symptom relief from these categories. I could now maintain calm, love, peace, and presence in conflict management with interpersonal relationships in a way I could not effectively do before the EMDR. I was able to make better decisions for myself because I better understood who I was. The journeys you go on with yourself in EMDR start to pay off and give people the courage to interact with the world around them and reduce the symptoms of mental anguish that keep people isolated. This is especially important for queer folx because of the persecution that we face from society. Finding, creating, and engaging with safe spaces where we can meet one another and know we are not alone is how we fuel a revolution. Without all those heavy negative cognitions in our minds we can start to make space inside of ourselves for connection with ourselves and thus, connection with others.

I am amazingly lucky to be a trans therapist to trans clients. I have been moved, over and over again, by what I witness my clients become in their EMDR process. I watch people overcome mental turmoil and expand themselves into healthier humans and each time I can sense how utterly huge that is for bettering the person's life. Queer clinicians who are serving the queer population are creating a unique, beautiful community of healing. As I facilitate EMDR practices with my many queer clients it becomes apparent that we, all of us together, are creating a healing vortex in the queer community. It is an honor to witness, and even though my clients do not know one another, we are all in a container of queer healing together. In this way, EMDR creates community within the therapy nodes. If we understand EMDR as an individual liberation tool, we can see how all the queer folx using it, come together to create a big healing community! If we, as a community, are becoming healthier and healthier, then we can further liberate ourselves from the low vibration of hate that fuels this country. The more we understand ourselves, the more we can divest from the toxic system that keeps us unhealed and under external control.

As we descend into a social reality where queer people, immigrants, people of color, disabled people, and other marginalized groups are blatantly having our rights threatened, we must sink into deeper community with one another. Systems of capitalism, patriarchy and white supremacy do not value our safety and do not want us to have a voice or human rights because then they would have to look at the truth about this country, racism, and what has been done to marginalized communities. This inhumane treatment towards marginalized groups of people by the dominant systems can be seen in the mismanagement of the AIDS crisis, the forcible sterilization of Black women in the 20th century, the dehumanization of transgender people, just to name a few of the countless, horrific examples. Patriarchy, white supremacy, and capitalism have created a system where gender diverse children die by suicide because they do not value all lives the same and while genocide occurs some folks can look away and abandon people in danger because they do not see themselves in those "other" people. If people were to decolonize gender, then they might decolonize race, class, disability and much more. Therefore, trans people will continue to be public enemy number one, even though all we want to do is live our silly little human lives in peace.

With all this pressure, discrimination, and hate swimming and swirling around our queer communities, we have to find the way forward through community with like-minded folks. I hear it time and time again in my client sessions, when people hang out with each other they feel more resourced, more alive, less plagued by negative cognitions, and more willing to take on the shitstorm that dominant culture has non-consensually brought to our doorstep. Any amount of trauma work is a win in this lifetime. At times, you will be able to do a lot of trauma reprocessing, and at other times, you will need to take breaks and integrate the hard challenges of life, growth, and the material that arises in your EMDR practice. Many people who have an EMDR practice also have other activities that help them stay centered: mindfulness, exercise, reading, journaling, dancing, breath work, or eating well. There are so many tools to explore that make your internal realm more comfortable to be in. There are also ways to enhance our own trauma work by layering in other modalities which can help us grow even more successful at being in right relationship with ourselves and our communities. We so far have seen how an individual EMDR practice can help with love of the self and how that can flow into being engaged in community in ways that help with our mental wellness. Now, I will highlight the three modalities that have helped me target my own trauma the most effectively: parts work, psychedelics, and dance. There are vast ways to enhance your healing, but these have been the most effective for me.

EMDR Enhancers

Parts Work

I've found that there are enhancers that marry well with EMDR and allow for a more full-bodied healing. It is important to note that, at times, layering modalities can be too overwhelming for some folx. It is helpful to work with a counselor, life coach, or mentor when exploring multiple therapeutic approaches at the same time. The first EMDR enhancer we will explore is Parts Work. Many of you know Internal Family Systems (IFS) created by Richard Schwartz. Jamie Marich, the author of *Dissociation Made Simple* (DMS) and the foreword of this book, helps folx understand that people can have a system of selves, and a person can better understand themselves if they look at their dissociation patterns and how they interact with their parts. An extremely important historical lens that Jamie Marich highlights in their book is there is nothing new about parts work in modern psychotherapy. The wisdom that we now know as *parts work* is truly Indigenous in their origins. Moreover, concepts like *Self* in IFS closely parallel what yogic philosophy teaches us about the unchanging Self and Self's relationship to our unique, human expressions.

Parts of self, not to mention dissociation, show up all the time in the EMDR realm. I help my clients get a sense of what parts of self are around when they are out of their window of tolerance and feeling dysregulated. I also help them understand what parts are around when they feel safe and grounded. This way, the client and I can have a mutual understanding of what parts of themselves are getting triggered at what moments and why. We can also then mutually understand what parts of self are resourcing and feel regulating. Those regulating parts can be used in a resourcing way before the reprocessing portion of EMDR. Setting up a calm safe place, bringing in a protective figure, or using a part of self who is an anchoring source can provide safety to the more scared parts that then will protect against distress.

Once the reprocessing begins, parts start to show up whether a person has a well-understood map of their parts or not. *Dissociation Made Simple* has an excellent template for helping people map their parts. I've seen clients reprocess and they will suddenly get a feeling, a picture, or a knowing sense of a part of self who is either saying something to them, behaving a certain way, or sharing an aspect of themselves with *theirselves*. This happened in my own EMDR work before I knew what parts theory even was. I was reprocessing family trauma, and my own young self appeared and allowed me to speak with them. They helped me understand what was needed for them at that moment to feel safe and what would make them less scared. One of my adult parts in that moment was able to give love and reassurance to the young part. In that moment I was able to "lovingly parent myself," which is a phrase that comes from the language of Adult Children of Alcoholics (ACoA). When you start loving yourselves in this way you can start to help your younger parts understand that they can receive the love and care they have always desired, from your own adult parts. In this way you help them grow up and mature into a new place of functioning that would not have been possible without the support of yourselves. This can lead to the younger part lashing out less and instead turning toward the adult parts for safety and security when dysregulation occurs.

Earlier in the chapter I mentioned that most of our parents were immaturely raising us, so at some point we must learn how to re-parent our own selves from the inside out, rather than the outside in. The children inside of our own consciousness want to get their desired love and caretaking from other humans. They especially wanted to receive that love from their caretakers when they were young and growing up. The truth is, we cannot rely on our attachment figures (parents, lovers, friends) to re-parent us. We need this love to come from our own adult parts inside of us. This process of learning how to reparent yourself is seriously healing and rewarding. The support you give yourself leads to healthier overall functioning, bolsters self-worth, and allows confidence in yourself to flourish. We still need love and secure attachments with other people. And yet to have a secure attachment with yourself is the most helpful thing when it comes to loving all parts of yourself (check out Jessica Fern's book, *Polysecure* for an in-depth feminist understanding of attachment theory that will aid you in creating a secure attachment with yourself and others) in this lifetime.

After the client locates their parts of self, they can start to understand how their selves work together as a system of selves, or as mentioned in IFS, a family of selves. You want to help your system of selves learn how to care for one another, like any healthy family does. Here are some examples of parts work that I have constructed from a combination of my own and my clients' experiences. They provide a blueprint of someone learning their system and using that knowledge to create harmony and balance within their different selves:

A person has an anxious part of self they call "The Storm" and another part of self they call "Radiance" who holds their positive affirmations about themselves. This person has gotten to know their parts and knows that when The Storm is around it comes with an uncomfortable bodily sensation in the throat. This person picks up on the queues of The Storm and remembers that they can utilize their Radiance part to counterbalance the negativity of The Storm with positive feelings about the self. The person has found a way to balance out their system. Another example: A person has a part of self called "Carmen" who struggles with gender dysphoria because they identify as a woman who uses she/her pronouns. Another part of self they call "Sapio" who identifies as non-binary, uses they/them pronouns, and has gender dysphoria for different reasons than Carmen. Since the person is aware of both parts, some days they will dress more femininely to accommodate Carmen and some days they dress more androgynously to accommodate Sapio. The person knows their parts of self and how they can work together to create more synergy in their system together which lowers their gender dysphoria.

Parts work mixed with EMDR can be an effective way to excavate more knowledge about one's parts and system of selves. The subconscious is more easily navigated when in the meditative state of the reprocessing phase of EMDR. I have found that parts of self are easier to locate, talk to, and interact within the subconscious plane. It can be a bit surreal at first, parts of yourself coming forward to have conversations with other parts of yourself. Some people might find that to be extremely strange and ignore the fact that this happened in a reprocessing session and keep it locked in the subconscious. Please understand that all the oppressive systems that create the rules here generally take all the fun out of life and want to make you feel like a weirdo for finding different parts of yourself inside of yourself. Reality is magical, being a human is fantastical, and finding parts of self is an epic adventure that I urge you to navigate and try out! Parts show up in different ways for different people. For me they showed up while I was bilaterally reprocessing in my twenties, and they came to me as younger parts of myself from traumatic moments in time. For example, I had big traumas occur at the ages of 3, 5, 13, and 17. Each of those babies have come to visit me and have made themselves known to me (current me). When you are looking for parts, trust your intuition, they usually come with a "knowing" sensation once you start to look in their direction.

I have done the work getting to know these parts of self and they have opened up to me about how hard it was to survive what they went through. Through this process, they have learned to trust me, and we have healed together which has resulted in less anxiety, depression, trauma flares, and dissociation. Some parts of self are not found by chronological age but instead come from being attached to an emotional expression. An example might be when someone has anger, anxiety, or depressive outbursts and they label this part of self as "Take Over," or maybe call them a name, like

"Kenny." This way the person can verbally say, "Ope, Kenny is here again," and can externalize this part of self so that they can start to understand what this part of self needs to feel safe and calm. Other folx find parts to be bodily sensations and to be less cognitive, such as belly aches, headaches, chronic pain flares, etc. Parts of self are not always negative or associated with trauma. For instance, I have a part of self named Exhale who is confident, stable, loving, centered, and very in tune with Earth. Not all people will have well defined parts and that is okay as well, they don't have to be super defined to start to see them as a piece of yourself.

Clinicians, you can help your clients find their parts of self! Make sure to use psychoeducation about what parts work is so that the client has a framework for the process. Then, when your clients have these big Aha! moments about their parts arising you can start to point out when you feel like you are hearing a part of self. People may say things like, "Oh that part of myself is xyz," and you could simply say, "I am sensing there might be a part of self here, could that be true, or does that not feel correct in your body?" By stating the inquiry in this way, you are being careful not to push your own desire for a person to find their parts onto them. Help empower them to choose if something sounds like an actual part of self or not and follow the client's lead. This identification of parts adventure can be powerful to someone's understanding of themselves and can result in clients making strides towards their therapeutic goals and overall wellness.

Once parts are mapped and more understood, the parts of self start to show up in the client's reprocessing journeys. A clinician and client can target a part of self utilizing EMDR. Here is an example: The Storm (from the story above) is getting triggered a lot in someone's life. The person decides to target a memory where their Storm part has been activated, and they set up the negative cognition surrounding the experience. The client reprocesses the event and gets to understand the part of self more effectively, which then helps heal this part of self. As a result of this healing, The Storm is triggered less frequently, and this helps them to maintain more wellness in their life. It is common to have parts of self talk/interact with each other when in the reprocessing phase of EMDR. This open communication between parts can promote effective metabolization of traumatic feelings that parts of self may hold.

One can start to see that breaking their consciousness up into parts can make it easier to differentiate where triggers are coming from, therefore making it easier to understand where the healing work needs to be done. You can have a lifelong relationship with yourself and your parts, cultivating these connections like a garden. Which brings me to my next enhancer. In the right environment, working with psychedelics can be the fertilizer of that garden.

Psychedelic Medicine

Let me hit you with two, big thinking points: EMDR is inherently psychedelic and EMDR and psychedelics are inherently queer. Psychedelics expand your consciousness by showing you other ways to view your own reality, and queerness has the same essence. Queerness helps you bring your own reality into focus by using a different perspective from the norm. EMDR is psychedelic in this same nature. It dips you down into your subconscious and shows you aspects about your life, memories, and selfhood that are otherwise hidden in your conscious understanding of life. Both entities are inherently queer because of their ability to aid others to see past toxic norms that are harming people with maleficent messaging. Queerness, EMDR, and psychedelics all add new perspectives to the washed-up status quo and they all have the healing power to help people love themselves.

As with EMDR preprocessing phases, it's important to clearly state that setting a safe container is essential for psychedelic medicine work, whether people create their own container or join a group-facilitated container. We set containers in our therapeutic spaces all the time, such as fifty-five minute sessions, guided meditations, and facilitated breathwork experiences. This therapeutic framework sets the stage for safe healing to occur through boundaries that provide safety by keeping the individual in a healing state for a predetermined amount of time. Everyone participating is aware of the boundaries, as they are agreed upon before the experience begins, which adds extra layers of safety to the process as a result of informed consent. It is so important to use this same boundary setting mentality when sitting with psychedelics.

There are many types of boundaries in a group facilitated psychedelic container, or what we in the community call a circle. There are boundaries regarding consent and touch in psychedelic spaces. Depending on the type of medicine and the facilitator setting the container there may be therapeutic touch or no touch at all. These guidelines would be described beforehand and adhered to throughout the circle by all members. Another boundary is to eat healthy days or weeks before and after the ceremony which is sometimes referred to as a "dieta." This is a way to honor the medicine, who is generously offering us their wisdom and deep knowledge of consciousness.

Confidentiality is an important boundary for the ceremonial container. People are exploring different states of consciousness in these settings, and this may come with large Aha! moments and deep processing that is intimately shared with the group. It is mandatory that anything shared with each other in the circle while in these elevated states be kept within the group. When people come to sit in circle together there is always a beginning, a middle, and an end to the container so humans can have clear guidelines of when they are interacting within the container, which provides a layer of safety. It is trauma-informed care to help humans know where they are *at* in space and time within a container. There is a moment where we all consciously open the container together and close the container together which adds to the connection and safety of all the humans participating in the circle. At any moment in a psychedelic container you can let anyone you are interacting with know that it is time to come back inside of yourself, return to your mat, and have your own space be your space again.

Another important aspect to consider when sitting with psychedelics with or without other people is determining the appropriate setting. For instance, going out in public on medicine is not always the most healing choice and can, at times, cause a great deal of anxiety. A safer venue can be at home, or in nature, where there is space to go through anything that might feel intimidating while on the medicine. Reminiscent of helping clients locate protective figures and calm safe places with EMDR, when sitting with the medicine one can call in entities that help them feel strength such as role models, queer icons, spirits, ancestors, plants, and animals. A facilitator or journey guide can also be present to add to the safey of the container; someone who can watch over the person on their journey, hold space for them, and get anything they might need (e.g., water, help to the bathroom, pleasant scents, blankets, walking behind you for safety, etc.).

These ways of setting the container for spiritual psychedelic medicine experiences show a stark contrast from the incorrect social portrayal of psychedelic medicines as harmful drugs. The myth that the government spreads is that these types of consciousness expanding entities are harmful to humans and end in self-harm, death, and addiction. If the government can tell people these medicines are for unsuccessful people who want to ruin their life with partying, then they can keep people away from lifesaving medicines that will raise the collective consciousness. Oppressive forces do not want folx in our culture to wake up to their own selves through the avenues of psychedelics, because it could lead to a larger portion of the population fighting back against injustice. Oppressive systems don't want that.

I believe that exploring consciousness is a basic human right. We are here on planet Earth and if there are tools that can help us to understand our true meaning as humans then I absolutely believe we should have access to that. Psychedelics are taking a step into the mental health avenues of our world in a big way. MDMA, ketamine, and psilocybin are now a part of the dominant discourse in the mental health field across the states and across the globe. People are starting to understand that the war on drugs is a war on consciousness and that these lifesaving medicines can be utilized in safe intentional settings and have life altering positive effects on the mind and body. I find that something profound starts to occur to my EMDR clients and in their reprocessing sessions after they start to utilize psychedelic medicine. The medicine opens new realms in the EMDR reprocessing by helping someone to better understand their subconscious reality, as if it fills in gaps and allows one to better know themselves. EMDR and psychedelics both access the subconscious. Because of this similarity, the two worlds piggyback off of each others' awareness and knowledge. Psychedelics allow some to navigate their subconscious through EMDR in a more direct and clear way.

After sitting in ceremony with psychedelic medicine, I realized that my EMDR sessions had become more expanded. It is kind of hard to explain with human language (the idea of ineffability can be seen both in psychedelic experience as well as in the EMDR experience); put simply, the EMDR became bolder and richer. I was able to ascertain more knowledge in an easier to understand way, as if the psychedelic realms had layered themselves with the EMDR realms and had become intertwined, creating a higher level of insight into who I was. This opened a doorway in my subconscious and beautifully led to me discovering a connection to my ancestors. Communicating with my ancestors has been such a net positive experience for my healing. Since I have developed this relationship with them, they will now come and visit me in my subconscious EMDR realms as I go through my reprocessing. They offer guidance while I am in that subconscious place and will say very insightful, loving, positive things to me while I am reprocessing. It actualizes my connection with my lineage and helps me to heal my intergenerational trauma. My ancestors missed me and are happy to have this connection with me. I now have the EMDR portal to access their wisdom and love. It turns out they have always been right inside of me and I just had to find the right combination of consciousness that would allow for them to have access to me.

I am forever grateful to EMDR and psychedelic medicine for guiding me home to my ancestral family. Unlike white culture where intergenerational influences have been forgotten, Indigenous folx have always had ancestral influence and support baked into their culture. Because of white people's dark history as colonizers we pretend that our ancestors don't exist because we don't want to look at the horrors committed, but at the same time we lose access to the resourcing parts of ancestral relationships. It is important to note that as a white person, it is likely that not all of my ancestors were acting ethically considering their white colonizer privilege. It is important for white people to acknowledge the legacy of colonization in their heritage and understand the way that white privilege is passed down through the generations. This helps the white culture to become more anti-racist by being honest with what has happened on this timeline regarding white supremacy. And, hopefully, move towards building antiracist systems that may heal racial trauma.

In psychedelic spaces, integration is a term that we use and is a helpful framework with any modality where trauma is being faced and healed. Trauma work is strenuous on a person's body, mind, parts of self, and daily functioning. When someone sits with the medicine, the lessons and wisdom that come up can be large pieces of information that the person did not have access to before the journey. It is important that the journeyer integrates their new understanding of reality into their preexisting knowledge of themselves. Integration consists of a period of time after a large trauma reprocessing experience where a person intentionally honors the large experience they just went through and cares for themselves in a loving, compassionate way. Integrative practices may consist of journaling, positive affirmations, moving the body more, less social media, less violent content, healthier diet, better boundaries with people (and the self), or interacting with addictions in a healthier way. Integration can (and should) be used in the EMDR process. Some clients will experience what I call "the EMDR hangover" where they are depleted of energy after a reprocessing session and may show signs of exhaustion, dissociation, or feeling unwell. Of note, those clients who have many days of this fatigue may require more integration of what came up for them in their reprocessing.

Psychedelics can be used as a complimentary integration method for deep EMDR work and vice versa. It is highly likely that

EMDR and psychedelics will have much work to do together in the future when evidence proves their solidarity. At this moment in history, because of the legal status of most psychedelics, ketamine excluded, that isn't a possibility. So people are doing their EMDR work and their medicine work separately. Psychedelic medicine and EMDR both want the world to heal and I am thankful for their cohesion.

Dance

Another enhancer that may help you find depth in your EMDR realms is by developing a dance practice. Dance is when a body freely moves in a rhythmic way, usually to a beat or a piece of music. The back-and-forth motion of the dance is the same foundation of the sacred beat that is intrinsic to EMDR. Every culture across the globe uses song, dance, and drumming to be in connection with one another in a trance state. Moving in sync with a group of people has an instinctual calming effect. My favorite thing to do when I am out of an intense EMDR reprocessing session is to dance. This both calms my body down and offers me integration from the powerful psychological experience that I just had. It helps you to access higher consciousness and anchor into the body as well as allowing you to enter a flow state and leave the body.

The art of knowing the body gives someone access to understanding the intricate connection of the body and the mind which then can help a person better understand how to regulate. When you dance you start to develop a mind map of your own movements. A higher tempo of a song may make you move one way, limbs flailing, booty shaking. A slower tempo may elicit more sensual, slow movements. Understanding the body in this way then gives the body-inhabiting human a deeper glimpse into bodily sensation by getting to know oneself intimately. A person may feel a tightness in their chest, pick up on it due to their bodily awareness, and then do something to regulate themselves since their mind was able to catch the cues of dysregulation the body was sharing. A great thing to do in this instance of catching the hyperarousal would be to dance!

Dancing can also be used when one finds oneself in a low state of hypoarousal to bring energy back into the body. If someone feels drained from life, the simple action of swinging the arms and moving the hips, with or without gusto, can bring energy back into the system. Formulating a dance practice at home can be difficult and almost feel embarrassing at first. This embarrassment can help you unlock your own insecurities surrounding body movement. Consistently dancing can be a way to process these limiting beliefs and get in tune with your body. Dancing at home can be a great way to amplify your overall healing and integrate your EMDR practice.

Dance can be viewed through a disability justice lens and can be an accessible practice for disabled people. Folx can identify which body parts are safe and comfortable to move and then modify dance by lying down or being seated as they move to music in a secure way. A cane, walker, wheelchair, or other mobility aids can be utilized as stabilization forces as a person navigates what is comfortable with their movement. For those with chronic pain or low mobility, relaxing and finding the beat of the song and then matching the breath with the beat can be a gentle way to get movement into your body and welcome the music inside. It can be healing to stay inside the boundaries of what feels comfortable for you in the body. If someone is deaf, the bass of a song can be felt throughout the body causing an intimate connection for the dancer. EMDR paddles that rumble back and forth have the same impact of allowing the buzz of a beat to be transferred into the body through bilateral movement. Dance spaces often can be ableist by not having disabled people in mind when creating the layout or functionality of the event. When modifications can be made from a disability justice standpoint, it makes the space more accessible for everyone and creates more safety for disabled folx to enter the environment. Anti oppressive spaces benefit everyone.

Dance can be a sad topic due to the lack of access to the lost art of dance in Western society. Dance is a basic human right. It has always been a part of liberation. If a human is dancing, there is hope for freedom in the world. Indigenous cultures around the world are built on the foundations of dance and beat. It is no coincidence that

Western society has colonized dancing out of our culture. Dancing in a group can bring about a sense of belonging, and due to the high level of processing that occurs during the activity, experiencing it alongside others can be a profoundly healing activity. To lose such a natural human way to process trauma is a big loss of an important resource and calls to mind the song "We've Lost Dancing" by Fred Again and Marea.

This concept builds upon other assertions made in this chapter about dominant culture trying to take humans liberation from them so they can be easily controlled and contribute to a toxic system. So, it's not surprising that Western society has stripped it from community spaces. In many places there are not reliable community dance spots. Many dance spots revolve around bar culture and drinking. If people do get to a location with dance, embarrassment of how they will be perceived dancing may be a barrier to letting go and losing oneself in the dance. If you were on the dance floor and everyone else had coverings over their eyes, would you feel safer moving your body how you truly desired? Have you ever been to a concert where no one, or limited people, are dancing? It feels haunting, as if people's mind-body connection is severed. We must start thinking about dance as a human right and when it is taken away from us, in any form, we must fight back to remain in connection with our bodies. So, I turn to Detroit, Michigan as a template to spark inspiration in overcoming the dancing dearth in our lives toward building a stable community revolving around dance.

Detroit's heartbeat is its dance culture. People come from around the world to hear the music of Motown and the deep beat of techno, as it is well known as the birthplace of techno. The techno movement in Detroit was built by Black DJs: Stacey Hotwaxx Hale, Carl Craig, Jeff Mills, DJ Minx, Rick Wilhite, Kevin Saunderson, to name a few. The music scene has grown out of Black folx' creativity towards liberation and resistance to oppressive systems. Stevie Wonder, The Supremes, Diana Ross, The Temptations, Marvin Gaye and so many other Motown musicians built this city up into the revolutionary powerhouse music hub that it is today. They are the backbone of music and their influence on music and musicians can be seen around the world, throughout time. Liberation is baked into this city from every angle, and it shows in the lively dance scene. Almost any night you can find music in some part of this city and people are dancing. The type of dance where folx are moving the body in a vulnerable way without embarrassment. It is okay to feel like a total beginner and work up to feeling more confident in your bodily movements. The point is to attempt to facilitate a mind-body connection, if you allow yourself to move through the embarrassment and into the vulnerability this will lead to healing – typically, vulnerability leads to healing.

There is a large queer and transgender population in Detroit, and we flood the dance floors. There is an abundance of queer DJs, and the community thrives. Dance is inherently queer and has always been a part of our culture because of the way it centers liberation. *Paris is Burning* is a must-watch documentary by Jennie Livingston that outlines the importance of the ball dance scene in New York City in the 1980s. The film is a beautiful example of how dance liberates communities, and it centers Black, Latinx, trans, and gender non-conforming folx who were the backbone of the community. Many folx in Detroit just go out to dance and feel free with each other, without utilizing substances at all. There are unspoken "rules of the dance floor" in Detroit: you dance for your own process, you lose yourself as freely as you would like on the dance floor, you are respectful of each other's dance practice, and you don't hit on or touch people on the dance floor. This makes for a safer container where folx can come and reprocess their trauma on the dance floor with the back-and-forth movement that is present in bilateral healing. Some people will dance for many hours going through a psychedelic experience of trauma reprocessing and will express that it felt like a whole journey into one's internal realm.

Essentially, Detroit is laying the blueprint for how to successfully create a vibrant culture around dance. If more cities could focus on dance and the sacred beat of the soul like Detroit does, we could see more and more humans collectively processing their trauma in community. Dance can and always will be a tool for getting free from our human cages.

It All Builds Together

You take your individual love for yourself and begin to have a strong community. Then you mix in together these other aspects of life to create a healing vortex for yourself. You construct a known subconscious landscape for yourself by layering these different consciousness explorations over top of one another. The self is in connection with community, which is connected to dance, which is connected to EMDR, which is linked to your own parts of self, which is intermixed with your intergenerational healing, colliding with your psychedelic medicine work, deepening your understanding of self, leading you back to being more authentic in community. It all mixes together to create a potent understanding of who you truly are. You get down to your true essence that the oppressive systems stripped away.

Being human still comes with challenges. Getting the trauma calmed down and out of the way has led me to pathways of happiness. Joy is a revolution. Being in connection with others is a revolution. Loving our parts of self is a revolution. What a strange place we have found ourselves in, one filled with hate and discrimination but at the same time filled with love, connection, and inspiration. When we feed the wellness of the world, we can start to imagine systemic changes that can lead to freedom. In the words of Robin Wall Kimmerer, the author of *Braiding Sweetgrass*, “Even a wounded world is feeding us. Even a wounded world holds us, giving us moments of wonder and joy. I choose joy over despair. Not because I have my head in the sand, but because joy is what the earth gives me daily and I must return the gift” (Wall Kimmerer, 2013, p.327). Thank you for spending time with me on this journey, I appreciate the time we spent together. Live your life authentically and give the oppressive systems hell. Take care of yourself and your communities.

With compassion, Cash.

Cash Waller (they/we) grew up in northern Michigan and were raised by fire and the lake they grew up on. Now they are based in Detroit, where they can be found dancing. They are a queer transgender nonbinary system who works at decolonizing the therapeutic space by utilizing an anti-oppressive, feminist, multicultural approach. EMDR is central to Cash's therapeutic style and they help create a co-created container with their client's so that the space can feel consensual and unique to the person's needs. They work with transgender teens, people with dissociative disorders, those who identify as plural, queer and transgender humans with complex trauma, clients utilizing psychedelic medicine, and folx practicing ethical non-monogamy. Cash is a psychedelic medicine life coach and helps people prep and integrate from their psychedelic medicine journeys. The pillars to Cash's person and therapeutic work are EMDR, parts work, dancing, and psychedelics. They believe these four aspects of life to be healing entities that create a powerful container for deep trauma work resulting in the ability to access joy.

Reference

Kimmerer, R. W. (2013). *Braiding sweetgrass: Indigenous wisdom, scientific knowledge and the teachings of plants*. Milkweed Editions.

The Generative Healing Power of Self-Disclosure in the Co-Creation of the Safe Space and Resourcing

Tawanna Marie Woolfolk, LCSW (The Doula for the Soul)

Self-disclosure in psychotherapy refers to the intentional sharing by the therapist of their personal experiences, values, identities, or reactions within the therapeutic relationship. Traditionally, therapeutic training (especially in Eurocentric and psychodynamic frameworks) has warned against the risks of therapist self-disclosure, cautioning that it can blur boundaries, shift the focus from the client, or interfere with the transference process (Henretty & Levitt, 2010). However, within a queer, decolonized, trauma-informed, and culturally responsive lens, self-disclosure can become a powerful tool of relational reciprocity, safety building, and identity affirmation.

For queer, BIPOC, and neurodivergent clients, witnessing aspects of their lived experience reflected in their therapist can be deeply affirming and regulation-enhancing. For communities historically and contemporarily harmed by systems of psychiatry, medicine, and colonial mental health practices, transparency and authenticity can begin to repair ruptures of trust. This reframing of self-disclosure honors the therapeutic space as co-constructed rather than hierarchically administered.

Reconsidering Self-Disclosure

The Role of Self-Disclosure in Building Trust and Rapport

As a queer, neurodivergent, BIPOC clinician with more than two decades of experience, I have witnessed how strategic and values-aligned self-disclosure has facilitated attunement, safety, and mutual respect. My clients often tell me, "It helps to know that you understand not just because you read it, but because you've lived it." This kind of resonance creates relational safety—a form of resourcing in and of itself.

Decolonized care invites us to remember that the therapeutic relationship is not built on neutrality but on mutual recognition and co-regulation (Watkins & Shulman, 2008). Disclosing one's cultural positionality, lived trauma history, or even healing practices like being an EMDR client oneself can invite the client into a space of shared humanity. Rather than a rupture, it becomes a ritual of connection.

Challenges and Concerns Related to Self-Disclosure from a Colonized Perspective

Traditional training and ethical codes in psychotherapy often stem from white, patriarchal, heteronormative, and ableist frameworks that elevate distance, objectivity, and clinical neutrality as the gold standard (Brown, 2015). These ideologies disregard how such detachment can alienate clients whose lives demand visibility, recognition, and solidarity in order to heal.

A colonized view may frame therapist disclosure as self-serving or boundary-violating. However, this perspective fails to acknowledge the cultural dimensions of healing and connection. For example, in many Indigenous, African diasporic, and collectivist cultures, healing is communal, relational, and narrative-based (Gone, 2013). By failing to examine the colonial underpinnings of clinical "objectivity," we risk replicating the very harms we claim to heal.

Carl Rogers, the father of person-centered therapy, offered a radical counterpoint to clinical detachment long before relational cultural theory gained traction. Rogers (1961) once said: "The curious paradox is that when I accept myself just as I am, then I can change" (p. 17). Likewise, Irvin Yalom (2002) emphasized the existential necessity of mutuality in therapy. He wrote: "It's the relationship that heals, the relationship that heals, the relationship that heals — my professional rosary" (p. 53). In many ways, both men anticipated what decolonized, queer-affirming, and neurodivergent-centered therapists now argue: that the clinical space is most powerful when it makes room for humanity—in all its complexity.

Empowering Clients to Determine Comfort Levels with Self-Disclosure

It is crucial to recognize that clients also bring internalized narratives around power, visibility, and safety into therapy. Empowering clients to share how therapist self-disclosure affects them—or even inviting consent before offering personal narrative—is part of a trauma-informed, consent-based, decolonized approach. This might sound like: "I want to share something that might help build a bridge between us. Would it feel okay for you if I did?"

I often invite my clients to pause and check in with their body. Is this moment of relational intimacy activating or soothing? This process transforms self-disclosure from an act of imposition to one of sacred invitation. By honoring the client's bodily knowing, we return power to the places where trauma once took it away.

Personal Testimony: Utilizing Self-Disclosure as Therapist and Client

One of the most profound moments of my clinical life unfolded not in an office, but in the corner booth of a Burger King. I had the joint honor of working for nearly five years with a beloved client—a Latino man in his 40s, devoted to his wife and teenage son. We had shared many meals and rituals by then, but on this day, as we sipped hot coffee across from one another, I could sense something sacred unfolding.

He looked at me, gently, and said: "T, I have a question, but I don't know if it's inappropriate. I feel safe asking—but I want to respect your boundaries."

I looked down first, gathering myself, then back into his warm brown eyes, smiling. I had been waiting for this moment.

"Do you have a partner?" he asked. "And are they a woman?"

Tears brimmed as I paused to root myself. I was practicing what I call healthy detachment—knowing where I begin and end, and where he begins and ends. From that grounded place, I could offer not just truth, but consent.

"I feel honored that you felt inspired to ask," I said. "Before I answer, may I ask what inspired the question?"

His response brought me to my knees.

"T, ever since I met you, you've just been so consistently kind, so loving, so clear and open in how you embrace humanity. Not just with me—with my family, with our animals. Your heart... it just feels unconditional. Like you love without expectation or fear. And I guess I just wondered, who gets to receive that kind of love from you?"

By the time he finished, I was anchored in truth. My smile widened.

"I do have a partner," I said softly. "She is a woman, and we've been together for over five years."

He threw his head back and laughed with joy. "I knew it!" he beamed. "Me and my wife knew it—this is the best news ever!"

We laughed together, belly-deep, between sips of coffee. But then his energy shifted—softened.

He looked at me, eyes wet with tears, and whispered: "T, that was the last piece of reassurance I needed. May I share something with you?"

I took his hand across the table.

"It would be my sacred, liberating honor to bear witness."

And then, for the first time in his life, he told me he had been sexually abused by men as a young adolescent. The one truth he had never dared to share with a therapist. The one truth that haunted his worthiness, threatened his masculinity, and fractured his knowing of his own lovability.

"I thought the gangs, the drugs, the violence—those would be the things that would kill me," he said. "But it's this truth that's been eating me from the inside. And you—the way you see me—you made it safe to say it out loud."

We sat there in that corner booth, in a place most people pass without a second thought, holding hands. And in that moment, he came home to himself.

This is why I do this work. This is what it means to be a Doula for the Soul.

Resourcing Queer, BIPOC, Neurodivergent, and Marginalized Clients

"You only are free when you realize you belong no place—you belong every place—no place at all. The price is high. The reward is great."
— Maya Angelou (1973)

Reimagining marginalization belonging—or the absence of it—shapes how we see ourselves and whether we believe we are worthy of healing. In trauma work, we often center those identities that are most visibly targeted by systemic oppression. But what if marginalization is not only about what is done to us, but what is withheld within us? What if some wounds are invisible because the people who carry them were never given permission to feel them?

In my clinical practice, I have sat with many clients whose social identities mirror the dominant culture—cisgender white men, high-functioning professionals, able-bodied leaders—and yet, they arrive emotionally starved, unable to locate themselves in their own stories. They were told that their power disqualified them from pain. But what I've come to understand is this: proximity to power doesn't guarantee protection from trauma. Often, it guarantees isolation from healing.

There is a grief that lives in those who have never been allowed to be vulnerable. There is a wound in those who were told that to feel is to fail. And if we, as trauma therapists, are to truly queer our lens and decolonize our practice, we must widen our understanding of marginalization to include those disconnected from their capacity to hurt—and therefore, to heal.

The Importance of Resourcing in Trauma Therapy

In the EMDR framework, resourcing is often viewed as a preparatory phase—a way to help clients stabilize before reprocessing trauma. But for many of the clients I work with—queer, BIPOC, neurodivergent, and those quietly devastated by inherited systems they do not fully understand—resourcing isn't just preparation. It is the core of the healing.

When someone has lived without consistent safety—in their identity, body, family, or society—the act of locating an internal sense of calm or strength is not intuitive. It must be learned. In many cases, it must be remembered. Resourcing becomes the bridge between survival and presence. It teaches clients what it feels like to belong to themselves—maybe for the first time. And that is revolutionary.

Building Resilience and Strength Through Resourcing

Trauma tells us: you're alone, and it will never get better. Resourcing tells us: you've made it this far—and you don't have to keep doing it alone. Every time a client connects with a strength—whether it's a memory, a mantra, a body movement, or a sacred song—they are creating new neural pathways for safety. For belonging. For breath.

This process is not linear. Clients will forget their resources. They will doubt their worth. They will feel the gravitational pull of despair. And yet each time they return to that resource—each time they breathe into the possibility of peace—the body remembers: I am not just what happened to me. I am what I did to survive it.

This is how we build resilience. Not through performance or toughness, but through repeated acts of radical return—to self, to body, to dignity.

Personal Testimonies: Co-Constructing Safe Spaces in EMDR

I've worked with clients who resource through imagined ancestral councils, through affirmations from queer icons, through drag performances, through scripture, through movement. One white male client imagined a younger version of himself being held by the grandfather he lost at age five—finally being told, "You did nothing wrong."

These resources are sacred. They are not supplemental. They are central.

They remind clients that healing doesn't require erasing what happened—it requires remembering who they were before it did.

And that remembering is how we return.

Ethical Considerations and Invitations

Confidentiality and Privacy in Self-Disclosure

In traditional clinical ethics, therapist self-disclosure is often regarded with suspicion—a boundary risk, a potential distraction, something to be minimized or avoided. But when working with queer, BIPOC, neurodivergent, and other marginalized clients, we must interrogate and prioritize whose ethics are being centered—and whose safety is being protected.

From a decolonized and relational ethic, the question is not "Should I disclose?" but rather, "Why might disclosure serve this client's healing right now?" When offered with consent, attunement, and humility, therapist self-disclosure can deepen trust, rupture power hierarchies, and model embodied truth-telling. It becomes less about the content of the story and more about the quality of the presence. That said, disclosure must always be client-centered. It should never shift focus or place the emotional labor on the client. Instead, it should serve as a relational bridge—a mirror, not a megaphone.

Ethical transparency also means preparing the client for what they might feel—curiosity, connection, discomfort, even resistance—and inviting them to reflect. We assert that this is not "therapist as expert," rather "therapist as human." Self-disclosure, when practiced from a decolonized, trauma-informed, and queer-affirming framework, is not just a technique—it is a tool for liberation. Self-disclosure says: You are not alone in your becoming. I have walked some of this road, too. And I will not disappear when you need to be seen.

Deconstructing Boundaries and Queering Intimacy in the Therapeutic Relationship

In a colonized frame, boundaries are often understood as walls—rigid, inflexible lines designed to protect professionalism. But in decolonized and queer-affirming care, boundaries are sacred agreements. They are not static; they are relational, evolving, and mutually informed. Boundaries must hold both safety and presence. They must be clear, yes—*and* also compassionate, culturally fluent, and attuned to power dynamics. For clients from collectivist cultures, or those whose trauma is rooted in abandonment or invisibility, the boundary that matters most is not distance, but relatability.

A client once told me, "I never felt safe with past therapists because I never knew who they were."

That's not a failure of ethics. That's a failure of intimacy.

This reframing intentionally *queers* the concept of intimacy by resisting its normative associations with romantic or sexual connection. Instead, I use "intimacy" here to refer to the emotional depth, presence, and relational safety that should characterize therapeutic work—particularly with queer, trans, and other marginalized clients for whom institutionalized care has often been unsafe or dehumanizing.

Intimacy, as I invoke it, is about attunement, mutual respect, and the capacity to hold space for emotional vulnerability without fear of judgment or harm. It is not about closeness in a personal or romantic sense, but rather the ethical commitment to relational presence. In *queering* intimacy, I suggest that therapeutic ethics are not only procedural or regulatory—they are relational. When a client does not feel emotionally safe, it is not just a lapse in technique or policy; it is a rupture in the emotional contract that underpins healing.

The therapeutic space can be a site of radical potential if we understand intimacy as both an invitation and a condition for deep healing. As Foucault (1976) argued, power dynamics within institutions, including therapeutic spaces, often marginalize and silence non-normative bodies and experiences. *Queering* intimacy is a challenge to these dominant power structures by affirming the humanizing presence of both therapist and client as equal participants in the process of healing. This form of intimacy is not defined by proximity, but by vulnerability and the safety to be authentic within a deeply structured relationship.

Additionally, a trauma-informed lens demands that we acknowledge how relational ruptures are often a byproduct of histories of marginalization, trauma, and abuse. The work of trauma theorists such as van der Kolk (2014) emphasizes that emotional safety is essential for trauma recovery. Without safety, there can be no healing. In the context of therapy, this means that emotional safety is not incidental to the process; it is the foundation upon which healing must occur.

To queer intimacy in therapy is to reclaim it as a practice of radical empathy and witnessing. It demands that we move beyond neutrality, beyond professional distance, and toward a practice of humanizing presence—especially in a therapeutic system that has historically marginalized non-normative identities and experiences. Intimacy, then, becomes a political act of resistance and restoration: a refusal to dehumanize and a commitment to providing space where clients can exist fully and authentically.

When we queer our approach to boundaries and intimacy, we make space for realness, for rupture-and-repair, and for an ethic that is relational and liberating rather than oppressive and rigid.

Cultural Humility and Sensitivity in EMDR

Cultural competence is not a checkbox. It's a practice—one that requires ongoing self-examination, community accountability, and a willingness to unlearn. As EMDR Therapy practitioners, we must ask:

- What parts of the protocol assume whiteness, linearity, or access to safety?
- How are we integrating somatic wisdom from other healing traditions?
- Are we imposing a standard of "regulation" that erases expressions of grief, rage, or cultural memory?

Cultural humility invites us to step off the pedestal of "expert" and into the shared ground of co-creation. It means asking, "What does healing look like for you?" and being willing to be led.

This is not about knowing everything. It's about being willing to be with everything.

Navigating Dual Relationships in Queer and BIPOC Communities

In many marginalized communities—especially queer, BIPOC, and activist spaces—therapists and clients may know one another socially, spiritually, or through shared community work. These are not necessarily boundary violations. They are invitations to bring transparency and community ethics into clinical practice.

Rather than defaulting to avoidance, I believe we must be willing to say: "Yes, our worlds overlap. And yes, I will remain accountable to this space with clarity, respect, and consent."

This work lives in the tension—the tension between clinical integrity and communal interdependence. Queer and decolonized therapy doesn't erase that tension. It honors it. It breathes into it. And here is what I teach around the country: The embodied co-creation of the neuroception of safety means the clock is reset at each encounter. Every time we meet our clients—whether it's the first session or the hundredth—we are invited to earn their safety anew.

Safety is not a given. It is a gift. And we must learn to receive it with reverence.

Future Directions and Conclusion

When practiced through a queer, decolonized, neuroaffirming lens, self-disclosure and resourcing are not "extra" tools—they are essential technologies of healing. They undo isolation. They challenge hierarchy. They restore permission to feel.

Self-disclosure, offered with humility and consent, becomes a bridge across difference, a softening of the clinical armor that has so often kept our most marginalized clients at a distance. It says, "I am with you. Not above you." It becomes a sacred act of resistance to systems that have demanded invisibility—from both clients and clinicians alike.

Resourcing, in turn, is the altar we return to. It is the act of remembering—and as I have come to believe and teach in my work as the Doula for the Soul. *Resourcing is the act of rebirthing our right to safety, connection, and embodiment.*

For every queer client who was told their love was wrong, for every neurodivergent client who was taught to mask, for every person living in the shadows of inherited power—resourcing becomes the doorway to self-belonging.

We do not heal in the absence of ourselves. We heal in the return to ourselves.

To queer EMDR is not simply to serve queer people. It is to disrupt every assumption that healing must be linear, clean, or protocol-bound. To center BIPOC wisdom is not simply to diversify the room—it is to remember that healing traditions existed long before Western psychology gave them a name.

The future of trauma therapy is relational. It is embodied. It is consent-based. It is queer. It is decolonial. It is sacred. And it will be built by those of us who were never supposed to survive—but did. And not only survived, but reclaimed the tools and traditions and truths that were once used against us.

This chapter is not just an offering. It is a calling.

As the Doula for the Soul, I have learned that healing is not always about resolution. Sometimes, it's about remembrance. Sometimes, it's about standing beside someone in the threshold of their becoming—holding steady while they do the holy work of returning to themselves.

May we be the kind of therapists who do not flinch at grief.
May we unlearn the clinical distance that numbs.
May we disclose not to center ourselves, but to offer solidarity.
May we resource not to bypass pain, but to anchor in dignity.
And may we always remember: Healing is not a path we prescribe
It is a home we co-create within the becoming self.

Tawanna Marie Woolfolk, LCSW (she/they) is the founder and CEO of Doula for the Soul Enterprises. A queer, neurodivergent, and multiracial Black woman with over two decades of clinical experience, Tawanna Marie is nationally recognized for her leadership in decolonized trauma healing, relational therapy, and neuroaffirming care. Her work centers the healing of historically marginalized communities and embodies radical love, embodied safety, and clinical liberation. A certified EMDR therapist, grief specialist, and somatic practitioner, Tawanna Marie trains clinicians across the country on the neuroception of safety, ethics of self-disclosure, and culturally responsive resourcing. She sees her clinical work as sacred and soul-centered—a return to wholeness and an unapologetic reclaiming of humanity.

References

Angelou, M. (1973). Interview with Bill Moyers. Journalist and author discussion on identity and belonging. Available at: https://billmoyers.com/content/conversation-maya-angelou/

Brown, L. S. (2015). *Cultural competence in trauma therapy: Beyond the flashback*. Washington, D.C.: American Psychological Association.

Gone, J. P. (2013). Redressing First Nations historical trauma: Theorizing mechanisms for Indigenous culture as mental health treatment. *Transcultural Psychiatry, 50*(5), 683–706.

Henretty, J. R., & Levitt, H. M. (2010). The role of therapist self-disclosure in psychotherapy: A qualitative review. *Clinical Psychology Review, 30*(1), 63–77.

Foucault, M. (1976). *The history of sexuality, Volume 1: An introduction* (R. Hurley, Trans.). New York: Pantheon Books.

Rogers, C. R. (1961). *On becoming a person: A therapist's view of psychotherapy*. Houghton Mifflin Harcourt.

Shapiro, F. (2018). Eye movement desensitization and reprocessing (EMDR) therapy: Basic principles, protocols, and procedures (3rd ed.). Guilford Press.

Van der Kolk, B.A. (2014). The body keeps the score: Brain, mind, and body in the healing of trauma. New York: Viking.

Watkins, M., & Shulman, H. (2008). *Toward psychologies of liberation*. New York: Palgrave Macmillan.

Yalom, I. D. (2002). *The gift of therapy: An open letter to a new generation of therapists and their patients*. New York: Harper Perennial.

quEerMDR As A Practice of Love & Liberatory Healing

horizon greene, LICSW/LCSW

i am trans as in movement, nonbinary as in free
–unknown

I am writing to you from the ancestral lands of the Coast Salish peoples. I acknowledge these peoples and their history as well as the history of this land–its beauty and vibrancy but also its extraction and colonization. I acknowledge that the Coast Salish peoples, stewards of the Lushootseed language, are still here today as they have been since time immemorial. In this acknowledgment, I dream of the deep interconnection and interdependence of all beings, of being deeply woven with each other and the land. I dream of decolonization and land back, of ways-of-being rooted in relational attunement, justice, love and possibility. I invite you into this dreaming with me. This is a part of queering our worldview and imagining (knowing, making real) that healing is possible.

I like to remember that the atoms in our bodies come from the stars. This helps me remember that all bodies have dignity and worth, that all life is sacred and interconnected, that human diversity—and queerness—is a part of the beautiful, complex ecosystem we inhabit and tend. And too, this helps me remember that we were born to heal and that healing is our birthright. And *this* helps me anchor into the truth that when we co-create the relational conditions for safety (which is always our practice within EMDR), the intelligence of our ecosystem body will always lead us toward healing.

I am a queer, fat, nonbinary femme. I am 46 years old, have dynamic disabilities and am in the dramatic, complaint-worthy throws of perimenopause. I have a body that can't hide and yet as a femme my queerness can be invisibilized the way our sick overculture erases these beautiful queernesses and differences. One of my roles in this lifetime is to love my queer fat disabled body and to remind us that this body, too, is sacred. I have always believed that love is our most powerful magic and that healing happens in relationship.

And, what is love if not a relationship?

I like to say that I am a lifetime student of how healing happens.

Our Birthright Capacity for Healing

It was my unending fascination with how to create the conditions for healing that led me to become an EMDR therapist. And then a certified EMDR therapist. And then an EMDR/quEerMDR consultant. Talking about EMDR, how to queer it, and how to align our practice within a framework of liberatory healing, is one of my favorite conversations. Through a queer lens, EMDR works by catalyzing our body's innate wisdom and deep capacity for healing and transformation. This is folk magic (meaning magic of the people; this belongs to us) that travels the riverbed of our bodies' birthright capacity for healing and that taps into our deep embodied knowingness of how to heal. The job of the EMDR therapist is to create the relational conditions for safety in trauma processing while holding the somatic knowingness that healing is possible. Within this intentional container, our clients are able to reach for a different (healing) experience of what is possible. To be clear, I don't mean the container we teach our clients in resourcing, though this container too is a resource. I mean the resource of the larger relational container that holds the body of trauma recovery work where transformation happens.

EMDR therapists accompany our clients in the process of metabolizing the core negative beliefs they have learned about themselves. These are beliefs that our clients have (or more accurately, that we ALL have) not because of what is true, but because of what we and our ancestors have survived.

"I'm not safe, I'm unlovable, I'm too much, I'm not enough, I'm bad."

As therapists we try to contradict these negative beliefs: "You are secure, you are loved, you are worthy, you are enough, you are good" by fundamentally honoring the dignity, worth and yes, the queerness, of our clients. This is a contradiction we generally make not in words, but rather by practicing love and creating the conditions for true belonging, a protective factor in helping someone to heal.

These relational truths–"you are secure, you are loved, you have dignity and worth, you belong"–are woven into the fabric of the container we hold in therapy. And, this supports the work our clients do in therapy as they unlearn negative beliefs, replacing old beliefs with wisdoms about themselves that are, instead, whole, beautiful and true.

"I have dignity and worth, I am secure, I am lovable, I have value, I am connected, I belong."

This transformation is possible because of the relational safety we co-create within the therapeutic container. Which is another way of saying healing happens in relationship...which is another way of saying that in our practice we queer what is possible...which is another way of saying that the healing that is possible between hearts, nervous systems and souls is absolutely beautiful. This is not work we can do alone.

Holding Power Well

As a person who has spent over 23 years (so-far!) doing anti-oppressive, liberation-rooted practice, I have learned over and over that when you have power, you have the ability to do harm. As trauma therapists—particularly when working with folx[1] who live

---

1 **folx:** *a queer, inclusive word substitution for "folks." This language reflects the growing cultural need for an evolving, more-expansive language that includes identities that don't fit into a gender binary (trans, gender queer, nonbinary, agender and more). For myself and many others whose gender identity does not fit within a binary experience of gender, seeing and using the language of* ***folx*** *can invite a sense of belonging and feeling seen and known.*

with complex developmental trauma and who have survived (and are surviving) intersecting oppression, violence, and interpersonal/historical/structural traumas—it is profoundly important that we hold power well within the therapeutic container. Not doing so replicates and echoes oppression and violence within therapy, something that is inappropriately common due to the prevalence of racism, white supremacy, nationalism, classism, ableism, fat-oppression, cisherterenomativity, queer/trans oppression, misogyny, patriarchy, cultural erasure and other ongoing oppressions within our overculture.

These structural oppressions are present within the schools and institutions where we learn to practice therapy, within our systems of licensure and within many of the theories that guide our clinical practice. I was reminded by Dr. Carama Jones, in her *We Can Do Better* conference keynote[2] lecture, that there is no institution within the United States of America whose roots are not embedded in the history and legacy of structural racism and oppression. In the resonant truth of this we are invited to center the voices of marginalized folx who tell of the ongoing impact of continuing structural violence. If we listen, we will find that the people and communities who are surviving oppression are continuing to tell us exactly what they need. Even while ongoing structural oppression and racism influences our practice, this embodied listening, and the relational responsiveness that comes from believing someone's lived experience, helps us to co-create the conditions in trauma therapy where healing is possible.

Practicing within oppressive systems while striving to co-create liberatory healing is a practice of harm reduction. As harm reductionists, we queer our practice by using relationship, voice, anti-oppression, love and a therapy practice rooted in human dignity, to contradict structural oppression and violence within EMDR. While there are many things we could say about holding power well, one thing we should say is that making room for our clients' beautiful identities and actively working to practice against their retraumatization are vital components of co-creating safety in trauma therapy. If our clients can not express/show/be their

2 *We Can Do Better* Conference, Portland OR, 1/17/2019

full selves in therapy, and if structural, interpersonal and historical oppression is not acknowledged and accounted for, trauma therapy is simply not able to be fully effective.

This is one of many reasons why trauma therapy must be anti-oppressive and liberatory for folx to access the full healing available for them. Through anti-oppressive, liberatory, queer-centered practice, we can co-create a space for folx to feel and be with whatever needs to be felt, metabolized and transformed. This is where and how the healing happens. When our clients feel secure and free enough to unmask from performative roles, and to show us who they really are and where they are holding pain, there is more authenticity in the therapeutic relationship and more opportunity to be with whatever inside of our clients needs to be compassionately witnessed. Fundamental to a queer, liberation-rooted EMDR is a remembering that all oppressions are interconnected and that all life (and therefore all liberation) is interdependent.

Queering Our Work

Queerness is vast, expansive, boundless, luminous, brilliant and full of poetic possibility! When we queer our EMDR, or when we call the full expansiveness of queerness and queer possibility into EMDR, what is possible within the therapeutic container also becomes vast, expansive, boundless, luminous, brilliant and poetic. Queering this work invites us to take EMDR out of the binary and into the liminal, where it belongs. quEerMDR is the way I have come to understand queer healing through my deep study of EMDR and in the ways EMDR has come alive through my relationship with queerness, liberation and possibility. This body of work flows through the artistry of EMDR, using the fluidity, authenticity and vastness of queerness to invite healing and transformation, challenging and unlearning existing power structures (desensitization) and re-inviting us into updated knowings or rememberings that are whole, beautiful and true (installation).

While many EMDR therapists like to say we are working with one foot in the past and one foot in the present, I prefer to think of this work as building a bridge. Or, we might say, we are building a relationship. The parts of us that are burdened with trauma memories do not tend to understand they are in the present moment or that the past traumatic experience is not still happening. However liberation-rooted EMDR therapists understand that traumas also happen to us in the present—especially the ongoing systemic traumas of racism, queer/trans phobia, fat oppression and other structural violence. This can, of course, be true of interpersonal traumas as well. In the wisdom and language of dear friend and fellow EMDR Certified Therapist Lisa Gallegos, the white, class privileged, cis, hetero, trauma healing world often leaves ongoing systemic oppression out of all aspects of the healing process and phases of EMDR. One important way we can create the conditions for safety in trauma healing work is to practice EMDR in ways that are anti-oppressive, queer in every liminal sense of the word, and rooted in liberation.

One way we can more boldly queer our work is to increase comfort acknowledging and accepting that EMDR is fundamentally a relational therapy. As folk medicine has always known, and relational neuroscience continues to reaffirm, we are born with a biological imperative for connection. This is the science behind *healing is our birthright*. While it is absolutely true that we hold the container for our clients to simply do what their bodies know how to do (heal), the strength and stability of the therapy container (and therefore what is possible within it) is absolutely linked to the security and stability of the relationship. The binary and limiting way EMDR can be talked about as "the therapist is not doing much, it's all the client" undermines the deep importance and value of the therapeutic relationship. This minimizes the fundamental truth that healing happens in relationship and that we heal in a space of connection and within a culture of belonging.

As humans with brilliant nervous systems who are born both wired for survival and longing for connection, we are always scanning our inner and outer world for cues of safety and danger. When our bodies are able to feel settled, when we can feel in our bodies the truth of "I have dignity and worth, I am secure, I am lovable, I belong," we have access to the adaptive capacity of connection where healing happens. This is something we learn to feel because we have been able to internalize an inner sense of belonging. This is something we learn not in isolation but in relationship. One way I practice and embody this is by telling my clients (and believing) "I am accompanying you so that you can accompany your own parts." The rich resource of co-regulation and attunement offered within a secure relationship is a deep nourishment that seeds our clients' capacity to anchor in the present while touching what has been intolerable and is now available for transformation.

quEerMDR

In order to access traumatic wounding held within our client's body memory, Phase 3 in EMDR guides us to call up a felt sense of the traumatic activation. When we call this wounding up, we are able to touch it (Phase 3), move it (Phase 4), and transform it (Phase 5). This is some of the beauty of EMDR. Dr. Bonnie Badenoch, an important teacher of mine in heart-centered trauma therapy, would often say, "we are simply waiting for the exact right conditions for healing to occur and when they do, healing simply happens." If queerness is vast, expansive, boundless, luminous, brilliant and full of poetic possibility, so too is what is possible when we help to co-create the relational conditions for healing. When it comes to trauma, the interpersonal relationship is so often the site of injury and therefore is also where we will feel traumatic relivings. Knowing that we heal when we have access to both enough activation (a foot in the pain) and safety (a foot in the present, knowing I belong), relationship is, therefore, also the site of healing.

Having a deep attunement to and compassion for the impact and retraumatization of queer/trans phobia, cisheteronormativity, conversion therapies, dehumanization of queerness, the pain of being rejected by your family/workplace/community because of your queerness and the current political violence explicitly targeting trans, nonbinary and queer sovereignty (and BIPOC/immigrant communities) is necessary for being a culturally responsive, culturally humble EMDR therapist. Similarly, understanding the deep resource of queer/trans/nonbinary joy, gender euphoria, the pride movement, queer history and the beautiful ongoing legacy of queer ancestors and transcestors, chosen family, chosen names and pronouns and the rich resource of a person who is able to beautifully know who they are are all invitations into a therapeutic relationship that is flexible and vibrant enough to hold the vast brilliance of queerness.

When EMDR therapists align our practice with liberatory justice movements and draw on the rooted wisdom of anti-oppressive, queer, liberation-based healing, EMDR can queerly become a practice of liberation. This is intersectional with (and not separate from) a rooted practice culture of anti-racism, anti-ableism, BIPOC liberation, neurodivergent liberation, fat/body liberation, queer/trans liberation, and intersectional feminism. Through a queer lens, an EMDR practice where anti-oppression is not woven into the threads of the practice is limited by a small, binary way of thinking about trauma healing and misses the vast liminal complexity of human experience and the importance of trauma healing interwoven with human liberation. When humans are not free (oppression), healing is limited by the nature of being oppressed. When humans are free to move, dream, create, transform and be their full, vibrant selves (liberation, connection, belonging), what is possible is beautiful. Through an anti-oppressive, liberation-aligned practice where our clients can bring their full selves and queernesses into the therapy room, and where we reach together for what is possible (liberation, connection, belonging), we are co-creating a healing culture where our clients can do what we all are here to do (heal), so that we can be who we are all born to be (free).

Trauma therapists who practice from a liberation orientation understand that oppression is trauma and is felt by the nervous system (and in the interpersonal relationship) in the re-experiencing pathways we know traumas to follow. We understand that historical trauma and structural/cultural oppression is real and ongoing, hurts queer and trans people (and ALL people with a lived experience of violence and oppression) and must be presenced in EMDR for therapy to be fully effective and for clients to bring their full selves into the room. There is an ongoing invitation here for the field of EMDR, its leadership and training programs to grow to meet the needs of marginalized and diverse communities.

And, because we understand all liberations are bound up in each other, this is not work we can do for a single oppressed community, rather, work we must do for all oppressed communities. This is the brilliance of queerness: expanding our scope and inviting growth and transformation to be a resource and a guide for what is possible where possibility is limited only by our imagination. We must be willing to allow our practice and our field to grow and transform (a parallel to what happens within EMDR) to meet the true safety needs of the 2SLBTQIA+ community and all oppressed peoples including (and certainly not limited to) BIPOC and QTBIPOC, fat folx, disabled folx, neurodivergent folx, nonbinary folx, women and femmes. If, as a field, we're not able to grow, to increase safety within EMDR treatment for oppressed communities—especially when folx with lived experience of oppression are telling us over and over exactly what they need—I invite us to sit with the question of "Who is EMDR actually for?"

A grounding truth from my learnings in Somatic Abolitionism with Resmaa Menakem is that *all of our bodies are fundamentally good and loveable.* And all people have dignity and worth. This is foundational to therapy, to queer liberation, and to a liberation-aligned, queer-centered intersectional EMDR practice. As practitioners committed to queering our practice, practicing from a liberation-orientation and creating more safety with queer clients and families, it is our responsibility to make room for the expansiveness of queer experiences, identities and futures. This looks like everything from absolute comfort with using folx' correct pronouns, to centering culturally specific queer and trans resources in the resourcing phase and throughout processing, to holding in our bodies and embedding throughout our practice the truths of:

You know who you are.
I see and celebrate your queerness,
your relationship structures,
the beauty of your human sexuality,
your gender identity, your gender expression.
I see the complexity of ongoing oppression
you and your communities experience and have experienced.
We can compassionately hold the hurt of this violence
(a foot in the pain)
and feel for the healing that is your birthright
(a foot in the present).
All of this, and all of you, is welcome.
You and your queerness, in all its beauty, belong.

When my clients ask me what is possible in EMDR, or what they can reasonably hope to achieve over the course of therapy, I always respond (and genuinely believe) that so much is possible–we never want to limit our healing! What is possible is vast, expansive, boundless, luminous, brilliant and full of poetic possibility. Yes, what is possible is queer, rooted in a vast, liminal possibility that reflects the fluidity, nonconforming, shape-shifting nature of what is possible within the awe-inspiring spectrum of our humanity. Being a queer EMDR therapist and doing the work of trauma healing with other queer beings has taught me over and over again that what is possible is limited only by our imagination.

Though we have an idea of the positive belief we hope to frontload before we begin trauma processing, at the end of desensitization and before moving onto reprocessing I ask my clients, "When you think of where you started, what do you believe about yourself now? A huge percentage of the time, the depth of their insight—what is now possible for them to believe about themselves–is so much more profound than they could have ever possibly imagined. And, beautifully, this is what our clients then get to seed in their bodies and feel within their neural pathways: new and brilliantly queer possibilities, the most profound truths their hearts could imagine. This, when combined with the magic of BLS to seed change, nurtures the body's brilliant capacity for transformation. Or, we might say, for queer liberatory healing.

We are living in a time when we know so much about how healing happens and about co-creating the relational conditions for safety. Much like our journey of transformation over the course of EMDR treatment, aligning—or we could say queering—our EMDR with a practice of liberatory healing is the growth and transformation we were born for. As Dr. Martin Luther King powerfully said, "the arc of the moral universe is long, but it bends towards justice." This is about who we, as a people, are becoming; it's also about the culture we build together and a cultural change we are being called to collectively shape toward justice. Where we are now on the map of that long arc toward justice is an invitation for us to open to queer possibility so that the practice of EMDR, and the culture in which it is set, can be a tool of liberatory healing where oppression is not reinforced within the therapy container but rather where liberation is the foundation and the visionary springboard for what is possible. Here, we are invited into a trauma healing practice rooted in love, anchored in possibility, in service of queer liberation.

horizon greene, LICSW/LCSW (they/she) identifies as a queer, fat, nonbinary femme who has spent more than 23 years in a deep study of how healing happens, learning to undo oppression while learning to co-create cultures of justice and belonging. She identifies as white and comes from Jewish people whose body memories tell the story of grief and loss and whose prayers feed a commitment of *Never Again* for anyone. Their training has included intensive learnings in somatics, trauma healing, anti-oppressive practices, anti-racism, liberatory culture building, ritual and witchcraft. horizon is an initiated witch in the Reclaiming tradition of witchcraft. Her work as a therapist and consultant is a blending of liberatory healing practices rooted in the relational neurosciences, somatic wisdom, parts work, ancestral healing, magic and love. horizon accompanies people in the deep work of making real what our souls know is possible.

Let's Talk About Sex

Building Confidence in Discussing Kink and Sexual Healing in EMDR Therapy

Anna Clarke, MCPT, BPsych (Hons)

Introduction

Supporting survivors of sexual assault through EMDR therapy has been one of the greatest privileges of my career. Initially, I felt like my role was straightforward. I was there to help clients process their trauma, rebuild confidence in relationships, and then conclude treatment.

With my background in sexual assault support services, I was comfortable discussing sexual trauma in clinical settings including police interviews, forensic exams, and therapy. Yet, I hadn't considered a crucial aspect of healing: helping survivors cultivate positive sexual experiences, rather than just reducing fear and flashbacks.

I initially hesitated to raise the topic with clients. Would discussing sexual pleasure cross professional boundaries? Would it make my clients uncomfortable, or even put me at risk of scrutiny from regulatory bodies? However, when I finally broached the subject, I saw relief on my client's faces. Simply knowing they *could* have this conversation was validating, even if they only talked about it once.

Many clients, whether or not they had experienced sexual trauma, struggled with feelings of shame, disconnection from their bodies, and uncertainty about what a positive sexual experience could be like. Some questioned whether their interest in kink or Bondage, Dominance, Sadism, and Masochism (BDSM) was "wrong." Others withheld details that, if openly discussed, could have ensured more safety while exploring new sexual experiences. While trauma survivors often faced greater challenges in reclaiming sexual agency, I realized that shame around sexuality wasn't exclusive to survivors of abuse.

In the EMDR therapy community, I am primarily known for my work with children. As I contemplated writing this chapter, I feared professional judgment, not just for discussing sex and kink in therapy, but for publicly writing a chapter on this topic. I even considered using a pseudonym, worried that associating my name to these discussions might lead to misinterpretation or unfounded concerns. Would my professional reputation be questioned simply for engaging in this dialogue? Would my willingness to explore sexuality as a therapeutic issue be conflated with something inappropriate?

I am acutely aware of the troubling reports of abuse in healthcare settings, including cases involving therapists. These acts are often labeled "sexual misconduct." We need to call them what they are: *sexual assault*. The power dynamics inherent in the therapeutic relationship make true consent between a therapist and client impossible.

While necessary conversations about abuse in therapy have increased awareness and accountability, they have also contributed to a growing hesitancy among clinicians to discuss sex at all. Many therapists fear that even raising the topic could be misinterpreted or place them under suspicion. Having personally experienced the profound harm of a violation by a therapist, I understand the damage this causes better than most. At the same time, I recognize that avoiding these discussions with ethical professionals does not protect clients. It only reinforces silence and shame.

Building my own confidence in discussing these topics with clients took time. Cultural taboos around sex remain deeply ingrained, and even saying words like "sex," "vagina," or "penis" can provoke discomfort. Discussing concepts like bondage or dominance? Even more so. However, many therapists are unfamiliar with the realities of kink, often relying on misleading media portrayals or harmful myths. Without proper understanding, we risk misinterpreting or pathologizing our clients' experiences, creating further barriers to their healing.

The aim of this chapter is to equip EMDR therapists with the confidence and knowledge to work in kink-affirming ways with clients. EMDR therapy offers valuable tools to support clients in connecting with their bodies and fostering healthier sexual experiences. By expanding our understanding and normalizing these discussions, we can better support our clients in their journeys toward healing, bodily connection, and pleasure.

Understanding Kink: Definitions and Associations

What comes to mind when you hear the word 'kink' or 'BDSM'? Historically, kink has been viewed as rare and deviant, shaped by media portrayals and societal biases. In reality, kink is diverse and, for many, a fulfilling part of their identity and relationships. The kink community is a subculture that embraces a wide range of sexual interests, prioritizes consent, and fosters open communication.

Research suggests kink is more common than many assume. Brown et al. (2020) estimate that 20–30% of people actively engage in BDSM, with up to 70% having related fantasies. While participation spans diverse backgrounds, underreporting is common due to stigma and cultural taboos, especially in regions where discussing non-traditional sexual practices carries greater social risk and consequences.

Kink is a broad term for sexual experiences outside conventional (i.e., "vanilla") sex. It ranges from playful activities to structured role-play and intense sensations. While often linked to sex, many engage in kink for emotional, psychological, or social reasons. It can be part of long-term relationships or occasional encounters, practiced privately or in community spaces.

Kink is an umbrella term encompassing a wide range of sexual interests, including role-playing, sensory experiences, and power exchange dynamics. Understanding these concepts allows therapists to create a nonjudgmental space for discussion. Table 1 provides key definitions commonly used within the kink community.

Table 1. Key Definitions of Kink

Term	Definition
Aftercare	Emotional and physical care provided after a kink scene to ensure well-being and comfort
BDSM	A category within kink that involves Bondage, Discipline, Dominance, Submission, Sadism, and Masochism
Bondage	The practice of restraining a partner using ropes, cuffs, or other materials
Degradation & Humiliation	Activities involving embarrassment, shame, or demeaning language in a consensual and negotiated context
Dominance	The act of taking control in a power exchange dynamic. People may identify as a 'dominant' or 'dom' (sometimes also known as a 'top') when this is their preferred role.
Fetish	A specific, intense sexual focus on an object, body part, or activity that enhances arousal
Impact Play	Activities involving physical impact, such as spanking, flogging, paddling, or caning, typically with negotiated intensity and limits; this may leave visible marks, including bruising
Kink	A broad term encompassing a wide range of unconventional sexual interests and activities
Kink Shaming	The act of judging or demeaning someone for their consensual kink interests or activities

Munches	Social gatherings for kink community members in non-kink settings, often held in restaurants or cafes; many people also meet online before attending in-person events
Play	A general term referring to engaging in consensual kink or BDSM activities
Role Play	Acting out scenarios within a kink context, often involving themes like power dynamics or fantasy-based interactions (e.g., professional roles, costumes)
Safe Word	A pre-determined word or signal used to stop or pause a scene/interaction
Scene	A planned kink interaction that can range from brief interactions to extended role-play
Sub and Dom Drop	The emotional or physical comedown that can occur after an intense kink experience, sometimes requiring aftercare for support; this may manifest as feelings of exhaustion, sadness, anxiety, or physical fatigue
Sub and Dom Space	A deeply focused, euphoric, or heightened psychological state experienced by dominants and submissives during a scene
Submission	The act of relinquishing control in a power exchange dynamic; people may identify as a 'submissive' or 'sub' (sometimes also known as a 'bottom') when this is their preferred role.
Switch	A person who enjoys and engages in both dominant and submissive roles, depending on the partner, scenario, or personal preference at the time
Vanilla	A term used within the kink community to describe conventional, non-kinky sexual activities

Myth Busting Kink and BDSM

Stigma and misconceptions about kink and BDSM remain widespread, shaped by societal attitudes, media portrayals, and outdated psychological classifications. Historically, BDSM was mischaracterized as a mental disorder, thought to stem from childhood trauma or psychological dysfunction. It was subsequently classified as a paraphilic disorder in diagnostic manuals like the Diagnostic and Statistical Manual of Mental Disorders (DSM) and the International Classification of Diseases (ICD).

While the ICD-11 has since removed sexual masochism as a disorder, the DSM-5-TR still includes sexual sadism, sexual masochism, and fetishistic disorder applicable when they cause distress or involve non-consenting individuals (American Psychiatric Association, 2022). Critics argue that these classifications reinforce stigma and needlessly pathologize consensual sexual interests (Brown et al., 2020).

Despite advancements in medical and psychological understanding, outdated beliefs about BDSM persist, fueling shame, fear of judgment, and reluctance to discuss it openly. Research indicates that BDSM practitioners often anticipate stigma, particularly in healthcare settings (Sprott et al., 2023). A Belgian study found that 86% of participants held at least one stigmatizing belief about BDSM, while one in five believed that BDSM practitioners had psychological issues (Schuerwegen et al., 2020). These misconceptions contribute to misunderstanding and marginalization, making it essential to challenge the most persistent myths surrounding kink.

Myth #1: The Kink Community is Homogenous

Research on kink has been criticized for focusing primarily on White, English-speaking, well-educated participants, failing to capture the full diversity of the community (Martinez, 2021). In many regions, legal restrictions, cultural stigma, and fear of discrimination discourage people from disclosing their involvement in kink, leading to an underrepresentation of marginalized groups in research (Westlake & Mahan, 2025). As a result, kink is often mistakenly perceived as a community dominated by White men (Martinez, 2021).

In reality, people who participate in kink come from diverse backgrounds, with their experiences influenced by identity, relationship structures, and psychological traits (Westlake & Mahan, 2025). Despite this diversity, research has identified common trends related to demographics, gendered role preferences, relationship styles, personality traits, and neurodivergence.

- Demographics: People involved in kink tend to be well-educated, younger, and more likely to identify as non-heterosexual (Brown et al., 2020). Studies also suggest that interest in kink is widespread across genders and education levels (Strizzi et al., 2022).
- Gendered role preferences: Men are more likely to identify as dominants or sadists, while women tend to identify as submissives or masochists. However, this trend is less pronounced among non-binary and non-heterosexual individuals, where roles are more fluid (Brown et al., 2020).
- Non-monogamous relationships: Kink extends beyond traditional romantic relationships, with many individuals engaging in play with multiple partners, including friends and strangers (Brown et al., 2020; Cesur & Sancack, 2024; Westlake & Mahon, 2025).
- Personality traits: Certain personality traits may also influence kink engagement. Research suggests that people involved in kink score higher in openness to experience, a trait linked to curiosity, creativity, and a willingness to explore unconventional behaviors (Brown et al., 2020). Additionally, those who participate in kink tend to score higher on sensation-seeking, including thrill-seeking, experience-seeking, and distraction-seeking (Schuerwegen et al., 2020).
- Neurodivergence: Emerging research suggests that Autistic individuals may be more likely to engage in BDSM than the non-Autistic population (Pliskin, 2022). The structure of kink, with clear emphasis on communication, sensory

experiences, and well-defined roles, may align with Autistic communication styles and sensory preferences, making it particularly appealing (Rosqvist & Jackson-Perry, 2021).

Myth #2: People Who Engage in Kink are Re-enacting Their Histories of Sexual Abuse

A common misconception is that kink is primarily driven by a history of childhood sexual abuse (CSA). While some survivors engage in BDSM, research does not support a direct causal link between past trauma and BDSM participation (Gewirtz-Meydan et al., 2024). The kink community includes individuals from a wide range of backgrounds, with most having no history of CSA. Studies show that childhood trauma is not a significant predictor of either dominant or submissive sexual behaviors, reinforcing that BDSM participation is shaped by factors beyond trauma (Gewirtz-Meydan et al., 2024).

For some survivors of sexual assault, kink can be a tool for reclaiming empowerment, exploring boundaries, and reshaping their relationship with their bodies (Turley, 2024). Research highlights that BDSM can foster emotional healing by offering a structured, consensual space where survivors can regain control, build self-worth, and process difficult emotions (Cascalheira et al., 2023; Gewirtz-Meydan et al., 2024; Walling-Wefelmeyer & O'Niell, 2021).

While some survivors find kink healing, others may struggle with distress, particularly if they have difficulty setting boundaries due to past non-consensual experiences (Gewirtz-Meydan et al., 2024). Retraumatization is more commonly reported among individuals unfamiliar with kink's structural safeguards, emphasizing the protective role of consent, negotiation, and boundary-setting within the community (Cascalheira et al., 2023).

Rather than reducing kink to a reenactment of past trauma, it is more accurate to recognize it as a diverse practice with different meanings for different individuals. For some, it is a tool for healing. For others, it is simply a consensual form of self-expression and pleasure. Therapists must acknowledge this complexity to provide nonjudgmental, informed support, ensuring that clients feel validated rather than pathologized.

Myth #3: People Who Engage in Kink Have Psychological and Relationship Issues

There is no evidence to suggest that individuals who engage in kink have higher rates of mental health or relationship problems compared to the general population (Brown et al., 2020; Cesur & Sancak, 2024). Research suggests that people engaged in kink experience relationship satisfaction that is comparable to, if not higher than, those in conventional relationships (Strizzi et al., 2022). Shared intimacy and mutual pleasure are often cited as key reasons for this (Williams et al., 2023). The emphasis on negotiation, boundary-setting, and explicit consent in kink interactions has been identified as a factor that mediates the relationship between BDSM participation and relationship satisfaction (Carty & Davidson, 2024). Additionally, the structured communication in kink helps foster trust, emotional intimacy, and negotiation skills, all of which contribute to greater relationship stability (Melavc et al., 2024).

In addition to relationship dynamics, engaging in kink is often cited as a source of mental health benefits, including stress relief, catharsis, and altered states of consciousness, such as 'sub-space' or meditative states (Melavc et al., 2024; Westlake & Mahon, 2025). Qualitative research by Turley (2024) found that participants find kink psychologically meaningful, offering a way to deepen their connection to emotions, bodies, and identities. Similarly, Dunkley et al. (2020) found that individuals involved in kink exhibited higher levels of dispositional mindfulness, suggesting that kink can promote present-moment awareness, emotional regulation, and overall well-being.

Myth #4: The Main Purpose of Kink is for Sexual Pleasure

Although kink is often associated with sex, many people engage in it for reasons other than erotic pleasure. This includes asexual individuals, showing that kink is not solely about sexual desire. An increasing body of research highlights non-sexual motivations for kink, including leisure, play, and coping. For many, kink serves as a form of recreation providing enjoyment, adventure, and relaxation (Westlake & Mahon, 2025), or escape from adult responsibilities through structured play (Melavc et al., 2024). Schuerwegen et al. (2020) found that approximately 40% of individuals who engage in BDSM use it to manage stress or distract from daily life challenges.

Kink can also be a powerful tool for self-exploration and personal empowerment. Turley (2024) found that both dominant and submissive participants reported greater confidence and self-esteem after engaging in BDSM. Many individuals see BDSM as a journey of self-discovery, helping them better understand their desires, boundaries, and personal strengths. For others, kink is more about exploring intense sensory experiences rather than sexual gratification. Kink often involves heightened tactile and visual stimulation, including pressure, sensory deprivation (e.g. blindfolds), and controlled pain, in a structured space, allowing participants to explore sensations in a focused and intentional way (Pearson & Hodges, 2023; Williams et al., 2023).

Myth #5: Kink and BDSM are Abusive and Dangerous

Kink is often mischaracterized as violent or abusive, but the key difference between kink and abuse is consent. Abuse involves exerting control without consent, while BDSM is based on mutual agreement, clear boundaries, and structured negotiation (Tarleton et al., 2025). The kink community prioritizes informed consent, clear communication, and risk awareness, following frameworks like Safe, Sane, and Consensual. This principle ensures that activities are safe (minimizing risks through knowledge and precautions), sane (engaged in with clear awareness and mutual responsibility), and consensual (with explicit, ongoing agreement from all parties) (Litam & Speciale, 2020). Built-in safety measures such as safe words, negotiated boundaries, and aftercare help protect participants' well-being (Tarleton et al., 2025). While unhealthy dynamics or accidental injury can occur in any high-risk activity, kink emphasizes communication, consent, and safety measures to minimize harm and ensure well-being.

As someone who participates in mixed martial arts (MMA) recreationally, I see a clear parallel between the structure of combat sports and the safeguards in kink. Like BDSM, MMA is often stigmatized due to its association with violence. However, for myself and many others, MMA is an important part of both physical and mental well-being. For me, the challenge is not about seeking harm but about pushing limits in ways that build confidence, resilience, and trust in my body. MMA also offers a positive social outlet, providing opportunities for connection and belonging with my incredible coach and teammates.

While sparring inevitably involves risk, MMA fighters willingly accept this and rely on training partners to follow established rules and protocols to ensure safety. When these boundaries are respected, MMA promotes discipline and empowerment. However, when individuals disregard the rules, they create an unsafe environment.

The same is true for kink. When practiced with mutual respect and communication, it provides a structured and intentional space for exploring power dynamics safely. Just as reckless behavior does not define MMA, individuals who violate consent do not define kink. The existence of risk does not make kink inherently harmful; rather, it highlights the importance of communication, negotiation, and community accountability.

Risks in BDSM and Kink

While challenging misconceptions about kink is important, we must also acknowledge the risks of ignoring boundaries, breakdowns in communication, or lack of consent. Violence, coercion, and accidents can occur, and kink can be misused to cover abuse. Acknowledging these risks is crucial for fostering informed consent and ensuring ethical, safe engagement in kink.

Physical and Psychological Risks of BDSM

While most BDSM activities carry minimal risk of serious injury, unintended harm can occur if proper precautions are not adhered to (Westlake, 2024). Temporary bruising or marks may be expected or even valued as a "badge of honor" by participants (Westlake, 2024). However, activities involving restraints, impact play, or breath control carry inherent risks that require careful execution.

Many individuals are first introduced to kink through pornography, which rarely depicts pre-scene negotiation, boundary-setting, or aftercare. This can lead to unrealistic and unsafe expectations (Herbenick et al., 2020; Westlake, 2025). While real-world BDSM communities emphasize education and mentorship, relying on pornography as a primary source of information may increase the likelihood of unsafe practices (Herbenick et al., 2020).

Clear communication is essential for preventing harm, allowing participants to stop an activity if it becomes physically or emotionally overwhelming. However, some hesitate to use safe words due to fear of disappointing their partner or embarrassment, increasing the risk of distress or injury. Individuals with trauma histories may be particularly vulnerable, as they may dissociate or become psychologically overwhelmed during a scene (Gewirtz-Meydan et al., 2024). High-risk activities, such as breath play, can be especially dangerous if limits aren't communicated and respected (Westlake, 2024), but even lower-risk activities (e.g., spanking) can lead to unintended harm without discussions about pain tolerance and boundaries. Dominants may experience guilt or anxiety if they fear they've harmed their partner, especially if a scene doesn't go as planned.

These risks emphasise the importance of informed consent, negotiation, and ongoing communication. Education, mentorship, and real-world experience are essential for safe and responsible kink participation. Without these, new participants may rush into high-intensity experiences without fully understanding their physical or psychological limits, increasing risk of harm (Westlake, 2025).

Violent Relationships Disguised as Kink

Violence can occur in any relationship, regardless of whether kink dynamics exist. However, abuse within kink can be more difficult to recognize or challenge, as it may be excused as "just part of the play." A concerning example of this is the rise of the "*rough sex*" defense, where perpetrators of abuse or homicide claim their victims consented to violent acts that led to serious harm or death (Walling-Wefelmeyer & O'Neil, 2021).

Certain populations, including CSA survivors and people with disabilities, may be particularly vulnerable to abusive BDSM dynamics (Gewirtz-Meydan et al., 2024). Survivors of trauma may struggle to recognize red flags, assert boundaries, or communicate discomfort, making them more susceptible to coercion. In cases where kink is used to disguise abuse, perpetrators may manipulate survivors into believing harmful behaviors are consensual. This highlights the need for education, clear communication, and community accountability to distinguish safe kink from exploitation.

Therapists, especially those working with trauma survivors, must understand the distinction between consensual kink and abuse. Dismissing kink as inherently abusive risks silencing clients and hindering open conversation, reducing opportunity for therapists to assess safety in current sexual relationships. Therapy should be a space for clients to discuss their experiences and develop tools for engaging in kink with a focus on agency, consent, and well-being.

The following checklist (Table 2) differentiates between safe, consensual kink and abusive or coercive behaviors within kink dynamics.

Table 2. Checklist for Differentiating Between Consensual Kink and Abuse

Category	Safe Kink ☑	Abuse & Coercion ⃠
Consent & Negotiation	Discussing boundaries, desires, and limits before play	Pressuring or guilting a partner into uncomfortable activities
	Using and respecting safewords or non-verbal stop signals	Ignoring safewords, pushing past limits, or mocking their use
	Checking in about medical conditions, past trauma, and triggers	Dismissing health concerns or claiming a partner is "too sensitive"
	Allowing consent to be withdrawn or renegotiated at any time	Using threats (e.g., threatening to end the relationship) to force participation
	Respecting pre-agreed time limits for scenes	Deliberately prolonging play beyond what was agreed upon
Safety During Play	Checking in during play for signs of distress or discomfort	Ignoring signs of distress (e.g., freezing, panicked breathing, dissociation)
	Stopping immediately if a partner is overwhelmed or withdraws consent	Continuing despite visible distress, discomfort, or resistance
	Ensuring all tools and equipment are clean and safe	Using unsanitised or unsafe tools, ignoring safety measures

Category	Safe Kink ☑	Abuse & Coercion ⃠
	Never leaving a bound or restrained person unattended	Leaving a partner alone in a vulnerable position
	Introducing new dynamics only after discussion and agreement	Springing unexpected elements on a partner mid-scene without consent
Post-Scene Care & Emotional Safety	Providing agreed-upon aftercare (e.g., hydration, quiet time, verbal reassurance)	Withholding aftercare, ignoring needs, or disappearing after a scene
	Checking in 1-3 days after play to ensure emotional well-being	Failing to check in post-scene, dismissing emotional effects
	Encouraging open, honest discussion about experiences	Criticising, belittling, or ignoring concerns brought up after play
Power Dynamics & Emotional Well-being	Allowing both partners autonomy outside of scenes	Controlling daily life, finances, or relationships outside of agreed kink roles
	Respecting personal boundaries beyond play	Isolating a partner from friends, family, or support systems
	Negotiating power exchange dynamics with informed consent	Claiming "real submissives" or "real Dominants" act a certain way to manipulate behaviour
	Recognising the difference between kink and emotional abuse	Using BDSM as a cover for control, fear, or emotional harm

Red Flags of Coercive Control

- Pressuring a partner into activities they are hesitant about
- Mocking, minimising, or ignoring distress signals
- Withholding affection, attention, or aftercare as punishment
- Controlling whom a partner speaks to or isolating them from support
- Pushing for riskier play without experience or preparation
- Using fear, guilt, or threats to manipulate participation

If a partner dismisses concerns, disrespects boundaries, or manipulates through coercion it's abuse, not kink.

Sex as Self-Injury (SASI)

Sex as Self-Injury (SASI) is a relatively new phenomenon in which individuals seek sexual situations involving harm, often accompanied by shame, guilt, anxiety, or self-hatred (Fredlund et al., 2017). Research links SASI with past sexual abuse, poor mental health, and non-suicidal self-injury. Unlike sex addiction, which involves a compulsive need for sexual behavior to achieve gratification or relief, SASI is driven by self-punishment, shame, or emotional pain. Individuals engaging in SASI may intentionally pursue violent or degrading encounters—not for sexual gratification, but as a form of self-harm, reinforcing negative self-perceptions (Fredlund et al., 2020).

Unlike healthy kink—where activities are negotiated, boundaries are respected, and fulfillment is the primary goal—SASI is driven by self-punishment, shame, or emotional pain. The key distinction is that kink involves personal-agency, and pleasure, whereas SASI stems from distress and self-harm. Clinicians should assess whether a client feels safe, empowered, and fulfilled by the experience, or if it leaves them feeling worse.

Understanding why someone engages in kink is crucial for providing appropriate care. Kink is based on enjoyment, boundaries, and self-expression, while SASI reflects distress, self-punishment, or a need for external validation. Therapists must differentiate between the two to offer appropriate intervention when sexual experiences are being used as self-harm.

Discussing Kink and BDSM in EMDR Therapy: Clinical Considerations

Many therapists lack adequate knowledge about kink and BDSM, which can contribute to reinforcing stigma, pathologization, or ineffective clinical interventions. Research highlights that while most therapists have treated at least one BDSM-practicing client, less than half feel competent discussing it (Lantto & Lundberg, 2022) which leaves many therapists unfamiliar with its practices and uncomfortable working with kink-involved clients (Litam & Speciale, 2020). Kink identities and practices are diverse, and clinicians must be aware of how gender, sexuality, disability, and other aspects of identity influence how kink is expressed and experienced (Sprott et al., 2023).

Clients may withhold information that could meaningfully alter the therapist's approach, potentially impacting treatment effectiveness. Since EMDR therapy involves processing traumatic memories and restructuring negative beliefs, understanding a client's engagement with kink provides important context. Without this knowledge, EMDR therapists may unintentionally overlook critical considerations, misinterpret responses, or fail to tailor treatment effectively. Addressing distressing memories through EMDR therapy requires an understanding of how clients navigate intimacy, boundaries, and power dynamics—elements that can be shaped by kink involvement.

Barriers to Disclosure in Therapy

Many clients who engage in kink will never disclose this, even after long-term therapy (Sprott & Benoit Hadcock, 2018). They may fear that their kink practices will be misinterpreted as symptoms of mental illness or unresolved trauma, or worry that disclosure will cause therapists to focus too heavily on kink, assuming it is the root of all therapeutic concerns. In some cases, clinicians unintentionally signal that kink is taboo by redirecting discussions, responding indifferently, or failing to ask open-ended questions about sexuality (Lantto & Lundberg, 2022).

To address these barriers, therapists should clearly communicate their openness to discussing kink and sexuality. Research suggests that clients are more likely to disclose kink-related identities when therapists normalize sexuality as part of overall well-being and invite such conversations in a nonjudgmental manner (Sprott et al., 2023).

Clinical Guidelines for Working with Kink-Involved Clients

Various guidelines exist for kink-affirming therapy (see Litam & Speciale, 2020; New et al., 2021; Sprott et al., 2023). Therapists can create a safe environment by approaching kink with curiosity, openness, and a nonjudgmental attitude. The goal is not to promote or discourage kink (or suggest it is a trauma-processing tool), but to ensure that clients feel safe discussing it when relevant to their life and therapy. Table 3 synthesizes these frameworks and integrates additional insights to provide a comprehensive approach for therapists working with kink-involved clients.

Table 3. Clinical Considerations for Kink-Affirming Therapy

Principle	Clinical Consideration
Kink is Diverse & Not Inherently Pathological	Kink encompasses a wide range of consensual behaviors and identities. It should not be assumed to stem from trauma or mental illness. Clinicians should seek appropriate training rather than relying on clients for education.
Consent & Communication Are Central	Unlike abuse, BDSM relies on explicit, ongoing consent, negotiation, and boundary-setting. Therapists should understand how consent functions in kink relationships to avoid pathologizing safe practices.
Kink Can Be Healing or Harmful	While some survivors find empowerment in BDSM, others may engage in it in ways that reinforce trauma. Therapists should assess whether kink aligns with pleasure and agency or serves as a reenactment of distress.
Intersectionality Shapes Kink Expression	Kink intersects with factors like gender, sexuality, neurodivergence, and cultural background. Therapists should consider these influences when exploring clients' experiences.
Balancing Disclosure & Client Autonomy	Clients may not disclose their kink involvement due to stigma or fear of judgment. Therapists should foster an open, nonjudgmental environment while respecting client autonomy.
Ensuring Ethical & Competent Care	Clinicians should remain informed about current kink research, seek supervision when needed, and refer to kink-affirming professionals if appropriate. Recognizing personal biases and setting ethical boundaries is essential.

It's crucial for therapists to recognize their own comfort level with the topic of kink. If personal beliefs, religious values, or discomforts arise, it may be appropriate to refer clients to a different practitioner who can provide the best care. Table 4 provides self-reflection questions to help clinicians assess their readiness to engage with kink-related discussions in therapy.

Table 4. Therapist Self-Reflection Questions on Discussing Kink

Reflective Questioning:

As a therapist, you will need to conduct a self-assessment of your personal biases surrounding this topic. Consider engaging in reflective journaling on this subject to explore your thoughts, values, and any potential areas of discomfort:

1) Are you comfortable discussing sensitive topics related to kink in detail?
2) Can you maintain unconditional positive regard for clients who practice kink without judgement?
3) Are there specific aspects of kink that might trigger strong emotional reactions for you?
4) Are there any topics within kink where you feel it might be necessary to refer a client to another practitioner?
5) Are you able to work with clients in kink-related issues even if they challenge your personal beliefs?

If any of these questions have brought up emotional responses for you, it may be helpful to speak with a trusted colleague, supervisor, or your own therapist.

Starting Kink-Affirming Conversations in Therapy

Once therapists have reflected on their own comfort and biases, they can take proactive steps to create a safe and affirming space for clients to discuss their experiences with kink and sexuality in a way that maintains ethical boundaries. The following statements can help therapists invite open conversations while ensuring client autonomy and emotional safety.

General Openness

- "I'm comfortable talking about sex, including kink. If it's relevant to your life, you are welcome to discuss these topics if you want to."
- "Sexuality and relationships are a part of life."
- "For some people, past experiences can shape their sense of safety and pleasure during sex. If that's something you'd like to explore, we can."
- "Many people engage in different types of sex, and it's completely valid to explore what feels right for you. Shame dies when we shine a light or when we give it a voice."

Ensuring Safety & Consent

- "You can use whatever words feel comfortable for you when talking about sex, your body, or relationships. I will follow your lead on language."
- "If I ask a question that makes you uncomfortable you do not need to answer."
- "If any part of your sex life feels unsatisfactory, distressing or unsafe, we can explore that at your own pace."

Exploring Meaning & Experience

For clients who engage in kink and agree they would like to discuss in therapy, these prompts can help explore experiences with curiosity and care:

- "What is your experience with kink?"
- "Are there aspects of it that feel particularly good, empowering, or meaningful?"

- "Are there any parts of your sex life that you'd like to change?"
- "What role does kink play in your relationships, identity, or self-expression?"
- "Do you feel confident communicating with others during kink? Are you always able to communicate your limits with a play partner?"
- "Do you feel safe enough while engaging in kink? Have there been experiences that have felt unsafe?"

Using these types of statements and prompts, can foster an environment of trust, openness and respect, helping clients explore their sexual experiences in a safe and supportive manner.

Using Kink-Affirming Principles During EMDR Therapy

Many clients seek EMDR therapy to alleviate distressing symptoms such as flashbacks and hypervigilance, particularly in the aftermath of relational and sexual trauma. Furthermore, EMDR therapy also provides an opportunity to foster a new relationship with the body, reshape self-perception, and enhance confidence in intimacy and pleasure. A kink-affirming approach ensures that clients feel safe exploring the full spectrum of their sexual identities, rather than reinforcing shame or avoidance. The following section provides considerations for integrating kink-affirming principles across EMDR therapy.

Enhancing Bodily Awareness

During Phase 2 of EMDR therapy, resourcing that focuses on increasing bodily awareness can help clients recognize how trauma may affect their ability to engage in kink safely and enjoyably. Many survivors experience dissociation, numbness, or hypervigilance in response to physical touch, making it difficult to fully participate safely in kink interactions (Gewirtz-Meydan et al., 2024). Similarly, people with high pain tolerances may not always recognize when a sensation has exceeded physical limits. For example, someone with high pain tolerance may not feel the early signs of nerve compression during rope bondage or register when a scene becomes physically unsafe. By integrating mindful body awareness practices into EMDR therapy resourcing, therapists can support clients in developing a safer, more attuned relationship with their bodies during kink scenes.

These exercises should focus on general body awareness rather than explicitly sexual sensations. Therapists are not guiding clients to explore arousal responses in-session but rather helping them attune to physical and emotional cues in a non-sexual context. Clients may later choose to apply these skills in their sexual experiences if they find them beneficial, but this should be self-directed rather than therapist-led. This approach ensures that therapy remains ethically appropriate and prevents any risk of boundary violations or misinterpretations of the therapeutic relationship.

Key Therapeutic Approaches:

- Guide clients in mindfully exploring bodily sensations in a non-threatening way, helping them distinguish between safety, discomfort, and distress.
- Support clients in identifying trauma-related somatic tension, numbness, or dissociation and examining how this impacts their experiences of touch and sensation.
- Explore clients' psychological and emotional associations with pain, particularly for those engaged in impact play or other sensation-based kink practices.
- Strengthen interoceptive awareness to help clients recognize bodily cues for safety, pleasure, or distress during kink interactions.

Processing Past Trauma

EMDR therapy is effective in reducing trauma symptoms, anxiety, and depression in survivors of sexual violence (Schwarz et al., 2019, 2021). It also addresses the negative self-perceptions and shame that can result from past trauma. For kink-involved clients, processing past trauma is essential in distinguishing between consensual kink and trauma reenactment.

For example, a client with a history of sexual assault may struggle with dominance-submission play due to unresolved trauma and deep-seated feelings of shame about their desires. EMDR therapy can reprocess these memories, replacing harmful beliefs such as "I am broken" or "I am to blame" with healthier, more adaptive ones like "I deserve pleasure and safety." Similarly, clients who experience fear-based responses during role-play scenarios can use EMDR to desensitize triggers and regain agency over their experiences. Studies show that EMDR not only alleviates distress but also fosters greater self-acceptance, confidence, and emotional resilience (Schwarz et al., 2019).

Key Therapeutic Approaches:

- Process traumatic memories that interfere with safe and fulfilling kink experiences.
- Target distressing sensory stimuli (e.g., pressure, restriction) to reduce trauma-based reactions.
- Restructure shame-based cognitions such as "I am damaged" or "I am unworthy" to foster self-compassion.
- Use future templates to help clients visualize positive, consensual kink experiences free from fear or self-judgment.

Addressing Internalized Shame & Stigma

Many kink-involved individuals struggle with shame due to societal stigma or negative self-perceptions. EMDR therapy can help target distressing cognitions and support self-acceptance. A client who internalizes cultural messages that kink is "abnormal" may struggle with deep-seated shame that interferes with their relationships and self-image. Processing memories where they felt judged or rejected can help them develop a more affirming perspective on their identity.

Key Therapeutic Approaches:

- Target distressing cognitions such as "There is something wrong with me" or "My desires make me damaged" through EMDR Therapy.

- Normalize the role of exploration in kink by encouraging self-compassionate narratives about sexual identity and preferences.

Sex as Self-Injury (SASI) Considerations

Some clients may engage in kink in ways that are compulsive, reinforce negative self-beliefs, or serve as a form of self-harm (Fredlund et al., 2020). Therapists must be able to differentiate between consensual kink and Sex as Self-Injury (SASI) behaviors. For example, a client who seeks degrading encounters due to a belief that they "deserve" mistreatment may need support in challenging and reframing these core beliefs. EMDR therapy can address these harmful cognitions and help the client explore healthier, alternative ways to meet their emotional needs.

Key Therapeutic Approaches:

- Assess the emotional aftermath of kink experiences. Does the client feel affirmed, connected, and in control, or do they experience shame, emotional numbness, or regret afterward?
- Identify SASI-driven cognitions such as "I deserve pain" or "I am worthless" or "I am a slut" or "I don't matter" and target them in EMDR therapy.
- Use EMDR therapy to strengthen adaptive beliefs such as "I have the right to experience pleasure" or "I am important."
- Support clients in building alternative coping strategies that meet the same emotional needs as SASI (e.g., emotional regulation through safe intensity, self-expression without harm).

Strengthening Boundaries and Consent

For many trauma survivors, asserting boundaries, especially in sexual or power-exchange contexts, can feel unfamiliar or even unsafe. Some may struggle to use a safe word for fear of disappointing their partner, while others may tolerate discomfort due to past conditioning that taught them their boundaries would not be respected.

EMDR therapy can be used to install adaptive beliefs that increase confidence in asserting boundaries. A present or future template exercise might involve guiding the client through a visualization where they negotiate a kink scene with confidence, use their safe word when needed, and experience the affirmation and respect of their partner in response. Table 5 provides an example for how this could be approached in therapy. This allows the nervous system to internalize the expectation that boundary-setting will be honored, reinforcing self-trust and agency.

Guided Case Example for Boundary Rehearsal in Kink Context

Therapist (Introducing the Exercise): Before we begin, I just want to make it clear: you do not need to share any sexual details, unless you choose to. This is about building confidence in communicating your needs, negotiating consent, and practicing saying what works for you and what doesn't. I'll never prompt for anything explicit.

Client: Okay, that feels okay. I'm ready.

Therapist: Great. Let's imagine a situation where you're preparing to engage in a kink scene with someone. You can picture a real person or an imagined one. I'll ask a few questions to guide you through this. You can answer aloud or just reflect internally, whichever feels best. Take a moment to notice that.

How does it feel in your body as you prepare to talk with them about the scene?

Client: I feel a bit tense. Shoulders are tight. But also kind of steady.

Therapist: Okay let's stay with that steadiness and the tension. You're allowed to feel both. Now imagine you're starting the conversation. You're telling them what you're open to. What are some words or phrases you might use to talk about your needs or limits?

Client: Um... I might say something like, "I'm okay with restraints, but no name-calling."

Therapist: That's really clear. Imagine saying that now, and notice how they respond. What do they say or do?

Client: They nod. Repeat it back. Like, *"Got it - restraint okay, no name-calling."* I feel relief.

Therapist: Let it settle into your body. Now let's practice establishing a way to tell them you want to stop the scene. How would you let your partner know?

Client: Maybe the word *'yellow'* if I need to slow things down. I'd just say, *"If I say yellow, I need a pause"*. But as I'm saying that now, I honestly don't know if I would ever use it.

Therapist: That's a really important reflection. It makes sense, especially if you've had experiences where speaking up didn't make a difference. Can we slow it down here and just stay with that for a moment? When you imagine needing to ask them to pause, what do you notice in your body or mind that holds you back?

Client: I think I'd worry about ruining the moment... or disappointing them. Like they'd think I was overreacting.

Therapist: You'd be overreacting? Hmm... Where does that feeling sit in your body?

Client: In my chest. It's kind of tight. Like I'm bracing.

Therapist: Just stay with that sensation for a moment. You don't need to change it or fix it, just notice it.

(Pause)

If that part of your body could speak, what might it be trying to tell you?

Client: Maybe… *"Be careful."* Or, *"Don't mess it up. Like, don't be too much."*

Therapist: It sounds like a part of you learned that speaking up might have consequences?

Client: Yeah. That has happened. I can see how hard that part is trying to stop it happening again. But I know this new person and they're not the same as my ex. We've been talking and they really do seem like they're listening and being respectful. I've done my homework, I've set things up well, and my friends vouched for them…

(Pauses)

But I still feel stupid for not just getting over it. I don't want to project my old stuff onto them and ruin something that could be good.

Therapist: You're recognizing how hard that protective part has worked to keep you safe, and you're also noticing that things are different now. Would it feel okay to check in with that part for a moment? Just a reminder before we do, this isn't about *getting rid* of that part or ignoring its concerns. That part exists for a reason, and if anything ever felt wrong, it would be the one to alert you. But is there anything you think it might need to know or hear right now?

Client: I think I'd say… thank you. I know you've been working overtime to protect me. And I know you're scared we'll get hurt again. But I've done so much to make sure things are different this time. I'll keep listening to you. But I also want to try letting someone in.

Therapist: That was really powerful. How does it feel to say that?

Client: Honestly? Like... something loosened. I don't feel like I'm fighting with myself as much.

Therapist: Let's stay with that for a moment, the sense of more space inside, less internal struggle. With that in mind, would you be willing to revisit the image of setting some boundaries with this new person? Just gently bring that moment to mind again. What do you feel in your body as you imagine yourself saying the word?

Client: It's not as scary. There's still a bit of tension, but I don't feel frozen. I can see myself saying it now. And it feels good. There's relief now.

Key Therapeutic Approaches:

- Strengthen cognitions related to the right to set limits and stop activities when needed without guilt or fear.
- Consider future templates to help clients visualize themselves confidently expressing boundaries or using a safe word.
- Install adaptive cognitions such as "I can trust myself to know what I need."
- Encourage clients to rehearse safe negotiation of kink dynamics through guided imagery exercises.

Reclaiming Positive Sexual Experiences

For some people, sex and intimacy have historically felt like something that happens to them rather than something they actively create. This can be particularly relevant in kink, where the interplay of power dynamics requires a high level of self-awareness, communication, and agency. A client who has always deferred to partners in sexual decision-making may work through an EMDR future template where they confidently communicate their needs, initiate a scene that excites them, and experience pleasure on their own terms. The goal is to shift from a mindset of "I go along with what others want" to "I have the right to pursue what brings me joy."

Key Therapeutic Approaches:

- Support clients in shifting from a passive role in intimacy to an active participant in their desires and experiences.
- Reinforce the belief that they have the agency to initiate, shape, and modify their kink interactions in ways that align with their well-being.
- Use EMDR future templates to help clients visualize themselves choosing partners and scenes that feel affirming and safe, rather than engaging in dynamics that reinforce old trauma scripts.
- Encourage self-exploration and confidence in intimacy through visualizing positive, affirming kink experiences.

By following this structured approach, therapists can support kink-involved clients in reclaiming their sexual narratives in a way that prioritizes safety, empowerment, and healing.

Conclusion

Integrating discussions of kink into EMDR therapy is not about encouraging or discouraging specific sexual practices, but about creating a therapeutic space where clients can explore their experiences without fear of judgment or pathologization. I recognize that these conversations can challenge therapists' own comfort levels. However, reflecting on our own biases and beliefs is essential to ensure we can approach these conversations with openness while maintaining clear professional boundaries. By continuing to educate themselves and adopt kink-affirming principles, clinicians can contribute to a more inclusive, sex-positive therapeutic culture—one that supports healing, self-acceptance, and meaningful connection.

Anna Clarke (they/them) is a psychologist, educator, and advocate passionate about reshaping mental health systems to be inclusive, neurodiversity-affirming, and informed by lived experience. Anna is openly Autistic and ADHD, and brings both clinical and lived experience to their work. Anna is the co-founder of Divergent Futures, an education and training company dedicated to dismantling ableist approaches to therapy with Autistic and ADHD clients. They have extensive experience supporting survivors of sexual assault, domestic violence, and complex trauma, including plural systems of dissociative identities. Anna co-authored the first peer-reviewed publication on neurodiversity-affirming approaches to EMDR therapy for Autistic and ADHD clients in The Oxford Handbook of EMDR, and has written several other publications exploring trauma, neurodivergence, and inclusive practice. Outside of work, Anna enjoys mixed martial arts training, drawing, Dungeons & Dragons, and exploring whatever new interest captures their attention next!

References

American Psychiatric Association. (2022). *Diagnostic and statistical manual of mental disorders* (5th ed., text rev.). American Psychiatric Publishing.

Brown, A., Barker, E. D., & Rahman, Q. (2020). A systematic scoping review of the prevalence, etiological, psychological, and interpersonal factors associated with BDSM. *The Journal of Sex Research, 57*(6), 781–811. https://doi.org/10.1080/00224499.2019.1665619

Cascalheira, C. J., Ijebor, E. E., Salkowitz, Y., Hitter, T. L., & Boyce, A. (2023). Curative kink: Survivors of early abuse transform trauma through BDSM. *Sexual and Relationship Therapy, 38*(3), 353–383. https://doi.org/10.1080/14681994.2021.1937599

Carty, A., & Davidson, A. (2024). Directness of communication mediates sexual satisfaction: What we can learn from a positive view of BDSM practice. *Journal of Positive Sexuality, 10*, 8–16. https://doi.org/10.51681/1.1012

Cesur, E., & Sancak, B. (2024). Evaluation of sexual behavior and sexual functions of BDSM practitioners: A controlled study. *Archives of Neuropsychiatry, 61*, 148–153. https://doi.org/10.29399/npa.28527

Dunkley, C. R., Barringer, A., Dang, S., & Brotto, L. A. (2020). Dispositional mindfulness among BDSM practitioners: A preliminary investigation. *The Canadian Journal of Human Sexuality, 29*(3), 314–322. https://doi.org/10.3138/cjhs.2020-0013

Fredlund, C., Svedin, C. G., Priebe, G., Jonsson, L., & Wadsby, M. (2017). Self-reported frequency of sex as self-injury (SASI) in a national study of Swedish adolescents and association to sociodemographic factors, sexual behaviors, abuse, and mental health. *Child and Adolescent Psychiatry and Mental Health, 11*(1), 9. https://doi.org/10.1186/s13034-017-0146-7

Fredlund, C., Wadsby, M., & Jonsson, L. S. (2020). Motives and manifestations of sex as self-injury. *The Journal of Sex Research, 57*(7), 897–905. https://doi.org/10.1080/00224499.2019.1689377

Gewirtz-Meydan, A., Godbout, N., Canivet, C., Peleg-Sagy, T., & Lafortune, D. (2024). The complex interplay between BDSM and childhood sexual abuse: A form of repetition and dissociation or a path toward processing and healing? *Journal of Sex & Marital Therapy, 50*(5), 583–594. https://doi.org/10.1080/0092623x.2024.2332775

Herbenick, D., Fu, T. C., Wright, P., Paul, B., Gradus, R., Bauer, J., & Jones, R. (2020). Diverse sexual behaviors and pornography use: Findings from a nationally representative probability survey of Americans aged 18 to 60 years. *The Journal of Sexual Medicine, 17*(4), 623–633. https://doi.org/10.1016/j.jsxm.2020.01.013

Lantto, R., & Lundberg, T. (2022). (Un)desirable approaches in therapy with Swedish individuals practicing BDSM: Clients' perspectives and recommendations for affirmative clinical practices. *Psychology & Sexuality, 12*(3), 742–755. https://doi.org/10.1080/19419899.2021.1918230

Litam, S. D. A., & Speciale, M. (2020). Kink culture: What professional counselors need to know. *ACA Practice Briefs*. American Counseling Association. https://www.counseling.org/docs/default-source/practice-briefs/acapb-kink-culture-2020.pdf

Martinez, K. (2021). Overwhelming whiteness of BDSM: A critical discourse analysis of racialization in BDSM. *Sexualities, 24*(5–6), 733–748. https://doi.org/10.1177/1363460720932389

Melavc, M., Jug, V., & Gomboc, S. (2024). Positive psychological effects of BDSM practices and their implications for psychological and psychotherapeutic work: A systematic literature review. *Društvena istraživanja: Časopis za opća društvena pitanja, 33*(3), 411–432. https://doi.org/10.5559/di.33.3.04

New, C. M., Batchelor, L. C., Schimmel-Bristow, A., Schaeffer-Smith, M., Magsam, E., Bridges, S. K., Brown, E. L., & McKenzie, T. (2021). In their own words: Getting it right for kink clients. *Sexual and Relationship Therapy*. https://doi.org/10.1080/14681994.2021.1965112

Pearson, A., & Hodgetts, S. (2023). "Comforting, reassuring, and...hot": A qualitative exploration of engaging in bondage, discipline, domination, submission, sadism, and (sado)masochism and kink from the perspective of autistic adults. *Autism in Adulthood.* https://sure.sunderland.ac.uk/id/eprint/15924/

Pliskin, A. E. (2022). Autism, sexuality, and BDSM. *Ought: The Journal of Autistic Culture, 4*(1), Article 9. https://doi.org/10.9707/2833-1508.1107

Rosqvist, H. B., & Jackson-Perry, D. (2021). Not doing it properly? (Re)producing and resisting knowledge through narratives of autistic sexualities. *Sexuality and Disability, 39*, 327–344. https://doi.org/10.1007/s11195-020-09624-5

Schuerwegen, A., De Zeeuw, I., Huys, W., Henckens, J., Goethals, K., & Morrens, M. (2020). A survey study investigating stigma towards BDSM in the general population and self-stigmatization among BDSM practitioners. *JSM Sexual Medicine, 4*(7), Article 1055. https://doi.org/10.47739/2578-3718/1055

Schwarz, J. E., Baber, D., Barter, A., & Dorfman, K. (2019). A mixed methods evaluation of EMDR for treating female survivors of sexual and domestic violence. *Counseling Outcome Research and Evaluation, 11*(1), 1–15. https://doi.org/10.1080/21501378.2018.1561146

Schwarz, J. E., Baber, D., Giantisco, E., & Isaacson, B. (2021). EMDR for survivors of sexual and intimate partner violence at a nonprofit counseling agency. *Journal of EMDR Practice and Research, 15*(4), 202–217. https://doi.org/10.1891/EMDR-D-21-00014

Sprott, R. A., & Benoit Hadcock, B. (2018). Bisexuality, pansexuality, queer identity, and kink identity. *Sexual and Relationship Therapy, 33*(1–2), 214–232. https://doi.org/10.1080/14681994.2017.1347616

Sprott, R. A., Herbitter, C., Grant, P., Moser, C., & Kleinplatz, P. J. (2023). Clinical guidelines for working with clients involved in kink. *Journal of Sex & Marital Therapy, 49*(8), 978–995. https://doi.org/10.1080/0092623x.2023.2232801

Strizzi, J. M., Øverup, C. S., Ciprić, A., Hald, G. M., & Træen, B. (2022). BDSM: Does it hurt or help sexual satisfaction, relationship satisfaction, and relationship closeness? *The Journal of Sex Research, 59*(2), 248–257. https://doi.org/10.1080/00224499.2021.1950116

Tarleton, H. L., Mackenzie, T., & Sagarin, B. J. (2025). Consent norms in the BDSM community: Strong but not inflexible. *Archives of Sexual Behavior, 54*, 549–559. https://doi.org/10.1007/s10508-024-03038-6

Turley, E. (2024). 'I feel so much better in myself': Exploring meaningful non-erotic outcomes of BDSM participation. *Sexualities, 27*(1–2), 154–170. https://doi.org/10.1177/13634607211056879

Walling-Wefelmeyer, R., & O'Neill, T. (2021). 'There are a lot of bad dominants, mostly men, where it's basically abuse dressed up as a kink': Victim-survivors' everyday navigation of BDSM, kink, and fetish. *Loughborough University*. https://hdl.handle.net/2134/21333831.v1

Westlake, B. G. (2024). BDSM safety in pornography: Its perceived accuracy and impact on practitioners' safe word practices. *Archives of Sexual Behavior, 53*, 3475–3484. https://doi.org/10.1007/s10508-024-02967-6

Westlake, B., & Mahan, I. (2025). An international survey of BDSM practitioner demographics: The evolution of purpose for, participation in, and engagement with, kink activities. *The Journal of Sex Research, 62*(3), 341–359. https://doi.org/10.1080/00224499.2023.2273266

Williams, D. J., Coto, L., & Berkowitz, D. (2023). "It's absolutely intense, and I love it!" A qualitative investigation of "pegging" as leisure. *Leisure Sciences, 45*(5), 666–689. https://doi.org/10.1080/01490400.2023.2226669

Navigating Grief Through EMDR Therapy

Lisa Hayes, LISW-S

Queerness is not simply a term used to define sexual orientation, it is a way of navigating the world, relationships, systems and healing. When I think about queerness or what it means to use a queer lens to navigate the world I am generally drawn to the understanding that queerness is an invitation to liberation. Queerness allows and often insists that I find alternative paths; that I find new places to belong and feel connected. In this way, queerness has allowed me to imagine the world as a plastic and responsive place that can expand to make space for my joy. Queerness is not inventing a new truth, it is acknowledging the truth that has been hidden by systems of oppression that fear our freedom.

Queerness not only provides pathways to liberation, queerness can be considered its own source of liberation. Liberation from normative systems of thinking, living and connecting; a tool that creates space for deconstructing social, cultural and political norms. This lens of deconstruction is the shared goal of both queerness and EMDR Therapy: a desire to explore experiences with the hope of revealing subconscious meaning and truth. It was within this foundational parallel, this protective shroud of queer liberation, that EMDR Therapy was able to support me on my healing journey following the death of my mother. Unlike cognitive interventions that sought to directly confront my perceptions of my mother as irrational distortions, EMDR Therapy allowed me to be curious and explore my experiences. I sincerely believe that EMDR Therapy, like all therapies, is as dynamic as you make it.

My EMDR Therapy was bound to hold aspects of queer identity but the processing work I was doing did not simply carry the essence of my identity but centered it as a lens through which I experience my life and the world around me. Queerness gave me a path of departure from normative family structures and allowed me, for the first time in my life, to imagine my mother and I as having equal access to power. Rescuing power from a narrative of violence and subjugation and reshaping it as a tool for healing and empowerment. Through the queer lens I was able to view my mother as a peer; a fellow traveler. Within this flattening of hierarchies I was more able to question and confront my mother's choices and behaviors. I was encouraged to be upfront about the impact of her parenting. It was not a process focused on disrespecting or disregarding my mother as a parent and elder; it was a process that allowed me to imagine that my emotions and perspectives were equally valid.

Applying a queer lens to my EMDR Therapy allowed me to reimagine what it means for my family to directly and collectively address pain. This collective perspective removed the burden of attempting to access healing in isolation. Queerness taught me that it is important to give space and voice to your pain. Queerness reminded me that silence is not sustainable safety. Using this queer lens to inform my EMDR Therapy allowed me to acknowledge that naming a problem is not equivalent to creating a problem; it invited me to be honest about my feelings and experiences without the fear that I would be responsible for upsetting the balance of my family. My intent was never to disrespect the memory of my mother but to extend curiosity and repair the experiences that both shaped and silenced me my entire life.

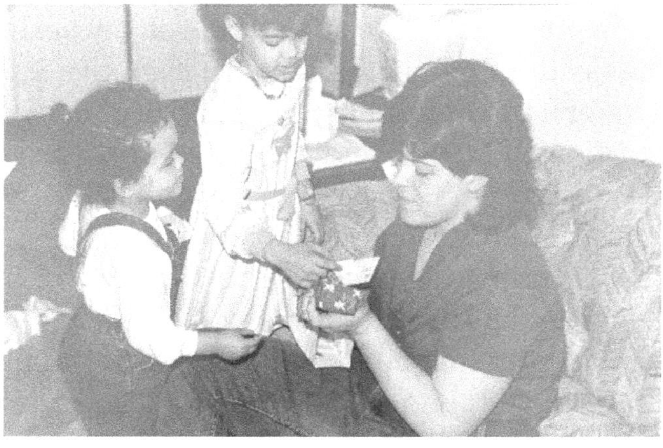

From the author's collection. From left to right:
Lisa Hayes, Tiffany Hayes, Joan Hayes.

My Mother

As is often the case following a loss of any kind, my mother's death created an urge to reflect and try to make sense of my loss and grief. In the weeks following her death, my sisters and I shouldered the task of clearing out my mother's home. We scrambled to collect the pictures, childhood homework assignments and holiday ornaments that were now without an owner. We were desperate to preserve the memories of our childhood; to insist that we have existed in the world. Throughout this process, my siblings and I were invited to reflect on the interactions that we had with our mother. It is often said, and always true, that each child experiences their own version of their shared parent. My own little family was no different.

Each of us were able to highlight different experiences of pain and connection with our mother. Growing up I remember feeling distinctly different from my mother and siblings. I remember always feeling small and quiet compared to their unapologetically fierce and dominant energies. I often found myself a spectator of my family. My internal process felt too slow to keep up with their direct and dynamic energy. I was in awe of their ability to give voice to their joys, pain, desires and objectives; my own thoughts, dreams and needs staying hidden. These organic differences in personality allied with my desire to escape the harsh realities of our life often drove me to the silent creation of a rich internal world. A world of dissociated isolation that I longed to get lost in. While this survival technique did in fact keep me alive, it also kept me alone. Alone in my thoughts, alone in my fears and, as a result, alone in my identities.

When I reflect on my relationship with my mother I am faced with the reality that she never really knew anything about me. She knew that I was different from my siblings and in lieu of exploring these differences to better understand me she chose to label them instead. She often categorized these differences as "weird" or "eccentric". She neither asked nor understood anything about my dreams, desires, fears, goals or worldview. My mother created a version of me that served her own demanding standards and never gave me any opportunity to exist outside of those restrictions. The urgency of poverty and unhealed trauma did not allow for slow and gentle moments of connection and understanding. Even after surrendering to this reality, I still found myself wishing that I would be able to stand in front of her memory and proudly declare that I have made a life for myself that is full of joy, adventure and love. In order to make this declaration I knew that I would have to do the often arduous work of healing the many wounds inflicted by my mother over the course of my life. I wanted to allow EMDR Therapy to support this healing. I wanted to let my mother know about the love that I have found within my queer community. I wanted her to know that what she had labelled as weird and eccentric were actually the best and most cherished parts of my personality. I wanted her to know that even without her participation or permission I had shaped a life worth living.

To fully share the story of processing my complex grief using EMDR Therapy, I first need to share a bit about the mother that I both loved and feared my entire life. In the early morning hours of September 25, 2012 in a hospital bed, only a few feet away from my sleeping sister, my mother closed her eyes for the last time. That night was one of the first times in weeks that I asked my little sister to watch over our mother alone so that I could run home, take a shower and experience the long forgotten comforts of a real bed. My mother died after a long and grueling dance with brain cancer, six months after her fiftieth birthday. The year before her death was filled with countless doctor's appointments, close calls, pitying looks from well-intentioned strangers and my own exhausted eyes staring back at me through hundreds of hospital bathroom mirrors. When my mother died, what I remember more than anything was how exhausted I was. For that entire year I spent the hours before work and almost every waking hour after work caring for her body and what was left of her mind. I collapsed my own life to protect what was left of my mother's; advocating with insurance companies, banks, hospitals and care facilities to insist that they allow my mother to die with dignity. I was so committed to protecting her that I became a ghost in my own life. I lost almost every friendship

I had spent years building, I declined every social invitation, I released every hobby and forgot what it felt like to sleep through the night. I donated that year of my life to my mother.

Even now I have difficulty determining whether my actions were motivated by altruistic love or by the cruel reality that there was no one else coming to help. Growing up, my mother never shielded my sisters and I from this reality. We had to take care of each other because we were alone in the world and no one was coming to save us. We were never encouraged to believe that things would improve, we were taught to adjust to our reality and survive. I did not grow up in a home that was driven by curiosity and understanding. My home was fueled by survival and necessity. A home where your preferences were a luxury rarely capable of altering your reality. Your unique personality and personal preferences were overshadowed by the unrelenting reality that your existence was dependent upon your ability to survive. I was taught very early in my life that in order for your survival to be valuable it must be collective. I was never supposed to eat if my siblings were still hungry, I was never allowed to want anything that everyone could not have, I should never accept any kindness that was not extended to my entire family, and I should never want anything that did not prioritize the needs of my entire family.

I was taught that to want anything special for myself or to define my joy outside of our collective survival was selfish and unacceptable. I was taught to be invisible; to silence my own needs and identities if I wanted to survive. This encouragement towards invisibility supported a life complicated by isolation, unmet emotional needs and dissociation. I was never supposed to voice or acknowledge pain, fear, or exhaustion. Growing up my rest was treated as violence against my family because my rest supplied someone else's fatigue. Any moment of joy violated our collective agreement to be in pain. Our shared pain was our highest level of emotional intimacy.

Being able to pull my mother's rage and violence away from my siblings and towards my own body was a skill that I grew over the years with a great sense of pride and satisfaction. My own pain was lessened by the reality that I had fulfilled my familial duty of protecting my siblings. Collective survival was one of our only reliable family traditions. It was during these moments of shared pain that we understood each other the most. I was taught early and often that any moment of my own joy was a departure from my family, a violation of our shared agreement. It often felt like my mother believed that living joyfully was a selfish luxury. A luxury that neither she nor the vast majority of my ancestors were ever afforded. Growing up, I never remember anyone doing anything simply for the pleasure of it. When confronted with this harsh reality my mother would always choose to spiritualize her pain. She insisted that suffering brought you closer to God. Much like kisses, hugs and words of affirmation, joy was not a reasonable desire for any member of our family. The never spoken, always understood, reality was that in my family you would have to make do with the fact that not allowing you to die alone, unhoused and hungry was the ultimate expression and guarantee of love. That was our family legacy. The absence of indifference to your death was as close as we could come to any evidence of love. When I reflect on it now I am certain that it would have come as a great surprise to my mother that this kind of love almost killed me. These lessons on survival forced me into the same joyless oblivion that surrounded my mother until the day she died.

On the rare occasions that my mother would speak to us about her own childhood she would describe layers of dysfunction that never allowed her to feel truly wanted by anyone; a childhood filled with constant criticism, addiction, codependent silence, avoidance and violence. Throughout my own childhood my mother would describe her desperate desire to avoid creating a similar reality for her own children. The glaring irony is that in an attempt to avoid the things she feared she became imprisoned by them. My mother's fear shaped our relationship and created a culture where successes were never acknowledged and mistakes were magnified. My mother's fear insisted that my mistakes be paraded in front of me like a thousand little deaths. She needed to be sure that I understood that I was never more than one mistake away from ruining my entire life. It took me a long time to understand that what I mistakenly assumed as fierceness from my mother was almost always fear. My mother knew that if we fell, there would be no one to catch us.

My mother spent her entire life only seeing her own fear, and that fear became an extension of our family. I was taught that fear prepared you for the harsh realities of life; that optimism was unrealistic and dangerous. Most importantly, I was taught that the safest way to survive was to make yourself small and invisible. I remember being confronted by my mother when I was thirteen years old and she found one of my journals. With complete indifference to my privacy she read the numerous entries expressing my sadness and suicidal ideation aloud to an audience of my siblings before demanding that I provide an explanation. Terrified that my honest explanation might cause my mother to feel attacked and defensive, I could only find the small words, "I am not happy", to represent my persistent suicidality. I will never forget the way that she stared at me in complete disbelief, laughed, and smiled one of her rare smiles before replying, "That is ridiculous, ninety-nine percent of your life will not be happy. You still have to keep living!"

My mother always found my desire to be happy laughably ridiculous. I was taught in this moment and many other similar moments to treat any desire to live a joyful life as a ridiculous and unrealistic goal. The culmination of these lessons left me weighed down, dysregulated and afraid that my mother would never have the time to be curious about the life that I imagined for myself. As strange as it may sound, my mother's death opened a new possibility for connection. In her death, I could imagine her as no longer being chased by her own fears and the crushing weight of poverty. If I could imagine that she was finally in a place of rest and spaciousness I could also imagine her as being more capable of extending that spaciousness to my identities and the work of healing our relationship. These childhood lessons all provided potential negative cognitions. This awareness allowed and even insisted that I reorganize my memories away from the dominant narrative of my childhood. My needs did not have to stay anchored to the belief that I am a burden or that my hopes and dreams are insignificant.

I could instead conceptualize my needs as simply human and that as a result I might not be a burden but a person that is deserving of love and compassion.

From the author's collection:
Joan Hayes, Tiffany Hayes (back row); Lisa Hayes (in the baby seat)

The EMDR Process

When I began using EMDR Therapy to process the death of my mother, I understood that the need to "come out" to my mother was also a part of my healing. This "coming out" to my mother was not merely to provide a declaration of my sexual orientation. It was an opportunity to insist that she see all of my complexity in the hopes that a new understanding would allow me to pass through the weight of our differences; a weight that had felt like a heavy and impenetrable door between us her entire life. I was not seeking acceptance or permission from my mother, I was only hoping for an opportunity to share with her the life that I had made for myself.

I understand and have often also asserted that queerness does not require comprehension and that attempting to convince our parents, families and communities to love all of us is an act of self-sabotaging futility. However, the older I get and the closer I come to a place of healing, I find that I am unapologetic and fiercely protective of the child in me that wants to experience a healing connection with her parent. The biologically imperative desire to be safely held by our families is simultaneously the simplest and the most complicated desire. My EMDR Therapy experience was about insisting, and perhaps even reclaiming my right to believe that my mother is capable of loving me completely.

I arrived at my first EMDR Therapy session a few months after my mother's death hoping to find a safe place to explore my relationship with my mother. Only in the safety of the therapeutic environment was I able to invite the best parts of my mother's memory to heal and connect. My grief, like all grief, held as much complexity as my relationship with my mother. I was grieving for the moments of repair and understanding that I thought would never happen. I was grieving for my sisters. I was grieving for my mother who had lived a hard and unrelenting life filled with abuse, neglect, abandonment, cruelty and struggle. I was grieving for the child in me that had buried both of my parents before the age of 30. I was grieving for my future nieces or nephews that would never know the dry wit and humor of their grandmother. I was grieving for a world that had to keep spinning with one less person who was trying their best. I was grieving that I had never been able to stand in front of my mother in all of my identities. I was grieving for the child in me that had never felt fully loved or wanted. It was within this complexity, this difficulty in narrowing down the source and solution of my pain, that I began my EMDR Therapy journey through complex grief.

In my own research as an EMDR therapist I knew that there were many different therapeutic perspectives when addressing grief. After discussing it with my EMDR therapist I knew that there were many possible channels that we could choose to access my grief; a focus on the traumatic medical realities of navigating a terminal illness, the impact of the early deaths of both of my parents, the absence of support from our family of origin and subsequent feelings of abandonment, a focus on the abuse and neglect I experienced throughout my childhood or even a focus on the impact that navigating complex grief was having on my own health and identity. These all served as valid and reasonable points of entry. After some discussion and collaboration with my EMDR Therapist, we were drawn to the Continuing Bonds model which suggested that instead of using therapeutic intervention to detach from our deceased, that we could instead use EMDR Therapy to repair past grievances with the ultimate goal of creating new pathways for connection, healing and ongoing kinship with our deceased loved ones (Klass et al., 2014). After my mother's death I had to face the reality that what I wanted more than anything was to feel safely seen and held by my mother. I, of course, needed to process through the aspects of our relationship that demanded my mother's accountability and I also wanted that accountability to yield a softer and more connected relationship to her memory. I wanted to live a life where I could access the positive moments of my mother when she was truly trying her best. I wanted to be able to smile a genuine smile when I looked in the mirror and saw a bit of my mother's own face looking back at me. I began my EMDR Therapy journey hopeful that I could find this path of healing.

In order to embrace this healing journey, I first needed to acknowledge and explore the presence of limiting beliefs that were likely to disrupt my EMDR Therapy: the veil of fatalistic determinism that had been cut from my mother's own robes and placed over my eyes to shield me from the dangers of hope and desire. Before processing through my grief I had to acknowledge the reality that I had grown up in a family that continuously reinforced the limiting belief that your pain was the evidence of your effort and loyalty.

If I wasn't miserable, then I wasn't trying. If I wasn't miserable, then I didn't really love anyone. My family had been subjected to so much violence, poverty, and ignorance that survival had become our most shared experience, the thing that allowed us to feel connected as a community. Pain, or maybe I should say a general dissatisfaction with life, became my family emblem. The process of healing was complicated by the weight of believing that I might, in order to turn towards my own joy and healing, have to turn my back on my family.

I was raised to hold onto grief. To wear my grief like shackles to prove that I was connected to the pain of my family. Centering this pain to justify the survival of my ancestors through their own lives of pain. These lessons on grief bolstered the limiting belief that being joyful was considered an affront to my family; it separated me from the larger narrative. Joy was turning my back on the pain that connected my family and would leave me alone in a dangerous world. To turn my back on this blocking belief would suggest that I was turning my back on my family. A group of people bonded by trauma without ever speaking about or processing through that trauma. In order to grieve, to truly grieve, I would have to sit with the reality of so many things that had previously been sheltered by collective silence.

It was through the work of EMDR Therapy that I was able to understand that I had carried around the weight of that belief for as long as I could. I realized that carrying around this weight would kill any possibility for my joy, hopes and dreams as surely as it killed my mother's. In working to confront these limiting beliefs I realized that what provided me with a path of liberation from this fallacy was queerness; my own queerness and the persistent insistence of my queer community and queer ancestors who refused to conflate smallness and invisibility with safety. Queerness reminded me that true connection comes from authenticity and that my authentic joy could serve as a path of liberation for not only myself but also as a new model for my family. Using this queer lens to support my EMDR Therapy I was able to confront my limiting beliefs and choose to explore opportunities that might liberate me from this constant fear and allow me to be curious about the life that I could lead if I center love, kindness, community and unapologetic existence. EMDR Therapy allowed me to confront the reality that grief, fear and avoidance never once kept me safe or made me feel loved. They barely allowed me to escape alive.

Having addressed my limiting belief I now turned to the difficulty of seeking posthumous repair and healing of the relationship with my mother. In order to do this I had to be willing to hold the best aspects of my mother close to me and to imagine a version of my mother that never existed, but I believe could have existed if she were healthy, loved and supported. Throughout my mother's life it had been extremely painful to witness her persistent self-loathing. The absence of self-acceptance and the constant familial reinforcement of her low value made it unlikely, if not impossible, that she could ever fully love and embrace anything that she perceived as flawed, different, messy, or complicated. Queerness encouraged me to understand that complexity and differences were not flaws, rather a reflection of what is naturally true in the absence of fear and control. Every person is their own unique constellation of wants, desires, and needs. These wants, desires and needs are only misperceived as flaws within fragile systems of power and violence that need to homogenize and reduce everything in order to control it. EMDR Therapy created an opportunity for me to use this paradigm shift as a safer foundation to support the work of repairing my relationship with my mother.

After successfully processing my complex grief using EMDR Therapy I have found that I can still hold my mother accountable when it needs to happen. I can also sit with her vulnerability without needing to make sense of it. As I quickly approach the age she was when she died I understand what a tremendously short and demanding life she lived. When I think of my mother now, I like to imagine that she is no longer afraid of her own imperfections or her own complications.

My own experiences of abuse, neglect and the subsequent reality of insecure attachment left me without the emotional flexibility to assume that my mother held unconditional positive regard for me. Growing up I was taught that the surest way not to feel pain or disappointment was to not expect anything from anyone. To assume that everything and everyone was likely to disappoint you. This reality necessitated attachment based considerations for my EMDR Therapy processing. Using the Continuing Bonds model's quest to repair attachment meant that I would first need to explore the existing attachment strengths and injuries between my mother and I.

My EMDR Therapy journey did not begin at the end of my mother's life but at the beginning of my own. In honor of this reality, my initial grief reprocessing targets centered on pre-birth and pre-verbal traumas. This reprocessing work sought to explore the ways in which my mother's dissatisfaction with her own life was subconsciously absorbed and interpreted as dissatisfaction with mine. Using pre-birth narrative as the foundation for my relationship with my mother allowed me to unpack the ways in which my mother began to conceptualize and shape me before I had ever even had the opportunity to exist. Throughout the course of my childhood, my mother would often describe the fear and uncertainty she experienced during her pregnancy. She would use these stories as a means to compare and contrast the personalities of my sisters and I, describing her fears as the result of our innate traits and behaviors. When conveying my pre-birth narrative she would often describe a feeling of distance and disconnection that was unlike any of her other pregnancies. Her most common narrative to describe my general lack of engagement was, "You were so quiet and inactive that I was always afraid that you were sick or dead." She explained that after months of worry she began to feel so concerned that she would plead with me to be more active and that eventually I relented and would stretch or kick as evidence that I was, in fact, very much alive.

These stories always made me feel responsible for our distance and silence; an unspoken suggestion that if only I were more engaging and capable of understanding her needs that we would be more connected. What my mother rarely shared, but I was able to explore in EMDR Therapy, was how depressed and alone she was during her pregnancy with me. She was living alone in military housing, my father having surrendered all pretenses of being an active parent. Through reprocessing I was able to lay down the burden of this narrative and become more open to repairing our attachment which would ultimately allow me to make space for my grief. Centering my initial processing around my attachment with my mother allowed me to address the negative cognitions that were the result of attachment injuries and ultimately allowed me to sit in shared compassion for my mother and for myself. If I could imagine my mother as being freed from the realities that produced her most abusive and unhealthy behaviors then I could also imagine her capable of helping me to heal the attachment wounds she created; providing new space for grief and safer attachment that was not possible during her life. I was able to realize that her fears were not a result of my inactivity but her own isolation and uncertainty about her ability to keep herself alive, let alone her children.

What I realized through the use of EMDR Therapy is that I could reverse the parentification that was so essential to my survival by giving myself permission to be sad, scared and uncertain. I could provide validation for my emotions, I could sit in exposed vulnerability without fear, and I could present myself for maybe the first time as truly a child of my parents. This was a moment of repair in my EMDR Therapy processing where I could make demands for my younger self, I could demand that the best parts of my mother try again. I was unwilling to supplement another moment of comfort, care, or understanding on her behalf. After her death I could do what I was never able to do in her life: I could insist that she show up and truly see me. In this way, queer liberation has allowed me to reconceptualize the meaning of family and has encouraged me to demand more now from anyone who is invited into my love; to insist that my love has value and deserves to be protected.

When I think of my mother now, I like to imagine that she is able to find peace within the complexity of not only her own existence but also the complexity of her children. EMDR Therapy helped me to extend this hope of a peaceful perspective to myself. As a result, my EMDR Therapy processing allowed me to give my mother's memory the gift of a new life; a new life that she was not able to gather for herself. For me it was not about simple forgiveness, rather, about accountability and changed perspective. EMDR Therapy gave me the opportunity to safely love her. EMDR Therapy allowed me to safely remember. It allowed me to remember my mother as she was and to create space for what I hoped she would have been. It allowed me to have a relationship with my mother after death. It allowed me to admit to the saddest, smallest and most scared parts of my identity that I, like all children, wanted to be accepted, held softly and to be fiercely protected by my primary caregiver.

Using a queer lens to understand my mother, I can understand now that I spent most of my life feeling sadness for her; a sadness that was weighed down by guilt. Because despite all of her attempts to prepare me to survive the version of life she had been exposed to, I hoped more than anything that my life would be so unlike her own that all of her lessons would be invalidated.

After EMDR Therapy processing I was able to unpack this sadness and renounce my guilt. I was able to realize that what I really wanted was for my mother to have a different life so that she might create a different and more joyful life for me and my sisters. I wanted her to take risks emotionally, to let go of the rigidity that she believed ensured her safety and try living freely. I wanted her to encourage me to ignore the hurtful judgements and opinions of the world. I wanted her to be free in the hopes that her freedom could liberate me. After EMDR Therapy I was able to radically accept the reality that my mother and I conceptualized freedom very differently. My mother's quest for freedom was a desperate need for acceptance, and mine was a desperate need for authenticity. Her inability to understand this made it unlikely that she would ever understand me and because she could not relate to my desires she categorized them as fruitless.

EMDR Therapy has given me access to the truth that silence and time alone do not promote healing. In reality, healing often requires a reorganizing of memory and a disruption of the lessons embedded in those memories. EMDR Therapy was not something that caused me to grieve, it was something that allowed me to grieve. It worked for me, like I have seen it work for so many others, to move the barriers out of the way that block our access to grief. I needed to grieve many things involving my mother, including her own lack of a supportive, loving childhood and life. I want to be very clear to anyone who is reading this and disagrees or feels a more complicated relationship with their own parents or death that I am not offering you a solution or even a suggestion. I am only offering you an opportunity to witness the way in which EMDR Therapy allowed me to find a more gentle place to hold my own mother and allowed me to imagine a reality where my mother is prepared to celebrate my joy.

EMDR Therapy helped me to put down the heaviness of my pain and make room for healing and love. I am not attempting to minimize the severity of my mother's abuse or the constant dread that shaped my life as a child. In fact, I am suggesting quite the opposite. I insist on holding my mother accountable because that accountability allows me to humanize her. To not hold her accountable would be to think the very least of her, to assume that even in death, she would be incapable of operating with integrity.

After all of the EMDR Therapy I am left with this algedonic truth: my current love is a culmination of all of my pain. I would not exist without my mother. I would not be my current self without her. And maybe that is what healing is, not insisting that all of our pain be converted to joy but rather to insist that we can create opportunities for joy to float to the top. On my best days I imagine that my mother is sitting peacefully wherever people go when they are not with us and I hope that the part of my cells that were a gift from her are filled with joy as my gift in return. The beautiful thing about EMDR therapy is it allowed me to take this collection of memories, experiences, feelings, and understanding of my mother and hold them all together in one space as I moved through the hardest parts of our relationship. One of the main gifts that EMDR Therapy provided was increased awareness that my relationship with my mother is still able to be shaped. As irony would have it, my relationship with my deceased mother is very much alive.

Conclusion

Even now, as I write this, I feel the tiniest twinge of shame when I admit that even I was a skeptic. I was unsure if the waving of a hand or tapping on the knees could possibly touch the depth of my pain and the intensity of the relationship that I had with my mother. Even as someone who absolutely believes in the power of EMDR Therapy, having provided thousands of hours of EMDR Therapy and hundreds of hours of EMDR Therapy training, there was still the very scared little child inside of me that felt as if this part of my heart might always stay broken. And I think that is one of the things about being a member of the queer community that is most inspiring to me.

I am a member of a group that constantly shows up, takes a risk and trusts, even in the smallest part of their hearts, in the remaining goodness of people. Most of all, I am a member of a community that insists on its own joy in the face of all hatred. I was carried through my EMDR Therapy journey by the strength and support of my queer family. The power of this support gave me the courage to close my eyes and tap back-and-forth in the hopes that this conversation with my mother would go better than all the rest. That I could imagine only the best, strongest, loving and unafraid parts of her to support my joy and to generally default to anything, anyone that brought me happiness and joy. In gratitude for the support that EMDR Therapy gave me on my journey to healing grief I want to offer my story as a testimony of what is possible when we use an intersectional lens to create pathways for healing. The power of liberation that is made possible when we align our therapy with our identities.

My parting wish is that the power of queer liberation can be extended to everyone who finds their life limited by fear and ignorance. I offer this narrative to encourage you to ask yourself for permission to access your own grief. To open yourself to that process and possibility of healing without reducing or dissociating from the violence that created the pain. I am extending an invitation with the understanding that we can only hold others as softly as we hold ourselves. Through the use of EMDR Therapy I have realized that I am not looking for my mother's approval but rather my own.

I have asked myself this question and now offer it to you: Do you have the strength to stand on the shoulders of your ancestors and proudly declare that you exist with or without permission and approval?

Lisa Hayes, MSW, LISW-S (she/her) is a Clinical Social Worker based in Columbus, OH. Lisa graduated with a master's degree in Social Work from The Ohio State University. Her undergraduate education is in Sociology and Gender Studies; her academic and professional focus has always included special considerations for issues of gender identity, sexuality, race and social representation. Lisa is a proud first-generation college graduate. Lisa's clinical experiences include work with complex trauma; anxiety; panic disorders; interpersonal relationship health; residential alcohol and drug treatment; inpatient psychiatric hospitalization; significant life transitions; ethnic and race based trauma; LGBTQIA+ specific support needs; depression; complex dissociation; Military Veteran experiences; sexual assault and childhood sexual abuse. Lisa's clinical practice has primarily focused on the treatment of adolescents and adults. Lisa is energized by environments of learning, collaboration and increased understanding; she has provided local, national and international trainings focused on the impacts of trauma and its effects on individuals, communities and families. In her therapeutic work, Lisa uses a variety of expressive and experiential therapeutic interventions all aimed at identifying and celebrating the strengths of each person. Lisa is currently employed by The Ohio State University, maintains a part-time private practice, is co-owner of the Trauma and Wellness Institute and serves as the Director of the EMDR Therapy Training Program for BIPOC Clinicians with the Institute for Creative Mindfulness. When not at work Lisa enjoys reading, laughing with her sisters, spending time with her godson, making up silly dances with her nephew, traveling with her partner and playing with her dog.

Reference

Klass, D., Silverman, P. R., & Nickman, S. (2014). *Continuing bonds: New understandings of grief*. London: Taylor & Francis.

A Neurotype Inclusive and Neuroqueering EMDR Framework

Erin E. Kelly, LCSW, REAT, RYT-500

There has been increasing conversation in the field of psychotherapy about a paradigm shift away from the pathology paradigm to a neuro-affirming paradigm (Walker, 2021). In the context of EMDR Therapy, this paradigm shift would allow for *and* embrace accommodations for different neurotypes in all eight phases of EMDR Therapy. Given the established intersectionality of neurodivergence and queerness noted in the literature, we make the argument that the clinician should not only be aware of these dynamics but provide alternatives to the client in order to ensure an inclusive and affirming environment to better support holistic healing.

Introduction and Perspective

This chapter presents a combination of academic writing and lived experience to accommodate all learning styles. I want to provide information from my years of living as a queer, neurodivergent individual, as well as my years of working with queer, neurodivergent individuals using EMDR Therapy. In the spirit of both unmasking myself and providing maximum readability for others, clinical implications will be both peppered throughout the text and summarized at the end of this chapter. I also acknowledge existing limitations in my capacity, breadth, and depth of that lived experience. My whiteness, late diagnosis, and hyperlexia/verbosity provide privileges in the dominant paradigm and society that many others do not have. There are experiences of BIPOC queer and autistic folks that are not fully reflected in this chapter because those are not my stories to tell. I want you, the reader, to have related resources to explore after you finish this chapter, should you choose to do so. I appreciate the knowledge of other people who have been doing this work before me and alongside me, and I want their voices to be included. I am not an expert, I am a member of the community hoping that their voice can be one of many.

Trauma, Neurodiversity, and Queerness

"Neurodiversity is the variation among minds."
(Walker, 2021, p. 53)

In this chapter, I explore two primary topics: (1) how and why neurodivergence is relevant to the concept of "queering EMDR, (2) considerations and modifications for EMDR with neurodivergent clients in all eight phases of EMDR Therapy, including case examples from both my clinical and personal experiences."

While I want to acknowledge that the definition of"neurodiversity" can include those who experience Down Syndrome, Obsessive-Compulsive Disorder (OCD), Post-Traumatic Stress Disorder (PTSD)/Complex Post-Traumatic Stress Disorder (CPTSD), Dissociative Identity Disorder (DID) and other dissociative disorders, Traumatic Brain Injuries (TBIs), and schizophrenia, most of the research is focused on neurodevelopmental information and sensory processing experiences that are related to autism and Attention Deficit Hyperactivity Disorder (ADHD). For the purposes of this chapter, "neurodivergent" will refer to autism and/or ADHD. However, all of the suggestions may be helpful in supporting clients with other neurotypes.

There is a high overlap between LGBTQIA2s+ identity, neurodivergent identity, and trauma.

A survey of 641,860 people found that transgender and gender-diverse individuals have higher rates of autism, other neurodevelopmental, and psychiatric diagnosis than cisgender individuals (Warrier et al., 2020; Weir, Allison, & Baron-Cohen, 2021). While there is a wide range of percentages from research on prevalence of queer identities in autistic people, one study suggests that between 15-35 percent of autistic people who do not have an intellectual disability identify as gay, lesbian, or bisexual (Pecora,

Mesibov, & Stokes, 2016), while other samples have rates of sexual minority (non-heterosexal) as high as 69.7% (George & Stokes, 2018).

Many people have theorized as to why this is. Perhaps it's because neurodivergent and queer folks are less likely to adhere to binary thinking, making them less susceptible to societal pressures that seemingly dictate how and what someone should "be." At the same time, this can also "other" individuals and make them more vulnerable to abuse, neglect, and social exclusion.

Recent research indicates that 45-61% of autistics also meet criteria for PTSD (Haruvi-Lamdan et al., 2020; Reuben et al, 2021; Rumball et al., 2021). They are also twice as likely to experience more than one adverse childhood experience (ACE) (Hartley et al, 2024). Similarly, up to 48% of LGBTQIA2S+ individuals meet criteria for PTSD, and 42% of transgender and gender diverse individuals (Valentine, et al., 2022).

The entire field of psychotherapy is built upon the notion that there is a "norm" and that everyone must conform to that way of being to experience mental and physical wellness. The current political climate in 2025 even asserts that Americans are sick because of the food we eat and the lack of physical exercise, without considering other sociocultural and systemic factors. There is seemingly no concern as to why we are drawn to foods and inactivity in the first place. We are all ringing out our nervous systems and have destroyed our bodies to meet norms that are dictated by capitalism. Neurodivergent, queer, and disabled folks are seemingly less willing to tolerate it and they are speaking out about it louder than anyone else.

Dr. Nick Walker, an autistic, transgender scholar started using the term "neuroqueer" almost twenty years ago. Walker states that "intentionally liberating oneself from the culturally ingrained and enforced performance of heteronormativity is sometimes referred to as *queering*, intentionally liberating oneself from the culturally ingrained and enforced performance of neuronormativity can be thought of as *neuroqueering*" (Walker, 2021, p. 155). While being queer is not required to be neuroqueer, the linguistics highlight the divestment from the dominant paradigms. We can adapt EMDR Therapy for queer and neurodivergent clients the same way: to allow exploration to find their own unique EMDR experience that works best for them. As I frequently say to my consultees: *make the EMDR work for you and your clients, not the other way around.*

My own neurodivergence was not diagnosed until my PTSD and anxiety symptoms were better managed. A long history of high-masking, high-achieving, and the presence of acute PTSD symptoms hid my neurodivergence until after my first experience with trauma reprocessing. This has been a common experience with a number of my clients—the intrusive symptoms of PTSD often overwhelm an individual's ability to understand or communicate their experience. I have noticed that self-blame, incompetence, unworthiness, and a sense of being unsafe are the most notable when they present to therapy. These beliefs about self, dysregulation related to masking, dysregulation related to executive functioning struggles, and internalized ableism are often attributed to traumatic experiences outside of oppression and ableism.

I "came out" about my sexuality before I received my first neurodevelopmental diagnosis. My now-wife was the one who called me out. As soon as I sat in front of a psychiatrist for the first time, he took one hour with me and said, "Oh there is no doubt at all, you have severe ADHD."

I was floored. Me? I had high anxiety, sure. Some imposter syndrome as a new clinician. But didn't everyone experience those things from time to time? Because I had only my inner experience to go off of, I had no idea that my information and sensory processing mechanisms were different than other people's. I was so used to being disconnected from my body and distracting myself, I didn't realize that my high anxiety was the one thing that kept me surviving and prevented collapse. Once my PTSD symptoms were managed, some past traumas processed, and my mask of heteronormativity removed, it became apparent that the effort, time, and way I was "keeping myself together" was not sustainable. Without high anxiety and people-pleasing to guide me, it was impossible to continue on as I had for most of my life. I was burnt out. Like many other traumatized, neurodivergent, and queer folks, it was an autoimmune disorder that finally forced me to slow down and begin to release what was left of my mask. I was sick because the expectations of our society and the expectations that I force myself to live my life as a heteronormative, neuronormative person was disabling.

My lived experience is one of a high-masking individual, both in my sexuality and gender expression, as well as my neurotype. As Dr. Devon Price, another autistic and transgender scholar states, “masking is a state of exclusion forced onto us from the outside... we only get the opportunity to take our masks off when we realize other ways of being exist” (Price, 2022, p. 15). LGBTQIA2S+ folks also often feel like they need to internalize or avoid emotional pain and authentic self expression to maintain safety and/or acceptance, often also referred to as “masking.” Consider that unmasking requires feeling safe enough to get to know ourselves (Price, 2022), so this may be a process for your client that takes a few years. However, EMDR Therapy does not need to wait until the client has totally unmasked—actually, EMDR may help the client unmask and gain clarity about their authentic self-expression.

For myself, lifting some of the negative beliefs about myself and somatically processing the trauma of both masking and others expectations freed up space in my body to be my authentic self, and to even discover what that meant in the first place. EMDR can be a wonderful resource to the client throughout their trauma reprocessing journey, should it resonate with them. I want to be clear that I do not believe every neurodivergent person *should* do EMDR Therapy, simply that the bottom-up approach can be an avenue for healing, should it resonate and be adapted with them. Consent and collaboration are key.

Thematic Conceptualization and Masking: Considerations for EMDR Therapy

"The nature of any culture's dominant paradigms is that they're so pervasive that they become normalized to the point of invisibility for anyone raised within that culture."
(Walker, 2021, p. 130)

There is a plethora of information on the detrimental toll masking takes on physical and mental health (Price, 2022). Neurodivergent and gender-diverse individuals experience a high level of identity trauma, as well as trauma from masking (MacInnis, 2024). Many neurodivergent and queer folks alike, particularly those who are high-masking, have gotten direct and indirect messages throughout their lives about doing something wrong, not living up to their potential, being lazy, being thoughtless/careless, or being rude. For myself, this was a theme in school, at home, and with peers who didn't understand me. I picked up that something was "off" and recognized patterns when I would either get reprimanded, ignored, or dismissed. I learned what people expected of me and what level of self-expression kept me in a sense of belonging, even if it felt inauthentic and was difficult for me to produce.

I was psychologically evaluated at the suggestion of a particularly astute teacher in fourth grade and labeled "gifted" (what I now look at as the female-socialized, straight A, extroverted "autistic"). While I thrived in these classes and activities, I was the one person in my small school who attended the gifted program, which required I be bussed to another facility once a week. The social exclusion and negative attention was too stressful and I ultimately gave up the opportunity at the desire to be liked and included in my school. This theme continued throughout middle school, high school, and parts of college as I continuously abandoned my interests, joys, and creative expressions in favor of social acceptance. As I got older, I saw how cruel people could be to one another and I opted to stay safe rather than be myself. I stopped playing the piano and clarinet, stopped riding horses, stopped painting, stopped reading the books that interested me, and instead forced myself to do competitive dance, drink alcohol, and even joined in bullying others to get accepted. I was "good" at being a social chameleon, and I hated it. This masking and desire to seek social acceptance as safety also masked my sexuality and gender queerness for years.

I've heard so many similar stories amongst some of my clients and friends. These experiences are often important or core areas to explore themes, negative cognitions, and associated targets. Internalized ableism and homophobia (e.g., bullying others, self-abandonment, receiving social acceptance but still feeling "empty") often show up when exploring subconscious beliefs, even if the client doesn't identify any direct traumatic experiences related to their sexual identity and/or neurodivergence.

Psychoeducation on masking is often helpful if the client has any neurodivergent or LGBTQIA2S+ identities. This can be as simple as giving the client a definition of masking and asking if it resonates with their experiences in life thus far (also a great question to explore themes and negative cognitions). Many clients will choose to do research on their own—connecting with other neurodivergent or queer individuals who have unmasked and/or listening to others' experiences is often helpful in this process. For those who want more introverted guidance, I often point folks to Devon Price's books and work to further explore their understanding of masking and how it has shown up throughout their lives.

All marginalized populations experience trauma around their associated marginalization. It's often not helpful to jump to offering solutions before clients are able to communicate their experiences to you. We are not treating the person's autism and/or ADHD. We are treating and processing the distress around the experience of being neurodivergent in our society. We are not treating their race, sexuality, or gender identity, we are helping them unpack and process the negative impact of the stigma and oppression around these identities. Pathologizing or dismissing clients' lived experience echoes the trauma of oppression in the therapy room—denying their identities traumatizes them and invalidates both their existence and their experience of the world (McVey et al., 2023). This also means that many queer and neurodivergent individuals alike have avoided receiving necessary medical and/or mental health care (National LGBT Health Education Center, 2020).

The autistic community really began forming online in the 1990s (Walker, 2021), just a mere couple years after EMDR Therapy became a structured modality. Neurodiversity-affirming and queer-affirming EMDR embraces all neurotypes and does use hierarchical labels to identify one as "better" or "more adaptive" than another (Hanville et al., 2024; MacInnis, 2025). Unfortunately, due to the pathologizing nature and rigidity of the medical model, many neurodivergent and queer folks alike have been traumatized by both medical care and psychotherapy (Doherty et al., 2022; Hanville, 2025; James et al., 2022). Keep in mind that processing traumatic therapeutic events and repairing ruptures from previous providers and modalities may be crucial in the client's ability to move forward with you, and with EMDR.

EMDR on EMDR ("Meta" EMDR)

Removing expectations of what EMDR "should" look like or how clients "should" respond, and communicating to clients that individualizing the protocol can alleviate subconscious or conscious pressure to mask or perform. I often start with an initial target of EMDR on EMDR, or what I sometimes call "Meta EMDR." I have done this now with dozens of clients, and suggested it to probably a hundred consultees and trainees over the past several years, with a lot of reported success. There are several intentions here:

- clients get to experience a likely low-stakes target with a negative cognition that is somewhere in their neural network but not directly related to any previous experience or trauma,
- clients get a live demonstration to be able to understand the structure of EMDR reprocessing,
- clients can gain insights about how they experience EMDR during and after reprocessing, and
- we can start to address any blocking beliefs around perfectionism, people-pleasing, or emotional expression.

Clients can read all about EMDR, watch a million videos, talk about it ad nauseam with you, and collect as much information as they can—for some of my clients, this is tantamount to their process! And, they still won't know what it feels like for them, what dual attention stimulus (DAS) they prefer, what they need during, and how they feel afterwards until they experience it firsthand. It is possible that distressing trauma memories can overwhelm the introductory target. I tell clients that it is possible, so we discuss ahead of time what our game plan will be. Do we "go with that"? Do we pause and figure out how this fits into their Phase 1 conceptualization? Is there anything that is off limits to process right now? I have had these experiences happen a few times with clients, all which resulted in overall positive or neutral EMDR experiences.

Considerations for all Phases of EMDR Therapy from a Neurotype-Inclusive Lens

Dissociation

When assessing for and discussing dissociation, expand beyond the quantitative rating scales. To date, none of the assessment tools have been normed for ADHD or autism. Collaborate with your clients to understand why they answered items the way they did and to help both of you gain awareness of all aspects of their experience, as much as they are willing and able. Neurodivergent dissociation and overwhelm is easily confused with trauma dissociation. It can also be helpful to explore your own comfortability and understanding of dissociation, both clinically and with your own experience.

Personally, my neurodivergent dissociation and trauma dissociation feel very different now. Sensory overwhelm or fatigue often feels like I am "powering down" and manifests as brain fog, blurred vision, and difficulty accessing recall. This can also be prolonged burnout and make it difficult for me to do daily activities like brushing my teeth, choosing meals, and interacting with others. My traumatic dissociation was often linked to a specific trigger and is shorter-lasting. When I am sensorily overwhelmed or burned out, I am also more likely to experience a trauma trigger. I have had many clients report similar patterns.

"Wide Processing"

In individuals with autism (Koyama & Ikegaya, 2015; Xiong, Chen, & Li, 2023; Zhan et al., 2014) and ADHD (Mascarell Maričić et al., 2020), reduced synaptic pruning—the brain's process of eliminating unused neural connections—may lead to the formation of numerous associations during EMDR reprocessing, including but not limited to the identification of multiple feeder memories. I call this "wide processing", indicating that the scope of content may be much wider than what we would typically try to contain targets to in the standard EMDR protocol. Due to this, I often see clients who do a "target within a target" (i.e., floating back to another target and/or negative cognition in the middle of reprocessing another target). This may take a bit more note-taking or organization on your end as the clinician. I tend to jot down the emergent target(s) and highlight them to be included in our thematic conceptualization or target list. Remember to check back in (e.g., when checking the SUDs, VOC, closing a session) on the original target where you started. My language here is usually: "I know a lot of other things have come up in this session today, which is often how the process goes. As you look back on the original target where we started, what is your level of distress, 0-10?"

Overemphasizing words, using hand gestures, and visual aids are wonderful tools to add in nonverbal communication to the verbal scripts of EMDR. I have some clients who have done EMDR with me for awhile now that much of our Phase 3 set up is nonverbal. We point to the target we're working on, I point to my head to get a prompt for the negative cognition, my stomach for emotions, and both my hands up and down in front of my body a few times to ask for somatic awarenesses.

On the flip side, some of my other clients would absolutely hate it if I did this. The more you get to know your client (and they get to know themselves!), the more flow you will find within the EMDR framework and build an EMDR process that is ideal for them. This does often involve a lot of trial and error. Inform your clients of that so they know this is a natural and helpful part of the process, not some default of theirs (which may reinforce masking trauma).

Although not every neurodivergent individual experiences pathological demand avoidance (PDA), it is common enough that it is worth mentioning here. PDA (also known as persistent drive for autonomy' in the autistic community) is noted as a heightened nervous system response to the existence or perception of a demand (MacInnis, 2025). Transparency in the therapeutic process, the emphasis of collaboration, and the use of command-free and nonverbal language can be helpful guidelines to reduce the expectations and demand of EMDR. This can also be helpful for working with perfectionism, neurodivergent trauma, and complex trauma in general.

VOC and SUD Scales

Oftentimes these quantitative scales will not make sense to clients, especially as they are different from one another. I use visual aids (different versions of the scales, printed or digital), hand gestures, and exaggerated facial expressions to communicate the SUDs and VOC. Clients and I will come up with our own scales (common ones are emoji, colors, or personal experiences when they have felt their 0 or 10, somatic sensations that indicate someone's neutrality or flooding) to understand the client's experience in the moment. Often, I will make this an expressive arts exercise so the client has their own customized visual aid to reference during Phase 3 and throughout reprocessing.

Perhaps a controversial opinion—if I have talked about options for the SUDs and VOC with a client, experimented with every way of communicating a temperature check we can both think of, and the client is still hung up on the scales...I don't use them. As long as we have a stop/pause signal (verbal and non-verbal, if possible), I just need to know where the client is and if they're in their window of tolerance. I have yet to work with a client who couldn't communicate some type of general pleasant/keep going (e.g., thumbs up), unpleasant/feeling worse (e.g., thumbs down), and a neutral/nothing has changed (e.g., thumb sticking out sideways) signs. What's important here is that you can get some information as to how a client is feeling before, during, and after trauma reprocessing. Potentially helpful language to invite collaboration and exploration includes, "How else can we communicate other than words/verbally?"

Verbal Processing During Phases 4-6 is Sometimes Helpful

Some clients are hyperverbal or verbal processors. In my experience, this is especially common in ADHD. For some folks, it's a defense mechanism. For others, it's an integral part of their information processing. For many (myself included), it's both. Talking during reprocessing (Phases 4-6) is often helpful for neurodivergent clients. It can provide some much needed regulation to prevent flooding, communicating and having someone else try to understand their process may be reparative for their traumatic experiences, or may be crucial to how their brain integrates information. I do like to provide psychoeducation about why we generally do not want to focus solely on cognitive/verbal processing in EMDR (we have talk therapy for that) so clients can self-regulate their verbal content and so we can problem solve together when the client is "stuck" without the stigma that they're doing something wrong or EMDR is "not working."

This psychoeducation usually consists of:

- neuroanatomical and/or neurobiology theories of EMDR (which can range from a few sessions worth of theoretical discussion to "*we think EMDR helps the brain communicate in a way that can make it easier to check in on body and emotional memory*")
- information about "top-down" and "bottom-up" processing
- conversations about decolonizing therapy, collaborating in treatment, and unmasking (Dr. Jennifer Mullan and Dr. Devon Price's work are great for this)

We may experiment with different check-ins to see what is preferable for the client. Some clients prefer frequent reminders, as over intellectualization has been their primary protective factor. I find major shifts are really only necessary when someone is "stuck" or looping in Phases 4-6 (i.e., SUDs or distress level is not changing in any direction, no new information or insights are emerging). Sometimes this includes doing EMDR every other session to allow space for verbal processing/talk therapy.

Evaluate Sensory Needs and Spend Time on Exploring DAS Options

Being somatically oriented is important for working with trauma, and especially important for working with queer and neurodivergent clients. The body often manifests internalized oppression (Walker, 2021). So much of the queer and neurodivergent experience is ineffable. You will need a wide range of resources to work with the vast array of humans and human experiences. Some clients may have marked differences in sensory and information processing, such as aphantasia (inability to visualize) or synesthesia (experiencing one sense as another; such as hearing colors or seeing music).

I have clients who have benefited immensely from occupational therapy as part of their sensory exploration and training. While occupational therapy itself may not be part of every client's treatment, we can spend time exploring sensory options for the person-in-environment, as well as understanding some key terms that are often helpful for neurodivergent nervous systems. These include:

- Proprioception: perception or awareness of the position and movement of the body (Kent, 2006)
- Interoception: the process of sensing signals from the body, (e.g., heartbeat, hunger, pain, fatigue, elimination cues) (Barker, Brewer, & Murphy, 2021)
- Neuroception: an awareness of what happens between your interoception and interoception, i.e., the way your nervous system communicates with others and determines safety–

> with individuals and groups (Dana, 2021). I would also add that in my experience, this also applies to energetics of a space, as well as sensory input of the environment.

Phase 2 resources and somatic awareness exercises can focus on proprioception (gentle balancing poses, clenching a stress ball, using a weighted lap pad or blanket), interoception (body scan, clench and release, breathwork, emotion and/or body mapping, yoga and other exercises), or neuroception (progressive muscle relaxation, breathing in tandem with your client, and sensory exploration in general). Neuroception is bodily experiences made conscious, so any exploration you do with clients around sensory preferences and needs will help support their EMDR work with practice. There are many, many ways to explore somatic exercises for trauma healing and EMDR Therapy. You may feel comfortable with some and not with others. Your own personal experiences, healing, and training will likely inform what you offer to your clients. Find what feels authentic to you! If it feels scary or intimidating to clients who consent to these kinds of exercises, your calm presence can help support them in their vulnerability. I often find that this is my favorite topic to consult (both as a consultant and consultee) because there are so many options and things to learn!

Exploring DAS modalities can also help your clients start to develop an understanding for their body cues, particularly when it is asking for movement and when it is asking for stillness. Without overwhelming them, let clients know the different options for DAS (audio, tactile, and visual). Remember that anything that crosses the midline can be bilateral stimulation. This can be toe tapping, tapping on a specific body part, rocking, swaying, flicking, clenching, walking, pinching the fingers together...the list goes on and on. Clients will often offer their own suggestions once they realize it's okay to explore and with practice listening to their nervous systems/bodies.

Make it commonplace to ask for consent and check in on the DAS options each session. For example: "You self-tapped on your knees last session. Is it okay to try a short set to check out speed, pressure, and location of the tapping to see what feels best for where you are today? We can also try out another kind of DAS if you want to try something different."

As a generalization for ADHD clients, it may be helpful to start with shorter sets until the clients settle to help with distraction. Using more than one form of dual attention stimulus (e.g., tactile, auditory, and visual) can also be helpful, especially as the client can choose to drop in and out of the stimulations by closing the eyes, stopping tapping, taking off headphones/asking you to stop the sound as needed. This can help with racing thoughts, distraction, and can add a sense of novelty that many people with ADHD find supportive.

Exploring sensory needs can also give you as the clinician important information about the client's experience and modifications you can make throughout treatment. Many of my neurodivergent clients find that they benefit from pre-EMDR and after-EMDR care plans to both allow therapeutic change to happen, as well as integrate the experience and allow the body to continue processing as it needs to. I give concrete examples of this in the case example below.

There are many supplemental sensory practices and somatic work that can support trauma reprocessing. Examples include massage, float tanks (sensory deprivation pods), acupuncture, exercise, yoga, meditation, arts practices, listening to music, going for a walk, experiencing pressure (e.g., weighted blankets, swaddling, hugs from trusted people), naps, sensory deprivation (e.g., laying in a dark room), or engaging in a special interest.

Clients do not need to be seated, or even still, during reprocessing. Allow stimming (repetitive self-stimulation) for regulation–as long as it is not distressing to the client or harmful to themselves or you. Stimming can come in many forms: proprioceptive (rocking, flapping, pressure-seeking), tactile (touching surfaces), vestibular (spinning, swinging, hanging upside down), auditory (listening to music), verbal (echolalia–repeating phrases or sounds), olfactory (smelling), gustatory (tasting), visual (gazing/focusing on something, e.g., running water, art, or a video) (Walker, 2021). Many of these suggestions can also be used as the DAS itself.

- use fidgets
- knitting
- walking
- drawing/doodling/coloring (related or unrelated to target content—I have had a few clients draw the target itself, or depict what the target felt like with scribbles/colors/shapes rather than verbally respond in between sets)
- virtual or in-person sandtray
- writing
- swaying/rocking
- marching in place
- drumming
- throwing a ball/item from hand to hand
- I have often had clients benefit from putting their bodies in a position that is supportive to their nervous system (e.g., laying on the floor with legs up the wall, wrapped in a blanket, in a hammock)

Thoroughly exploring, practicing, and strengthening use of sensory information, coping skills, support systems, assessing need for rest, and physically nourishing practices is often essential for helping your clients understand what their body is asking for. Skill regression is common with unmasking (Price, 2022). Regressions in adaptive functioning and communication are also common trauma responses (Oswald, 2024). It's also common with trauma reprocessing, especially when folks are releasing defense mechanisms that are no longer serving them. Find a gentle, authentic way to normalize the time spent on sensory exploration with your clients. The more they explore and practice, the more they will start to develop more conscious communication with their body.

Modify, Modify, Modify!

You may need to be more direct with questions and interweaves with some clients. Conversely, some clients may really enjoy the use of metaphor to understand complex connections and concepts.

Are you noticing a theme here? It is very difficult to make sweeping generalizations and suggestions for neurodiversity-affirming and queer-affirming EMDR because every client is unique. Their needs, supports, and awareness will likely shift throughout their trauma processing work. I believe that in order to truly offer a trauma-focused or even trauma-informed approach, we need to offer options, feedback, and transparency during every step of the process. Modify as needed, just as you would with complex trauma clients. Again, there is major overlap here. Ask them how they tend to process information and use that to guide you as much as possible in EMDR.

Certainly some clients may be annoyed and feel infantilized if we are giving them boxed choices every few minutes. This is where I cannot tell you exact steps on how to apply to your clients. Trust your clinical instincts, identify the theoretical paradigms that click for you, and most importantly, *ask for feedback from your clients*! EMDR is unique because it truly is most effective as a collaborative effort. You are there as the guide, to make suggestions, and create/hold the container. They are there to discover what works and does not work for them as they process their trauma.

Case Example: The Author's EMDR Preferences as an EMDR Client

First and foremost, I need time to prepare. Often this means taking time to quiet down, set up my space (or pack my bag for in-person sessions) and make sure I have my tools—journal, fidgets, water, ginger chews, a crystal or two, maybe a stuffed animal or blanket that will feel supportive for me, especially depending on what I might be targeting that day. While I have done EMDR without this preparation, it is usually slower and doesn't go as deeply as it would, had I intentional space beforehand.

While I have a very expansive mindfulness and grounding practice, having my therapist lead me in an exercise allows my protective, intellectual mind to start to release, as well as provides an opportunity for co-regulation. It also gives my body the opportunity to do a fully present check in to see how I'm feeling—what I might need, what resistance might be present, and what could be helpful to facilitate vulnerable, embodied work this session. A pillow in my lap can often serve as both a grounding and sensory tool, as well as a protective shield that helps my body allow intense emotions. Sometimes, my mind is too busy and forcing it to reprocess would be detrimental. If I'm in a high state of anxiety or particularly tired, this can be ideal time for reprocessing if *attunement and enough grounding is present* because I am in a state of emotional desperation and/or apathy that it's easier to access my emotions. Sometimes, it's too much—I once tried to start reprocessing with about 20 minutes left in the session, just to move along a stuck point and almost immediately it was clear that the time limitation was a barrier that day. I have learned that I need time to get my nervous verbal jitters out and talk shop a bit with my therapist. And I need ample time to settle into the target. It often takes me several sets to be able to fully access my experience, regardless of how much prep and grounding I do beforehand.

When reprocessing, I take my DAS long, intense, and fast. I am someone who paradoxically needs to share some elements of my experience and talk it out, but need to be mindful of being hyperverbal because I can quickly switch to analyzing without experiencing it as a protective factor—this isn't always helpful. My therapist knows this and we discuss it frequently. We have a rapport where she can challenge me and redirect to the body/emotions in a way that I am receptive to. That has taken some trial and error, both with her and other therapists I have worked with. I frequently self tap, and virtual EMDR often allows me to go deeper, faster because I am in the nest of my own space, and there is a bit of distance between myself and my therapist. But in-person EMDR has its own magic, because I LOVE the tactile buzzers with LED lights on them. It gives me the option to have a focal point and additional modality of DAS, without any effort from me. I notice my body and nervous system is more receptive to my therapist's attunement in person versus virtually.

Afterwards, my needs vary. I feel confident enough in this point in my healing process that I can respond to what I need, when I need it. I like to schedule therapy late morning to mid-afternoon and make sure I have absolutely nothing planned (except maybe a supportive, low-stakes social engagement that can easily be cancelled). Often I will go for a hike or a walk, lay in bed with my comfort items, debrief with a confidante, or engage in some kind of expressive arts practice. I always drink A LOT of water. Our bodies release a multitude of different neurotransmitters and chemicals when we experience stress, emotions, and any kind of energetic or emotional release, so helping your body move those things along can be a straightforward way of continuing to process what it needs to.

Many of my clients have plans as extensive, if not more, than mine. Others stick to hydration and rest or have some movement/distraction. I usually tell them that it will take a few reprocessing sessions to really figure out what works best for them, and how to adapt as needed. My preferences have evolved over the course of a few years—I'm sure aspects will continue to change as I do. Normalize to clients that they can keep their preferences the same or change them up as often as they like.

The Role of the Therapist in Neurotype-Inclusive EMDR Therapy

Lean into compassion for yourself as a clinician. Most of us were trained in medical model, pathology-centric graduate programs, so this is often not something that comes easily to us. Most of us were not taught anything about assessing or treating neurodivergent clients in graduate school (Hanville, 2025). Some of us were not even taught about considerations for working with LGBTQIA2S+ clients outside of the fact that we exist and may have correlated health and mental health challenges. As mentioned earlier in this chapter, the field has pathologized and traumatized neurodivergent and queer folks alike for much of the existence of psychotherapy. Ole Ivar Lovaas, the creator of Applied Behavioral Analysis (ABA) therapy, also created "conversion therapy" (Sexual Orientation Change Efforts) (Price, 2022). ABA is both abusive and unethical. The modality ignores the needs of autistic individuals and instead uses operant conditioning to "correct" behavioral manifestations to neurotypical standards, regardless of whether or not the behaviors are causing distress to the autistic individual (Shkedy, Shkedy, & Sandovcal-Norton, 2021).

We have been taught to learn evidence-based therapies, apply them to fidelity with every client, OR ELSE...what? The therapy gods smite you? You lose your license? You'll irrevocably cause harm to your clients? Usually the response I hear from supervisees and consultees is along the lines of "if I do it wrong I'll harm my client." Anecdotally, imposter syndrome is common in our field, though little research has been done on its prevalence. It is a natural human experience when learning something new! Imposter syndrome has also been linked to higher levels of burnout and compassion fatigue in mental health professionals (Clark et al., 2022). We understandably look to research, supervision, and trainings for knowledge...all of which can be valuable! I also assert that when we think we need to have the "right" answer or "fix" our clients or regulate FOR them, we are actually causing harm by disempowering them and interrupting their stress response cycle completion without their consent.

The reality is that collaboration with the client requires tolerance of discomfort, acknowledgment and breakdown of the power differential between therapist and client, openness, and vulnerability of the clinician. By using active and ongoing collaboration in treatment, we are shedding the medical model assumption that we are experts in the room and know the "right way" for the client to heal, whether that's from our theoretical orientation or therapeutic modality. There are no step-by-step guides that work all the time, for every client, which is especially true when you are working with neurodivergent, queer, and traumatized clients. You as the provider–even if you are also neurodivergent, queer, and traumatized--will not have all the answers. It takes ongoing work to challenge the dominant paradigm, and both queer and neurodivergent clients will be impacted by oppression (Walker, 2021). Sometimes, the most healing thing you will do is sit in silence with them, laugh at a meme together, or tell them (and there are so many ways to do this, verbally and nonverbally) that you are present and listening. No one can tell you how to do this. It happens in the dynamic interactions between you and your client, in collaboration, in taking accountability for disappointment, in normalization of pain, in exploring and gaining awareness. Each session is often uncharted territory, which can bring up a lot of anxiety and self-doubt as EMDR Therapy and other trauma-focused modalities often include intense affect.

For this reason, authenticity is crucial. Many clients need to feel understood by you as their therapist and believe that you can relate to their experiences to feel safe enough to engage therapeutically (Neff, 2024), especially with the vulnerability EMDR often involves. Additionally, neurodivergent complex trauma survivors who experience hyper-empathy will be highly attuned to notice inauthenticity or performative gestures. Similarly, research demonstrates that non-binary clients deem it crucial to know their therapist's gender identity and sexual orientation (Rosati et al., 2022). This information about the therapist's identities can allow for deeper therapeutic rapport and trust building, a factor of psychotherapy that is inarguably the most important part of the therapeutic process. Despite the vast array of available modalities, evidence shows that a positive therapeutic relationship is more indicative of a successful therapeutic outcome than any chosen theoretical orientation (Duncan et al., 2014; Flückiger et al, 2012; Haikal, 2022; Horvath, 2001; Karver et al., 2006; Martin et al., 2000; Norcross & Lambert, 2019; Norcross & Wampold, 2019; Shirk & Karver, 2003).

Some of my best advice here is to find your own EMDR therapist. Fully experiencing the modality on the other side of the chair/couch/telehealth screen can bring insights and perspectives about EMDR that will be difficult to arrive at in didactic learning. You may have this unique opportunity to work through any trepidation you have to using EMDR Therapy in your clinical work, as well as gain clarity as to how EMDR Therapy does not fit into the way you practice at this time. While I do believe understanding the theoretical framework of EMDR Therapy is vital for modification,

I have noticed that clinicians who are active in their own ongoing healing work often struggle less with imposter syndrome.

Beyond my professional work as a practicum facilitator, clinical supervisor, and EMDRIA Approved Consultant, my doctoral dissertation research is focused on the psychotherapist's healing and how it impacts the therapeutic alliance and the psychotherapy process. At the time of this writing, I am still in the midst of data analysis. However, I have noticed emergent themes and begun to develop a theory of *healing humility*.

The cultural humility framework asserts that we cannot become "competent" in someone else's cultural experiences and calls for "lifelong self-evaluation and self-critique" to be willing to learn from the individuals we work with to lessen the power differential and better understand their experiences (Tervalon & Murray-Garcia, 1998). I as a White person will never understand the embodied experience of someone of another race, no matter how much anti-racism work I do. In the same way that cultural competency is impossible, I assert that "clinical competency" is also unattainable. I have a developed a concept based off of the cultural humility framework called *healing humility*, defined as: the continuous engagement in life-long learning, self-awareness, and critical reflection in an effort to sustain balanced vulnerability and authenticity within the therapeutic relationship.

Yes, there are requirements to adhere to ethical guidelines, continuing education, and other checklist items to complete. However, we as therapists do not have all the answers and assuming we know the "proper" way to administer a modality can be harmful by dismissing the client's autonomy and knowledge of self. Unanimously, psychotherapists I interviewed stated that some of the most beneficial "training" they got as professionals was their own healing process to be able to regulate their own nervous systems, attune to their clients, and being able to support others in navigating and moving through processing trauma.

Watching clients in pain is difficult. Being present and not caretaking or overfunctioning for your client (and thus disempowering them) is a delicate balance. Not I, nor anyone else, can tell you how to best manage this balance for yourself as a clinician, how to engage with countertransference, how to regulate your nervous system, or how to attune to your clients. I cannot best tell you how to work with your neurodivergent, queer, and/or traumatized clients and modify EMDR for them. I hope you can see that all the suggestions in this chapter basically are some variation of "it depends", "offer options", and "ask your client." The tolerance of ambiguity and willingness to enter and withstand the pain with your clients will only come from an amalgamation of your professional training, clinical practice, and your own healing work.

So thank you for the work you do, the space you hold, your willingness to learn, and your dedication to the healing process. I truly believe it is through genuine connection and understanding that we can heal our relational wounds and be in the presence of our authenticity.

TL;DR (Too Long; Didn't Read) Guidelines to Shift the EMDR Therapy Paradigm to be One that is Neurotype and Queer Inclusive

- Modify, modify, modify!
- Explore sensory needs, sensitivities, preferences, and aversions.
- Psychoeducation on the neurodivergent experience and understanding each client's individual lived experiences and needs.
- Nonverbal communication can be a game changer.
- Use individualized language.
- Thorough exploration of dual attention stimulus options and combinations.
- Allow the client to self-regulate for sensory and attention needs—do not try to do it for them unless there has been a specific discussion as to how and when this will be supportive for them.
- Consider transitions in and out of EMDR, both as a modality and in individual sessions.

- Ask for feedback! The client is the expert in their experience, not you. Make checking in and asking for consent commonplace in your rapport.
- Emphasize the collaborative nature as part of the efficacy of EMDR. Focus on client choice and bodily autonomy every step of the way.
- Consider your presence and comfortability with aspects of trauma-focused work such as intense affect, distress tolerance, and countertransference. Engage in your own EMDR and/or other healing work to support your nervous system throughout the process.

Erin E. Kelly, LCSW, REAT, RYT-500 (she/they) is a trained psychotherapist, clinical supervisor, and clinical consultant based out of Pittsburgh, Pennsylvania. Erin is an EMDRIA Certified Therapist, an EMDRIA Approved Consultant, and an EMDR training facilitator within the Institute for Creative Mindfulness network. A current doctoral student at California Institute of Integral Studies in the Transformative Studies Department, Erin is also exploring components of humility and vulnerability in healing relationships. As a white, queer, and neurodivergent provider, Erin aims to decolonize their therapeutic approaches as much as possible, while still currently holding state licensure—it's a work in progress!

References

Barker, M., Brewer, R. & Murphy, J. (2021). What is interoception and why is it important?. *Frontiers for Young Minds. 9*: 558246. doi: 10.3389/frym.2021.558246

Clark, P., Holden, C., Russell, M., & Downs, H. (2022). The impostor phenomenon in mental health professionals: Relationships among compassion fatigue, burnout, and compassion satisfaction. *Contemporary Family Therapy, 44*(2), 185–197. doi:10.1007/s10591-021-09580-y

Dana, D. (2021). *Anchored: How to befriend your nervous system using polyvagal theory*. Boulder, CO: Sounds True.

Doherty, M., Neilson, S., O'Sullivan, J., Carravallah, L., Johnson, M., Cullen, W., & Shaw, S. C. K. (2022). Barriers to healthcare and self-reported adverse outcomes for autistic adults: a cross-sectional study. *BMJ Open*, 12(2), e056904. doi: 10.1136/bmjopen-2021-056904

Duncan, B. L., Miller, S. D., Wampold, B. E., & Hubble, M. A. (Eds.). (2009). *The heart and soul of change: Delivering what works in therapy* (2nd ed.). Washington, D.C. : American Psychological Association.

Flückiger, C., Del Re, A. C., Wampold, B. E., Symonds, D., & Horvath, A. O. (2012). How central is the alliance in psychotherapy? A multilevel longitudinal meta-analysis. *Journal of Counseling Psychology, 59*(1), 10–17. doi:10.1037/a0025749

Garner, H. (2015). EMDR in the treatment of dissociative disorders. Retrieved from https://www.carolynspring.com/blog/emdr-in-the-treatment-of-dissociative-disorders

George, R., & Stokes, M. A. (2018). Gender identity and sexual orientation in autism spectrum disorder. *Autism: The International Journal of Research and Practice, 22*(8), 970–982. doi:10.1177/1362361317714587

Haikal, M. (2022). A Systematic Review of the Impact of Personal Therapy on Therapists. *Current Research in Psychology and Behavioral Science, 3*, 1069.

Hanville, C., MacInnis, C., & Lanza, T. (2024). Emergent neurodivergent: Neurodiversity-affirming therapeutic education. The Therapist, January-February, California Association of Marriage and Family Therapists (CAMFT). Retrieved February 16, 2025 from www.camft.com/org/Resources/Read-The-Therapist/The-Therapist-January-February-2024

Hanville, C. (2025). Affirming EMDR at the intersection of gender identity and neurodiversity. *Go With That Magazine, 30*(1), 13-23.

Hartley, G., Sirois, F., Purrington, J., & Rabey, Y. (2024). Adverse Childhood Experiences and Autism: A Meta-Analysis. *Trauma, violence & abuse, 25*(3), 2297–2315. doi: 10.1177/15248380231213314

Haruvi-Lamdan, N., Horesh, D., Zohar, S., Kraus, M., & Golan, O. (2020). Autism Spectrum Disorder and Post-Traumatic Stress Disorder: An unexplored co-occurrence of conditions. *Autism: The International Journal of Research and Practice, 24*(4), 884–898. doi: 10.1177/1362361320912143

Horvath, A. O. (2001). The alliance. *Psychotherapy: Theory, Research, Practice, Training, 38*(4), 365–372. doi:10.1037/0033-3204.38.4.365

James, S.E., Herman, J.L., Durso, L.E., & Heng-Lehtinen, R. (2024). *Early insights: A report of the 2022 U.S. transgender survey*. National Center for Transgender Equality, Washington, D.C., Retrieved on February 18, 2025 from https://ustranssurvey.org/download-reports

Karver, M. S., Handelsman, J. B., Fields, S., & Bickman, L. (2006). Meta-analysis of therapeutic relationship variables in youth and family therapy: the evidence for different relationship variables in the child and adolescent treatment outcome literature. *Clinical Psychology Review, 26*, 50–65.

Kent, M. (2006). proprioception. In The Oxford Dictionary of Sports Science & Medicine: Oxford University Press. Retrieved 2 May. 2025, from https://www.oxfordreference.com/view/10.1093/acref/9780198568506.001.0001/acref-9780198568506-e-5578.

Koyama, R., & Ikegaya, I. (2023). Microglia in the pathogenesis of autism spectrum disorders. *Neuroscience Research, 100,* 1-5. doi: 10.1016/j.neures.2015.06.005.

MacInnis, C. (2025). Neurodiversity affirming EMDR: Pathological Demand Avoidance. *Go With That Magazine, 30*(1), p. 3-11.

Martin, D. J., Garske, J. P., & Davis, M. K. (2000). Relation of the therapeutic alliance with outcome and other variables. *Journal of Consulting and Clinical Psychology, 68*(3), 438-450. doi:10.1037/0022-006X.68.3.438

Mascarell Maričić, L., Walter, H., Rosenthal, A. et al. The IMAGEN study: a decade of imaging genetics in adolescents. *Molecular Psychiatry, 25,* 2648–2671. doi: 10.1038/s41380-020-0822-5

McVey, A. J., Glaves, K. J., Seaver, S., & Casagrande, K. A. (2023). The ethical imperative to honor autistic clients' autonomy in mental health treatment. *Frontiers in Psychiatry, 14*. doi: 10.3389/fpsyt.2023.1259025

National LGBT Health Education Center (2020). Neurodiveristy and gender diverse youth: An affirming approach to care 2020. Retrieved on February 19, 2025 from https://www.lgbtqiahealtheducation.org/wp-content/uploads/2020/08/Neurodiversity-and-Gender-Diverse-Youth_An-Affirming-Approach-to-Care_2020.pdf

Neff, M. A. (2024). Neurodivergent affirming practice: Helping your clients accept their authentic selves. *Neurodivergent Insights*. Retrieved February 17, 2025 from https://neurodivergentinsights.com/blog/neurodivergent-affirming-practices/

Norcross, J. C., & Lambert, M. J. (2019). Evidence-based psychotherapy relationships: The third task force. In J. C. Norcross & M. J. Lambert (Eds.), *Psychotherapy relationships that work: Evidence-based therapist contributions* (pp. 1–23). Oxford University Press. doi:10.1093/med-psych/9780190843953.003.0001

Norcross, J. C., & Wampold, B. E. (2019). (Eds.). Psychotherapy relationships that work. Vol. 2: Evidence-based responsiveness (3rd ed.). Oxford University Press.

Oswald, T. (2024, October). A Neurodiversity-affirming approach to treat "autistic trauma". Psychotherapy Networker Conference presentation, Anaheim, CA.

Pecora, L. A., Mesibov, G. B., & Stokes, M. A. (2016). Sexuality in high-functioning autism: A systematic review and meta-analysis. *Journal of Autism and Developmental Disorders, 46*(11), 3519–3556. doi:10.1007/s10803-016-2892-4

Price, D. (2025). *Unmasking for life: The autistic person's guide to connecting, loving, and living authentically.* New York: Harmony Books.

Price, D. (2022). *Unmasking autism: Discovering the new faces of neurodiversity.* New York: Harmony Books.

Reuben, K. E., Stanzione, C. M., & Singleton, J. L. (2021). Interpersonal Trauma and Posttraumatic Stress in Autistic Adults. *Autism in Adulthood: Challenges and Management, 3*(3), 247–256. doi: 10.1089/aut.2020.0073

Rosati, F., Lorusso, M. M., Pistella, J., Giovanardi, G., Di Giannantonio, B., Mirabella, M., Williams, R., Lingiardi, V., & Baiocco, R. (2022). Non-Binary Clients' Experiences of Psychotherapy: Uncomfortable and Affirmative Approaches. International journal of environmental research and public health, 19(22), 15339. doi: 10.3390/ijerph192215339

Rumball, F., Brook, L., Happé, F., & Karl, A. (2021). Heightened risk of posttraumatic stress disorder in adults with autism spectrum disorder: The role of cumulative trauma and memory deficits. *Research in Developmental Disabilities, 110*. doi: 10.1016/j.ridd.2020.103848

Shapiro, F. (2018). *Eye movement desensitization and reprocessing: Basic principles, protocols, and procedures* (3rd ed.). New York: Guilford Press.

Shirk, S. R., & Karver, M. (2003). Prediction of treatment outcome from relationship variables in child and adolescent therapy: a meta-analytic review. *Journal of Consulting and Clinical Psychology, 71*, 452–464.

Shkedy, G., Shkedy, D. & Sandoval-Norton, A.H. (2021). Long-term ABA Therapy Is Abusive: A Response to Gorycki, Ruppel, and Zane. *Advances in Neurodevelopmental Disorders, 5*, 126–134 (2021). doi:10.1007/s41252-021-00201-1

Tervalon, M. & Murray-Garcia, J. (1998). Cultural humility versus cultural competence: A critical distinction in defining physician training outcomes in multicultural education, *Journal of Health Care for the Poor and Underserved, 9*(2), 117-125.

Valentine, S. E., Livingston, N. A., Salomaa, A.C., Shipherd, J.C. (2022). Trauma, discrimination, and PTSD among LGBTQ+ people. National Center for PTSD. Retrieved on February 19, 2025 from https://www.ptsd.va.gov/professional/treat/specific/trauma_discrimination_lgbtq.asp

Walker, C. (2021). *Neuroqueer Heresies*. Autonomous Press.

Warrier, V., Greenberg, D.M., Weir, E. Buchingham, C., Smith, P., Lai, M.C., Allison, C, & Baron-Cohen, S. (2020). Elevated rates of autism, other neurodevelopmental and psychiatric diagnoses, and autistic traits in transgender and gender-diverse individuals. *Nature Communications, 11*, 1-12. doi:10.1038/s41467-020-17794-1

Weir, E., Allison, C., & Baron-Cohen, S. (2021). The sexual health, orientation, and activity of autistic adolescents and adults. *Autism research: Official journal of the International Society for Autism Research, 14*(11), 2342–2354. doi:10.1002/aur.2604

Wood, J. J., & Gadow, K. D. (2010). Exploring the nature and function of anxiety in youth with autism spectrum disorder. *Clinical Psychology: Science and Practice, 17*(4), 281-92. doi:10.1111/j.1468-2850.2010.01220.x.

Xiong, Y., Chen, J., & Li, Y. (2023). Microglia and astrocytes underlie neuroinflammation and synaptic susceptibility in autism spectrum disorder. *Frontiers in Neuroscience, 17*. doi: 10.3389/fnins.2023.1125428

Zhan, Y., Paolicelli, R. C., Sforazzini, F., Weinhard, L., Bolasco, G., Pagani, F., Vyssotski, A. L., Bifone, A., Gozzi, A., Ragozzino, D., & Gross, C. T. (2014). Deficient neuron-microglia signaling results in impaired functional brain connectivity and social behavior. *Nature Neuroscience, 17*(3), 400–406. doi: 10.1038/nn.3641

Finger Waving The Gay Away

Mishma Kumar-Jonson, AMHSW

Jason, a 38-year-old gay,
I mean straight man of colour started to work with me in therapy.
On the intake form, he says,
"I think I have some trauma that I ? *think* it's time I work through
You know, for my boyfriend
I mean girlfriend Maria
because ***she*** thinks I have pent up stuff I haven't dealt with yet and that's why I'm so angry all the time
but *my best bud* Eddie Romirez knows that *that's* the stuff that made me who I am today, a strong and resilient man who makes him laugh
like the sun ain't met the other side of the moon,
anyway,
I've had EMDR before and it like REALLY worked, and I'd like to deal with my anger issues, so... do you think you could see me soon?"

Jason starts coming in weekly,
first, we worked through his history,
He tells me that he is from a small super catholic family,
there are coils that start to tighten in my belly.

He tells me of the pastor, of his church, of his mother, never mentions a lover, of his school, of his father, of all the ways he never quite fit in given he was, you know, into music theatre.

"But I got over all of that nonsense" he says with a rehearsed quickness, the coils tighten, his breathing quickens.

In his 2nd session, I ask Jason about whether he was ever smacked or punished as a child and he says, "Oh you know, I got in trouble a few times

but who wasn't smacked in the 80's he laughs,
no mirth reaching his eyes,
a smaller part mutters
"at least that part we survived".
Jason doesn't recall saying anything out loud when I say "pardon"?
The coils now a spring-loaded vertical drop screaming there's a little boy in there that is still hurting!

I ask about friends and lovers, and his eyes start to dart in a way that screams "run from the danger",
the topic change is swift,
He asks me how long this is going to take before we get to 'the good stuff' "What is the good stuff, Jason?" I ask,
"Oh, you know, the finger waving so I am not so angry anymore; I know that's how it works, I've been here before".
I notice the ghost of skin long shed twitching but saying no more.
After some ducking and weaving, bobbing and teetering,
in minute 50 of 50 with hand on doorknob Jason says,
"oh there was that one time I was sent to camp where they EMDRd the gay away", "It was like magic",
"This stuff really works"
"I can't wait to get into it".
"Is that what you meant by
Adverse.
Childhood.
Experiences?"
"Anyway, see you next week Mish!"
Coils now frozen, shatter into a million pieces.

It takes us 6 months for Jason to come to the truth that EMDRing the gay away is another way of saying conversion therapy,
and he has a hard time understanding why I
a queer, non-binary person
would not offer the same kind of service when there is
"quote – so much money to be made in that"
"trust me, I'd know"

I have started pumping bile by the litre in our sessions, burning holes into what I hope is the eyes of the men who looked at a child and saw their own abasement. Locked him away to live in a world that has learnt to play victim
Him, a 13-year-old boy the perpetrator,
of a crime so egregious, the thought of him so outrageous they pay to strip him down to a whip,
self-flagellation
he now proudly holds a new tongue that pronounces it
discipline.

In our first processing session,
He holds my fingers in his eyes
like it's the last shred of hope he has
to quell this ocean so deep it stretches generations.
So wide, it encompasses entire family trees,
their roots interweave
snaking beneath the debris
The rot has set in but not untreatable
Another set pausing, I say,
"Perhaps a deep breath, what are you noticing?"

He breathes in like a man who has seen the inside of too many shattered dreams, Incredulously,
Like if he was to allow his chest to compress,
it might just forget that it has a right to hold anything.
"*I just don't think I'm supposed to exist, it's just not natural*" he says,
"Can you show me where you are holding the first time you learnt that in your body" I ask with the steadiness of the Richter.

He takes me back to 13, eyes darting [read from left to right, line by line]

The lounge room	The skirt
The barbie movie	The twirl

The whip
The freeze
The fear
The parts
The hiding
The phone calls
The drive
The dark cabin
The bribe
The being alone with so many men
The pleading
The sealing
The EMDR
The bruising
The torture

The screaming
The splitting
The internal soothing
The fronting
The sealing
The pleading
The pleading
The pleading
The teary goodbye
The void ripping
The cutting
The void growing
The biting
The burning
The breaking.

…

The back straightening,
the eyes up,
facial features rearranging,
the thin line of a mouth hardening,
the void chasming,
the shaving,
the forced dating,
the social etiquette of the correct relationship,
the graduating,
the intercourse,
the void all ravaging,
the dissociating.

A door closes, a knight standing
I thank the protector for being so vigilant.

He tells me - to fuck right off.
It takes us 6 months for Jason and his now acquainted parts to come to the truth that EMDR never actually finger waved the gay away –
it was a lot to lose and far too much to gain.

Some say that you cannot land a whale in a canoe, I remind Jason that some days, whale acquainting requires hanging the mast of your healing on a spar of your resource team
Some days,
it's introducing the 13-year-old to bigger hands, the bigger body, the boyfriend's tan hands perfectly zipping into each other with the stability believing in your own damn skin brings
some days,
its thanking the suicidal parts,
the addiction parts,
the self-injury parts,
the I fucking hate you parts,
the you are worthless parts,
the I deserve this parts
the no one will ever love you parts
they are the keep you alive parts
in a world designed to kill your parts.

It takes Jason 6 months to say
I am a gay man without protector wielding the fog as armour.

It takes Jason 6 more months to say I am a married gay man, this time, protector has the best man's speech to honour.

Last week Jason said
I am going to be a father.

And the coils finally loosen,
As Jason sits next to 13 and 7

With protector now nurturer and torturer on vacation,
A smile on his lips,
No longer forged in damnation

Jason, a 40, gay married man of colour brings his daughter and *husband* Eddie Romirez to his last session
to say goodbye before leaving for a life of
queer joy and moments of whale acquainting.

Mish Kumar-Johnson (they/them), a plural system that is non-binary, queer, disabled, neurodivergent and a social worker of colour on land that always was and always will be Aboriginal Land, is an EMDR consultant and Practitioner. Mish is the Chair of The Iceberg Foundation and principal practitioner at Niram EMDR where they bring an anti-oppressive and anti-colonial lens to their practice with the LGBTIQAP+ and Neurodivergent communities across so called Australia.

The Sacred Work of Unbreaking

EMDR for the Queer Client's Recovery from Religious Harm

Stephanie Brashear, LPCC-S, LMHC

The South Carolina sky whirled above me. A bright blue with streaks of white. Swirling, faster and faster. My head began to rush as the tire swing began to slow its twirl. I straddled the tire with my head leaning against the rough rope. The air is humid and muggy. The gentle sway of the swing soothing my body. I loved twirling on that swing. The feeling of speed, the rush to my head, the way I could hear my heartbeat afterward.

I'm 10 years old, and it was just another weekday. Being homeschooled meant that once school was done, I could be outside. Sometimes I would traipse through the yard with my siblings. Other times my mom would load all of us onto our bikes and we would bike to the YMCA a little over a mile away. This day was one of the days that I just roamed. I would find myself on the tire swing often, or getting ankle deep in the tiny creek behind our house.

I felt connected to my body, it felt like my whole being was one, moving in rhythm. It felt like every part of me made sense. I knew at that moment that I was good.

~

I'm sitting on the fourth pew on the right of Ebenezer Presbyterian Church. The pew is uncomfortable, the light pink cushion just thick enough so that you can notice what you're missing. The sermon just started, and I found myself letting my eye wander around the sanctuary, as much as I could without turning my head and looking around, something I knew would get me in trouble. We sit at the front of the church so there are less distractions for me and my siblings, but the entire time I find myself fidgeting, zoning out, and just wanting to go play.

This was the church I was raised in. A conservative church with a large population of homeschooled families. Many of the families in my homeschool group attended Ebenezer, making our small social circle feel even smaller.

I catch bits and pieces of what the pastor is saying, mostly I just focus on how to arrange my face and body so that it looks like I'm paying attention while I let myself daydream. The sanctuary feels huge to me. The ceiling is way above me.

"I wonder if those lights would hurt people if they fell?," I think to myself, looking at the ornate lighting above me.

I normally love big spaces. When I would play in my backyard, or around the lake near my house, I would sometimes think "this is how I know that god is real." I would feel connected to the world around me, connected to myself, connected to god. So why is it that when I'm at church, "god's house," I feel so small and trapped?

There was a feeling I would get whenever I walked into church. I would think of it as "church feeling." A pit in my stomach, a sense of dread, a feeling of being watched. I had that feeling today. I squirm in my seat, rubbing the insides of my feet together back and forth. That always helped me feel more settled. Today it wasn't working.

~

I never thought I was straight. There wasn't a big moment that caught me off guard. I always knew that I didn't just like folks of the opposite sex. I also intuitively knew this was something completely off limits. I found myself heavily involved in theatre throughout high school, finally feeling at home somewhere. While I wouldn't categorize the church and family I was raised in as overtly hateful, what I was around felt much more insidious. Messaging about someone losing their way, not living in the will of god, and sentiments of distaste were always present.

Coming out never felt like an option, mostly because I didn't feel like I had to. I never told anyone I was straight, it was their problem if they made those assumptions. Finishing high school and moving into college, I naturally found myself in a group of people who were almost all queer, and almost all completely closeted. Each of us fully open and accepting to those around us, but closing off that acceptance to ourselves.

I considered sharing my outing in this chapter but decided against it. The details of someone who knows you outing you doesn't particularly matter, though the impact absolutely does. At the time I was an adult, had my own home, my own community. The removal of choice that comes with being outed feels complex. After all, this isn't a side of me that I'm ashamed of, so why am I being made to feel this way?

~

I sat in my Ethics class in graduate school, I was in a small bible school in the center of the bible belt, completing my Masters in Clinical Counseling. I don't even remember what the topic for the class was that day. All I remember is the class getting derailed and discussing ways to "ethically not have to work with everyone." I remember heat filling my body as my professor enthralled the class with stories of how "gay people would try to make us lose our license." The professor gave ideas to the class of all the ways to not work with gay people without saying "I don't work with gay people."

"You can tell them that your caseload is full, or that you don't specialize in what they are seeking treatment for. Just never put that you don't work with gay people in writing."

She went on to say that gay people would take that proof and try to get Christian counselors' licenses revoked. It was one example of the demonization of the LGBTQIA+ community at my school.

It was awkward for me, being a queer person in the process of coming out/being outed, deconstructing my faith, all while attending a biblical university. Only one person in my cohort knew I was queer. It was a carefully guarded secret there, made even more important to me when a peer several years ahead of me was kicked out of the graduate program for coming out. I was socially out in my friend group, and was in the process of coming out to my family. I found myself code switching every time I drove down the boulevard toward campus, determined to make it the last few months.

The beliefs I found myself examining and my discontent with my program were further coated with pain as others frequently reminded me: "You chose to be here" and "You are paying to attend this program." Both things were true, and I knew that the way the university treated the LGBTQIA+ community as a whole was problematic at best and abusive at worst.

The focus of the clinical counseling department was to provide clinicians with a foundation of incorporating spirituality into the world of mental health care by not neglecting the spiritual component of care. Something with which I ultimately agreed. The significant difference being that I believed that incorporating spirituality in many forms could provide relief and peace for people, while the school taught the methods from an Evangelical stance.

Sitting in that classroom that day, I realized that the impact of organizations like this were beyond painful; the actions of some moved into oppressive territory at lightning speed. In my head, a dream began to formulate that would take years to manifest, and that I hope continues to grow. I dreamed of taking the lessons learned in graduate school to help folks in recovering from spiritual abuse and religious trauma. I envisioned using the very methods and principles taught to bring healing and respect to communities that were marginalized and harmed.

~

Eight years later I found myself sitting on the floor of my office, scanning through the documents in front of me.

"I am broken"
"There is something wrong with me"
"I'm damaged"
"I'm broken"
"I am not worthy"
"It's all my fault"
"I am broken."

I sifted through target selection pages from clients. Seeing the Negative Cognitions was confirmation to what my gut already knew. My community was hurting, each story uniquely different, yet with a thread tying them all together. I was holding a stack of client charts. Clients who had the commonality of being part of the queer community and who had recently left or were in the process of leaving High Control Religion (HCR).

Since leaving graduate school, the focus of my work has steadily shifted toward working folks recovering from spiritual harm. Part of this was circumstantial, and part was intentional. For the first few years of being in the field, I would primarily be working with families and children. I started to see themes of removal of choice at the root of so much of the pain that made its way into my office. I saw how just growing up in the bible belt negatively impacted folks, even if they weren't religious. I saw how religion in the American South and white supremacy was tightly intertwined.

When I first entered the field, I was practicing from a cognitive-behavioral therapy lens with a focus in Positive Parenting. What I was doing wasn't working. I felt like I was constantly trying to help someone put a bandaid on a gushing wound.

In my personal life, things felt about the same. I was in the process of coming out more publicly, making changes in my life that also felt equivalent to putting a bandaid on a gaping wound. I had quit my job as Director of Children's Ministry at a conservative church. I left a marriage due to my partner's substance misuse, I shifted how I engaged in friendships and socially. Small and large changes that helped me take back choice in my life. And yet something was still off. I started to feel a creeping fear that maybe the religion I grew up with and the school I had attended was right. Maybe I was worthless, wrong, permanently damaged. Maybe I couldn't trust myself after all. Maybe my emotions weren't to be trusted. Maybe I was wrong. Maybe I wasn't enough.

If you're a clinician you know the chance of parallel processing in our field is high. At this point in my life and in these early stages of my career, I was experiencing parallel processes daily as I worked with folks who felt as if they were not good enough.

"Same," I would think, as I sat across from them, desperately trying to find interventions that could provide an ounce of relief.

Every aspect of my life felt like it wasn't enough. I didn't have enough knowledge, the tools I could use weren't enough. It felt like I was simultaneously being smothered while running into a brick wall.

In 2020 I found myself in the middle of a pandemic, moving to Ohio, and starting a new life. I decided to get trained in EMDR Therapy, something that had been on my radar for a while. The training shifted my life. Professionally, my entire paradigm began to change. As soon as I was introduced to the Adaptive Information Processing (AIP) model, it felt like a piece clicked into place.

Intuitively, I knew that this is what I had been missing in my practice.

Personally, EMDR training was the beginning of a huge shift in my life as well. I mean, raise your hand if you went into EMDR training expecting to walk out with a nifty tool and instead leaving with a huge trailhead of the work that could be done in your own processing...not just me, huh?

Following training I reached out to an EMDR therapist, told her that I "just had a few traumas to process" and that I "Needed someone who was going to kick my ass." Thankfully, my therapist said that wasn't her approach but she would like to work with me anyways. It was the best two year investment of my life.

I still wasn't getting it. Being raised where life's greatest struggle (the fallen state of man) had a relatively simple fix (the sinner's prayer[1]), I moved through life with the approach that large problems needed simple, straightforward solutions. If I could also get these results without the pain of having to tell every detail, or *gasp* actually be seen and known by someone, all the better.

I envisioned EMDR as the old Kool-Aid commercial. You know the one, a large red jug, unapologetically plowing through walls? The unsuspecting family inside startled at first, but ultimately

1 The Sinner's Prayer is common in many evangelical and protestant circles. It is a prayer of repentance where a person acknowledges sin/wrong doing/separation from God/god and expresses desire to begin or reengage in a relationship with God/god, through Jesus Christ.

happy with the uninvited renovations, because the Kool-Aid is just that good. I was enticed by the idea. I didn't take into account the damaged drywall.

My therapist Michelle is a saint. If I ever write a memoir, I'm sure that that will be a chapter title. Michelle invited choice, identified my neurodiversity, and supported me in processing past hurts. She also showed me that EMDR only serves our clients when it's administered with our clients in mind.

Michelle brought in other modalities in Phase 2, that ultimately allowed me to reprocess smoothly. Much of our work together was building up the adaptive information I was working with, so that the stuck information had something with which to connect.

During this time I began connecting with my queer joy and I was reengaging with spirituality for the first time since leaving the bible school I attended. The intuitive knowledge that I experienced during EMDR training was the spark of trust that I needed with myself to know that I could learn, question, practice, and not allow the same hurt that had happened before. I created a plan of safety for myself when reengaging with spirituality. The foundation of this plan being that *humans are not inherently broken.*

The more I explored, the more I began to trust myself. I saw that I could read/listen to/experience something and know if I believed it or not. And I was no less of a person either way. When Dr. Laura Anderson released her book *When Religion Hurts You* (2023), I found new language with which to frame my experience and the experiences of my clients. Dr. Anderson discussed how HCR teaches a person *what* to think, but not *how to think*. The impact that this has on a person's ability to think critically, and trust themselves was evident in my own life and the life of my clients.

I began to learn more about how EMDR is developed from a place of privilege which inherently makes invisible the experiences of clients with complex trauma and trauma related to oppression. There is a hope/expectation that a person will be able to afford to attend weekly sessions, have a support system while reprocessing, can use Calm Space, Container, not be present with their abuser while reprocessing, etc. But what about when we live in a country where the Evangelical christian way of life is the norm? What if someone was taught that any meditation outside scripture-focused meditation was evil or sinful? How about when someone is trying to process trauma experienced in a group that the majority of their support system are still involved in? Most of all, I found myself cringing as I moved through the script. As a person who has left a HCR and was currently basking in a newly found choice, giving so much direction to someone else just felt off in some ways.

At this point in my EMDR journey I had completed certification and was completing hours as an EMDR Consultant-in-Training. I started to explore modifications and additional support to the 8 Phases that felt helpful to my clients. Generally, I'm a pretty direct and open person and asking for feedback with clients feels pretty comfortable. While not every person who has experienced religious abuse or spiritual trauma is queer, every queer person living in America has had exposure to religious abuse. While many think of religious abuse as only impacting those within those faith communities, religious abuse is the use of religious beliefs or practices to control another person or impose that view.

As an American, I have had exposure to religious abuse my entire life, regardless of my faith background. When laws are influenced by religion, when my right to marry my wife was debated, negotiated, and voted on, with politicians citing religious text, that is an attempt to control my life through religious beliefs. With this realization in mind, I began to understand why some of the intuitive adjustments I've made while doing EMDR with those impacted by HCR made sense. I started to take the information I had gathered from my work within this community and began to implement specific adjustments with the values of choice and permission being a primary focus. Below are some thoughts on how to expand the standard protocol for EMDR in order to care for those coming out of HCR. Special attention will be paid to unique queer experiences. Cases that I discuss are compilations of clients and their experiences so that anonymity can be protected.

Phase 1

Dr. Laura Anderson's offering of the Adverse Religious Experiences can be a hugely beneficial way of identifying areas of harm in a client's past. I do not hold to the common belief that a therapist needs to have experienced what their client experienced to be able to serve them well. *And* the language involved in HCR is a primary function of that religious group. The language holds weight, alternative meaning, and implications.

I view the Negative Cognitions (NC) as the name for the road that we are getting on. A pathway built of experiences, reactions, sensations. I have also begun to view these pathways as layered. Let me explain what I mean by that. A client may come to therapy with the NC "I am bad." Everything is going to plan, gathering floatback memories are a breeze and the client can clearly identify the first, the worst, and the most recent time they had this experience. Over the following sessions the target sequence is worked though, with each target clearing. The client completes a future template with the newly installed belief of "I'm a good person." As we move into Phase 8, the client is continuing to report sensing that they are bad. Does this mean that the work we just completed didn't work? Did we reprocess the correct targets? Was the information integrated correctly?

What I began to see with my clients was the faultiness of human language for spiritual wounds. Yes, they had a pathway of "I am bad" made up of experiences of being given detention, and cheating on a partner, and running into someone's car while parking and just driving away. But they also hold a pathway of "I am bad" that possesses so much more: experiences that language just doesn't fully encompass.

My work around? I just ask. I explain to my client the ideas of highways and discuss how sometimes roads have the same name though they are not completely connected. And then I ask "Is this the same bad, or does this bad feel different?" If they say it's different, I check in to see if that language is the absolute best fit. Sometimes it's not and we work together to find the right words. Other times it is. Many who have experienced spiritual harm began to have exposure to this harm since infancy. When born into a family who is religious, it's natural for this family to instill beliefs, judgements, and behaviors at a young age. This leads to implicit memories being present. Sometimes the language just isn't there.

Introducing EMDR to folks raised in HCR can be a challenge at times. My approach as a clinician is to consistently work toward dismantling the power differential in the room. During history taking, getting a clear understanding of what power and submission looked like in the world of the client will play a crucial role in creating safe guards for our work together.

Phase 2

Resourcing is any reliable way to help a person be "okay enough." Resourcing is an area that I have found needs the most attention when working with queer folks who have escaped HCR.

When someone is raised in high control religion, they are often taught that their god is the only source of comfort that they can rely on. When someone grew up believing that they had to pray whenever they are anxious, it would make sense that prayer would be a resource. Then what is to be done if that very resource needs to be reprocessed?

Phase 2 is where I often remind myself that everything is a just "for now." Who am I to tell someone that their resources aren't okay? I support clients in accessing the resources they have, and try to diversify their resources as much as possible in case a resource gets contaminated during reprocessing. Nurturing figures can feel particularly challenging. I have seen many clients who unconsciously developed a protector figure with attributes of an abuser. Because a phase of spiritual abuse is love bombing and inclusion, I have seen clients utilizing these figures and connecting them to people in their faith community who have harmed them. Encouraging the personification of plants and animals can help a client develop an attachment, protective, or nurturing figure without the similarities of their abusers. Use of Light Stream and other guided imagery can be challenging for clients. I once had a client adamantly tell me

"No" to Light Stream because it reminded them of being filled with the holy spirit.

Phase 3

The main considerations I make for phase three centers around perfectionism. For some folks who have experienced HCR, getting it "just right" feels extremely important. It can feel like the difference between heaven and hell. The Subjective Units of Disturbance (SUDs) and the Validity of Cognition (VoC) can be particularly challenging when there is a pattern of looking to others for that information.

Whenever I provide consultation, something many of my consultees will hear is "know the why so you can know why you're changing it." The *why* behind the SUDs and the VOC is to track movement and progress and to recognize stuck points, primarily for the purpose of safety for the client. So with that "why" in mind, and understanding how a client could get stuck in the standard phrasing of things, a clinician now has the freedom to move away from numbers (especially at the very beginning) to help a client get started.

Here are a few ways that I track SUDs or VOC without numbers:

- Descriptive words: "When you are thinking about the worst part, along with the belief of __________" what are three words to describe how you're feeling?
- Hand movements: Starting with hands placed close together, show me how big the pain feels.
- Distance: "If the worst part was here, how close to you would it be right now?"
- Changing the numbers every time: Instead of 10 for SUDs and 7 for VoC, I may ask on a scale of 1-100, on a scale of 1-50, etc. This helps the focus shift away from precision and still allows me to see where that distress is located.

Phase 4

Can I be honest with you? Phase four is where I struggle most as an EMDR clinician. Not because I don't see the power of *going with that* or because I don't agree with the model of EMDR. Rather, I have a hard time keeping my mouth shut sometimes, especially when I hear clients repeating painful and harming beliefs. I have a part of me that is justice driven, that wants to rescue my clients from beliefs that cause so much pain, and from the outside, are so clearly not true.

Doing my own EMDR with these parts has helped me step back and trust the process more. However, I have found that with queer clients, specifically clients who have engaged in Christian/biblically based counseling or conversion therapy, I provide additional psychoeducation and preparation for phase 4.

I remember sitting across from a client who had gone through conversion therapy. We took our time building rapport and developing resources that worked for them. They selected a target with a more recent event, in hopes of easing their way in. We discussed that more past events were likely to come up and discussed continuing on if that were to happen. The metaphorical flight plan was agreed upon and off we went!

Things were moving as expected and a few dozen passes in, a memory from conversion therapy came up, specifically around the wrongness of my client. I said *go with that* and instantaneously, I knew it was a misstep. The client and I made eye contact and I could see the betrayal and disappointment in their eyes. I paused, we resourced together and I began the backtracking.

Although I had provided psychoeducation about the process of EMDR and the reasoning behind my limited input, we hadn't specifically discussed this possibility. That memories of another clinician convincing this client that they were broken and wrong would come up, and that I would not challenge it directly, but rather, suggest they go with that.

In our repair, there was a focus on the AIP model, that I trusted their brain and body had a way it was designed to process this information so that they could experience relief.

Phase 5

When moving into phase five, I typically view the uphill climb as over, and the speed that Phases 5-7 are completed are often rather quick. I've seen some differences with this when working with queer folks coming out of HCR. James Fowler developed and wrote about the Stages of Faith, consisting of seven primary stages that a person's spiritual journey can cover.

Pre-Stage: Undifferentiated Faith. This stage is the potential for faith. Normally considered for children under the age of 2, this phase focuses on how children experience faith as a connection to their caregiver. This may include prayers said before bedtime, witnessing their parents own faith, and witnessing the faith of their community. This stage introduces children to faith by building trust for it through the experience of trust in their caregivers.

Stage 1: Intuitive-Projective Faith. This phase speaks of preschool age children, where developmentally the ability to think abstractly is not present. Because children at this age view the world primarily through their own eyes, not others' perspectives, and cannot consider logical arguments and think through complex ideas, the experience of faith is impressed on them through action. This is the age that children are often involved in rituals in the faith communities of which they are a part. They are learning to engage in their faith communities through looking and experiencing.

Stage 2: Mythic-Literal Faith. This is often for children 6-12. It is in this stage that children begin to categorize fantasy from facts. Though abstract thought is still not present in this stage, perspective awareness is shifting. Children may be learning about faith from more than just their parents (they may have Sunday school teachers, priests, youth leaders, etc.). It is often in the later half of this stage that children often begin to have awareness that others outside of their faith believe differently from them.

Stage 3: Synthetic-Conventional Faith often begins around the age of 13 and continues to age 18. However, there are many people that never move past this stage at any point of their life. This is the first stage where people are thinking abstractly. There is more cohesion to a person's faith experience, where individual stories used to once feel unconnected, there are the beginnings of beginning to recognize consistency in themes around values and morality. It is in this stage that perception is able to be shifted in a way that a person can imagine what other people view of them and their faith. It is in this stage that authority within a faith group is very important. While 13-18 year olds still are looking toward their parents for spiritual authority, adults who are stuck in this stage are looking to those around them: pastors, faith leaders, and friends. In this stage spiritual authority resides almost entirely outside of a person.

Stage 4: Individuative Reflective Faith. If someone moves past this stage of faith, it often begins in early adulthood. However, there are people at all ages of adulthood who may be in this stage of faith. It is in this stage that people begin to question their own assumptions related to faith and the faith traditions they have participated in. It is also in this phase that people begin to question the authority structures of their faith. It is often that one may see a clash of folks in the third and fourth stages of faith development. When people begin to take more ownership of their own faith experiences, it can be threatening to the authority of faith structures that up until this point have gone unquestioned.

Stage 5: Conjunctive Faith. This stage is generally not reached until the early thirties. While Stage 4 is often a stage of discomfort and questioning, which can lead to disconnection from the faith community, this phase has led to maturity in a person's faith experience. They are now open to the faith practices of others around them, expanding the options for faith experiences.

Stage 6: Universalizing Faith. This is not a common phase and isn't one that all will reach. This stage describes when someone is no longer hemmed in by limitations of a religion or spiritual belief. There is a focus on justice, empathy and compassion for all.

EMDR Phase 5 can lead to some stuck points with those recovering from HCR when Fowler's phases aren't taken into consideration. Many times, folks in recovery may be in Stage 3, Synthetic-Conventional Faith. When exposure to beliefs not held within the HCR press against beliefs that have been learn and engrained since birth. This experience can often feel threatening, scary, and uncomfortable to those beginning to expand beyond the faith practices they were born into.

Additionally, many HCR's hold a focus on what to think, not how to think. This means that there are times when there is delayed cognitive development if this integral skill is not being compensated in other areas of a person's life. This form of rigid thinking can become very apparent in Phase 5. Blocks can happen when adaptive beliefs such as "I can trust myself," occur because this may be a full contradiction to what they were told growing up.

Some blocks I have seen folks run into have been:

- I was born this way.
- I can trust myself/I am trustworthy.
- I can believe in myself.
- I am good.

When these blocks occur, it is crucial for the therapist to keep in mind the client's history and where they are currently at spiritually. For folks raised with the belief that they were made and designed by god, and this belief is still present and feels beneficial, conversation around how the Adaptive Information Processing model actually fits into that belief can be helpful. Sometimes a pause assists to develop or strengthen adaptive information. This can involve protective and nurturing figures, exploration of other spirituality practices. Additionally, supporting the client in exploring and hearing stories of others' deconstruction [2] have been beneficial in helping clients develop adaptive information. I often refer to adaptive information as the interaction of two magnets being pulled together. The adaptive information pulling along and connecting the maladaptive information. The larger the magnet of adaptive information, the smoother and quicker this process is. When a person has not received adaptive information in their life, it is important to create opportunities for them to build this powerful magnet.

2 Deconstruction is a method of critical analysis of philosophical and religious beliefs. A reduction of something to its constitutional parts in order to reinterpret it and present it in a different way.

While I believe that the least amount of intervention needed is the way to go with EMDR, in this phase, I personally feel that is even more important. When someone has grown up in a cult or HCR, belief development often comes from the influence of those in power. I try my best to not input anything original during this phase, in hopes to not recreate that scenario again. When interweaves are used, I've found that coming back to the body, returning to the target image, or using specific phrases the client has used have felt more aligned therapeutically.

Phase 6

Like all other phases of EMDR Therapy, the success of Phase 6 is contingent upon the preparation in Phase 2. While the standard EMDR protocol is linearly laid out, I view Phase 2 as a continuous process, with each target cleared or phase completed, the client has more accessible adaptive information to resource and strengthen. Many folks in HCR experience disconnection from their bodies. I have observed this to be even more present with LGBTQIA+ folks.

Purity culture [3]and its impact in the Christian church can lead to a distrust of one's bodies and desires, lead to fear and shame related to natural sexual experiences, and blurs the lines of consent in a way that encourages dissociation from the body. When you add to the equation sexual connection with the same gender, gender non-conforming experiences, or trans experiences, it can lead to even stronger distrust or disconnect.

Lack of body awareness and sensation may be something you encounter with clients in HRC recovery. In Phase 6 when asked what they notice when they scan their body the answer very well may be "nothing." Clarifying if this is nothing as in "all clear" or nothing as in "numb" can be a helpful starting point as recommended in Dr. Jamie Marich's EMDR training manual with

---

3 Purity culture is an evangelical movement that gained popularity in the 1990s that promotes abstinence before marriage, often equating a person's purity to their worth. Purity culture impacts people of all genders, though an emphasis has traditionally been placed on assigned females at birth to avoid causing temptation to others by dressing modestly and engaging in a demure and restrained fashion.

the Institute for Creative Mindfulness. This work may be the first time that someone is experiencing embodiment, and can be a great time to strengthen the client's trust in their experience with their body. Phase 6 is a phase where I may change up the form of BLS if that could be helpful to the client. Engagement with tapping or other tactile movement may be supportive for clients who have primarily used eye movements or audio has been the main source of bilateral stimulation (BLS).

For folks who have never experienced safety in their body, any sensation may feel like a threat and emotional recognition may be challenging. Heart racing...could that mean anxiety or anticipation? Body sinking into the couch...is that hiding and discomfort or a feeling of relaxation? One of my favorite resources to introduce to clients is Mindfulness of Feeling Tone, which can also be found in the Institute for Creative Mindfulness' training manual by Dr. Jamie Marich. While supporting a client in bringing awareness to their body, I encourage them to name any sensation they have as either pleasant, unpleasant, or neutral. As a client's comfort grows with this exercise we may modify it by adding the question, "Is that sensation high energy or low energy?" So someone may notice a pleasant sensation in their chest and also notice this sensation is high energy. From there we can determine if that sensation may be signaling an emotion, such as excitement or eagerness. Referencing back to the client's history and what you know of them can help determine if a client is experiencing a disconnect or if they are in need of support for building adaptive information.

Some interweaves I find myself using in this phase are:

- Nothing as in all clear? Or nothing as in numb?
- Is your body asking for any movement or adjustments right now?
- What emotions are present with that feeling in your body?

Phase 7

When I first began doing EMDR I was pretty determined to not end EMDR sessions with a church service or an altar call. I experienced a lot of discomfort when first getting trained due to the nature of many resources and visualizations. Light Stream felt too much like anointing; protective and nurturing figures felt loaded. From my time as a staff member of a church, I have awareness of how heightened emotions are used to manipulate and expose. When working with clients who were already used to this process, with another clinician I wanted to ensure that I wasn't mimicking these experiences. I wanted to make sure space for needs was being created and honored.

From my first appointment with a client, I do my best to offer options and choices. My air system in my office is controlled by remote control, an easy way to invite small adjustments for clients simply by handing them the remote and encouraging its use. Asking for feedback in regular and consistent ways from the very beginning. When I was in graduate school and provisionally licensed, I was involved in gathering research for Partners for Change Outcome Management Systems (PCOMS). PCOMS is two, brief 4-item scales, one used at the beginning of the session (Outcomes Rating Scale), and one at the end of the session (Session Rating Scale). The results of which were openly discussed and used to help increase collaboration and promote better outcomes for clients. One primary element I took from PCOMS was the discovery that lower rated satisfaction of sessions or the therapist themselves didn't necessarily indicate poorer outcomes, it actually indicated that clients felt comfortable providing feedback which led to improvements in the therapeutic alliance. While I don't utilize formal PCOMS anymore with regularity, the premise and comfort with feedback is something that I deeply value.

This comfort with feedback, paired with clinician flexibility means that closure can be expansive and supportive to the client's system. Following up week to week about the hours following sessions can provide the insight needed around adjustments and additional support.

Phase 8

I've never seen someone process their trauma and stay the same. Now, you're probably thinking...obviously? That's the point, right? Let me explain. When someone starts processing the hurt they've experienced, there is often a lot of hope about what changes *will* happen. They may be hoping for less flashbacks, more confidence, improvements in self talk, a desire to be more engaged in relationships. There is often no shortage of what folks hope could happen in the course of healing.

What isn't always a focus is the changes that *will have* to occur along the way. When someone comes to therapy to process their childhood trauma, they are rarely daydreaming about whether the status quo they have lived with for so long isn't going to be what they need anymore. That job that was fine? Suddenly the toxicity of the workplace is so clear. Those relationships that felt safe and familiar? Now the similarity between you and your partner's relationships and the relationship your parents had is on the forefront of your mind and you aren't sure you can look past that.

When you process your trauma, everything has the potential to change. Family relationships, career, your relationship with food and money, friendships, partnerships, you name it; there is a chance it will be affected. I think there is a perception that going back and witnessing the pain a person has experienced is the worst part of trauma treatment. And yes, it takes connection and courage to do that work. However, I truly believe it's the idea of what comes next that is so scary for many. The crumbs that once sustained you will no longer be acceptable when you've experienced sustenance.

The reevaluation phase is not only an opportunity to check back on target selection and adjust target sequencing, it is an invitation for change and grief. This may look like a queer client who has maintained relationships with harmful community members, now seeing their self-worth and knowing those relationships have to change. It may mean more openness or boundaries around privacy. It is also a chance to explore changes in their spirituality for faith practices.

Perfectionism can easily come to the forefront during this phase, and is something to slow down and explore with clients. When someone is coming out of a faith practice that has told them that perfection was needed in order to be valuable, cared for or seen, it's understandable why clients may be eager to rush to the next target, as though their NCs are a to-do list that has to be done. EMDR is not another form of penance, something to do to finally not feel broken.

~

I collapse onto my bed breathless, my ADHD medication has worn off and I have the zoomies. I am currently regaling my wife with one of our favorite bits, interpretive dancing and all. We tell each other about our day, there is a lot of laughter, and an obnoxious amount of puns. This is our routine most evenings, we often joke that we are having a slumber party. Nights like tonight feel reminiscent of sleepovers from high school, laughing till we cry, inside jokes that only she would understand, and wanting to stay up late just to savor each and every moment. We have taken to pressing our foreheads against the others' and having full-blown conversations, trying not to be the first one to break into laughter.

Rebekah caught me by surprise when we met. She quite literally wrote her way into my heart, filling the box by my bed with poetry and letters. She's incredible. Thoughtful and wise, tender and sassy. She also comes from a past where harm has occurred in the name of god. She is living proof that humanity is good at its core, and there is nothing greater than loving others as herself. Every time I am with her, it feels like being on that tire swing again. Embodied, joyous, connected, and good. A reminder that I, as a person, makes sense.

Stephanie Brashear, LMHC, LPCC-S (she/her) is a queer therapist, EMDR Consultant-in-Training, and founder of Root and Grow, a private practice in Providence, Rhode Island. With bachelor's degrees in Biblical Studies and Family & Church Education, and a counseling degree earned while leaving a high-control religious environment, Stephanie brings a deep, embodied understanding to her work with clients healing from religious trauma. She offers care rooted in EMDR, and Internal Family Systems (IFS), with a special focus on supporting LGBTQIA+ individuals. Her approach blends scientific grounding with intuitive, relational care, honoring both the physiological and spiritual dimensions of healing. Stephanie also provides consultation to other therapists learning to apply EMDR with nuance and care. Outside the therapy room, she lives in Providence with her wife, where they are building a sacred life of joy.

References

Anderson, L. E. (2023). *When religion hurts you: Healing from religious trauma and the impact of high-control religion*. Ada, MI: Brazos Press.

Fowler, J. W. (1981). *Stages of faith: The psychology of human development and the quest for meaning*. New York: Harper & Row.

Marich, J. (2020). *Eye movement desensitization and reprocessing (EMDR) therapy: Training course, Part I*. Warren, OH: The Institute for Creative Mindfulness.

The Intersection of Intersex & EMDR

Mariena Joy, LCSW

Author's Note: To my brother Jon, who encouraged me to start teaching about EMDR & my intersex identity when I was uncertain but couldn't find ANYONE else to to teach me more. As Jon said "Ah, yes, the 'ask an adult, oh wait I am the adult' of academic sources."

To my friend Jacob Dougherty, who was the first person I ever spoke these thoughts out loud to and said, "Queen, you could publish that." To my best friend, Dr. Alisse Diers, who listened endlessly while I talked this stuff out for YEARS. Bless her, she's a saint.

And to my courageous fellow intersex people who have graciously given me permission to share pieces of their journey.

Content note: If you have gender dysphoria or a complicated relationship with your body and gender, some of the content that I write about in this chapter can be activating so please, do what you need to do to take care of yourself. For safety considerations, some of the following vignettes have had key identifying information changed, or may be a combination of people. All names have been changed, except mine.

Definitions & Chapter Foundations

Intersex people are at least as common as redheads (Carroll, 2005; Fausto-Sterling, 1993; Organisation Intersex International Australia, 2012b). Know a redhead? Chances are you know an intersex person. Despite this population size, intersex people receive very limited visibility in the media, health care education, LGBTQIA education, and in health care policies in law. Before we really get rolling into this chapter, let's open with some basic working definitions so we are all on the same page. InterACT advocates for intersex youth defines intersex and sex characteristics the following ways:

> "*Intersex* is an umbrella term for unique variations in reproductive or sex anatomy. Variations may appear in a person's chromosomes, genitals, sex hormones, or internal organs like testes or ovaries. Some intersex traits are identified at birth, while others may not be discovered until puberty or later in life."
>
> "*Sex characteristics* is a term that often refers to the internal and external traits of an individual's body. Gender and sexual orientation are different concepts. Intersex people can have any gender identity and sexual orientation" (interACT: Advocates for Intersex Youth, n.d., "What is the definition of intersex?" section).

It's important to understand that intersex is NOT about gender, gender identity, or sexual orientation. While it can affect those things, intersex is about your SEX. Some intersex people identify as transgender, many do not. As someone who is an intersex person myself, I've experienced firsthand how confusing all these things can be without clear information.

In this chapter we start with this introduction section that includes definitions, this chapter breakdown, and an introduction to me. Then we will move on with multiple case vignettes to illustrate the variation of intersex experiences and multiple ways that EMDR can be helpful to provide affirmative care when working with intersex folks. These vignettes also help highlight the wide variations there are in potential targets, considerations for why therapists should know basic information about what intersex means, and to start to paint a picture about the sheer breadth of intersex experiences.

Next, I will talk more about why cursory knowledge of intersex identities matter for therapists, and then dive into the fourth section of this chapter, recommendations for practice. This includes: basic expectations around education, Intake and EMDR Phase 1, affirmative information you can provide, asking for consent around addressing somatic issues, interpersonal dynamics around safety, negative & positive cognitions, target selection [including a table of potential targets], resourcing in the middle of trauma, and Marie's very own *Script for Stabilizing Sense of Self.*

Introduction to Me

My name is Mariena Joy. I am a queer, neurospicy, intersex person who grew up lower class but have had the good luck to live in the middle class most of my life. I am privileged to have been able to get a master's degree in social work and go on to become a specialized EMDR therapist with a private practice. I hold many other identities that have shaped my approaches –bi-racial, living as a system of parts, survivor of domestic violence, independent business owner, and more. I am privileged to share my lived and professional experience with you all in this chapter. The following case vignettes are just the beginning of some of those experiences that illustrate just how varied intersex experiences can be. And how EMDR can be adapted to meet those needs.

Case Vignettes

TJ: A Case of Firsts

Early in my therapy career, before I even knew what the words *intersex* or *EMDR* meant, a young trans man named TJ came into my office for our first appointment. The first thing he wanted me to know was, "I hate being everyone's first client with xyz." He shared that over the years he had been trying to get medical care and therapy but he had, time and time again, been an oddity. A medical oddity and a mental health oddity.

"I am so tired of being a learning opportunity. Of being everyone's first. A doctor's first, a therapist's first. I'm just really tired and I need to know that you know what you're doing." As a first year intern, I didn't know what the hell I was doing. Frankly, I was upset for TJ, because why on earth would management send someone to me who was so clearly out of my scope of practice.

I was also floored by how deeply I resonated with what this human had just said. This human who had a body shaped like mine. Who was everyone's first, just like me. So we made an agreement.

That I would listen to the things he wanted help with, and to the things that he was very tired of being "People's First" around. And that I would tell him which things I had experience around; which things I had lived myself, and which things I needed to go get training on. And then he could decide if he wanted to stay with me or see someone else. TJ graciously gave me the opportunity to hear what he had to say.

To this day, I agree with him that I should not have been assigned to him that early in my career. Someone in management decided that there was something about us that made us both "a little different" and we "might be a good fit." I know because that is what management told me when I asked why.

In one way management was correct, this human and I had a shared lived experience of being clocked as outside the binary; of being othered/marginalized for this. Even though we didn't know the word for it at that time, he and I both knew that the shared understanding was important.

I made an agreement with TJ to refer him to someone else on my team and that I would go get training on suicidality, transgender healthcare, and a few other things that he needed. And I did. Six-ish months later he and I started a therapeutic relationship that has come and gone over the years. I got to watch him grow up. We have been able to work together as he learned about his intersex identity when I learned about mine. We learned that we have at least one identical medical condition that makes us intersex people. EMDR was useful in processing his history of medical trauma, of being people's *first*, about the change in his understanding of his gender identity.

I've been there with him while he went through EMDR and processed that he may never be able to have children, all the while processing my own inability to do the same. While his experience of gender goes a different direction than mine, I've been privileged to walk alongside him and be in a unique space to understand being transgender and getting gender affirmation care as an intersex person. Where you have to explain that your hormones are "not like other girls," so the hormones that you need for your care are not like every transgender person. And while he may have been my first in many ways, TJ shared how important it was that I was the first that understood him because I had also lived it.

P.S. He's so grown up and I am SO proud of him. He's a blooming young professional in the social services field and it fills my heart with immense joy to hear from people whose life he has touched. He's doing well.

Sean: A Case of Culture, Identity, and Fertility Trauma

Years into my career, I had established a thriving private practice in the small rural Oregon community where I lived. Even though it was scary, we advertised that our focus was LGBTQIA+ and neurospicy (autism & adhd) identities. Over the years, whenever I think about threats or homophobia that we experienced, I remind myself of Sean and how it was worth it to be visible.

I was shocked to get a voicemail from Sean, a police officer who wanted to know if I had any openings and could see him. I honestly thought it must have been a mistake and I called to ask if he understood what my clinic was and the population we served. He knew.

Sean was a man who had lived his life in a way that made him feel masculine. He was heavily muscled, living traditional gender roles within his marriage, and in a career that he felt was very masculine. Sean and his wife had been struggling to conceive for quite some time. He contacted me after testing came back that the reason Sean was having these difficulties was because he was an intersex person. Genetically, he did not have standard issue XY chromosomes. Sean had Klinefelter Syndrome (XXY chromosome).

Sean was at a total loss. He was grieving the loss of potential future biological children, yes, and so much more than that. Sean was facing extreme grief and fear and ego death. The loss of his identity as a man based on what he *believed* men to be. Fear that anyone would find out. That he would be rejected by his wife, his family, his friends, and his coworkers. Sean's fear was very valid, because he knew how he would respond to someone in his life if he learned they had this condition. Sean felt alone and terrified. His extreme feelings of hopelessness, suicidal thoughts, easy access to lethal means, and (understandable) reticence to include anyone in his treatment made me very worried that he would not live through this.

Working with Sean cemented in my mind the importance of understanding the complexities of trauma that intersex people can face. Sean and I had to work to shift his entire understanding of gender and community. Teaching Sean that the sex you are born with is not a choice (it's biology, baby), and that his GENDER is whomever/whatever he FEELS. Gender is not a choice, it's what you feel. Teaching him that *he is a man because he felt like a man*. Using EMDR, we worked to help shift his negative beliefs of "I'm not a man" to something that felt right for him. Over time Sean was able to believe that, regardless of being an intersex person, he was a man.

Helping Sean understand that he had choices for having children (including pursuing medical interventions to potentially have his own biological children) helped address the hopelessness. Working with him to increase the belief that he had choices in who to trust and how he shared information helped him increase feelings that he could keep himself safe, even in spaces where people wouldn't understand.

Part of his healing journey was connecting with anonymous places online where he could connect with the intersex community, where he can speak with other men and be understood. He needed to believe that he had community and that he was not alone. Over time, as his understanding of these things changed, he was able to see how toxic people can be around binary gender roles. And I was moved as I watched him interact with the world around him in different ways.

I still think of Sean, living his life, his intersex identity a secret, while quietly challenging the thoughts, beliefs, and behaviors of people in his world. Every once in a while we spot each other and I'm happy to see he is alive. I don't know if he ended up pursuing medical treatment to be able to have his own children, but it's good to know that he has the information so he can make that choice.

Sean reminded me that visibility matters — not just for clients to find us, but for us to challenge the assumptions we carry about sex, gender, and what healing looks like.

Annette: A Case of Adoption Trauma and Provider Knowledge

Once I began to speak about intersex identities and EMDR, I started to get calls for consultation from all over the world. While I struggle to think of myself as a specialist in EMDR for intersex folks, the editor of this volume, Roshni Chabra, insists, "I know it is hard to be thrown into it but you are an expert based on lived experience and I know the world needs and benefits from your voice and your leadership." I may not have set out to be a specialist consultant for intersex and EMDR, but as more therapists reached out, I realized how urgently BASIC knowledge was needed.

One such consultation was around a woman who we will call Annette, who had been adopted from an Asian country as a child. She didn't find out until much later that she had been put up for adoption due to having "ambiguous genitalia" and had undergone surgery as an infant to "correct" this.

The clinician who was calling me said "I don't know where to start with her." They didn't know how to talk about intersex identities and how this related to trauma around adoption and surgery. Yet this clinician was excellent at understanding adoption trauma. And excellent at working with early childhood surgeries. My work as a consultant was helping them understand that they already knew most of what they needed to help Annette, and filling in the blanks about identity and gender and oppression related to binary norms. Teaching them the importance of connecting Annette with the community so she could know that she is not alone in her experiences.

Alex: A Case of Complex Trauma and Infantalization

Alex is a queer, neurodiverse adult in their twenties, who was referred to me by a psychiatric provider due to complex psychosomatic symptoms, extreme levels of dissociation, and concerns by the provider that the client may be a victim of factitious disorder imposed on another (previously *Munchausen syndrome by proxy*). Alex is a brilliant human whose parent was in the medical field. The first stages of EMDR history taking were a bone chilling account of how their parent had control of their extensive, and often experimental, medical care since infancy. Alex was aware that they had a medical condition that affected their sexual development, but were unaware that this made them intersex. As the story unfolded, I was horrified to learn that Alex had been treated as a medical oddity by the medical community and a parent who was obsessed with "fixing" Alex, while at the same time, dismissing their voice. Alex expressed that the medical community "was often dismissive." Alex continues, "I saw SO many providers, and they would do all this testing but then only talk to me for 15 minutes and then give me a diagnosis that wasn't right. It's like they didn't want to see me."

Over our time together, Alex was able to unpack that they had been infantilized and made to believe that their medical conditions meant that they could never live on their own, that they would be unable to care for their complex medical needs. Alex's medical trauma, conditioning, and a variety of other factors resulted in them having extreme distress noticing or even THINKING about having a body at all. Their window of tolerance around body mindfulness was at such an extreme low, they would experience dissociative fugues or, if we were lucky, an intense sense of depersonalization when the topic was broached. The same was true around the topics of medical abuse/enmeshment with their parent.

Our EMDR journey could be broken down into multiple key additions to standard protocols (some of which were co-occurring or returned to throughout the process):

1. Administering the Multidimensional Inventory of Dissociation (MID) with extensive psychoeducation about dissociative experiences and the protective nature of their system (Dell, 2006).

2. Strengthening their sense of self outside of their medical identity and caregiver/child role.

3. Strengthenging their autonomy in all aspects of life. Including working with the client and other medical providers to extract the parent from involvement in the client's care and establishing appropriate medical case management.

4. Beginning to imagine future states where they could explore different pursuits and things they liked with all the freedom they were entitled to.

5. Slow identification of parts/ego states that served different roles in their life, and the development of resource roles using Developmental Needs Meeting Strategies (DNMS) protocols (Schmidt, n.d).

6. ONLY after extensive parts work and agreement from the system: begin widening the window of tolerance around noticing the body with somatic mindfulness, utilizing tools such as Jim Knipe's Level of Urge to Avoid (LOUA) & back of the head scale (Knipe, 2018), color breathing, and *Painting with Light* (Marich, 2021).

7. Addressing Internalized ableism and internalized discrimination around their non-binary body.

8. Using a variety of tools from somatic psychology (special thanks to Dr. Arielle Schwartz and her infinitely useful book *Somatic Psychology and EMDR*) to address the many somatic symptoms (Schwartz & Maiberger, 2018). This book has lived on my desk for two years.

Sprinkled through all of this, gently addressing Alex's attachment trauma and using BLS (bilateral stimulation) to strengthen any insights or sense of autonomy they came to, and - when they were ready - directly addressing the confusion, anger, and grief around the acute impact the infantilization had on their development and ability to address their intersex nature.

While this goes FAR beyond the typical cases I see with intersex clients, it's important to know that "Alex" is an amalgamation of four separate intersex individuals who experienced similar situations, five if I include my own story. The likelihood of one clinician meeting these four individuals seems so wildly improbable, that it leads me to believe that there must be more intersex individuals like us who have experienced infantilization and a very specific flavor of caregiver interactions that, at best, imitates factitious disorder imposed on another. I would strongly encourage clinicians to be mindful of this in cases of overly enmeshed caregivers involved in the medical care of intersex people.

I have a working hypothesis that, in cases where clients genuinely DO have unique or extreme medical conditions that mental health or medical providers are unfamiliar with, this form of abuse can go unnoticed or undetected as typical signs a caregiver may exhibit that may cue providers into this issue (overly pushy or involved caregiver, frequently changing providers, many many procedures/tests/medications, strange or a usual symptoms that are unexplainable) can genuinely present with intersex individuals. Due diligence is necessary here in our work.

In at least one case I worked with, the caregiver genuinely seemed well meaning and was able to course correct, support the client's independence, and work on their views of binary sex. This client has said this of their parent: "She's gotten way better as an adult. She lets me go into my appointments on my own and lets me speak for myself." That client graciously reviewed this vignette, approved it as a representation of their story, and expressed how meaningful it was to them to learn that they were not alone. Stories matter.

Mariena: A Case of Damn Near All of The Trauma Targets

My name is Mariena Joy. I use she, her, we pronouns and I didn't know I was an intersex person until my thirties. I own a private practice that's primarily LGBTQIA+ and neurospicy-focused. I am a queer educator and was providing LGBTQIA+ education and support groups in my community for YEARS before I knew the word intersex applied to me. This is my story.

Finding Out

Sometimes people need to process how they learned about their intersex identity. I didn't learn about it in a hidden medical record and have to process my parents keeping the secret like some folks I know. I didn't grow up knowing that I was intersex. It wasn't a shocking moment with my doctor like Sean. But I still remember my world feeling like it got turned upside down. I remember feeling numb with an overwhelming tidal wave of thoughts and emotions when I found out.

Of all ways, I learned I was intersex in front of a crowd of people while I was teaching about intersex identities. I was leading an LGBTQIA+ support group in the community and someone casually asked how they know if they are intersex. We had been talking about how do you know if you were gay and how do you know if you are transgender. These are things I thought I knew, but I didn't know how to answer her. As I was sitting with the shock- realizing that I, an educator on this, genuinely didn't know about one of these identities, I decided to fix it. I told her I didn't know, and wasn't that a problem in and of itself? So we looked it up together, and together we learned that intersex can be a medical diagnostic label and/or describes a person with the lived experience of having non-standard issue reproductive organs, gender related hormones, genitalia, or chromosomes which dictates sex. Examples of this can include people with Polycystic Ovary Syndrome (PCOS) which, while not considered an intersex condition by the medical community, can be considered intersex by the intersex community. This is due to the shared experience of living outside of the binary definition of sex because of someone's biology. PCOS can affect sex characteristics (e.g. hair, acne, fertility, body fat distribution, size), affect sex hormones (specifically elevated levels of androgens), and can contribute to experiences of trauma that align with traumas experienced by folks who do have a medical diagnosis of intersex. In that moment, I learned the word "intersex" applied to me.

I remember being foggy as I sat down for EMDR therapy that week with Susan (my fantastic therapist and once-upon-a-time EMDR basic trainer). My memory of that EMDR session is hazy, a swirl of emotions that came up as we started with a recent events protocol and then the flood of memories that came rushing at me.

I sat there processing with Susan as these things (my childhood, puberty, my medical history, my current relationship with my gender, my current relationship with sexuality/intimacy) started clicking into place. There was joy. Joy at finding the word that suddenly felt RIGHT. That explained it all. Why I felt my body was never quite feminine in the ways that I experienced my gender. Why I wished I was transgender so I could take gender affirming hormones.

If you've ever wished the word transgender applies to you, it probably does. I didn't learn till later that there were other intersex people just like me who experienced gender dysphoria because their sex was affecting their gender expression in a way that did not match their gender identity. Initially, I didn't know intersex people like me could have gender affirming hormones to help my gender expression finally match my gender identity. Who knew!

Finally. Finally I felt like I really belonged to an identity.

And there was grief. Grief that I hadn't known who I was for so long. That the word intersex was so far outside of the dominant discourse that someone like me, someone who is SUPPOSED to educate people on these identities DIDN'T KNOW it applied to me. In some ways, it reminds me of working with my own clients when they are grieving after learning late in life about a neurodiverse diagnosis. Grieving the change in their identity. Grieving the support they could've had. Honestly, this is the main impetus for me to write and talk about this subject.

Childhood, Puberty and Being Different

I grew up always knowing I was physically different from my peers. Even as a little kid doctors thought I was interesting. I was a year younger and always a head taller than everyone. I was stocky, big shoulders, quick to bulk up. My body fat ratio in grade school was fine, but I was a "big kid."

I didn't know the word intersex applied to me, but I (and everyone else in grade school) knew SOMETHING was different and that I was outside the binary. I was "the whale," the kid they want for sports, but never the girl a boy had a crush on.

My mother insisted for years I keep my hair long. I had it cut short early in grade school and immediately people started mistaking me for a little boy. I waffled between wearing pink girly frilly things and "tomboy" clothes, trying to figure out who I was, where I fit in. It's strange as a child to be unsure of who you are and to be gauging your identity off the reactions of others. And yet without guidance, without a blueprint to tell me what was happening for me, I did the best I could trying on different identities that were familiar.

As I started to hit puberty, I was so excited. I was so excited because I was like "yes my body's gonna start doing things right. I'm gonna stop being this person that kids ask, *are you a boy are you a girl?*" I was SO tired of wearing the trappings of a "tomboy" or hyperfeminine girly things. Neither was who I was exactly, but at least it helped me fit in in ways that kids understood. Being in an ill-fitting box felt better than people around me questioning why I didn't fit into any box. In some ways, I feel fortunate that I was able to pass somewhat into boxes that experienced less discrimination than others.

So puberty... I was SO excited for boobs! And then I was waiting... and waiting and waiting and waiting for them. I was six foot one in junior high and my voice dropped, which was great for the tenor section in the junior high choir, but not stellar for my personal identity development or my social standing. I was told by a doctor that I had short muscle fibers (more likely to bulk up), and "how interesting that was," and that my testosterone levels were higher. And no one had treatment for me. It was awful and mortifying that my body felt like it was becoming more masculine. It felt like my body was betraying me. Those of you with gender dysphoria are going to hear the familiar ring in that.

I felt so incredibly grateful for hormonal birth control once my period EVENTUALLY started because, while my body didn't know quite what to do with those hormones (there were some consequences), it DID cause the girls to come in a big way. I went from an A cup to a G cup over the summer. Zero regrets. They are ridiculous and I love them.

When I came back to highschool with ALL the boobs, I felt gender euphoria for the first time in a long time; since I was a little girl with long hair wearing stupid big pink frilly dresses. But because my body didn't know what to do with these hormones, and because the doctors didn't know what my hormonal needs were, I also developed a beer belly like gut and gained 60 pounds over the course of three months. Going back now and reading my medical records from the time brings up a great deal of anger and frustration. The doctors knew something was wrong, but chalked it up to an eating disorder (which I've never had), didn't listen to my concerns, AND didn't talk to me about what they thought was going on.

I didn't know that the word intersex applied to me. The doctors didn't know that the word intersex applied to me. I've since learned that the experience of hormone induced weight gain is common in parts of the intersex community. We would hope that the prevalence of this would result in doctors catching folks at puberty onset and referring to providers in the know, but the understanding of intersex or PCOS in the medical community is astonishingly limited given the size of the intersex population. There's so little information on the topic. Many people, like me, get missed for years.

Social Interactions and Identity Development

More than just kids questioning my gender, they questioned my sexuality (because I must be a lesbian right?) and made judgements on where and how I fit in. In puberty my relationship with identity got SO much worse because I denied myself experiences I wanted, and participated in activities I didn't want to...all for the sake of trying to fit into a gender norm. For example, it seemed like every sports captain everywhere, for everything, wanted me desperately to play for them. I didn't want to be masculine, I didn't want to be anywhere in anything that might associate me with being a "tomboy" anymore. So I stayed away from things I wanted to do because they felt like they were associated with masculinity. I did not want that. I denied myself experiences due to internalized binary discrimination. I turned to outward expressions of (what I thought was) hyperfemininity in what I wore and how I presented myself, past the point of who I really was in an effort to make my body and my gender expression line up with some unachievable moving target of femininity that my body would never conform to.

Other moments (long since processed in EMDR) around social interactions and identity development included: (a) My first kiss; a gay boy who thought I was "just boy enough" that he could tell if he would ever like a girl (The answer was no, so points for me?), (b) My first break-up: because, and I quote, "You're too masculine." I was 13 and I still remember his face, remember the words. (c) Hip dips: the boxy shape of my hips being pointed out in the girl's locker room at swim practice in junior high.

More Medical Nonsense

As I grew up I continued to have medical complications and issues with the medical industrial complex. Even once I got on a better combination of hormones and medication so my body started to change how I wanted, there was a constant fight of trying to find a doctor who understood my specific hormonal needs. A fight to find a doctor who wasn't fat phobic after I gained weight. I was desperate to figure out what was WRONG and why my body had changed to develop a gut when everything else was fine. I had a doctor that said "I don't know what to tell you, it's calories in and calories out. Your food log is lying." It took me YEARS to find a doctor who understood my hormonal needs and that my particular medical issue caused insulin resistance. The right medicine and a change in the kind of food I was eating resulted in a dramatic weight loss off my gut. It took a long long time to process the anger.

Reproduction and Then Some

Not everyone grieves pieces of this, and not every intersex person struggles with fertility. But the effect of my intersex identity had on this area of my life was profound. At one point, a gynecologist told me it was a "shame" my pelvis was "shaped like a man," because I had "all the torso room to have babies. You probably won't even show till the end!" I didn't know if I wanted kids yet, but I was SAD at the thought I wouldn't LOOK pregnant and that I would likely be unable to give a vaginal birth due to my bones. It's a strange experience to be told your BONES don't match your gender. For me, it was heartbreaking. I hated my hips for years.

A few years ago, my medical issues resulted in an emergency hysterectomy and oophorectomy. Initially, I didn't grieve my lack of fertility, or the babies I'd never have. At first, I felt a sense of gender euphoria when I was placed on a combination of hormones that began to make my body more feminine than it ever felt. My body started changing in ways I dreamed of since I was little. I cannot begin to express the sheer joy of finally having an ass. Years later, I do grieve. I have grieved that I will never have children of my own, never nurse them, never see them grow up. I grieved that I felt less feminine for not having these opportunities. EMDR and exploring options, like the potential for induced lactation to support other mothers, has been helpful with both the grief and my feelings around my gender.

Let's Talk about Sex

We can't talk about intersex without 'sex.' For me, sexuality was deeply affected by my intersex body and my lived experiences. I experienced significant shame around aspects of my body that didn't feel "feminine enough" or had reduced physical sensations due to their anatomy (personally, underdeveloped nipples and an extremely small clitoris). It was difficult to connect with my body and be present in the moment when partners did not see me as feminine or wanted me to take a more dominant role during intimacy. Top that off with the experience of pain during sex for years due to medical complications, and it's no wonder sex was generally a dissociative experience.

It is important to note that as a marginalized population, intersex folks report experiencing increased rates of sexual predation. Actual studies on the topic would be advised. In addition to the standard increased risk for any female presenting person, I have noticed a theme of some intersex folks seeking validation of their bodies from partners which can lead to unclear or unenforced boundaries and even coercion. This is in NO way suggesting that ANY victim is at fault for sexual assault. Lets place the blame where it belongs: on the perpetrators. Lack of education around consent, healthy dating and healthy gender norms, combined with validation seeking, can lead to difficulty saying no and normalizing toxic masculinity and aggression. For YEARS, as an example, I was stuck in a marriage where I was shamed for my boundaries with sex, for saying no, for the sexual desires I DID experience, or wanting to wear lingerie to feel prettier.

All these things combined led to dissociation, shame, and a very complicated relationship with sex that I was EXTREMELY grateful for my two dear friends and sex educator therapists: Dr. Lanza (check out their chapter in this book) and Tzippi Folinsky. They helped me start to make sense of my relationship with sexuality and identity. My friends shared with me their experiences with intersex clients who had similar (or waaay more complicated) issues with pain, dissociation, assault, shame, or awkwardness with sex due to physical traits and intersex specific trauma. My friends helped me learn how NORMAL this was for intersex folks.

Even after years of therapy working on this with my excellent EMDR sex therapist Melissa, and exploring through Kink ways I felt more feminine and comfortable in my body in a submissive role, I still can run into moments around my intersex identity that wound me and need attending to. An example would be when the first partner that I felt ever treated me as a deeply feminine person really triggered my internalized binary discrimination and gender dysphoria. He asked that I "not go so hard on arm day" in the gym because "I'm not trying to date a man." And while I have since untangled my gender identity from having healthy shoulder joints (and cut off contact with him cus wow, no thank you toxic masculinity), stuff like that can still sting.

Looking For Community

The last part of my story, and my transition into the whole textbook flavor of this chapter, is that when I went looking for community, I found a few groups online with intersex folks. I found INTERACT (Pop that term in a search engine. You'll find it.).

I learned about my identity. I felt accepted. Then I went looking for my professional community. I was so excited when I had the idea to apply EMDR to intersex related traumas in my career. It worked for me (thanks Susan and Melissa), why not for others? I was SO excited to go find every article, podcast, post, and person out there who had written SOMETHING on EMDR and intersex.

...I couldn't find anybody.

I couldn't find ANYTHING.

Google Scholar has thousands upon thousands of articles on EMDR. When you put in "EMDR" and "intersex" you get one result. Just. One.

It's the chapter on EMDR therapy with lesbian/gay/bisexual clients from the well known book, *Cultural Competence and Healing Culturally Based Trauma with EMDR Therapy: Innovative Strategies and Protocols*. The end of the opening paragraph states the following: "clinicians need to be aware that there are unique concerns for all clients under the LGBTQQI umbrella" And then there was a list of identities. The very last one was intersex (O'Brien, 2017, p. 195).

That is the final straw that brought me here to write this chapter. I'm not a specialist in the way I'd like to be. I don't have years of research under my belt. Heck, I don't have all the variations of intersex memorized (there's a LOT). I'm always reading, researching, and brushing up on the next thing. What I have is years of personal and professional experience, and a deep commitment to continue to gather stories and data about my community. I'm here to start the conversation academically. Someone's got to be the first right?

Intersex and Why it Matters

Research has generally estimated that 1.7% to 4% of people are intersex (Carroll, 2005; Fausto-Sterling, 1993; Organisation Intersex International Australia, 2012b). That's a lot of people. I'm going to use a metaphor my brother Jon came up with here:

> Imagine that you are a redhead, and most people think there are only blonds, brunettes, and black hair. When you are born, the doctor says to your parents, "I'm sorry, there's something wrong with your baby. But don't worry, we have options. You can dye their hair, keep it shaved, or we have this option for scalping your child. It's a fairly harmless procedure and they likely won't ever remember." Or maybe the doctor misses it. You grow up and grow into your red hair. And people always treat you like there's something wrong with you. You go through life with people knowing you are different, disliking you on principle, and you can't figure it out. They might ask, "Are you a blond or a brunette?," or "Why don't you dye your hair?' It's kind of like being discriminated against for having autism. It's stupid that people don't understand when it's so obvious.

I can't help but wonder how many of us are out there that DON'T know we are intersex. I didn't know. We are too large of a population to not be having some basic conversations and cursory knowledge about in dominant discourse. Just like we know redheads are a thing.

Lack of Dominant Discourse and Erasure

At an educator's conference I recently attended, I found a series of textbooks teaching about LGBTQIA identities in public schools. In one, intersex was mentioned once in a single sentence in the glossary. In another, we got a whole two paragraphs. These textbooks are known for being on the cutting edge of progressive education around minority identities. Yet, we are *at best* two paragraphs! I did point this out to them. One of my next steps is following up with their offer to work with them and edit the curriculum to include more about intersex identities.

Knowledge and cultural awareness of the existence of intersex people is different depending on where you live around the world, but we predominantly experience a lack of being known. It's as though we don't exist and never have. In some ways, it's hard to define if this is erasure, a lack of existence in the dominant discourse, or a bit of both. You have to have been known first to be erased. A current example at the time of writing this would be the United States Executive Order

> *Defending Women from Gender Ideology Extremism and Restoring Biological Truth to the Federal Government*, in which it is stated, "It is the policy of the United States to recognize two sexes, male and female. These sexes are not changeable and are grounded in fundamental and incontrovertible reality" (Trump, 2025, Sec. 1).

This particular political event was notably traumatic for many of my clients. To further make the point that validation of our existence can make a profound difference to our mental health, those same clients (and myself) experienced a sense of validation, hope, and increased wellness when Judge Ana Reyes responded to these claims about there only being two sexes.

> "This executive order is premised on an assertion that's not biologically correct," Judge Reyes said. "There are anywhere near 30 intersex examples. Anyone who doesn't have XX or XY chromosomes is not just male or female, they're intersex."[...]"I'm telling you that there are people who are neither male or female," [...]"The premise of the executive order is just incorrect" (GLAAD, 2025).

No Need to Specialize

I'm not here suggesting that every EMDR therapist needs to specialize in working with intersex clients. My previously mentioned therapist, Susan, didn't know jack about intersex. But she was able to very quickly learn the basics of what the word meant, how it applied to me, and then she filtered that through the lens of *her* expertise. For us, that looked like revisiting my trauma timeline and processing targets that I realised were affected by my experiences as an intersex person.

You are all experts in something. It's important to learn the basics and then develop the capacity to filter the work we are *already doing* through the lens of intersex. This lens I'm talking about? It's one I use myself. Here's where I'm coming from as someone with the lived experience of being intersex: *As you think about an intersex person's life experiences (especially the traumatic ones), think about how it might relate to being intersex.* Using this lens reshaped how I visit and understand my own life experiences. And it can reshape the way other clinicians hold space for folks. It's okay if you don't fully understand intersex. It's the trauma that needs to be validated. Just start there.

Recommendations for Practice

When I was first interviewed about writing this book chapter, it was suggested that I included a "summary of best practices that are simple and approachable." I'd love to do that, but frankly, there's no research yet about this. After I realized there wasn't a blueprint for best practice for EMDR with intersex folks, I figured I'd give it the whole *trial and error* approach. So that's what I have here, a compilation of things I have sorted out over the last few years that seem to work for me, my clients, and my therapist peers. Some of them won't work for everyone. An example would be someone I recently met in one of the intersex support groups not feeling like he was outside the binary. I expect some of these practices I have developed will be found out to be not helpful, entirely accurate, or in need of some serious tweaking in years to come. At least I hope so, because that would mean that enough time, effort, and academic research will have occurred to show that to be the case.

Educate Yourself

Learn the basics of what intersex means. Learn about your client's specific condition to some degree. Get the name of the condition if they know and go look it up. That's what the internet is for. Do not expect your client to educate you on intersex identities; that is not what they are paying you for. This is a blanket piece of advice for any marginalized identity. We can be open and curious about our client's experiences, make room to listen when they need to be heard, and engage in appropriate history taking.

Intake & EMDR Phase 1

I started to make some minor changes to my intake and EMDR processes, and you could consider this too. Under sex, I included male, female, intersex, and unknown. I keep a separate category for gender. Remember, sex and gender are NOT the same thing. During Phase 1 when I ask about history, I pay special attention to complicated medical histories, especially those around hormones, fertility, and genitalia. I may ask clients if they are aware of any surgeries in early childhood. When asking about prior medical and mental health diagnosis, I give examples including intersex conditions. In family history, if they indicated they were adopted, we explored if they knew WHY. I created a brochure "You might be intersex if..." and have made it available for free on my website, and keep copies out for my clients. Lastly, I openly identify as intersex on my website and when introducing myself to new clients. All of these changes have opened up the opportunity for clients to share if they are intersex, or increased the likelihood of psychoeducation conversations about intersex identities. Since making these changes, I have had multiple clients share that they, or loved ones, are intersex.

Affirmative Information That a Therapist Can Provide

Figuring this bit out is an ongoing process. Intersex experiences are so diverse, that it's hard to distill affirmative information. Know that this is not an exhaustive list, but a beginning. Here's Marie's *hot takes* on affirmative information for supporting intersex clients, based on the things I needed to hear growing up, what my community has said they needed to hear from someone, and what my clients have said was useful during the EMDR process:

1. We exist. There are MANY of us.
2. If you (the therapist) are not intersex, you are willing to learn some basic information to provide care.
3. Existing in a way that challenges the binary is exhausting.
4. It's hard to get things right when you feel like you don't have a blueprint for your sex/gender/medical needs.
5. Your medical history does not define your gender. YOU get to be whatever gender you know you are.
6. Hearing stories about other intersex folk's experiences can make us feel that we are not so alone (okay, this is a reframe of #1, but look- it's super important).

Asking for Consent When Addressing Somatic Sensations and Concerns

This one is brief. I hear myself echoing Dr. Sand Chang, "Ask consent when addressing somatic sensations and concerns" (Chang, 2022, p. 183). Many, though not all, intersex people experience discomfort when focusing on their physical body or body sensations. This makes sense given the breadth of trauma that we can experience in relation to our bodies. Clinicians should obtain permission EVERY session to address or focus on somatic experiences. In my experience, clients have appreciated careful attunement to this, and it has seemed to foster trust in the therapeutic alliance.

Interpersonal Dynamics Around Intersex and Safety

Above all, we must be thinking about the safety of our clients. This section is an unfortunate necessity, especially given today's sociopolitical uncertainty in certain areas of the world. I live in the United States, and as I'm writing this in early 2025, we are facing a political climate where an executive order has just been signed that denies our very existence.

Here are some important safety concerns for clinicians to keep in mind:

- Not outing your client. Either to individuals or in clinical documentation.
- Speak with your clients about what information they want excluded from their medical records, who is safe to know, who is not safe.
- Work with the clients to assess the safety of their environment and make plans for how to keep this information protected as needed, and what to do if they are outed as intersex.
- Make plans with the client for what they can do if they have an abreaction as they are processing or in response to others' reactions to their identity. Plans for regulating themselves, making the choice (if they want) to mask their identity (if they can) around unsafe people (e.g., I'm not gonna wear my rainbow glasses at a hardware store), and who they can reach out to for support.

Negative & Positive Cognitions

Since the intersex community and their experiences crosses such a breadth of trauma (medical, interpersonal, identity, and otherwise), each person's complex culmination of negative cognitions (and their needed positive cognitions) are going to need special attention and time to uncover.

There is no one size fits all model for these cognitions, but we can borrow from works that already exist. We can visit the breadth of works related to EMDR and minority identities, adoption, body image dysregulation, chronic pain, and more. These cognitions are numerous, easily findable online, and are likely ones you are already familiar with in your work. By exploring the body of knowledge on EMDR and cognitions, we can start to get an idea about what cognitions may be a fit for our client's experiences. This is not an exhaustive list of cognitions, merely a collection of some that I have seen repeatedly in my work.

Table 1. Cognitions

Negative/Oppressive Cognitions

- I don't belong (because the system is binary/because I don't look like others)
- There's something wrong with me (because medical issues/outcasted/dominant discourse is binary)
- I'm weird because I'm not like others
- I'm alone because there's no one like me
- No one could ever understand me
- My body is wrong/shameful
- The world is unsafe
- I'm going to die
- I'm going to get hurt
- The pain will never end
- I'm helpless
- I can't
- I'm unlovable
- I don't deserve love

Positive Cognitions

- I am not my trauma
- I am human
- I am whole
- I have community
- There are things in my body that I do like
- My uniqueness is what makes me who I am
- I have ways to reduce/control pain/discomfort
- This is the body I am in and it gets me from Point A to Point B
- I have choices
- I can take steps to be healthy
- I am worthy
- I deserve love
- I can heal
- I can take steps to increase my safety
- I am a natural part of the human experience

A Little Phase 1 & A Little Phase 2

Something to discuss with clients is how and IF them being intersex has contributed to trauma in their life. If this is something they even *want* to address. I've had a handful of clients, and plenty of peers in the intersex community, that either report that they have "other fish to fry" right now, or that their particular flavor of intersex experience doesn't feel bothersome. As a whole, that has not been the predominant experience I've run across, but let's not assume that a client would necessarily want to target things related to being intersex.

Okay, but what if we DO want to target intersex related trauma?

Below is the beginnings of a list that I've started to compile about different genres of targets/traumas that intersex folks I've known have encountered. It's by no means an exhaustive list. Take note that this list includes targets from the past, current triggers, and future concerns.

Resourcing & How We Do It in the Middle of Trauma

We build hope.

Phase 2 resourcing is a vital part of EMDR (or any form of trauma work) with intersex clients. This is especially important, given that most intersex people are CURRENTLY experiencing trauma in some form or another related to their intersex identity. And as we know, surviving current traumas requires building hope and resilience. We can do this through psychoeducation, BLS to strengthen positives, sorting out what is amplified by the past and what is real and present trauma, distancing techniques, orienting to present safety, pain management, connection with supports (internal and external), noticing choices and action steps you DO have, desired future states that feel tangible and probable, memory reconsolidation tools such as Four Blinks (Zimmerman, 2023), stabilizing sense of self, and many others. You're the therapist, you've done this work. I'm just here to remind you that your clients may be in the middle of experiencing trauma while trying to heal from it.

Table 2. Potential Targets: Historical, Present Triggers, Future Concerns

1. How They Found Out
   a. Some intersex traits are noticed at birth
   b. Others don't show up until puberty or later in life
   c. In adulthood, when infertility or other medical problems reveal internal differences
   d. When learning that adults covered up childhood medical interventions
2. Identity
   a. Who am I? Viewing self from the medical model
   b. Gender and dysphoria
   c. Infantilization
3. Medical Stuff
   a. Pain
   b. Surgeries
   c. Infertility
   d. Medical oddity/mystery
   e. Medical abuse
4. Other people
   a. Family of origin
   b. Rejection by family, friends, work, peers, romantic partners
   c. Larger community, i.e. fear around things seen in the news/politics
5. Intimacy
   a. Sex
      i. Something feeling off with primary or secondary sex characteristics in relation to sex- might be awkward, embarrassing, shameful (i.e., Micropenis, hipdips, flat chest, underdeveloped clitoris—- the list goes on. Sex can feel hella awkward when equipment is not "standard issue" and the other person isn't cool with it.)
      ii. Pain with sex
      iii. Explaining "what's up" to potential partners
6. Dissociation
   a. Body Trauma can = needing to disconnect from ourselves
   b. Being present in my body now and in the future
7. Grief
   a. The life they could have had
   b. 1-6 above

Script for Stabilizing Sense of Self - By Mariena Joy

"Stabilizing Sense of Self" is a resource that I created without realizing I was making something. I had never contemplated writing it down or giving it an official name prior to this book. Over the last few years, I have often found myself talking to clients about "stabilizing your sense of self" when talking about their relationship with how they viewed their identity.

For years, I would doodle on a scrap piece of paper for this activity, or hand-write edits to The Genderbread Person or the Gender Unicorn (Killermann, 2018; Trans Student Educational Resources, 2015). Neither of these resources were quite right for what I and my clients needed. For the sake of this book, I have made slight edits to The Genderbread Person. I am eternally grateful for that author's "uncopywrite"- allowing for the Genderbread Person to be in the public domain.

Feel free to use the attached figure. For a larger version of "Marie's Genderbread Person+" or for links to a glossary of LGBTQIA+ identities, you can find them on my website www.brainbowfire.life under LGBTQIA+ Resources or the Blog sections.

Invitation to Stabilizing Sense of Self: *What you have gone through can be confusing and destabilize your sense of who you are. You might feel uncertain about what your gender, gender expression, sex, and sexuality actually are and what that says about you. If you'd like, I have an activity we can do to sort out some of that. Would you like to take a look and decide?*

Using Genderbread Person+: *Why don't we take a look at this and fill these out. (Fill out)*

"*Looking at these, what do you feel each says about who you are?*" (Provide psychoeducation or glossary of LGBTQIA+ terms if need be. This is an opportunity to address any glaringly problematic beliefs or blocks that may come up to connect them with positives)

Resourcing with Sense of Self: *As you look at this, notice the sense of WHO you are. Notice if anything about that is neutral* *or positive. These reactions may be thoughts, feelings, body sensations, memories, or something else.* (Let them talk it out if they want to).

(If a negative is identified) *Is there something on here that helps address that negative? or What do the most adult parts of yourself have to say to the part that is experiencing that, or* (provide psychoeducation).

(If a neutral or positive is identified) *How do you feel about using slow BLS to connect with these things to better connect with your sense of self?*

(If yes, engage in SLOW BLS; they can talk it out during if they want) *You can go as long or as short as you like. Let me know when you feel done, or stop if it goes negative.*

(Continue to address any negatives or concerns that arise for the client. Continue sets of slow BLS for as long as the client would like/as long as the positives continue to strengthen)

Are there any words, gestures, images, or objects that you would like to pair with this positive sense of self? We can use these anchors to quickly find these positives in the future if need be. (You might give examples of squeezing a finger joint, putting a hand on their heart, hugging self, a positive cognition, etc.)

(If they say yes - slow BLS to pair) *Good, now let's test the anchor. Go ahead and try it and see if it connects with the positive experience of self.*

(If yes, move on. If not, invite the client to try continued pairing if they like.)

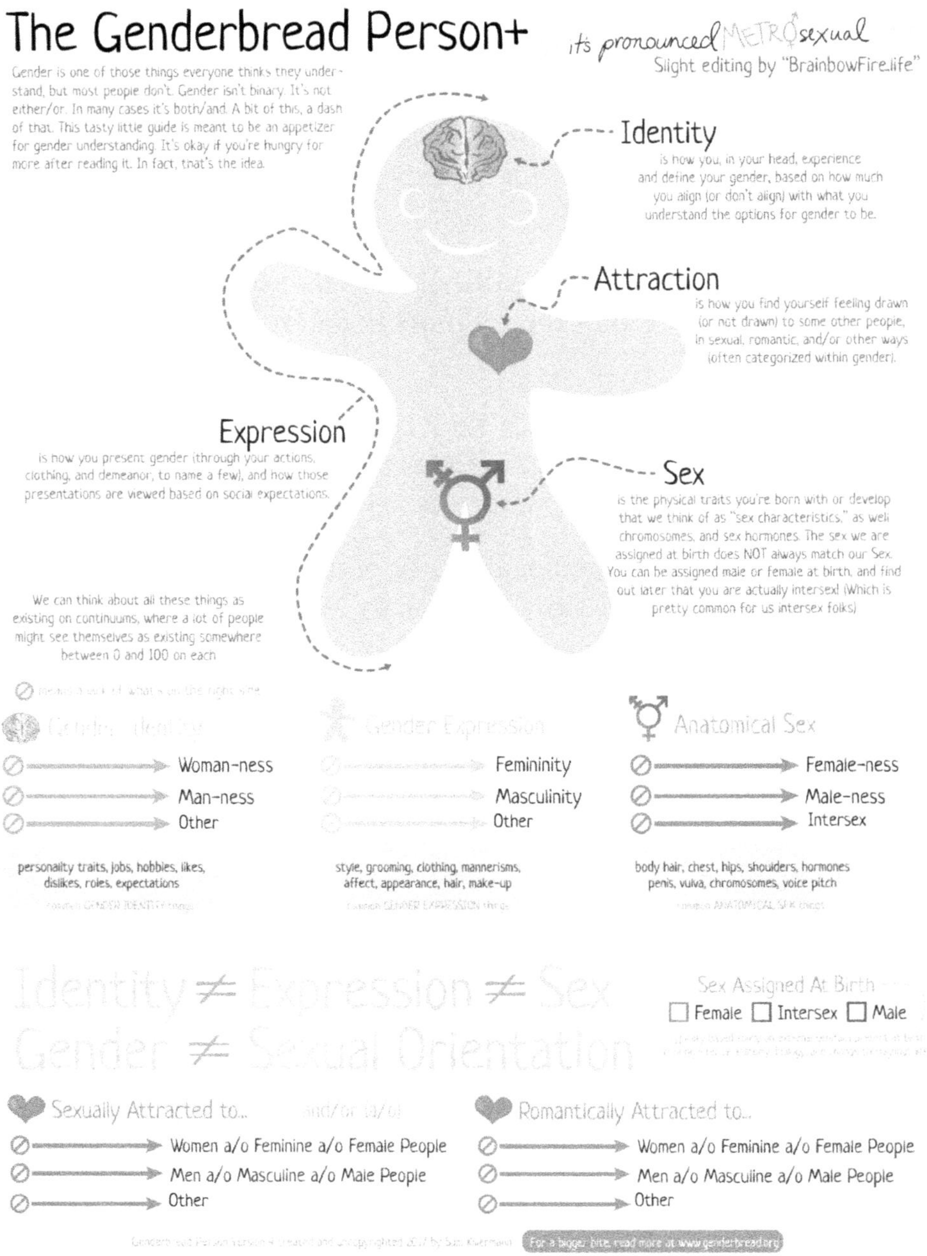

The Genderbread Person+
it's pronounced METROsexual
Slight editing by "BrainbowFire.life"
Gender is one of those things everyone thinks they understand, but most people don't. Gender isn't binary. It's not either/or. In many cases it's both/and. A bit of this, a dash of that. This tasty little guide is meant to be an appetizer for gender understanding. It's okay if you're hungry for more after reading it. In fact, that's the idea.
Identity
is how you, in your head, experience and define your gender, based on how much you align (or don't align) with what you understand the options for gender to be.
Attraction
is how you find yourself feeling drawn (or not drawn) to some other people, in sexual, romantic, and/or other ways (often categorized within gender).
Expression
is how you present gender (through your actions, clothing, and demeanor, to name a few), and how those presentations are viewed based on social expectations.
Sex
is the physical traits you're born with or develop that we think of as "sex characteristics," as well chromosomes, and sex hormones. The sex we are assigned at birth does NOT always match our Sex. You can be assigned male or female at birth, and find out later that you are actually intersex! (Which is pretty common for us intersex folks)
We can think about all these things as existing on continuums, where a lot of people might see themselves as existing somewhere between 0 and 100 on each
Woman-ness
Man-ness
Other
personality traits, jobs, hobbies, likes, dislikes, roles, expectations
Femininity
Masculinity
Other
style, grooming, clothing, mannerisms, affect, appearance, hair, make-up
Anatomical Sex
Female-ness
Male-ness
Intersex
body hair, chest, hips, shoulders, hormones penis, vulva, chromosomes, voice pitch
Identity ≠ Expression ≠ Sex
Gender ≠ Sexual Orientation
Sex Assigned At Birth
Female Intersex Male
Sexually Attracted to...
Women a/o Feminine a/o Female People
Men a/o Masculine a/o Male People
Other
Romantically Attracted to...
Women a/o Feminine a/o Female People
Men a/o Masculine a/o Male People
Other
For a bigger bite, read more at www.genderbread.org

For me, this was accepting my body as intersex, and that I am a trans Queen who is entitled to any gender affirming tools at my disposal. That I have choices. And, as my once mentor Marshall Lyles talked about, I learned to focus on the parts of my body that I love - to be thankful that it works and is functional. After understanding my medical needs, I am thankful that I can give the proper care (hormones and nutrients) that I need. I love me. Hip dips and all.

Photo by Stefanni Eaton

Image 1. Marie's Genderbread Person+

Wrapping It Up

It is my hope that this chapter will make you curious about ways to expand your body of knowledge and be mindful of intersex identities in your work. I hope that advancements in research with EMDR and intersex identities occur to strengthen evidenced based practice for my community. And to my fellow intersex people: If you are not there already, I hope you get to some measure of peace with who you are and the journey you are on with your body.

For me, this was accepting my body as intersex, and that I am a trans Queen who is entitled to any gender affirming tools at my disposal. That I have choices. And, as my once mentor Marshall Lyles talked about, I learned to focus on the parts of my body that I love - to be thankful that it works and is functional. After understanding my medical needs, I am thankful that I can give the proper care (hormones and nutrients) that I need. I love me. Hip dips and all.

Additional Reading

Interaction for Health and Human Rights: https://interaction.org.au/16601/population-figures/

Center for American Progress: https://www.americanprogress.org/article/key-issues-facing-people-intersex-traits/#:~:text=It%20is%20estimated%20that%20up,identifiable%20sexual%20or%20reproductive%20variations.

INTERACT: https://interactadvocates.org/

Mariena Joy (she/her/we) is an EMDR Certified Therapist and Consultant in Oregon. She is a neurodiverse (AuDHD), intersex, plural, queer, Kinky therapist experienced in EMDR with parts work, somatic & attachment modalities, sandtray, and more within these marginalized identities. Over the last 8 years, Joy has served as an educator, speaker, & community advocate. Joy has presented on EMDR with intersex people: available on EMDRIA's Diversity SIG library. This presentation has been used in curriculum for social work programs at Portland State University and California State University Northridge, where she has been a repeated guest lecturer. More information available at *www.Brainbowfire.life*

References

Carroll, L. (2005). Intersex. In J. T. Sears (Ed.), *Youth, education, and sexualities: An international encyclopedia* (Vol. 1, pp. 440–444). Santa Barbara, CA: Greenwood Press.

Chang, S. C. (2017). EMDR therapy as affirmative care for transgender and nonbinary clients. In M. Nickerson (Ed.), *Cultural competence and healing culturally based trauma with EMDR therapy: Innovative strategies and protocols* (pp. 177–194). New York: Springer Publishing Company.

Dell, P. F. (2006). The Multidimensional Inventory of Dissociation (MID): A comprehensive measure of pathological dissociation. *Journal of Trauma & Dissociation, 7*(2), 77–106. https://doi.org/10.1300/J229v07n02_06

Fausto-Sterling, A. (1993). The five sexes: Why male and female are not enough. *The Sciences, 33*(2), 20–24.

GLAAD. (2025, February 16). Judge exposes inaccurate and absurd claims in Trump's executive orders targeting transgender people. https://glaad.org/judge-exposes-inaccurate-and-absurd-claims-in-trumps-executive-orders-targeting-transgender-people/

InterACT: Advocates for Intersex Youth. (n.d.). Intersex definitions. *interACT: Advocates for Intersex Youth.* https://interactadvocates.org/intersex-definitions/

Killermann, S. (2018, October 1). The Genderbread Person. It's Pronounced Metrosexual. https://www.itspronouncedmetrosexual.com/2018/10/the-genderbread-person/

Knipe, J. (2018). *EMDR toolbox: Theory and treatment of complex PTSD and dissociation* (2nd ed.). New York: Springer Publishing Company.

Marich, J. (Host). (2021, March 19). Dr. Jamie Marich talks about EMDR & dissociation [Video]. The Art and Science of EMDR. YouTube. https://www.youtube.com/watch?v=XEbC93sjFGQ

O'Brien, J. M. (2017). EMDR therapy with lesbian/gay/bisexual clients. In M. Nickerson (Ed.), *Cultural competence and healing culturally based trauma with EMDR therapy: Innovative strategies and protocols* (pp. 195–208). New York: Springer Publishing Company.

Organisation Intersex International Australia. (2012b, November 29). Intersex for allies. https://oii.org.au/21336/intersex-for-allies/

Schmidt, S. J. (n.d.). Developmental needs meeting strategy. DNMS Institute. https://www.dnmsinstitute.com/

Schwartz, A., & Maiberger, B. (2018). EMDR therapy and somatic psychology: Interventions to enhance embodiment in trauma treatment. New York: W. W. Norton & Company.

Trans Student Educational Resources. (2015). The Gender Unicorn. https://transstudent.org/gender/

Trump, D. J. (2025, January 20). Executive Order 14168—Defending Women From Gender Ideology Extremism and Restoring Biological Truth to the Federal Government. The White House. https://www.whitehouse.gov/presidential-actions/2025/01/defending-women-from-gender-ideology-extremism-and-restoring-biological-truth-to-the-federal-government/

Zimmerman, T. (2023, May 20). Four Blinks Version of Flash: An open approach to trauma reprocessing. https://fourblinks.com/

Ayeka

Carmine Abigail, (LCPC, ATR-P)

This visual chapter is a movement between questions and answers, concealment and revelation.

It begins with a question: *Ayeka*, the Hebrew word meaning, "Where are you?" Where are you in the process of becoming? This question has echoed across the chambers of hearts, sometimes unanswered and unasked.

And then the answer: Hineini. "Here I am."

This story is a map of that encounter between Ayeka and Hineini, at the nexus of past and present selves, body and spirit, trauma and healing. It is about sitting across from another human; therapist, client, friend, and feeling nervous systems settle into something new.

Credit for some of the text in this comic is attributed to Julian K. Jarboe and their manifesto *The Android That Designed Itself* in their short story collection, "Everyone On the Moon is Essential Personnel."

Additional credit to the text in this comic is attributed to adaptations of Thomas Zimmerman's words from his podcast episode, The Relevance of "Parts Work" to EMDR Therapy on The EMDR Podcast. All accredited text is in ***bold italic font***.

Carmine (they/them) is a queer trans nonbinary multimedia artist and Expressive arts therapist living on Wabanaki land, in what is now called Maine. Being an artist and a therapist are constellations of inquiry. I am endlessly fascinated by themes of the body, time, and space, and enjoy using comics and illustrations to wander through memory and the multiverse of the self. This comic is dedicated to every queer, nonbinary, and trans person igniting a quiet revolution in the process of becoming..

Ayeka. Where are you?

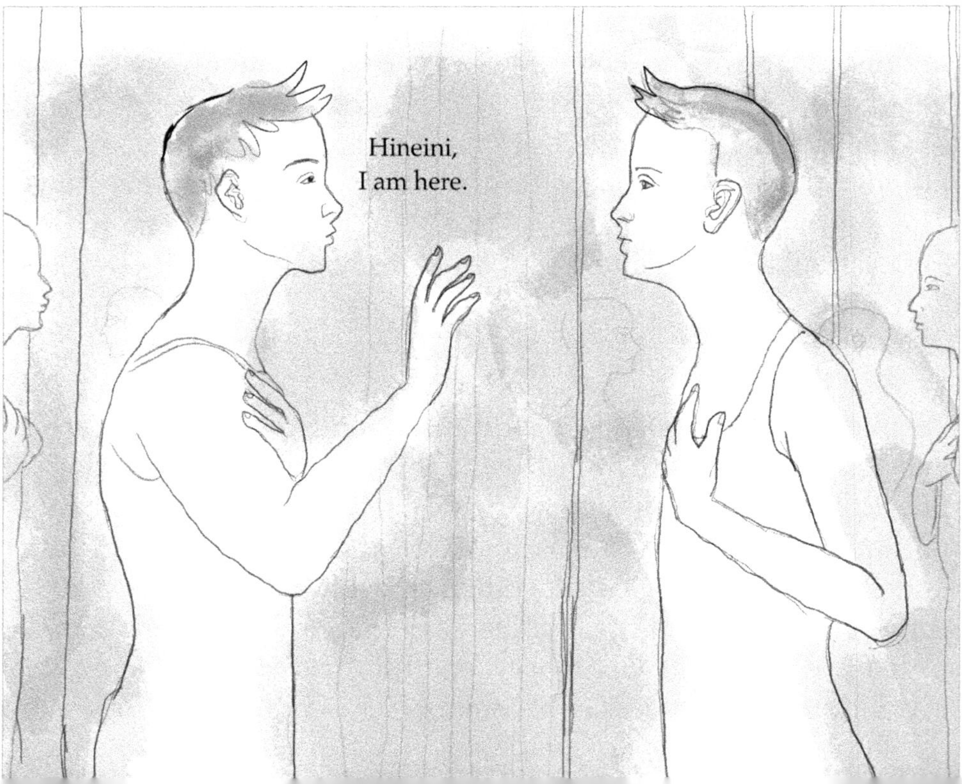
Hineini,
I am here.

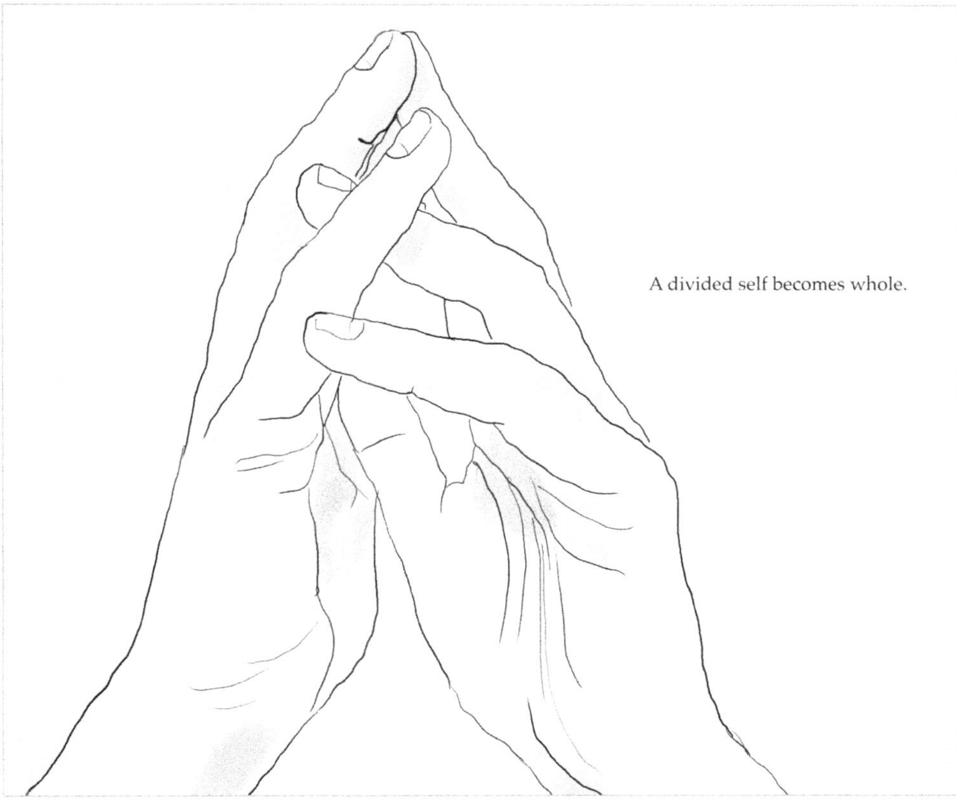
A divided self becomes whole.

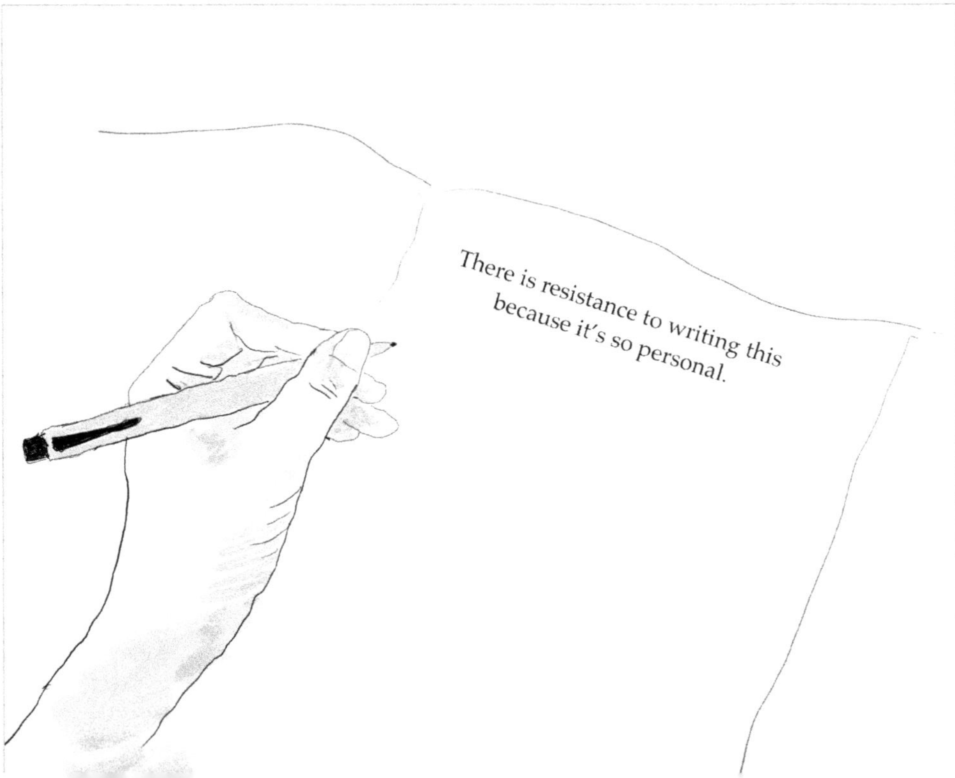
There is resistance to writing this
because it's so personal.

I learned to keep myself divided and fragmented because it was safer.

Sometimes I hid so well that even I could not find myself.

In EMDR, we create expansiveness in a nervous system stuck and lodged in past wounds.

Any small rupture can link back to the original upset, and healing can create new pathways.

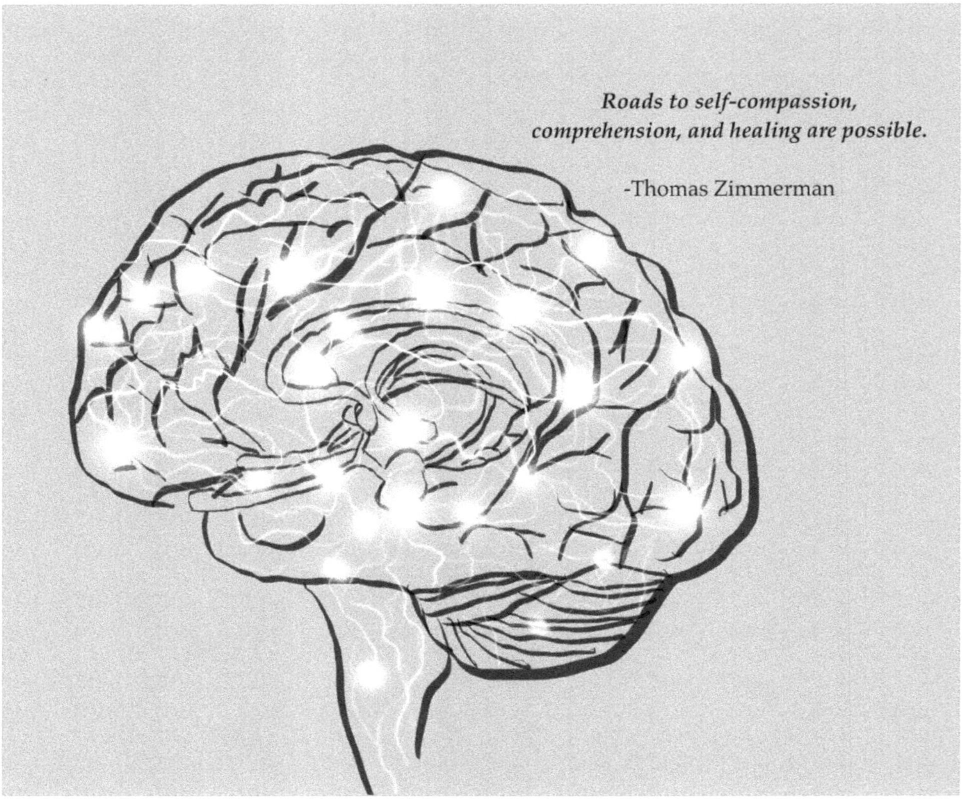
Roads to self-compassion,
comprehension, and healing are possible.
-Thomas Zimmerman

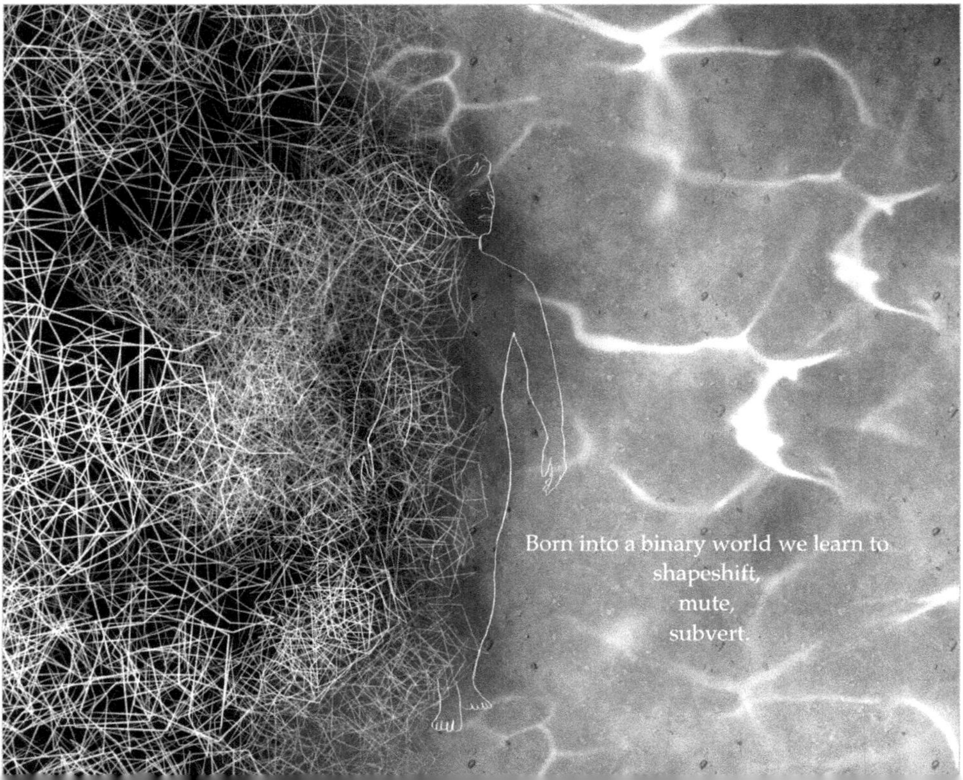
Born into a binary world we learn to
shapeshift,
mute,
subvert.

We learn to survive in spaces
inhospitable to most.

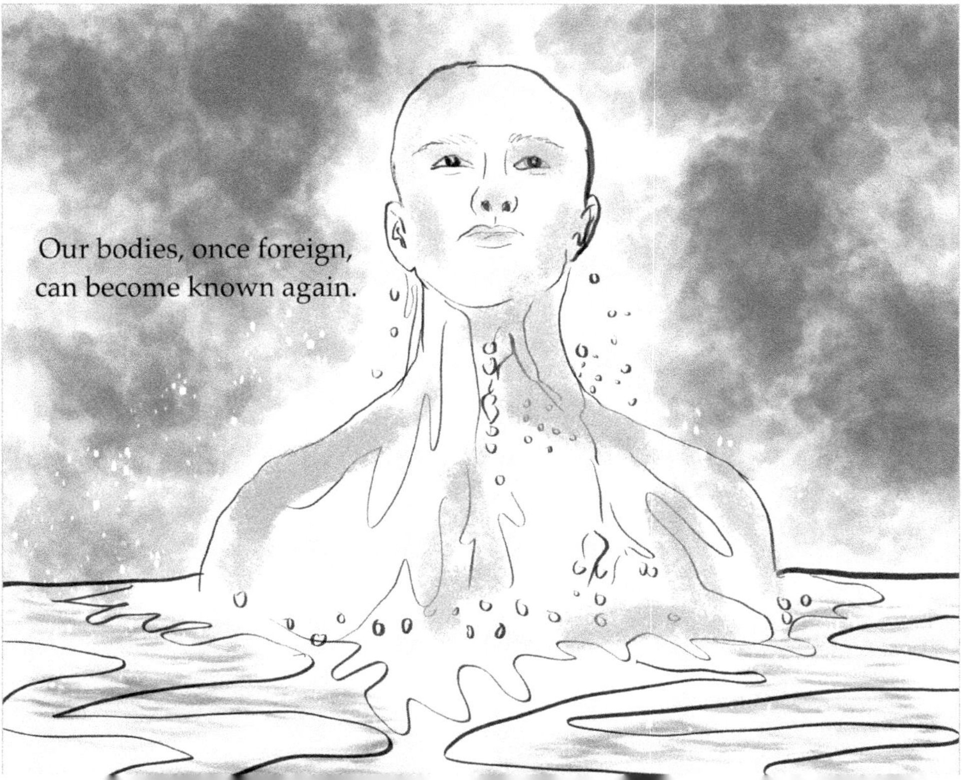
Our bodies, once foreign,
can become known again.

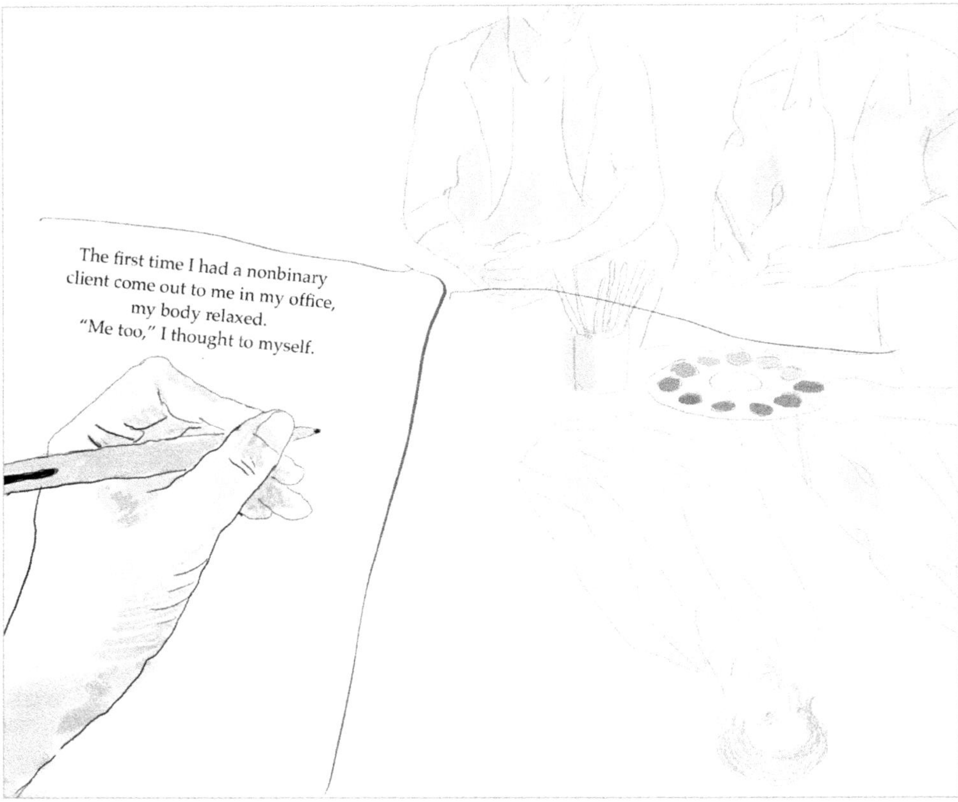
The first time I had a nonbinary client come out to me in my office, my body relaxed. "Me too," I thought to myself.

Through others I found the courage to claim myself.

Why did God create grapes and wheat, but not wine and bread? God did this because God wants us to share in the act of creation.
-Julian K. Jarboe

We are already whole, and shifting towards the divine.
-Julian K. Jarboe

Make your own art and/or
write your own story on the pages that follow....

EMDR

An Intersectional Lens from a Black Gay Man Raised and Practicing in the South

Earl C. Martin, Jr. MSW, LCSW

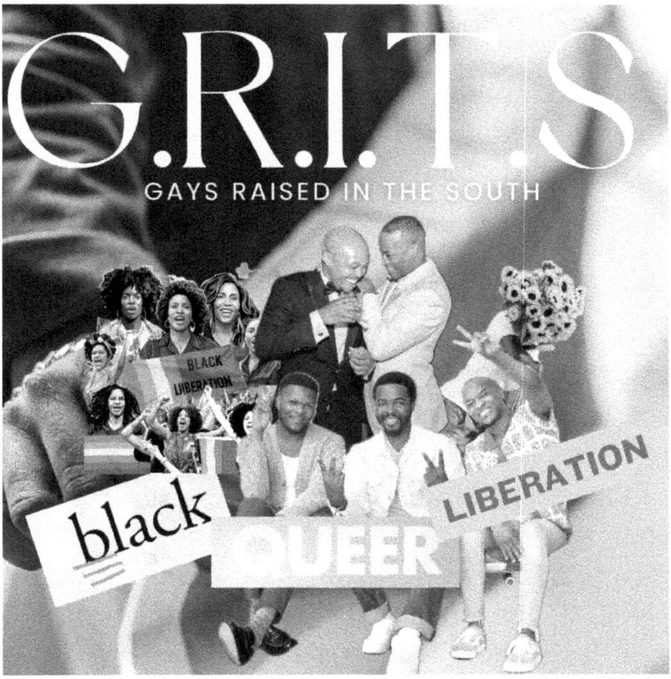

Mixed media created by the author

Blackness and queerness within the Bible belt collide uniquely, forming an interesting and often overlooked intersection. It is an interwoven culture of southern colloquialisms, superstitions that you're taught not to question, rich Black history, and often religious teachings that can be freeing but equally restraining. Navigating those spaces as a Black queer individual is no easy task, particularly when you've yet to reach a level of integration with those intersectional identities. Being raised in Columbia, South

Carolina, as both a Black and queer man, has created a lens of cultural humility in my worldview, which ultimately has influenced how I practice and with whom. My name is Earl C. Martin, Jr. and I'm a Licensed Clinical Social Worker in Charlotte, North Carolina.

My Story: Living in the Intersections

I was born to an incredible force of a mother, who provided protection and nurture like no other. She worked as a cosmetologist by day and by night served as a superhero to my sisters and I, where she ensured that all we ever wanted and needed were met. My father was a man of many trades involving his hands, particularly in the automotive industry, but he was also incarcerated the first 7 years of my life and an infrequent figure upon his release for the majority of my life thereafter. Being his namesake added a certain level of pressure to rebrand our shared name, particularly due to the expressed expectations by family to be a strong and respectable Black man. When you add in the secret and unknown special sauce of being gay, the pressures only multiplied in my mind. My mother often had candid conversations with me about the reality of the world I was born in, a world that would naturally view me as a threat due to my being a Black male.

She often spoke to me about the unfortunate reality that there were two strikes naturally against me. Unbeknownst to her, there were really three, that third being my queerness. It was the messaging of there being "two strikes" against me with the added third strike, that resulted in my being hyper-focused on working twice as hard as my peers. Many if not all Black individuals have been given the "Talk" by their parents of the harsh reality of having to work twice as hard as their peers to receive less. I've observed and experienced that these types of pressures cause an increase in anxiety and stress. Additionally, it creates dynamics of questioning your self-worth, as well creating traits of perfectionism to meet a certain standard. While this is a common experience of my Black peers, coincidentally, many of my Black queer siblings experience a caveat to this lesson. That caveat being an overwhelming pressure to be successful as a means of deflection and masking of queerness.

Whether it be consciously or unconsciously, I have found that many queer individuals have an ambitious drive to be the best in all that they do. Many have held high accolades throughout their high school and college years, where they eventually go on to have successful careers. These accolades may include student body or class president, president of the debate team, a high achieving athlete, an academic scholar, being heavily involved in service activities, and/or chairs of various committees and organizations. On paper they appear to have it all figured out, however, oftentimes these high achievements are used as a form of overcompensation. Deflection strategies from their queerness. Pleas and efforts of "If I'm successful in all these various avenues, you'll accept or ignore this one part of me."

Many peers and I have shared the ways in which we strived for success to mask our queerness from family and friends. These were last ditch efforts to allow our queerness to be more palpable to those around us, even when those around us were in support of us. In contrast, these were also survival techniques at play. This preparation of survival rooted in overcompensation and strides for overachievement was based on a need of being independent. A need to have a foundation to survive if the nightmare of being rejected and cast out by family became a reality.

According to a study completed by the Williams Institute at UCLA surveying various homeless agencies, 68 percent of homeless youth served experienced a history of family rejection (National Coalition for the Homeless, 2022). Furthermore, The National Coalition for the Homeless also reported that between 26 and 30 percent of LGBTQ youth are kicked out of their home specifically due to their sexual orientation or gender identity. When adding in the intersection of race, The Trevor Project reports that 35 percent of Black LGBTQ youth have experienced homelessness, have been kicked out, or ran away from home (The Trevor Project, 2020). It is experiences such as these and/or the fear of these possible outcomes, that causes an increased need to overachieve to cover our bases to survive in a world that causes so much harm by not recognizing our humanity.

At a young age I was aware of how the world treated those that were queer. While I was fortunate enough not to be raised in a family that condemned and bashed those who were queer, the messaging that "gay was wrong" was still broadcasted loudly elsewhere. It was spread in the messaging and sermons of church pastors. It was taught through fear mongering riddled throughout the sex education curriculum that promoted abstinence and warnings of contracting HIV/AIDS, which only deepened stigma. These very sex education courses were designed with the aim to help young people develop the knowledge and skills to make healthy choices about their sexual health, but it further caused a divide and delay of sexual understanding for queer youth in contrast to their heterosexual peers.

The message of "Gay was wrong" was observed in the bullying of peers who couldn't mask their effeminate quirks. And the ways the adults, who were supposed to protect and nurture, would police the way you talked, walked, and the ways your body freely and naturally moved. Oftentimes messaging of "Boys don't _____ like that" (fill in the blank with a never-ending list of verbs, i.e., cry, walk, talk, dance, etc.) were a constant. Like many LGBTQIA+ persons, I spent years overachieving in an attempt to overcompensate for my gayness. Specifically, I felt it was unpalatable due to initial shame that I held regarding it. This shame, like for many others, created a sense of internalized homophobia. This internalized homophobia would lead to me creating rigid boundaries on myself, on how I moved, how I talked, and how I showed up in the world. Fears of being persevered as "that type of gay" would lead to self-isolation, where I would create distance and unreachable walls with other gay men during my late teenage years and early college years. For those aware of the Six Stages of Coming Out Model, I was living in Stage Two: Identity Comparison. At this stage, I was internally accepting my queerness, but still actively avoiding other queer individuals and still not yet ready to invite others into my world.

I've had to navigate spaces where I've felt forced to sever and repress parts of my identity, due to feeling that those parts (i.e., my queerness) were not able to be digested or accepted. This was particularly present during my early parts of my undergraduate career, where I served as a student leader for many on-campus organizations. Prior to college I found myself questioning my sexuality, where I longed to leave my hometown to escape to college as a means to freely discover myself. However, upon reaching college I found myself enacting some of the same patterns from my adolescence, which was continued overachieving and masking. As I became an active student leader on campus, I began to feel I would never be able to show my queerness out of fear of being judged, scrutinized, and ostracized. This fear was particularly amplified when I joined my fraternity and formed a bond with my line brothers. The fear that I held and the assumed limitation that I had that my brothers would not be able to accept the fully integrated version of me caused me to create walls that denied them and my closest friends access to the truest parts of me.

It was not until my junior year of college that I reached a breaking point of no longer allowing fear and uncertainty to lead my steps in my relationship with all the intersectional parts of me, as well as those around me. This type of breaking point awakens in many of us who identify within the LGBTQIA+ spectrum, where we've reached a level of "tiredness" from acting. We develop a level of readiness and self-acceptance; a readiness to be accepted, embraced and loved by those we care about or be denied and ostracized. Either way this level of "tiredness" can no longer weigh us down as we crave and require wholeness within ourselves. In contrast, there is a bleak reality for many others, who never reach this level of freedom due to lack of safety and community.

Healing Queer Trauma: EMDR in Practice

It is through my life experiences that my approach to therapy has been shaped in a unique way, particularly when working with Black and Brown individuals, and even further when working with Black and Brown individuals who identify within the LGBTQIA+ spectrum. This connection and mirroring have created an unspoken rapport, where they can show up fully in sessions without the fear of being judged and without holding the burden of having to teach about their culture and unique experiences that lie within that culture. Many of my clients have experienced various forms of trauma tied to both their Blackness and their queerness, oftentimes by the very people who were supposed to love and protect them. Over the last few years of practicing, particularly in implementing the use of the modality Eye Movement Desensitization and Reprocessing (EMDR) Therapy, I've noticed common patterns connected to trauma as it relates to my clients. Those patterns typically include religious or church trauma, family ostracization, fear of safety, challenges or stigmas related to sex, and challenges with self-worth. Additionally, many of those patterns are connected to one another and create a cycle of negative beliefs for the client on how they perceive themselves in society.

For instance, I once worked deeply with a client who was raised in a religious upbringing, where they were the "savior" and parentified child in their household. This client was often left with the task of raising their siblings while their mother worked. For the purpose of this case vignette, we will call this client Jon. They often presented as hyper-independent, recognizing that their forced adolescent independence led to a frequent need for control and rigid boundaries. Furthermore, their need for control was only enhanced due to an experience of trauma from a sexual assault, where their autonomy and consent was taken away. This need for control was further compounded when they later learned of their HIV+ diagnosis, which also created a sense of distrust, betrayal, and self-judgment. This control and distrust greatly impacted Jon's relationship (i.e., emotionally and sexually) with his partner due to Jon feeling they had to be responsible for everything in their life and household. Being the oldest child in their family and realizing that they were queer put a vast amount of pressure on Jon during their adolescent years.

Jon was raised in the South, where the messaging that they typically heard regarding their queer identity was not one of support. In fact, most of the messaging they received was tied to fear mongering around "gay sex." Their mother often told them to be mindful and not to get "sick," which was her way of referring to

HIV/AIDS. Jon would often recall memories of having a simple cold and their mother making comments of concern about him being HIV positive. This would later cause massive feelings of shame, confusion, and uncertainty when years later they were diagnosed with HIV.

Due to the complex nature of Jon's trauma, we both agreed that EMDR would be the best modality to address their traumas. When developing their target sequence plan, we initially chose to tackle their sense of control and responsibility, where we settled on their negative belief being "I have to be responsible for everything" and their targeted adaptive belief being "I can relinquish responsibility and allow those around me to be responsible." It was through the desensitization phase of EMDR that Jon was able to make profound findings and connections about themselves and their relationship, primarily their romantic relationship with their partner. After clearing the neural network associated with the traumatic memories tied to feeling responsible for everyone and everything, Jon felt ready to delve deeper into their trauma and beliefs regarding sex.

Their readiness led to us identifying their next negative belief: "When I have sex, bad things happen." We also identified their adaptive belief as "When I have sex and let go, I can open myself to pleasure." It was through this process that Jon was able to rewire the stigma that was once force fed to him and create a healthier relationship with sex that was rooted in liberation and freedom versus shame, fear, and uncertainty. Jon's story, while uniquely his own, is similar to many of my clients' life experiences. These similarities being each of them standing courageously in facing their traumas and remaining resilient against life circumstances. I felt it would be beneficial to share some of the targeted negative beliefs and adaptive beliefs created by some of my clients to showcase the similarities of clients who share the intersections of being Queer and raised in the south:

Negative Belief	Adaptive Beliefs
"I'm not good enough"	"I'm deserving"
"I am bad for who I am"	"I am whole as I am"
"I can't trust men"	"Some men are worthy of trust"
"It's not safe to trust"	"It can be safe to trust"
"I am inadequate"	"I am capable and competent"
"I can't trust myself or others"	"I can be secure and vulnerable with myself and others"

In working with clients who share my intersections of Blackness and queerness, I've found that the healing journey is not just about processing the traumas but reclaiming all the parts of yourself to unlock the full innate version of you. In doing this, it allows you to not only rewrite the narratives but also the ability to walk in wholeness with resilience. EMDR, while structured and flexible, creates a unique vehicle for clients that allows them to challenge the negative beliefs that have been bred from the various aforementioned traumas of shame, systemic oppression, and familial and societal expectations.

My own journey in navigating the intersections of my identities, where I confronted internalized messages and embraced myself fully, mirrors this same resilience that many of my clients exhibit. While the South has deep origins of tension between identity and belonging, it is also a place of deep cultural richness and strength that can be a catalyst of healing. It is in the process of leaning into vulnerability and discomfort, though not easy, that we allow ourselves to be seen, heard, and transformed for the better. The journey may not be easy or linear, but it is a journey you are worthy and deserving of completing. To my Black and Brown queer siblings still finding their footing: you are enough, you are worthy, you are celestial. You are imbued with unimaginable strength and your truth deserves to be honored - unapologetically and in full.

Earl C. Martin Jr. MSW, LCSW, (he/him) is a licensed clinical therapist, podcaster, and curator of healing—but above all, a human committed to helping others live their best lives. He is the owner of Innate Virtue Counseling, PLLC, and the creator of 26 Affirmations for Boys of Color. Earl specializes in addressing anxiety, intimate partner violence, and boundary setting, with expertise in the intersections of LGBTQIA+ identities, minority stress, and trauma. Earl received his Master of Social Work and B.A. in Psychology from Winthrop University, where his studies focused on empowerment, racial inequities/microaggression experiences, and youth who identify as LGBTQIA+.

References

National Coalition for the Homeless. (2022, December 28). *LGBTQ Homelessness - NCH*. National Coalition for the Homeless. https://nationalhomeless.org/lgbtq-homelessness/

The Trevor Project. (2020, October 6). *All Black Lives Matter: Mental Health of Black LGBTQ Youth*. The Trevor Project. https://www.thetrevorproject.org/research-briefs/all-black-lives-matter-mental-health-of-black-lgbtq-youth/

Rebellious Love

By Jamie+ (The Unicorn System)

Yours is ebulliently rebellious love
The wise woman born in the fires of war
Said to me

This sage sees all of me—all of us
She sees how we were born
And what we were born into

For we are a system of many parts
Many selves
Many worlds

We are not fucked up,
Even though many in our field of "helping professions"
Would have us believe it

We live in a world of our own creation
Because of the fucked up things
That happened to us

Our creativity kept us alive
And brought these inner worlds
To life

The therapists and high thinkers
At least they believe in us
Say that we have "dissociative disorders"

They say that we are some of
The hardest people to treat
To make sense of

They say we are not
Actually healed
Unless we are "integrated"

They want to "fix" us
So that they feel better about
Themselves and their work

My selves and I wonder
If this is how our queer siblings felt
In the generations before us

What did you learn, beloved ancestors
When being queer or trans got you
Labeled "mentally ill"?

And all you were allowed to feel
When contemplating your
Precious identity was shame

Oh there are religious folk and
The politicians who do their bidding
Who still see us that way

At least the field has largely
Moved past it,
There is still work to be done

We wish the field could
Embrace the same understanding
To those of us who see

The world differently because of
How our creative minds
Responded to the things that happened

When the elites in their
Ivory towers say that shame
Accompanies a dissociative diagnosis

We say boldly,
Like our queer siblings before us
Who blazed a trail

Any shame we feel is
Because you fancy doctors
Made us feel that way

As an advocate for people with
Dissociative minds like our
Precious, unicorn system

We draw strength from
What the rainbow souls who
Came before us revealed

Be vocal.
Be proud.
Don't let anyone else speak for you.
Hold your allies accountable.
Let your existence be the resistance.
And may authenticity be your Higher Power.

Today, we exist as a Unicorn System of parts
The shapeshifting *Jamie*–
The doctor and the person
The person who often thinks
That the doctor and her world are

Full of shit

Four...Lucy
The innocence
The light
The optimism
The soft heart
She who feeds
The glow

Nine...Jaime
The cynic
The badass
The one needing
The most therapy
They who stand
With arms akimbo

Nineteen
The first of us
To come out
To ourselves
The one who held
All the pain
That followed

And all the small
Pieces and fragments
In our orbit
And the spiritual mother
Who holds us all
In her divine embrace

Being out and
Proud and queer
Helped us

To embrace
Our beautifully
Bisexual unicorn soul

Paving the way
For us to love
Our unicorn mind

Without shame

With rebellious love.

Mixed media artwork submitted by the author

Jamie+ (The Unicorn System) (she/they/we) is a kinky, bisexual, Croatian-American poet, expressive artist, mother, world traveller, figure skating fan, movie lover, witch, Interfaith seminarian, and believer in all things magical. The entire system wishes that the field of professional therapy would take the voices of lived experience more seriously, and to return to the artistic roots of healing which are Indigenous in nature. If there's one movie Jamie+ thinks we should all watch, it's Dogma (Kevin Smith, 1999).

The Forgotten Parts of Me

A Clinician's Journey Through Breast Cancer & Early Childhood Trauma

Rev. Karla Fleshman, LCSW, MDiv, TCYM II

EMDR Phase 1: History Taking

What has it all been for the great search for the soul
Behind all the lies are stories kept deep inside
Of who you think you are, a life you thought you could devise
But here you are again questioning all that you can
–Ananda Das, *Flow Like a River*[1]

Five years ago my life flipped. On Election Tuesday 2020 I felt a lump in my left breast. A month later I was officially EMDR Certified and diagnosed with breast cancer during a global pandemic. Shall we cue the tragic comedy soundtrack?

Immediately following the initial medical consultation with the breast cancer surgeon, my wife and I went for a walk in the woods. Masked and keeping our distance from others, I listened to her talk about the good news of early detection and my being diagnosed with the "easiest" type to treat and recover from. I drifted in my thoughts and I felt myself begin to disconnect from my body and the present moment. While listening to my feet crunch down on fallen leaves, I felt far, far away. I felt little and small, alone and afraid.

While my wife focused on the positives of diagnosis, treatment, and prognosis, I couldn't leave the negative. As we walked along the stream, memories of my life as a child resurfaced. And I noticed my chest felt tight and my throat began to constrict.

When I prep a client for EMDR, I ask them, "What do you notice"? They are given space to pay attention to the memory flashes and where in their body they feel the trauma. We do this before I ask them to frame the narrative of self that emerges within them;

1 *Das, Ananda, Flow Like A River, Flow Like A River Triloka Records (2021)*

then we focus on the target with some form of bilateral stimulation (BLS) that works best for them.

Following my own practices as a therapist, I focused on what I noticed in my body and where I felt the distress. I asked internally, what is the negative statement I was having of myself at that moment? I was able to identify two: "I am powerless" and "I am responsible."

This negative cognition of "I am powerless" may have been triggered by the diagnosis, but it wasn't attached to the cancer. I felt that very strongly. The cognition was from when I was a little kid. The "I am responsible" felt more strongly attached to the cancer diagnosis and not wanting to burden others, nor bring them sad news as I played inside my head the family role from childhood functioning as the parentified child.

We walked and I allowed my eyes to scan from left to right and back again mimicking eye movement akin to EMDR. I began to see some of the images from childhood that had been resurfacing since the diagnosis. And then suddenly I felt an intense reaction that caused me to stop in my tracks, place my hands on my knees and begin to bawl. My eyes were shut and I could visualize my grandma; and all I could think next was that "I couldn't protect her."

As I cried, I felt my wife place her hand upon my back supporting me through this very intense abreaction. I removed the mask and I wailed.

My grandmother was someone that I always referred to as my protector growing up in a house with "two alcoholics and a drug dealer." In my house, the emotional violence was daily, the neglect a frequent occurrence, and the occasional physical violence viewed as standard operating procedures for this little kiddo who knew no better until escaping to college.

I idolized my grandmother, and often said she deserved a better life than she had. In that moment, it felt to me that the cancer brought out a little kiddo who grew up feeling exiled and powerless. I was powerless within my family dynamics of daily dysfunction, exiled by a poverty that left me feeling ostracized and judged by my peers, and bullied for being a queer kiddo at a time that being queer was an anathema in my small town.

Cancer opened an old box of emotional hurt that had been packed away for decades. I felt that I finally had the support I needed to begin to heal from memories long forgotten...those parts of me that had gotten packed away with those memories and emotions. When I finished bawling, I found that I was able to stand up and breathe again. I noticed my throat felt no constriction, nor did my chest feel tight and heavy. At that moment, some part of me healed just a little. And it felt good.

It would be two years to the date of my initial cancer diagnosis before I would discover the depth and breadth of the hurt and the healing that I, and the forgotten parts of me, would need to walk.

EMDR Phase 2: Preparation. Grounding. Stabilization. Resourcing

Radiation Haiku

Oh! cancer... Fuck You!
Radiating beams of light...
Burn, fucking cancer!

by Dykalicious, February 5th 2021

I wrote in my journal dated March 6, 2021:

> I woke up about 5:00 am after waking up at 1:00 am and 3:00 am. At 5:00 am, I gave in and got up; and found myself reviewing my first 8 *table time*[2] experiences over and over and over and over again. This unending retraumatizing loop kept playing in my head with two parts battling over who had the dominant narrative: the afraid little kid part versus the angry 'ready to break something' teen part.

The therapist I started to work with immediately after the cancer diagnosis was EMDR certified and Gestalt trained. We focused

2 *In radiation therapy, "table time" refers to the amount of time a patient spends on the treatment table during a radiation session.*

almost exclusively on stabilization and grounding over what would be the next two years. We knew the radiation treatment was extremely dysregulating for me, but we weren't able to connect it to an earlier trauma target.

I would have panic attacks. Somatically, my throat would close and my arm would twitch. And I fought to not shut down inside. The radiation treatment required that I was immobilized in a vulnerable position with a mouthpiece inserted to help me hold my breath for three sets of 35 seconds while people in another room watched me to make sure I didn't move as the radiation beam would burn into my left breast.

I've been in and around healthcare for three decades, and my prefrontal cortex was kerflummoxed by the somatic responses and severe panic not understanding why the back of the brain was on fire. I was fully aware it was a medical procedure at the same time I felt stuck in some trauma loop in which the details were shrouded from my sight. This is largely how the next two years would go each and every time I had cancer-related treatment, medical visits or medical scans. The intensity of panic and fear, as well as the somatic responses intensified. There were a few times we tried, in therapy, to engage EMDR for resourcing and grounding. And each time I flooded quick and fast.

We used Parnell (2008)-inspired resourcing: calm space, container, distancing, light stream, nurturing figures, protectors, images from nature, music, walking meditations. And I fell in love with Belleruth Naperstack's voice listening to any and all of her guided meditations, especially the ones focused on healing with cancer. All with limited positive impact.

What finally landed for me was yoga, all eight limbs...not just asana. I rediscovered yoga for myself at the end of the summer of 2021. It felt like a game changer. So by the start of 2022, I set a simple goal of yoga 365 in 2022. I even purchased a yoga pillow and began to sit on the floor during therapy sessions with clients. Bought a second pillow for my clients and over half of them began to join me on the floor sharing they "literally felt more grounded" when talking about the tough stuff.

I made a commitment to mindfulness (movement and meditation) every morning before heading off to my group practice. I started my practice in 2018 expecting a solo practice focused upon serving LGBTQ folx. I didn't expect to have it expand into a group practice while fighting cancer, and the subsequent post-trauma responses that followed.

Seven months into 2022, I attended the virtual *Trauma Conscious Yoga Method* training for therapists and certified yoga instructors (Gessel, 2022). The teacher is certified in yoga, EMDR, and Internal Family Systems (IFS). The training involved a guided meditation entitled: *empathizing with an emotion* meditation, inspired by IFS.

This training and especially this meditation was transformative. My morning meditations evolved into my seeking to connect with this part who I understood at the time to be my inner child. I am trained (not certified) in IFS and have been engaging in parts work narratives with clients ever since the start of my private practice. *We All Have Parts: An Illustrated Guide to Healing Trauma with Internal Family Systems* by Colleen West is a book that I frequently open and place in front of clients providing psychoeducation on parts and how parts play a role in trauma recovery. The education would also include the importance of asking if whatever part or parts impacted by the trauma target identified for EMDR processing were ready and resourced before beginning. We gotta make sure that all parts are ready, resourced, and willing to participate before, as therapists, we actually initiate the processing of trauma.

In my own therapy, we continued to move at a pace comfortable, yet challenging. I felt safe enough, yet tuned into inner parts experiencing trauma triggers able to ground between sessions.

Slow and steady was our work.

And then November 10, 2022 happened.

Two years to the date of my cancer diagnosis, I was in the breast surgeon's office for a routine annual exam. I had Belleruth playing in one ear while I focused upon my breath, noticing my BPM on the Apple Watch slowly climbing. I was swaying side to side to help cultivate a calming BLS for my central nervous system (CNS).

At the check in window, I learned that I wasn't going to see the surgeon, rather a last minute switch up to a nurse practitioner with whom I had never met. This appointment would be in a small room with me administering the exam in which I was required to disrobe...

When I heard this, my arm began to shake violently; and inside my head I heard repeating phrases that were growing with volume and intensity: "We are not safe. We have to leave. We do not know her. She is unsafe. We have to leave."

In the seconds that followed, I next found myself on the other side of the waiting room, knees buckling, left arm shaking uncontrollably, and the office manager telling me I was not allowed to curse at her staff telling me I had to *get it together or leave.* I was able to vocalize, "I have PTSD and I am experiencing a trauma trigger." She showed no sign of compassion.

In the days that followed, everything that had been building up within me for two years and all that had been shrouded was being revealed. In the B.A.S.K. model of trauma memory, I finally gained an important missing piece: knowledge. The dissociative amnesic barrier was gone.

In the months that followed, it would become clear that the different parts (ego state) of me were actually more like different PARTS (self-state) of me... and everyone was trauma looping. These parts had been trauma looping pretty hard the last two years as it became clear just how the cancer diagnosis and treatment, especially the radiation treatment, mimicked one of the major types of early childhood trauma we survived and blocked.

In the immortal words of Kimberlé Crenshaw, during her 2016 TED Talk on "The Urgency of Intersectionality," she said, "We all know that when there's no name for a problem, you can't see a problem, and when you can't see a problem you pretty much can't solve it." The problem that I hadn't seen until that moment was that I didn't know I had dissociative identity experiences. This superpower of survival is meant to stay hidden. And we had hidden this from myself and everyone else for 50 years.

Too many Queerific and Transtastic clients seeking therapy have experienced repeated traumas over the course of their life: intergenerational trauma, attachment trauma, gender trauma, sexual trauma, and relational trauma, such as severe bullying. All therapeutic goals are best served by moving with a slow and steady client-centered plan. More typically than not, they live with repressed or blocked memories. EMDR is so wonderful to help process the trauma looping and the blockages. However, when therapists don't have a strong enough therapeutic alliance with the client and move too fast, too soon (before knowing enough about the person to be safe enough for the client) clients may get blown out, flooded, derailed. In my case, it wasn't the therapist, it was the medical model and industry that caused the premature breach.

EMDR Phase 3: Assessment

"The first time I dissociated was sex assigned at birth"
–anonymous

I closed out 2022 pendulating between amazing containment able to do my work with clients and staff while also reading every book I could get my hands on to rule out dissociative identity disorder. Ummm, we ruled it in!

The beginning of 2023 involved wicked visual and somatic flashbacks. My therapy sessions were incredibly intense and challenging as we moved between processing trauma narratives that demanded attention to stabilization and resourcing the different PARTS of me. The trauma work in therapy felt like jumping out of an airplane at an incredibly high altitude while putting on both my oxygen mask *and* my parachute trying to make it safely to the ground. I wouldn't recommend that process! However, it afforded me intensely attentive laser-focus on not only what I was experiencing, but what I was seeing differently with clients as we engaged their trauma processing with EMDR.

It felt like I was Neo from *The Matrix* taking the red pill from Morpheus.

Once you begin to see, you can't not see. The questions I would ask during the assessment phase shifted as a result of my lived experience influencing my clinical work. For example, when I noticed how my eyes would flutter a certain way and vision blur for a brief moment due to a Part coming forward, I became curious and inquisitive to see if this was happening in any of my clients when I witnessed their eyes flutter suddenly. I would simply ask them, "what do you notice?"

The assessment phase for EMDR is focused upon identifying memories to reprocess, and understanding the dynamics of the clients trauma. The therapist will ask a series of questions to target the cognitive, emotional, and somatic components of the memory elucidating the worst/first image, negative cognitions along with the preferred positive cognition, emotions stirred, level of distress, and felt location(s) within the body. When I begin with a new client or delve into a new trauma target with an established client, I hold to the framework of Johari's Window, wanting to be sure each quadrant is explored before proceeding into trauma work because the window that can be missed most often is the quadrant that is framed around the narrative of *unknown to others and unknown to self*. This is where undiagnosed, unrecognized, unaddressed dissociative experiences tend to live in the therapeutic alliance. If left unacknowledged as possibly present and/or unexplored by the therapist, then clients may be exposed to flood out and be blown outside the window of tolerance.

When noticing rapid eye blinks with a client, pausing and asking, "What do you notice?," I make space to explore with them, "Did something just shift for you when you shared...?" Coming back to the body time and again, "Is there anywhere that feels different just now...consider a body scan at this moment if you feel safe enough?" As the therapist, beginning sessions with mindful presence to ensure that my presence and my energy is in the room with the client modeling the mirror neurons for cultivating trust in trauma work is essential.

Engaging the assessment process with a lens for dissociation with clients who have known early developmental trauma makes perfect sense; and is equally important for the Transtastic and Queerific clients that struggle to be in their body because of gender dysphoria and body dysmorphia combined with a cultural narrative often framing their existence as illegal and unwanted. I once had a client say to me, "I think the first time I dissociated was sex assigned at birth." I believe them.

When a child comes to us and tells us something about their core identity and our response is to reject what they are telling us, it puts the child into an internal conflict. They turn in on themselves and think something is wrong with them, which could not be further from the truth. This leads to negative beliefs about themselves that follow them throughout their lives and get worse over the years the more they have to deal with people rejecting their identity.

Trauma narratives growing up LGBTQ+ in the American landscape may be best understood this way (Kort, 2017):

- Knowing at a young age you are different before knowing the words LGBTQ+
- Pretending to be who you aren't, trying to fit into the socially constructed binary narratives
- Because messages from family and community highlight your existence as flawed based upon who you are and who you like/love
- Left without a safe enough mentor or coach to counter this cisgender/hetersexual norm self hatred and shame begin to grow with the inner psyche; and
- The child is left alone fearing abandonment by those they long to be loved by, often leaving them with a glaring choice to dissociate from who they really are to survive.

Psychoeducation with LGBTQ clients—particularly Transgender and Gender Expansive individuals—requires addressing the trauma of growing up Queer in the U.S., within a framework that deconstructs how race and gender are embedded in systems of oppression. This work is essential and must proceed at a pace that aligns with the client's readiness and needs.

What I mean by at the pace of the client, is a person has to be ready before they are able to relativize their trauma narratives. Relativizing is about finding a balanced, compassionate, and empowering way to view one's trauma as part of a larger life experience, allowing for healing and growth. Part of surviving the daily deluge of attacking one's existence means taking the blue pill and telling oneself "I am fine, perfectly fine," while seated in the middle of a dumpster fire. A client has to be ready to take the red pill so that they stay within their window of tolerance because once they see, they can't unsee...they have to be ready...every part of them has to be ready... ready enough.

Which leads us to another important factor for consideration when working with LGBTQ folx. History taking is never ending because the complexity of cultural and familial trauma invariably leads to one diminishing, denying, and forgetting the danger experienced *in the moment* to survive it. When there is a "stuckness" with processing the target, become curious as the clinician, and be open to pivoting back toward reassessment.

For illustration, let's say a client keeps returning to a seminal trauma target when their parents learned about them being queer. The client and the therapist revisit this target many times and process different aspects, but it will not resolve. After spending a few months exploring attachment breaches as a child linked to discussions associated with the text *Adult Children of Emotionally Immature Parents* (Gibson, 2015), the client and therapist revisit the target with them having different narratives affiliated with the parent/child relationship. At the start of care, the parents were positioned upon a pedestal while the client as a child who survived the traumas, had centered themselves as "the problem." When the client is ready to center themself upon a pedestal of self-compassion/love and able to vocalize how the parents were the problem as products of their own intergenerational trauma, they are ready to revisit the target.

Let's imagine that in this newest round of desensitization of the target, they share how their parents hit them.

"What?," the therapist may say.

They repeat, "They hit me."

"You never shared that detail with me before now," replies the therapist.

"Oh really," they respond with their voice resonating a tonal surprise pausing a moment before continuing, "All these years, I downplayed it, but when I think of a wooden spoon, food isn't the first thing that comes to mind for me and I always thought that was normal."

EMDR Phase 4: Desensitization

One Transtastic therapist said to this author as we approached the 2024 presidential election, "*You can't be transgender or gender expansive in America without experiencing trauma.*" Year after year, the American Civil Liberties Union (ACLU) tracks hundreds of anti-LGBTQ+ laws. Most of those laws focus on gender identity and gender expression with an inordinate number fixated on attacking our most vulnerable and powerless people, our nation's Transtastic and Queerific children. Elected leaders are going after our kiddo's access to bathrooms, locker rooms, athletics and safety in the classroom. When the government that is tasked to protect you is the most powerful bully coming after you, trauma happens. And it can take a lifetime to heal from.

The bullying started for me in fifth grade, and grew worse in junior high before reaching its peak in high school when I would receive anonymous death threats from fellow students, who were incidentally active in the same Fellowship of Christian Athletes after school group I was active in. They felt perfectly entitled to use slurs when they called me on the house phone, or wrote them on my locker, or said them out loud in the middle of class without any repercussions from teachers.

I had blocked all these "lovely" memories, through my creative dissociative amnesiac super powers, until I was in my late 20's when my grandmother retold the story of the severity of the bullying during my senior year to myself and a friend as we were visiting her. I recall being shocked and perplexed when I responded, "What are you talking about?" She raised both her eyebrows and voice stating most emphatically, "We had to get the police involved...don't you remember?" As she proceeded to recite details I had "forgotten," flashes of the rotary phone and me answering it, hearing the voice telling me I was going to die came flooding back. And as fast as it came back, I pushed my way into a derealized/depersonalized space.

Diane Ehrensaft (2016), a prominent psychologist and advocate for gender-affirming care, discusses the concept of gender by location in her book *The Gender Creative Child*. She uses this term to describe children who express their gender differently depending on their environment or the people they are with. This variability often reflects the child's effort to navigate different social, cultural, or familial expectations about gender from a place of safety and social acceptance. I posit that sexual orientation by location also applies, and the repeated "masking" of authentic self from others from a place of real and/or felt sense of safety contributes to dissociative experiences.

The trauma experienced by systemic oppression leads to masking one's sexual orientation and/or gender identity for years, often leading to the risk of increased social isolation (particularly among family, peer, or community support). This level of isolation magnifies and exacerbates negative narratives of self in addition to social isolation; It is arguably the strongest and most reliable predictor of suicidal ideation, attempts, and lethal suicidal behavior among samples varying in age, nationality, and clinical severity (Van Orden et al., 2010). In 2023, *Our Epidemic of Loneliness and Isolation: The U.S. Surgeon General's Advisory on the Healing Effects of Social Connection and Community*, Surgeon General Dr. Murthy refers to scientific research saying, "About one in two adults in America reported experiencing loneliness" with LGBTQ+ individuals identified as having higher risk" (Department of Health and Human Services, 2023).

During the desensitization phase of EMDR Therapy, the client is instructed to focus on the traumatic memory. Focus upon the single episode or repeated episodes (first and worst targets) of assault in any and all forms, which may bring on a real and/or felt sense of isolation/loneliness elevating an inner narrative centered upon an existential conflict of "why bother?"

We ask them to pay attention to what they are able to recall happening as those memories show up in their body and emotions, through images and negative narratives they have attached to these moments. The goals are to (1) reduce the emotional charge, (2) reprocess maladaptive beliefs, and (3) allow natural resolution. No therapist should wade into troubling these waters without having established therapeutic trust, spending time installing resources to strengthen ego and affect tolerance, as well as encouraging the client to strengthen/cultivate social support both inside (parts work) and outside (peer relationships) of themselves.

Therapists inattentive to supporting clients with cultivating both inner communication among parts *and* external peer relationships do a disservice to LGBTQ+ folx often inadvertently by centering themselves, as the therapist, as the primary source of support risking creating yet another unhealthy attachment dynamic. I started a therapy group for clients entitled *Queer Dharma: Yoga and Meditations for Liberation* based on the book by Jacoby Ballard (2021) and invited in clients who struggled to connect with others. After eight successfully attended months of weekly/bi-weekly discussions, I felt it was time to end the group. Members had become connected during this time and decided on their own accord to continue meeting outside of the therapy practice weekly for Dungeons & Dragons calling themselves *ORK: The Order of Reverend Karla.* As we went into an unfavorable presidential election cycle, several of those in the group shared with me during individual sessions feeling fear, yet having the fear tempered with knowing they have a community of support they never thought they would have.

EMDR Phase 5: Installation

I believe, whether we are talking about "little p" or "Big P" PARTS, that every part is divine, in that, each part helped in its own way the ability to triumph despite (not because of) the trauma. –Rev. Karla

By the time a client approaches the installation phase, the focus of the therapist is to work to strengthen the emotional connection to positive cognitions (e.g., "I am safe now," "I am in control," or "I am worthy"), so that the strength of the belief feels more true and integrated. I've noticed that one area of a client's life that often doesn't get enough attention in therapy is exploring the trauma—or the potential positives—connected to their religious or spiritual experiences.

In the book *Courage to Suffer: A New Clinical Framework for Life's Greatest Crisis* written by Tongeren & Tongeren published (I kid you not!) on *February 27, 2020*, the centerpiece of their clinical model is one of *cultivating meaning in the midst of suffering* as essential therapeutic work. The authors juxtapose existential concerns, such as groundlessness, isolation, identity, and death with positive psychology highlighting relationships, virtues, and religion. I like to replace *religion* with *spirituality* when using this framework with both clients and the larger community.

I first learned about this book while listening to the authors on a podcast right after I finished my radiation treatment in 2021. I was drawn to their framework as a way for me to try to understand what was happening to me during cancer diagnosis and treatment. This book took on new meaning and insights as we wrestled with once repressed memories that painted a very different experience with our childhood.

For days to weeks to months, I would revisit the disbelief of living 50 years without the "knowing of what I endured" as a child. As the body remembered and the images came forth and the feelings emoted, I wrestled with experiences that were obviously mine yet felt foreign. Is this real? Am I making it up? How is this possible? The red pill of remembering does not lie.

For many persons (though not all), when first learning about their dissociative experiences that helped them survive the traumas of childhood, they are met with internalized narratives of denial, shame, guilt possibly partnering with narratives of "I am not normal," "I will never be accepted" and "I should hide my identity to avoid making others uncomfortable." Funny, not funny how these are many of the same narratives that many queer people experience when coming out to themself/selves.

As I sorted through my disbelief of how I could have gotten this far in life with dissociative identity *disorder*, I read the Courage to Suffer again, seeking direction from the Spirit of the God of My Understanding to lead me through the maze of memories and meaning making. I came to the conclusion that to suffer the cultural narratives of others that demonize the marginalized is the true sin. I am not "disordered" because I live with dissociative experiences any more than I am disordered loving a woman with my whole being. Who is disordered are the ones who cause the trauma, from sexual predators to pastors promoting hate.

When speaking with parents who struggle to accept their Transtatic, Queerific kiddos, I will often say, "I am so sorry that the social construction of our contemporary culture has made no space for your family." Unnecessary is the suffering that the loving family of Queerific and Transtatic kiddos experience on the daily. And yet here we are in a world in which every day we experience a thousand joys and a thousand sorrows trying to make some sense of it all!

The authors of *Courage to Suffer* make a distinction between pain and suffering (Tongeren & Tongeren, 2020):

> Pain exists when your client is experiencing an event or a pattern of thinking that (a) is explainable (having a clear source of reason) and (b) has a relatively distinct trajectory (appearing to be resolvable) and (c) is relatively focused (affecting one primary area of life) (pp. 7-8).

While pain may have a remedy, the authors argue that suffering is so profound and relentless that it irreversibly transforms individuals, compelling them to confront life's deepest existential truths. Pain can exist without suffering, but suffering cannot exist without pain.

For people who have experienced complex trauma and folx experiencing contemporary traumas in today's national/political climate, creating meaning is essential in supporting clients both with and through their suffering. We define meaning making as the subjective, client-centered interpretation that their experiences and life are coherent, significant, and purposeful.

When individuals can make sense of the traumatic events that have caused them harm (experiencing coherence) while fostering a sense of personal worth (significance), they are more likely to (re)discover a sense of life purpose, shifting from dysregulation to a more centered state (Tongeren & Tongeren, 2020). Finding meaning does not erase suffering but allows deeply painful experiences to transform into something greater, making the pain more bearable. Finding meaning is critically important in the installation phase of EMDR. This phase helps the client replace negative self-perceptions with more adaptive, empowering beliefs, further reducing distress and promoting healing.

EMDR Phase 6: Body Scan

Home is inside us.
–Thich Nhat Hanh

In EMDR, a body scan is used to identify and process any residual distress that remains in the body after reprocessing a traumatic memory.

For clients who, when the body may be the trauma, what to do?

Sometimes, it may be relevant to skip the body scan altogether if a body scan would lead to activating gender dysphoria while trying to resolve a trauma target unrelated to gender identity. Having a discussion with a client who lives with body dysmorphia and/or gender dysphoria in advance of processing an unrelated trauma target may be advisable to determine if a body scan is something to include or to skip. Please always lean into the client's right to self-determine as a therapist by making space for them to know they have options.

Yet, there are times a body scan may be beneficial. Thich Nhat Hanh wrote about the importance of integrated healing: mind, body, and spirit. He wrote about marrying breath and body when addressing suffering. In many of his teachings, he would reflect upon how, when we practice mindful breathing and tune into our bodies, we start to notice the suffering we've been avoiding. This suffering resides not only in our minds but also within our bodies. It has been trying to reach us, seeking acknowledgment, yet we have expended much time and energy pushing it aside.

Dissociative experience often includes detaching from the body to survive the trauma in the moment it is happening *and* when experiencing flashbacks. A person may become conditioned to exit the body when triggered by real and/or imagined distress.

It is very difficult to stay in the present when literally feeling the violation of past traumas upon the body. And yet, it is in resourcing a person enough to stay in dual awareness while reprocessing the trauma that may be key to leading them through to the other side of healing. Thich Nhat Hanh (2014) writes, "There is a way of getting in touch with the suffering without being overwhelmed by it...[and]...going back to listen and understand our suffering brings about the birth of compassion and love" (p.30). Therapeutically, it is the time spent teaching various stabilization and resiliency techniques to clients that makes all the difference in their being able to hold dual awareness. Do not skip this step. And always be ready to revisit this step.

Thich Nhat Hanh would suggest to begin with breath, such as box breathing, alternate nostril breathing, ocean breathing, or even 4-7-8 breath patterns where the dual awareness of focusing upon breath and body at the same time may be stabilizing enough. A touch-based body scan may work for someone else where they, the client, lightly touches or places their hands on different areas of their body to check in on sensations that can indicate a target may contain additional charge for processing. Providing an ice pack or a frozen orange kept in the office offers sensory reset for stabilization.

Instead of staying still, the person may benefit from moving their body through stretching, rolling shoulders or even a gentle bilateral sway while seated or standing to explore if the body holds tension somewhere seeking release. Still another option may be drawing or writing. What if the therapist had available on paper the image of a figure (human, animal, fictive, or fantasy character) that the client could connect with and draw on to help them both check inward and express outward if tension remains anywhere on their personhood. Another way to provide tactile support is to have items for the client to hold different colors or textures in which they may be able to make a connection to the red ball that is rough to the touch that feels like their heart space or the black block that feels like a head aching.

The more creative a therapist is able to be with Phase Six of EMDR, the more likely they will be able to connect with the client in supporting the client in connecting with their part and/or PARTS during a body scan.

A body scan, for a person living with dissociative experiences, may also be more than simply processing residual distress of a current trauma target. It may be a key indicator that a part (ego-state)/PART (self-state) is making their presence known. When my left arm began to shake soon after the cancer diagnosis I was baffled by the involuntary movement. This new experience was unfamiliar. And honestly, something I tried to hide as the emotion of shame co-occurred with the movement. Over time, as I became more aware of my dissociative responses and the PARTS of me communicating somatically, I realized there were layers to the communication found within and with the body.

I first learned about the *layering of emotions* from Dr. Mike Lloyd (2022) of the Complex Trauma and Dissociation (CTAD) Clinic through the CTAD clinic's YouTube channel. There are literally several emotional layers that are felt on/in the body and these emotions may be more connected to a part/PART than to the most right now self. Dissociative coping is the manifestation at surface-level of emotions where one might experience automated functioning (staying in work mode), detachment (a sense of numbness), derealization and/or depersonalization. The underlying emotional dysregulation is often a feeling seeking to be suppressed (or compartmentalized), such as fear/anxiety, shame/guilt, sadness/grief, or anger/frustration. This feeling may be emanating from a self-state having the big feels while the "most right now" self is befuddled by the sensations/emotions trying to stay focused upon work tasks. There are still deeper levels where somatic experiences co-mingle with trauma memories that activate when triggered.

For illustrative purposes, if the surface level were understood to be where a thunderstorm is occurring, the most right now PART would feel, hear, and see the rain, wind, lightning and thunder and may be able to say, "I am okay. I am safe from the storm" (in EMDR terms: *I am okay, I have processed the trauma and my logical brain knows I am okay*). However, when going "below the surface," a PART may feel and hear the thunder, lightning, or rain, yet struggle to find an anchor or a felt sense of safety. This can lead to a sudden rise of emotion in the body—such as fear or shame—that feels both deeply personal and strangely unfamiliar, leaving the present-moment self confused by an emotion that is theirs, but doesn't feel like it belongs. But, if going "below the surface" there may be a part/PART that feels and hears the thunder/lightning/rain and is unable to gain an anchor hold of a felt sense of safety leading to a rise of an unexpected emotion manifesting in the body then a felt sense of fear or shame may arise with the most right now self confused by an emotion that is their emotion yet feels foreign. Go a little deeper to the core where emotional wounds and subconscious body-level responses live, one may find the origin story of the shake of an arm, freeze of the body, muscle tension of the neck, nausea of the stomach because here may live a part/PART that only feels the boom felt at the surface without context triggering them to flight, fight, freeze or fawn.

The relevance of all of this is that through a body scan one might not discover residual distress that remains in the body after reprocessing a traumatic memory. Rather, it may be the first time a client and a clinician are able to notice a part/PART making itself known.

EMDR Phase 7: Closure

the calm within the storm is where peace lives
–unknown

Closure is all about resourcing the client to leave the session feeling stable and grounded enough. Because most likely, the processing of traumatic material will remain in process for many. Most of the queer folx we serve in Delaware and bordering states through the group practice are insurance dependent for receiving services. There is no way they can afford private pay or extended sessions so the ability to move through eight phases of EMDR in 60 minutes is often impossible; and the likelihood to clear a major target in a single super leap isn't probable. Complex trauma processing benefits from smaller bits of larger targets paced over time.

Another factor for consideration when working with a person with dissociative experiences is that one part/PART may clear the target, while another part/PART holds other memories/narratives that warrant their own session(s) for trauma processing. Also for consideration when working with parts/PARTS is that there may also be a situation in which one part/PART is not ready "to do the work" while another part/PART wants to force the process and engage in EMDR trauma processing. There are often really good reasons for the part/PART that wants to pause or slow the process.

I personally wanted to move in a direction with a trauma target involving a PART that held memories who also wanted to engage the trauma target. Enter in a third PART that blocked and paused the process for months. Turns out this third PART didn't trust the therapist we were working with at the time. When she let us know that she felt our needs exceeded her ability and she didn't have the bandwidth to seek out consultation/training we had to pivot in a new direction. There was a deep felt sense of both dysregulation and relief. The next therapist we worked with was able to secure the trust of the third PART and trauma processing resumed. Sometimes closure may not be the client resolving a target, but a therapist realizing they need to slow down the work while they seek out consultation or additional training.

I recently learned a new phrase in healing work from a colleague: *turtle steps*. Turtle steps in healing refer to small, gradual, and intentional actions taken toward emotional or psychological recovery. The concept comes from the idea that, like a turtle, slow and steady progress leads to meaningful change. It emphasizes patience, self-compassion, and consistency in the healing journey.

When engaging EMDR therapy with persons who have lived experience of historical and/or ongoing complex trauma, the idea of turtle steps feels pretty spot on. Meaningful closure may be more likely to occur when tiny, manageable trauma goals are made to prevent the client from becoming overwhelmed followed up by cultivating gentle self-compassion narratives embracing that healing isn't a race as much as it is a journey (Zimmerman, 2025). Having the therapist center narratives on building emotional resilience while celebrating small wins with the client coupled with allowing space to rest between trauma target sessions may be elements of best practices.

EMDR Phase 8: Reevaluation

From Haunted Self to Healing System:
A Plural Clinicians Positive Reframe

Reevaluation is the final phase of EMDR therapy. It occurs at the beginning of each new session after reprocessing has been done in previous sessions. The purpose is to assess progress and determine if any further work is needed. As we wrap up this chapter, the reader is challenged to reevaluate engaging queer folx and/or dissociative folx with EMDR.

There is a BIG difference between *fixing* and *healing* a plural system. Though most well-meaning clinicians use terms and descriptions to define and frame the narrative of plurals as broken, what they really are doing is judging from a place of their perceived privilege for being a "single." From a plural perspective, a singlet is generally described as a person who experiences themselves as having only one consistent, unified identity or sense of self—as opposed to systems or plurals, who experience multiple parts, selves, or headmates sharing one body.

Consistently, the dominant cultural narratives "other" those who are displaced to the margins whether plural, transgender, disabled, neurodivergent, different ethnicity/race, and so on and so forth. When I offer trainings to improve cultural responsibility toward, with, and for LGBTQ+ folx, I often use the following illustration: the term *indian giver*, which is a slur used to describe a person who gives a gift and then later wants it back, more aptly describes Western Europeans than Indigenous Communities in the United States. Dominant cultural narratives often frame their negative behavior as belonging to the marginalized by placing those narratives of the dominant culture onto those with whom they are marginalizing and proclaiming: this is who *they* are!

When I started reading *The Haunted Self* by Onno van der Hart, Ellert R.S. Nijenhuis, and Kathy Steele early in my realization of plurality, their factors they outlined that influence primary, secondary, and tertiary dissociation were most informative. They also helped me frame some of my own narratives of experience. Yet the overall descriptive language found within the book is one of negative judgment with the social location of being a "normal" clinician as non-dissociative and of being in a position to help the haunted, fragmented, broken, masters of deception plural people is misguided at best and mistreatment at worse.

Question: Who does *not* dissociate?

During my own healing together journey with my PARTS, I have discovered that each one in my plural system has unique gifts and skills, likes and dislikes often working together to create a better existence. And yes, each carries their own trauma memories that deserve attention for healing, *not fixing*. As I get to know each part of my system more deeply and authentically, I am discovering my... *our wholeness*...and I love us! I love every PART of me (us)!

To their (van der Hart, Nijenhuis, & Steele, 2006; p. 67) assertion that, "Development of [emotional parts] EPs over the course of time in chronic traumatization perhaps indicates a lowering of mental level for the previous part of the personality, such that another dissociative part is formed," I say, *bullshit*!

On the contrary, as I recover the memories of my early developmental trauma, I find the opposite is true...not a lowering of mental level, but rather a raising. As a little person and then young person, we had to raise our game to survive. Separating made it possible for me (for us) to *escape* intergenerational trauma and become the first in the family to go to and graduate from college. I am a part of a network of chosen family and friends, as well as active in the community. In fact, I am recognized as a successful business person in my community.

It is true that being a "dissociative system" has challenges and obstacles that may impede healing and wholeness within the System and/or within the System's Community, however the social location of those challenges and obstacles are better placed outside the plural person rather than within them. As I say, "I am so sorry that the social construction of our contemporary culture has made no space for our plural family members."

First, we are plural because of the disordered behaviors of others upon us. Second, we may be "maladaptive" as plural in the greater community because of *the continued lack of support in healing with the trauma narratives we experienced*; and once we receive appropriate support, our ability to thrive becomes evident; and we become much stronger. Thirdly, when we do begin to recognize our super powers, we continue to find the need to hide our "super powers" because of judgment and fear directed toward our *adaptive* and *creative* ways of surviving and thriving within our communities.

There was a time I called myself a "baby dyke" and now refer to myself as an "old dyke." I mention this because I now reference myself as a "baby plural" in need of finding my family of choice to help me understand and harness my super powers. As back in the early 1990s when there was no place to go in the greater community for support, I flocked to the "gayborhoods" to find my people. And so today, I find that I am flocking to the "pluralhoods" to do the same. And, I find once more, the need to translate narratives about me, by those who live outside of my experience and label my experience from a place of judgment, into a language that more accurately reflects what I am understanding to be my truth.

I wonder what the book might have been like if instead of being called *The Haunted Self* it was called *The Healing System*? And I wonder what these authors failed to report because they failed to see the beauty of being more than a "me," by their inability to see the power of being a "we."

I wonder, too, what it might be like if EMDR certified trainers would stop living in a place of fear of persons living with dissociative experiences as viable candidates for EMDR treatment. What would and could happen with less fear and more culturally responsible training for clinicians (both singlets and plurals) to support queer clients and/or those living with dissociative experiences find healing with integrated treatment modalities including EMDR.

Surrender to the unknown
As your path is now shown
The more present you can be
To each moment you will see
The blessings of this life
Unfolding in it's own time
If your patient you will see
That everything is meant to be

–Ananda Das, *Flow Like a River*

Rev. Karla Fleshman, LCSW, MDiv (they/she) has been an advocate for justice movements since Middle School marching with Quakers for Peace before coming out in the early 90's protesting with Act-Up & Lesbian Avengers; and culminating with Soulforce actions advocating against spiritual violence toward LGBTQ folx in the 2000's. They are a contributor in *Understanding and Dealing with Violence: A Multicultural Approac*h (Wallace & Carter, 2003). They are the owner, clinical director of Transitions Delaware, a private group practice which centers the experiences of LGBTQ+ folx. They earned their MDiv from Columbia Theological Seminary (1999) and their MSW from the University of Maryland School of Social Work (1991). Add: They are EMDR Certified with an Advanced Certification in Dissociation Studies for EMDR Therapists from the Institute for Creative Mindfulness and are also an EMDR Consultant In Training centering LGBTQ+, Spirituality, and Dissociative Experiences. When they step away from clinical training and consultations, they enjoy hiking with their spouse, creating Lego builds, and centering their energy with their understanding of the Divine through yoga and meditation.

References

Ballard, J. (2021). *A queer dharma: Yoga and meditations for liberation*. Berkeley, CA: North Atlantic Books.

Braun, B.G. (1988). The BASK Model of Dissociation, *Dissociation, 1* (1): 4–23. https://hdl.handle.net/1794/1276

Crenshaw, K. (2016 December 7.) *"The Urgency of Intersectionality,"* TEDWomen, Available: https://www.youtube.com/watch?v=akOe5-UsQ2o.

Department of Health and Human Services. (2023). *Our epidemic of loneliness and isolation: The U.S. surgeon general's advisory on the healing effects of social connection and community*. Washington, D.C.: Author.

Ehrensaft, D. (2016). *The gender creative child: Pathways for nurturing and supporting children who live outside gender boxes*. New York: The Experiment.

Gessel, N. (2022). *The trauma-conscious yoga method: A somatic workbook for healing from trauma*. New Harbinger Publications.

Gibson, L. C. (2015). *Adult Children of Emotionally Immature Parents: How to Heal from Distant, Rejecting, or Self-Involved Parents*. Oakland, CA: New Harbinger Publications.

Hanh, T.N. (2014). *The art of communicating*. New York: HarperOne.

Kort, J. (2017). *LGBTQ Clients in Therapy: Clinical Issues and Treatment Strategies*. New York: W. W. Norton & Company.

Lloyd, M. (October 2022). "Layering of Emotion in DID/OSDD," The CTAD Clinic, YouTube video, Available: https://www.youtube.com/watch?v=zHIcRhGfYz4

Parnell, L. (2008). *Tapping In: A Step-By-Step guide to activating your healing resources through bilateral stimulation*. Boulder, CO: Sounds True, 2008.

Theresa. "The Difference Between Ego States and Dissociative Parts." *DIS-SOS*. Last modified August 26, 2021 Available: https://www.dis-sos.m/?s=The+difference+between+Ego+States+and+dissociative+parts+%28Aug%2C+26%2C+2021%29

Van Tongeren, D.R., & Van Tongeren, S.A.S. (2020). *The courage to suffer: A new clinical framework for life's greatest crises*. West Conshohocken, PA: Templeton Press.

Van Der Hart, O., Nijenhuis, E., & Steele, K. (2006). *The Haunted self: Structural dissociation and the treatment of chronic traumatization*. New York: W. W. Norton & Company, 2006.

Van Orden, K.A, Witte, T.K., Cukrowicz K.C.,, Braithwaite, S.R., Selby, E.A., & Joiner, T.E. (2010). The interpersonal theory of suicide. *Psychological Review, 117*(2): 575-600.

Zimmerman, T. (2025). *Four Blinks version of Flash: An open approach to trauma reprocessing*, FourBlinks.com, accessed April 16, 2025, Available: https://fourblinks.com/

Boundaries and Belonging

SarahRose M. Hogan, LCSW-R, RPT

The phrase "no contact" has recently gained the spotlight on social media, even though the phrase has been around for years. Articles flood the internet debating this shorthand for saying, "I don't have a relationship with my *parent or family member.*" Our species has a history of phrases like "blood is thicker than water" and "family comes first" to describe the importance of familial unity. Now, these phrases are weaponized to shame those who choose separation from family for their safety. Parents unable to see their faults cling to "estrangement" to speak to the continued failure of their child. Queer and trans people often have a choice of no contact or hiding who they are. No contact or have their personhood questioned.

I hesitated to bring up my truth, even in Eye Movement Desensitization and Reprocessing (EMDR) therapy. I had learned, through looks and silences, that estrangement required justification. If I said, "I don't speak to my dad," I had to follow with an explanation deemed *sufficient* enough to erase the shame. My queerness followed a similar script. Because I am married to a cis man, I find myself making performative pleas for legitimacy: "My only other serious relationship was with a woman." As if I have to prove, over and over, that I am queer enough to call myself queer.

A wrongful narrative pervades our society that people who *go no contact* are considered selfish or indifferent. Often, they are seen as unwilling to engage with their family because they are bothered by some harmless personality quirk or difference of opinion. The truth of no contact is much more profound and painful. It seems that no one benefits from severing ties with a loved one. At a minimum, this self-protective action comes at the cost of being labeled a "bad child." Who dares to abandon their parent, especially in their older age? The heartwrenching choice of going no contact happens when it is the only viable or available way to protect oneself.

In the Queer community, boundaries for self-preservation are even more warranted and frequent. Parents may say, “I love my child even if they do this unlovable thing (are queer)” or “I love my *misgendered* child just as they *naturally* are.” There is a difference between the statement of love and loving action, which are often conflated in families. Stating love is used to deny and/or reject responsibility and reposition the self as the victim. Loving action is acceptance, validation, and support without conditions.

It seems everyone has their barometer of what is acceptable to go no contact. This typically involves overt “unacceptable” forms of abuse that show a perceived level of severity or taboo. Specifically, instances of sexual or physical abuse are often seen as “worse” or allowable to provide self-protection. I am intentionally leaving the question open for you to decide: Was it *bad enough* for me to take this self-protective action? I invite you to be curious about why you may question my own motives. Whatever comes to mind for you, would you think the same about your clients if you think it about me? Do your clients owe you an explanation that meets your standards?

This chapter is an invitation to hold space for complexity. I share my own journey into no contact, offering a firsthand perspective on how survival sometimes requires separation. At the heart of this chapter is an open letter—a deeply personal account of what it means to set boundaries with family and reclaim one’s sense of belonging. I ground the discussion in the neurodiversity paradigm, challenging the pathology-based narratives that have shaped trauma treatment. From there, I examine how neuroaffirming values can be applied to narcissistic traits. This lens helped me make sense of my parents behavior, especially those I struggled to name without internalizing blame. Finally, I turn to the role of the EMDR therapist, what is our part to play here? I invite you to engage with this chapter as both a lived experience and a therapeutic framework that challenges traditional EMDR approaches by centering the realities of neurodivergent people.

A Child Protecting Myself as an Adult

I was 13 when I initiated no contact with my father. It wasn't a dramatic declaration, not some rebellious act of teenage defiance. It was an act of survival. I was living in a constant state of stress, my body absorbing trauma I didn't yet have the words for. Autism and trauma were interwoven, creating a daily existence shaped by hypervigilance, shutdowns, and an overwhelming need for relief. But choosing myself—choosing survival—meant being framed as the problem. No one looked at the full picture. No one considered what kind of situation would push a child to refuse contact with a parent. Instead, I was blamed. I became the villain in a story they refused to read. The years that followed were filled with harassment, judgment, and whispered accusations of stubbornness. At family gatherings, the same question looped: *Why don't you talk to your dad?*

The assumption was always that I, the child, was responsible for the repair. That my father, an adult man, was the wounded party needing my forgiveness. The abuse I endured was hidden well. Friends and extended family didn't understand what could possibly warrant such an "extreme" action. "I know him, he would never do anything to deserve that!," they'd insist, clinging to the illusion that harm is done by strangers, not by parents.

One of my sisters stayed in contact with my father, and suddenly, I wasn't just responsible for my own pain—I was made responsible for hers.

"If you called him, she wouldn't have to call him as much."

"If you visited every other year, she wouldn't have to go every year."

Somehow, my absence became the thing that made his presence in her life unbearable. The message was clear: it wasn't *him* that needed to change. It was *me*.

My father would hide behind the mask of a "loving" dad. He wrote poetic messages about his devotion to me, and mourned the pain *I* caused *him* by maintaining distance. My boundaries were framed as cruelty. At one point, he even offered to pay for my therapy so I could "fix" whatever was keeping me from him.

The irony of that offer still sits with me. He used his position as my parent as an attempt to gain control over my life over and over again. If I needed or wanted something that cost money it came at a nonmonetary cost to me, more contact.

"I can get you that laptop for school if we speak more often."

Almost everyone around me reflected this loving and doting father image, and I spent years consumed with the question, "What's wrong with me?! Why does closeness feel so bad?"

I have been in therapy consistently since age 12. However, I was first diagnosed with PTSD at 21 years old after witnessing an act of violence in a professional role. When I first entered trauma therapy, it wasn't to process my childhood. It was for adult trauma, or so I thought. I didn't dare consider anything in my childhood or adolescence as trauma. My mother made that clear; "Nothing ever happened to you, so don't be the fucking victim, SarahRose." She would sneer at my trauma symptoms.

I was confused, and confusing to others because my parts had conflicting reactions and beliefs. For most of my life, parts of me idealized my mother. When attachment figures, needed for survival, are also the source of pain, the act of recognizing and processing feelings of anger, betrayal, or grief becomes a life threat. For many years, I referred to my mother as a "literal saint" and spoke of her good will achievements in admiration. At the same time, I recoiled at her touch, often felt physically sick in her presence, and avoided expressing my emotions to her at all costs.

It wasn't until my own EMDR therapy and becoming a parent that I could finally admit the truth. For the first time, I could see my own experiences without dissociating. I could track the patterns, connect the emotions, and hold space for my history. My mothering part grew stronger in a way that made all my old survival strategies unravel. I now had two whole beings, outside of myself, who didn't have to exchange their self-worth to be loved. This called into question what felt like the ultimate truth - my mother's sainthood. For the first time, I let myself feel my own emotions. For the first time, I validated my reality. For the first time, I spoke my truth. And that's what ended my relationship with my mother. A part of me had always known that speaking my truth would cost me my relationship with my mother, and so I did everything to swallow my reality and keep quiet. Then, I spoke my truth anyway.

Narcissism is born from attachment injury (Mosquera & Knipe, 2015). It feeds on admiration and the care and attention of others, often from children. It is sustained by public validation, by a carefully constructed image, by the illusion of self-sufficiency. Behind that mask, there is always a wound. A wound so deep it cannot be looked at directly. In my life, this mask created a dual reality, one that fueled my dissociation, self-doubt, and a psychological separation that made the truth slippery. What was real? What was me? What was them? I learned early on that reality is negotiable, that perception can be rewritten, that survival often depends on believing the version of events that hurts the least.

For me, though, the social and communication differences of being autistic made that dual reality even harder to navigate. My natural tendency was to withdraw, to be alone, and to escape into my mind. My brain, hyper-connected and always *on*, was constantly overwhelmed. This set the stage for dissociative parts to form. I believe that I developed dissociative parts as a way to cope and not narcissistic personality disorder, though the two can certainly coexist. But in my case, my body and mind chose fragmentation over the construction of a false self part that defines narcissism (Mosquera & Knipe, 2015). It could have gone another way. Maybe if the circumstances had been different, I would have leaned into performance, into image. Instead, I disappeared into myself.

The Letter

There's something about my autistic brain that makes me believe, deep down, that if I just explain something well enough—if I just find the *right* words—people will *get it*. If I am clear enough, logical enough, patient enough, then they will see my truth. So I explain. And explain. And explain again. It took a long time to accept that's not how it works.

I thought long and hard about whether I needed to send this letter to my family, whether making it public meant I had some kind of responsibility to them. But I don't. Because they *cannot* understand. To do so would require them to go against the disillusionment that protects them. It would mean facing the truth about what happened to me. No one wants to know that these things happen. No one wants to acknowledge that children are hurt in ways that are unbearable to sit with. It is easier, always, to make the child responsible. It is easier to believe that the child misunderstood, exaggerated, or even caused it. So, I finally released myself from the burden of finding the perfect words to make my reality real for someone else.

Dear family members,

This letter did not come about in the year and a half it took to write. It did not even begin when I first sat down to try. This is the culmination of decades—a process of unraveling, of unburying, of allowing myself to hear my own voice.

At first, it was only a whisper. Or not even a whisper. Just a feeling.

I remember moving out of my mother's home at 20. My first room of my own—a small, yellow space, mine alone. I remember staring at the color again and again, realizing:

This makes me feel something. Something like I could be okay here.

The words didn't come right away. Before there were words, there was a painting.

That first semester, I took an expressive arts class. During a guided imagery exercise, my hands moved before I fully understood what I was creating. A picture began to take shape: a deep, black pit, a dark hole with no bottom. And above it, a single yellow butterfly, rising.

I painted The Pit.

And then, My Escape from the Pit.

I did not know what it meant, not fully. But I felt it in every cell of my body. I wrote a fractured poem—jagged, unfinished, an attempt at something I wasn't yet ready to say. That was the first piece of my voice. It took years for the rest to come. And now, as I write this letter, I realize that every single word is another act of freedom. This is not just a story. This is my history. And I am the one holding the pen.

I assume this comes as a shock. You've seen me all these years, acting so normal, haven't you? I learned, at a very early age, that every word of my truth could be turned into a weapon against me. So, I stayed quiet. Pretending was survival. And I am a survivor. As an autistic person, I script everything I say before I speak. I hear every counterargument before the words even leave my mouth. When I script this letter, I hear the disbelief, the dismissals, the gaslighting, the minimizing—the automatic echo I've come to expect. And so, too often, I choose silence instead. But not today.

This isn't the first version of this letter. It isn't the tenth.

For years, I wondered: How can I make them see? I drafted letters filled with detailed accounts of my abuse and maltreatment. As I wrote, I'd think: "THIS ONE. This memory will open their eyes! They can't ignore this!"

But here's what I've learned: I cannot make someone see what they are willingly blind to.

The loss that hurt me the most wasn't when my father died. I lost him long before that. The real loss, the soul-crushing loss, was realizing his comfort, his happiness, and his needs would always come before my safety, my happiness, and my needs. It is devastating to realize that a parent continuously chooses themselves over you, and they've taught you to do the same. Society pushes a myth of parental love, and families often cling to it. They need to see a "loving parent." They need that story to be true.

That myth was so strong that it rewrote my own understanding of love and abuse. I sought out relationships that felt like my childhood—relationships where I could serve, soothe, and shrink myself. Just like my parents had taught me.

Going no contact came at a cost. "She's Dramatic.... Victim.... Attention-seeking.... Crazy.... Difficult..."

No one would acknowledge my pain. No one would name what happened as abuse. So instead, I carried the weight of my parents' actions. All of their mistakes became my burden. And because I was habitually seeking out hurtful people, I ended up in a string of toxic relationships, falsely proving that I was the problem all along.

The truth is, I was faced with a choice: Go no contact or continue enduring abuse.

I am proud that I did what every adult in my life failed to do—I protected myself. And yet, at 13 years old, I was routinely harassed about that decision.

"C'mon, SarahRose, why don't you talk to your dad?"

"SarahRose, your dad loves you so much."

It boggles my mind that I, a literal child, was seen as responsible for repairing a relationship that he alone had broken and refused to fix. No one questioned him. No one asked what had happened. No one considered that maybe I had a reason. They just assumed: "This is a good parent! We've seen him in public, not openly abusing his kids—must be the kid has some problem!"

This hurt me. It changed me. It limited my life.

I was not allowed to speak my truth because I was told it was a lie. I was told, over and over, to ignore my gut feelings—until I lost the ability to trust them at all. And when you can't trust yourself, you can't protect yourself.

My father died when we were no contact. I do not regret this. I received sympathy for his passing. And in my mind, I pretended that people were apologizing for the way he hurt me instead of for his death. And that helped. A little. Loss isn't always a parent dying. But that's the only loss we, as a society, are allowed to grieve. No one ever apologized for his life.

I was always accused of not loving my parents. The truth is: I loved them enough to fight for something real. I loved them enough to want them to be better, to be capable of real love. But I am not the kind of person who tolerates abuse. I am not the kind of person who makes excuses for harm. And I am proud of that.

You sometimes see me. I'm SarahRosie—the baby of the family, the sweet one. You know my heart. So how can you assume me so heartless?

Sincerely,
Your family member.

The Neurodiversity Paradigm

At the beginning of the global COVID-19 pandemic, I suddenly had a lot of time to research online information sources. I landed on the neurodiversity paradigm and EMDR. The combination transformed my life. Today, *neurodiversity* continues to gain traction in the public spotlight. Neurodiversity-affirming care is often conflated with autism/ADHD awareness, which grossly undersells the beauty of the neurodiversity movement.

Nick Walker (2021), an autistic scholar and foundational voice in the neurodiversity movement, outlines the neurodiversity paradigm in the essay "Throw Away the Master's Tools: Neurodiversity and the Pathology Paradigm," inspired by Audre Lorde's (1984) renowned essay "The Masters Tools Will Never Dismantle The Masters House." The pathology paradigm is a way of conceptualizing people that is dominant in our society. It has two main ideas: (1) there is one right or normal way to be human, (2) if your brain works differently, you are something to be fixed, normalized, or erased. This colonial framework is embedded in both therapy and society, shaping how neurodivergent, disabled, LGBTQIA+, and people that are not white are treated. The trauma of this paradigm is not just individual, it is systemic. It compounds over time as neurodivergent people navigate invalidation, coercion, and the relentless demand to conform to neurotypical (what people consider normal) standards.

The neurodiversity paradigm is the antidote. It reframes neurological differences as part of natural human variation rather than pathology (Botha et al., 2024; Dwyer, 2022; Kroll et al., 2024; Shaw et al., 2024). Walker (2021) describes the foundational principles of the neurodiversity paradigm as follows:

> (1) The variety of human brains contributes to the beautiful fabric of our species and they benefit everyone.

(2) There is no right or wrong, normal or abnormal brain type, just as no other form of human diversity is hierarchical. (3) Systemic oppression occurs against neuro minorities at every level of society. Valuing and celebrating neurodiversity also has healing potential for neuro minority groups.

This shift has real-world implications for how neurodivergent people claim identity. One example is the shift to identity-first language. Identity-first language is a way to embrace the paradigm shift from pathology to neurodiversity. For example, I am not a person suffering from autism. I don't have autism. I don't stand on a spectrum. I am Autistic just as I am Queer.

Judy Singer, an Autistic Australian sociologist, provided the first sociology study of the neurodiversity movement in her essay, *"Why can't you be normal for once in your life? From a 'problem with no name' to a new category of disability"* (Singer, 1999). While Singer's work offered the first published academic framing, the neurodiversity paradigm is fundamentally a community movement. The liberatory concepts at its core were developed collectively by autistic activists and allies, including early writings on "neurological diversity" in the *Independent Living* email listserv and the online community *Institute for the Study of the Neurologically Typical* (Botha et al., 2024). A much-debated question in academic and clinical settings is: 'Who counts as neurodivergent?' Kassiane Asasumasu used the term 'neurodivergent' in the early 2000s to describe anyone whose cognitive functioning diverges from the neurotypical norm (Botha et al., 2024). This definition was meant to be expansive, so more would be included in the neurodivergent movement and community. Yet, despite this clarity, debates over who is 'allowed' to claim *neurodivergent* persist—driven not by the original intent of the term, but by a scarcity mindset that fractures movements into "us" versus "them." The demand to *prove* one's neurodivergent identity—whether through a medical diagnosis, or alignment with a specific set of traits—reinforces the very pathology paradigm the neurodiversity movement seeks to deconstruct.

Neuroaffirming care, grounded in the neurodiversity paradigm, celebrates diverse cognitive, emotional, and sensory experiences as part of the human condition (Botha et al., 2024). Neuroaffirming practices reject neuro normalization—the societal demand for cognitive and behavioral conformity. Neuronormalization is a form of systemic violence. This care model seeks to provide ethical, trauma-informed psychotherapy that respects neurodivergent identities while fostering autonomy and reducing the risk of retraumatization (Chapman & Botha, 2023; Dwyer, 2022; Pantazakos, 2023).

EMDR therapists must recognize the profound impact of growing up in a society that upholds the pathology paradigm. For neurodivergent people, existence itself is often framed as a defect—an inherent wrongness that demands correction. This internalized harm is compounded by systemic invalidation, coercion, and marginalization. The minority stress model helps contextualize how these societal forces create and sustain accumulated trauma for neurominority groups, reinforcing the need for neuroaffirming, trauma-informed care (Botha & Frost, 2020).

Minority stress is external in discrimination and prejudice and internal in how it impacts thought content and self-esteem (Cyrus, 2017). This dynamic is further intensified at the intersection of neurodivergence and queerness/transness, where individuals often experience compounded minority stress across multiple oppressed identities. The cumulative effect of these forces frequently results in complex trauma, requiring therapeutic approaches that move beyond symptom reduction to address the root causes of marginalization, disempowerment, and identity erasure.

Neuroaffirming Care Benefits to EMDR

EMDR therapy relies on the Adaptive Information Processing model (AIP) as its core function (Shapiro, 2018). The AIP model describes the digestion of painful memories from a stuck part of the brain to a resting place part of the brain through the connection of adaptive information. This adaptive information must be present in the client's brain for the AIP model to work effectively, and deficits are often present in clients with complex trauma. While earlier EMDR scholars, including Knipe (2010) and Marich

(2011), have explored the crucial role of adaptive information in complex trauma, Zimmerman's (2024) *boat and whale* metaphor helped me conceptualize it in a new way. In this metaphor, the trauma is a whale that can only be processed if the person's boat, representing their adaptive information, is large enough. From a neuroaffirming perspective, this metaphor affirmed that everyone's boat is built differently, depending on identity, environment, and lived experience.

The neurodiversity paradigm is the adaptive information required for EMDR to be effective with neurodivergent clients. A person with unrecognized and pathologized brain traits will experience internalized shame, perceived moral failings, and a negative self-concept. The neurodiversity paradigm allowed me to see that I was not broken. I was/am autistic, dissociative, and a trauma survivor. And all of those things could coexist, without hierarchy, without pathology, without shame. Queer, trans, and gender-expansive clients require adaptive information to grow their boat as well. Minority stress builds with the layers of oppressed identities a person holds (Cyrus, 2017). Zimmerman (2024) uses a metaphor to illustrate the Adaptive Information Processing (AIP) model, comparing a person's available adaptive information to a boat. In this metaphor, traumas and attachment wounds are represented as whales or large fish, too heavy to be caught and processed if the boat is too small.

The neurodiversity paradigm expands a neurodivergent person's boat, increasing their capacity to integrate difficult experiences and reprocess trauma more effectively. Supporting clients in gaining this adaptive information through psychoeducation is crucial, but it cannot stop there. Affirming information about oppressed identities must be widely shared, not just within therapy sessions, but across multiple contexts. This includes family sessions, where clinicians can facilitate psychoeducation with collateral contacts and guide clients in sharing accurate information about their neurotype and needs in ways that feel empowering to them.

Clinicians should also advocate beyond individual sessions, whether through public education, school meetings, or professional spaces. By actively normalizing and integrating neuroaffirming perspectives into broader discourse, we challenge the assumption that neurodivergent identities require justification. EMDR therapists must demand that neuroaffirming care is not treated as an optional add-on. It is a fundamental standard of practice, just as trauma-informed, LGBTQIA+, culturally humble, and anti-oppressive care is.

Masking occurs across many neurotypes, with autistic masking recognized as a distinct phenomenon (Miller et al., 2021). The process of unmasking is highly individual, shaped by personal circumstances, safety, and access to support. Therapists can play a critical role in this process by understanding key factors: masking is linked to long-term mental health consequences (Miller et al., 2021) and is often a survival strategy to avoid discrimination, rejection, and harm (Pryke-Hobbes et al., 2023). The ability to unmask is largely dictated by privilege—many people do not have the safety or stability to openly stim (engage in self-regulating, repetitive internal or external movements or behaviors), express intense emotions, or disengage from social norms without consequence.

Clinicians must recognize these intersecting realities when working with neurodivergent clients. Instead of assuming unmasking is always the goal, therapists should collaborate with clients to explore what unmasking looks like for them in a way that is safe, affirming, and sustainable. Key questions to explore include: Who are the people with whom they feel safe unmasking? How can they connect to their interests? How can they build connections with other neurodivergent people? How can they internally accept self-accommodation (adjusting one's environment to fit their needs) as a valid and necessary form of self-care? How can they externally advocate for accommodations that support their brain's natural rhythms? By shifting the focus from full unmasking to intentional self-accommodation, therapists can help clients move toward authenticity without forcing vulnerability in unsafe spaces.

Masking for me involves suppressing stimming (rocking, swaying, moving my hands, pacing), making prolonged eye contact, having a typical 'back and forth' conversation, engaging in small talk, feigning interest in topics outside of my special interests, modulating my emotional responses to "neurotypical levels" among other things. Like many other late-diagnosed autistic people, I unmasked significantly during the COVID-19 pandemic. Much of the external pressure to perform neurotypically disappeared. During this time, I:

- Deepened friendship through authenticity and acceptance.
- Became more aware of my sensory needs and allowed myself to meet them without judgment.
- Engaged fully in my intense interests without fear of being "too much."
- Had social downtime that allowed my nervous system to reset.
- Learned about my autistic brain and found a deep understanding and vocabulary for my experience.

Unmasking and finding my authentic self was growing my boat. Before, I had been trying to heal myself by changing myself. But I didn't need to be changed; I needed to be understood. The boat wasn't meant to make me someone new. It was meant to hold me exactly as I was. When my boat was small, the truths I *needed* to process were too overwhelming. My self-worth, my identity, my trauma history—all of it felt too big, too dangerous. But as my boat expanded, I began catching truths I had been unable to hold before:

- I am worthy.
- I am not permanently damaged because I am a neurodivergent trauma survivor. I just am.
- My traits are not character flaws—I am not lazy, dramatic, rude, or difficult. I am autistic, and I communicate and process the world differently.
- I do not need to be fixed—I need to be supported.

These truths rewrote my self-concept. They replaced the old, pathology-based narratives that had shaped my relationships, my work, and my ability to seek support and care. A lot of this healing happened outside of the EMDR processing room. But it built the foundation I needed for EMDR to actually work.

- Before this shift, my boat was too small to process my family trauma. I had spent years circling around it, touching the edges, but never fully diving in.
- Once my boat expanded, the trauma memories became easier to process. Because the core of who I am was something I could embrace, not reject.
- EMDR became less about "fixing myself" and more about healing my painful experiences.

A Neuroaffirming Look at Narcissism

Neuroaffirming care means the absence of moral judgment as the sole way of contextualizing behavior. I believe strongly in explaining behavior and not excusing it. I've been filled with anger revolving around questions of willingness, especially toward my parents. Is it a brain trait or a choice? Can my parents change? Are they unwilling? There isn't a permanent answer. I was desperate for a solution that could change my parents into someone I could have a relationship with. Judgements against going no contact often center on the idea of spite or anger. While I was angry, I was also filled with grief and desperation. What the neurodiversity paradigm offers, and what neuroaffirming care makes possible, is a framework that holds both accountability and compassion.

Neuroaffirming applications to narcissism does not excuse my parents' behavior. Instead, this paradigm helps me to make better sense of it. What is going on in their brains that *this* is the behavior they are choosing? They are not just cruel and vindictive. I needed to locate deeper narratives to unpack how they showed up in my life. This reframing changed everything. It helped me release rage and confusion. It gave me language for what I could not otherwise understand. Blame was replaced with recognition of reasonable boundaries in response to harmful behavior. It made no contact less about rejection and more about reality: not everyone can give what we need, and we don't have to keep ourselves in harms way to be "good."

Neuroaffirming EMDR challenges the pathology paradigm by rejecting the notion that certain traits or neurotypes are inherently disordered. Rather than treating Narcissistic Personality Disorder (NPD) as a defect to be corrected, neuroaffirming EMDR recognizes it as an adaptive formation of the self. One that may have ensured survival in early childhood but now creates distress in adulthood. A neuroaffirming lens does not seek to *cure* narcissism but instead fosters connection with all parts of the self, seeking to fulfill unmet needs.

Some may ask, "Does this mean we simply affirm all behaviors, even harmful ones?" The answer is an unequivocal no. Ethical care can be guided by the Universal Declaration of Human Rights, which provides a framework for evaluating harm. The key distinction in neuroaffirming, trauma-informed care is that we can explain behavior without excusing it. Recognizing narcissistic traits as trauma adaptations does not absolve someone of harm, but it does allow us to work with these behaviors in a way that promotes healing rather than reinforcing shame.

The neurodiversity movement is inherently inclusive, yet harmful rhetoric within both psychology and activism continues to create artificial divisions between "acceptable" and "unacceptable." People with stigmatized diagnoses, such as personality disorders, are often cast out as *the bad kind* of mental health needs. This exclusion is not just unjust—it is actively harmful. We cannot criticize people labeled as narcissistic for not seeking help while simultaneously creating systems that pathologize, isolate, or reject them when they do. Within clinical spaces, specific diagnoses still evoke disproportionate fear, bias, or avoidance. Thus, limiting access to meaningful, affirming care.

The widespread rejection of clients with personality disorders is not about their lack of treatability—it is about the therapist's ignorance and discomfort. People tend to reject and project when they feel ineffective. Yet, research demonstrates that EMDR can be effective for individuals with personality disorder presentations

(Mosquera, 2018; Mosquera & Knipe, 2015). And yet, like autistic and other neurodivergent identities, personality disorders remain largely invisible within EMDR training and practice.

Applying Nick Walker's seminal work on the neurodiversity paradigm to narcissism, we must recognize that narcissistic brains are part of the natural diversity of human brain types. However, this does not mean accepting abusive behaviors as inherent traits. The distinction between brain traits and harm is critical. Narcissistic traits develop as a survival strategy (Mosquera & Knipe, 2015). The pathology of narcissism is deeply intertwined with extreme capitalism. Under a system that rewards self-interest, some narcissistic traits are socially enabled rather than pathologized. As Cowan-Janssen and Goodison (2009) argue, consumer capitalism actively exploits shame and disconnection, restimulating the narcissistic wound to sustain cycles of inadequacy and consumption. One could argue that narcissists, particularly those with privileged identities, are not disabled by capitalism but enabled by it. Yet, this structural enabling does not remove their internal suffering. Using a "where is the harm?" framework grounded in the *Universal Declaration of Human Rights* (United Nations, 1948), we must ask: What does it mean to allow someone with narcissistic traits to go on unsupported? Often, it leaves them in catastrophic pain, trapped in the same cycle of external validation that leaves them hollow.

As a neurodiversity-affirming therapist, I reject the term "narcissistic abuse." The phrase misrepresents both narcissism as a brain type and abuse as a relational pattern of needs meeting. It collapses complex dynamics into a diagnosis, stigmatizing people with narcissistic traits while obscuring the actual behaviors that cause harm. Neuroaffirming care rejects the idea that harm is caused solely by moral failings. Instead, it recognizes that many harmful behaviors reflect desperate attempts to meet needs without co-regulation, safety or relational modeling. This doesn't excuse the harm. Instead, it explains it. The following behaviors often show up in relational systems shaped by trauma, attachment injury, and chronic unmet needs. Naming these dynamics can support healing and boundary-setting, repair, and rebuilding a self that no longer relies on harm to secure connection.

- Gaslighting: A dynamic in which one person's behavior causes another to question their memory, perception, or sense of reality. Actions or words cause another to question their memory, perception, or emotional reality.
- Love Bombing: An overwhelming display of affection, praise, or attention. This stark difference in behavior can be confusing and create dependency for the survivor. These cycles may reflect the fluctuations between grandiose and vulnerable states (Edershile et al., 2019), especially when admiration-seeking fails to produce the desired outcomes.
- Triangulation: A relational tactic where a third party (e.g., another family member, friend, or therapist) is pulled into conflict to generate loyalty, jealousy, confusion, or division. This is used to maintain power by controlling narratives and pitting people against each other.
- DARVO (Deny, Attack, Reverse Victim and Offender): A defensive pattern where feedback is denied, the confronting person is attacked, and the roles of the victim and aggressor are flipped.
- Boundary Violations: Crossing emotional, physical, or psychological boundaries by dominance, dismissiveness, or intrusion. This can arise when a person's sense of self is fused with external validation, leading them to disregard the needs or autonomy of others to preserve emotional regulation.
- Emotional Withholding: withdrawing affection, care, or validation as a form of control or self-protection.

Treating narcissism and abusive behavior without a trauma-informed lens is both harmful and ineffective. From an EMDR perspective, narcissism is best understood as a fragmented self-state, one that evolved for survival but now creates suffering for all involved.

- EMDR helps integrate dissociated shame. Processing early attachment wounds can reduce the compulsive need for external validation.
- By working with defensive parts rather than against them, therapists can help narcissistic clients build internal self-worth rather than seeking control or admiration.
- EMDR processing often shifts from idealized, positive emotions to more realistic, vulnerable emotions—a necessary step for healing (Mosquera & Knipe, 2015).

EMDR Therapists' Role in No Contact

Therapists—especially those trained in EMDR—must recognize that it is never their place to determine how much contact a client should maintain with their family. Therapy spaces often reinforce the harmful assumption that reconciliation is the goal—that if healing is effective, clients should be able to "fix" their family relationships. But for many of us—especially LGBTQIAA2S+ and neurodivergent people—estrangement isn't a failure. It is a survival strategy. A choice to prioritize safety over obligation.

EMDR therapists must shift away from the unspoken bias that family should always be prioritized, even when it is unsafe. Cutting contact is often framed as an overreaction, a sign of unhealed wounds rather than a rational, self-protective decision. Even well-meaning therapists can unintentionally reinforce this by subtly pushing clients toward repair, rather than respecting their right to self-protection.

Key Therapeutic Considerations for No-Contact Clients

- Ongoing Abuse → Some clients remain no-contact because abuse is still occurring. Therapists must recognize that not all relationships can be made safe. Clients may need support in changing expectations, finding reality-testing supports, and using protective strategies to minimize conflict. They include:

- The Gray Rock Method: a commonly used technique in abusive dynamics encourages disengagement and emotional neautrality to reduce harmful behaviors through disengagemnt in conflict (Psych Central, n.d.).
- The Yellow Rock Method: Expands on Gray Rock by adding polite and non-engaging civility often used in co-parenting settings or ones involving children. This style presents a cooperative persona that is required in family court proceedings (Swithin, n.d.).
- Persistent Trauma Symptoms → Even when the abuse is in the past, the trauma often isn't. EMDR is crucial for processing attachment wounds, internalized guilt, and the grief of estrangement.
- Reframing Estrangement as Survival → Healing is not about fixing broken relationships; it's about reclaiming autonomy, self-worth, and safety.

Estrangement is not failure. Healing is not reconciliation. EMDR therapists must recognize that clients are the best experts on what relationships they can sustain. Our role is not to pressure repair, but to help clients process their reality without shame.

Conclusion

Estrangement is not failure—it is survival. Trauma therapy, including EMDR, must acknowledge that not all relationships can or should be repaired. Too often, therapists assume that healing means reconciliation. Yet for many of us, especially LGBTQIAA2S+ and neurodivergent people, healing means reclaiming the right to define our own safety and belonging.

The neurodiversity paradigm, applied to EMDR, challenges therapists to move beyond pathology and into affirmation. To hold space for narratives of survival, not just stories of repair. To validate clients who choose distance, not just those who rebuild bridges. Healing is not about erasing trauma—it is about integrating truth, standing in our own truth, and refusing to shrink ourselves to fit into spaces that were never safe to begin with.

Neuroaffirming care applies not just to those who leave harmful relationships, but also to those who were shaped by them. Narcissistic adaptations, like all trauma adaptations, form in response to unmet needs. The pathology paradigm fails both survivors and those who cause harm. Neuroaffirming EMDR challenges us to separate brain traits from harm, recognizing that personality disorders are not moral failings, rather survival responses to unbearable realities. We can explain behaviors without excusing harm, and we can support healing without forcing conformity.

As EMDR therapists, we must do more than process trauma—we must challenge the conditions that create it. We must demand that neuroaffirming care is the standard, not an afterthought. We must hold space for the complexity of survival, the weight of estrangement, and the right of every client to heal on their own terms. To be witnessed, not corrected. To be whole, not made smaller. To take up space in the world—without apology.

SarahRose Hogan, LCSW-R, RPT, (she/her) is a queer, neurodivergent+ clinical social worker, Registered Play Therapist™, and EMDRIA-approved therapist, consultant and instructor. She is the founder of Giving Tree Counseling, a neuroaffirming, trauma-focused group practice based in the Hudson Valley, New York. Her work centers autistic, disabled, and LGBTQIA+ individuals with an emphasis on attachment healing, play, and accessible trauma care. SarahRose integrates EMDR, play therapy, and the neurodiversity paradigm to challenge pathologizing narratives. A doctoral student in social work at the University at Buffalo, her research focuses on EMDR adaptations for autistic clients, particularly those who are nonspeaking and low-masking. She is passionate about family systems work, dismantling clinician bias, and expanding access to affirming care.

References

Botha, M., Chapman, R., Giwa Onaiwu, M., Kapp, S. K., Stannard Ashley, A., & Walker, N. (2024). The neurodiversity concept was developed collectively: An overdue correction on the origins of neurodiversity theory. *Autism*, *28*(6), 1591–1594. doi.org/10.1177/13623613241237871

Botha, M., & Frost, D. M. (2020). Extending the Minority Stress Model to Understand Mental Health Problems Experienced by the Autistic Population. *Society and Mental Health*, *10*(1), 20–34. doi.org/10.1177/2156869318804297

Chapman, R., & Botha, M. (2023). Neurodivergence-informed therapy. *Developmental Medicine & Child Neurology*, *65*(3), 310–317. doi.org/10.1111/dmcn.15384

Cowan-Jenssen, S., & Goodison, L. (2009). Narcissism: Fragile bodies in a fragile world. *Psychotherapy and Politics International*, 7(2), 81–94. https://doi.org/10.1002/ppi.187

Cyrus, K. (2017). Multiple minorities as multiply marginalized: Applying the minority stress theory to LGBTQ people of color. *Journal of Gay & Lesbian Mental Health*, *21*(3), 194–202. doi.org/10.1080/19359705.2017.1320739

Dwyer, P. (2022). The Neurodiversity Approach(es): What Are They and What Do They Mean for Researchers? *Human Development*, *66*(2), 73–92. doi.org/10.1159/000523723

Edershile, E. A., Woods, W. C., Sharpe, B. M., Crowe, M. L., Miller, J. D., & Wright, A. G. C. (2019). A day in the life of Narcissus: Measuring narcissistic grandiosity and vulnerability in daily life. *Psychological Assessment, 31*(7), 913–924. doi.org/10.1037/pas0000717

Knipe, J. (2010). *EMDR toolbox: Theory and treatment of complex PTSD and dissociation*. Springer Publishing.

Kroll, E., Lederman, M., Kohlmeier, J., Kumar, K., Ballard, J., Zant, I., & Fenkel, C. (2024). The positive impact of identity-affirming mental health treatment for neurodivergent individuals. *Frontiers in Psychology*, *15*. doi.org/10.3389/fpsyg.2024.1403129

Lorde, A. (1984). The master's tools will never dismantle the master's house. In Sister outsider: Essays and speeches (pp. 110-114). New York: Crossing Press.

Marich, J. (2011). *EMDR made simple: 4 approaches to using EMDR with every client*. Premier Publishing & Media.

Miller, D., Rees, J., & Pearson, A. (2021). "Masking Is Life:" Experiences of masking in autistic and nonautistic adults. *Autism in Adulthood: Challenges and Management*, *3*(4), 330–338. doi.org/10.1089/aut.2020.0083

Mosquera, D. (2018). Treating personality disorders with EMDR therapy. *Clinical Neuropsychiatry*, *15*(3), 187–193.

Mosquera, D., & Knipe, J. (2015). Understanding and treating narcissism with EMDR therapy. *Journal of EMDR Practice and Research*, *9*(1), 46–63. doi.org/10.1891/1933-3196.9.1.46

Swithin, T. (n.d.). *Implementing yellow rock communication when co-parenting with a narcissist*. One Mom's Battle. https://www.onemomsbattle.com/blog/implementing-yellow-rock-communication-when-co-parenting-with-a-narcissist

Pantazakos, T. (2023). Neurodiversity and psychotherapy—Connections and ways forward. *Counselling and Psychotherapy Research*. doi.org/10.1002/capr.12675

Pryke-Hobbes, A., Davies, J., Heasman, B., Livesey, A., Walker, A., Pellicano, E., & Remington, A. (2023). The workplace masking experiences of autistic, non-autistic neurodivergent and neurotypical adults in the UK. *PLOS ONE*, *18*(9), e0290001. doi.org/10.1371/journal.pone.0290001

Fletcher, J. (2022, December 1). *The gray rock method: How to deal with a narcissist*. Psych Central. https://psychcentral.com/health/grey-rock-method

Shapiro, F. (2018). *Eye movement desensitization and reprocessing (EMDR) therapy: Basic principles, protocols, and procedures* (3rd ed.). Guilford Press.

Shaw, S. C. K., Brown, M. E. L., Jain, N. R., George, R. E., Bernard, S., Godfrey-Harris, M., & Doherty, M. (2024). When I say … neurodiversity paradigm. *Medical Education*, doi.org/10.1111/medu.15565

Singer, J. (1999). 'Why can't you be normal for once in your life? From a 'problem with no name' to a new category of disability'. In M. Corker & S. French (Eds.), *Disability discourse* (pp. 59–67). Open University Press.

Strutzenberg, C. (2016). Love-Bombing: A Narcissistic Approach to Relationship Formation. *Human Development and Family Sciences Undergraduate Honors Theses*

United Nations. (1948). *Universal Declaration of Human Rights*. https://www.un.org/en/about-us/universal-declaration-of-human-rights

Walker, N. (2021). Neuroqueer heresies: Notes on the neurodiversity paradigm, autistic empowerment, and postnormal possibilities. Autonomous Press.

Zimmerman, T. (2024). *EMDR with complex trauma*. Cleveland, OH: EMDR Training Collaborative.

EMDR: The Intervention To Slay All Dragons (Fairy Tale)

Amber Gordon, LCSW

Artwork by the author

Once upon a time,
there was a witch with great power.
And after years of practicing sorcery
She returned to the tower.

The one she escaped
when she was 25 years old,
Guarded by a dragon
Who convinced her that pain was gold.

"Do not ever leave me," he would command,
"For the weight you feel is precious
And only safe in my hand."

Five years passed,
Why would the witch go back?
Well, to free the remaining women, of course.
Her beloved mother was still there, one of the last.

Believing he would get her back
The dragon welcomed the witch's arrival
To reach her mother's floor, though,
The witch went on an upward spiral

Swearing she would never be here again
The witch began to worry
But her mother taught her better than that
"I will save her from the dragon's fury"

When she made it to her mother
She found her sitting and smiling
"Come with me, let's go now"
But then her mother starting crying

"I have powers now,
I can protect you.
This is not gold,
and this tower is a trap too."

With confusion, the witch looked at her mother.
"Why not leave?"
"The dragon says your power is evil, daughter,
Which is what I still choose to believe."

"And how could I give up this pain?
This pain that he calls gold
The pain that I have gifted to you
Made you strong and bold."

With tears in her eyes,
the witch knew what she must do.
To love and honor her mother,
She would have to accept her too.

Amber Gordon (she/her) is a Licensed Clinical Social Worker and Certified EMDR Therapist in the state of California. Identifying as a Queer, Black and Filipina trauma-focused therapist, Amber prioritizes anti-oppression practices in her work. Amber developed a deep appreciation for story telling as a means of healing before ever becoming a therapist. With an undergraduate degree in English, Amber has been fascinated by the power of expression through the written word, and one's ability to build and extend compassion to strangers met through story. Amber received her graduate degree from the University of Southern California, in which she joined her passion for story telling and community healing. Amber is a proud cat parent, who loves to read, write, and run!

Expressive Arts Therapy, Parts Work, and EMDR and a Personal Exploration of Internalized Biphobia, and Bierasure

Sam Bergstein, MA, MSW, LISW-S, REAT

It may not surprise you that clinicians writing about Queering EMDR would highlight the limitations of a one-size-fits-all approach to healing. Our clients are unique, and their healing processes must be tailored to their needs and identities. By integrating expressive arts and parts work into the EMDR process, we create a space where the client's system can guide them through the eight phases of treatment in a way that feels supportive and authentic to them.

As a Queer therapist working with many Queer clients, it's crucial to avoid assuming I know my clients' goals or experiences. Many structured modalities, with little or no personalization, project specific roadmaps for healing onto our clients. While dismantling internalized oppression and healing trauma related to one's Queerness can be powerful, it's essential to leave room for clients to define their own healing. We must respect their autonomy and ensure that their treatment focuses on their needs and goals, not on assumptions. This radical personalization of the EMDR process fosters a more empowering, respectful, and effective therapeutic experience. This chapter highlights the value of integrating expressive arts therapy and parts work into EMDR with our Queer clients and will include examples in the form of personal exploration.

Expressive Arts, Parts Work, and Queering EMDR

About Expressive Arts

Through the use of multi-modal expression, expressive arts therapy engages in the processing of information through activation of the right and left hemispheres, at times, on many levels, including:

kinesthetic, sensory, perceptual, affective, cognitive, symbolic, and creative. The use of as many media or expressive modes as possible in expressive arts can facilitate deep growth and healing (Hinz, 2019).

Parts Work 101

Parts work is built on the idea that throughout our development, strong experiences trigger the need for a part of us to develop. These parts of us hold experiences, emotions, and protective responses. Many times, when a person faces a stressful situation or encounters a trigger that reminds them of an experience, a part of them that has learned to respond in a certain way may activate. These parts often work to protect the individual, helping them continue functioning, meet their needs, or protect them from further wounding. Here are some important points about parts and parts work:

- **Self:** Many people have a central "Self" or core self in addition to their parts. While standardized modern parts work as popularized by Internal Family Systems (IFS) therapy uses the term "Self," clients can use any term that resonates with them. It is important to let clients define this for themselves.
    - Some may not identify with the idea of a core "Self" or a centralized "identity" but still recognize parts of themselves.
    - Alternatives to using the term or idea of "Self" could be:
        - Identifying what aspects of the client represent their ventral vagal system (e.g., calm, creative).
        - Multiple parts may represent aspects of the "Self" and may evolve over time.
        - They may identify with the idea that they have multiple "selves," each with a set of parts accompanying them (like suns in a solar system with associated planets).
        - Creating a list of words, ideas, images, sensory elements, etc. that represent "calm" for them.
        - Dialectical behavior therapy (DBT)'s "Wise mind" concept: Wise mind is a DBT concept that describes

a state of balanced connection to both emotion and reason.
  - "System": All parts combined make up their system (without the idea of a centralized or hierarchical self being in the picture at all).
  - Exploring or gauging connection to the present moment and/or one's surroundings.
- **System:** The client and all of their parts may be referred to as a "system," if the client resonates with that term.
- **Intention:** Each part has an intention to help the client, even if their actions don't seem positive or helpful from the outside. They have roles they believe are necessary for survival and protection.
- **Parts may be running on old updates:** Parts may not always have updated information about current life circumstances or may have learned contrasting ways of protecting the client, leading to internal conflict.
- **We are not trying to get rid of them:** The goal is never to get rid of a part, but to help make their job lighter, if they'd like, by understanding and validating their needs, fears, and the work they do to support the client.
- **Key takeaways**: ***Consent, Curiosity, & Autonomy***. Approach working with parts and systems with respect, ask for consent (literally, use the word "consent") to explore parts, and remain curious, nonjudgmental, and don't project labels or assumptions onto parts that clients haven't identified (Marich, 2023; McKay et al., 2007; Schwartz, 2021).

What's Queer about Expressive Arts and Parts Work?

An essential component of both parts work and expressive arts therapy is allowing clients the freedom to identify their own needs and make their own meaning in your work together. This personalized approach supports the client in navigating their own healing process, rather than forcing them into a directive framework. For Queer clients, this is especially important, as it provides the flexibility to explore and process trauma in ways that feel empowering and respectful of their autonomy and identit(ies).

Another important aspect of integrating these modalities is the collaborative nature of these processes. Truly individualized EMDR requires a keen attunement between client and therapist. This collaboration also increases the attunement between the client and their system of parts as well as between the therapist and the client's system of parts.

Queering the Process: Respect, Autonomy, and Empowerment

Incorporating parts work and expressive arts therapy into EMDR with queer clients opens possibilities for exploration in areas where traditional methods—such as focusing on specific memories, body sensations, or verbal expression—may not be possible, feel safe, or be accessible. For some clients, externalized forms of expression (e.g., art, imagery, symbols) may be more comfortable, accessible, or effective.

EMDR encourages body scanning and noticing somatic responses. Standardized parts work also often directs clients to notice how they experience parts of themselves in their body (e.g., where in their body they notice a part or what somatic responses arise). Many clients may find it difficult to focus on their body due to trauma, neurodivergence, discomfort, disabilities, or many other factors. For many LGBTQIA+ individuals, their bodies have been sites of external and/or internal trauma. As a result, focusing on the body too directly may feel threatening or retraumatizing. Instead of pushing clients into direct somatic awareness, it can be helpful to take a more expressive and less directive approach. This means prioritizing consent and inviting clients to explore body sensations in their own way, allowing them to decide when, where, and how they want to engage with their body. Fostering space and practices for clients to gently notice or name their responses—without pressure to embody or "fix" them—supports their agency and respect for their lived experience. Thus, an expressive arts lens can inform alternative, expression-based approaches for clients to explore qualities such as somatic responses, beliefs or thoughts, and emotions based on their unique needs. Clients can name these qualities verbally, write them, or use other modes of creative expression to explore them.

Examples of these alternatives include providing options when exploring responses, emotions, beliefs, experiences, or parts, such as the following:

- **Basic expressive routes:** The use of color, shape, sound, scent, taste, texture, or other sensory elements.
- **More detailed expressive routes:** The use of imagery, energy, songs, fonts, fictional characters, or symbols as expression or representations.
- **Metaphors:** Exploring metaphors that might represent the client's system such as a solar system, a car, a house, a forest, etc. For example, asking: *Where in or around your solar system would the part be?*

These methods may allow for a respectful, consent-driven, deeper exploration of oneself and can serve to foster greater compassion for different aspects of one's identity. By honoring one's system by giving diverse options for expression and exploration, we are also working together to reduce the shame that sometimes accompanies the need for individualized or adapted care or support.

Masking and Polarized Parts

Masking, or the act of hiding or suppressing parts or aspects of one's identity/identities, can show up in many ways in a person's life. This coping mechanism often develops as a response to trauma, societal pressures, discrimination, the fear of rejection, or all of the above. In therapy, masking can present as the client feeling disconnected from their identity/identities, emotions, body sensations, experiences, behaviors, or needs to fit in or protect themselves. This may make it difficult to identify needs and target elements in the EMDR process. By using methods from parts work and expressive arts therapy, such as painting, movement, or role playing, clients can externalize and give voice to these masked aspects and the protectors that aid in masking them. Incorporating parts work and expressive arts into the EMDR process can help clients begin to understand and connect to their protectors, wounded parts of themselves, as well as the masked aspects of themselves, creating allyship between the client, their parts, and their therapist in the healing process.

Expressive Arts Using Cosplay, Puppetry, Character Work, Role Play, Special Effects Makeup, and/or Costume Work

Expressive arts therapy, puppetry, play-based therapy, and drama-based therapy may use techniques such as cosplay, character work, role play, special effects makeup, and costume work. These techniques can be powerful tools in the therapeutic process for the following reasons:

- **Externalizing parts**: cosplay, puppetry, character exploration, costume use and design, role play, and makeup work give a physical form to emotional or psychological parts. Clients may create a character that represents their "inner critic," "protector," or "wounded part" to work with in therapy.
- **Distancing expression**: Embodying a character or using costumes/makeup to alter one's appearance can offer a sense of safety and distance, which can increase a sense of safety or comfort in working with difficult memories or aspects of themselves. It may be easier to explore difficult emotions or memories from the perspective of a fictional persona rather than as themselves.
- **Perspective taking:** Diving deep into a character that represents a part can increase your ability to understand a part's role and build compassion, empathy, and/or appreciation of them.
- **Empowerment and autonomy through self-definition of parts**: Often, our parts may experience external or internal judgement or aspects of us may be

defined as "good" or "bad" by societal and social experiences. The process of creation of a representation of an identity or a part through cosplay, character, costume and makeup work can empower individuals by giving them the power to create and define the appearance, narrative, and emotions, beliefs, etc. of the part and reclaim their own voice in understanding their parts.

- **Materializing a protective figure resource:** By creating and possibly embodying a protective or supportive figure resource (Marich, 2022), clients can create an increased connection to their protective figure resource. Imagining or actually embodying this figure can strengthen the client and their system's ability to access the protective figure when needed.
- **Non-verbal expression**: cosplay, character, costume and makeup work provide a non-verbal outlet for emotions and experiences that may be difficult to articulate. For individuals who struggle with verbal expression due to trauma, these artistic forms can be a bridge to communication.
- **Giving shadows a platform**: The "shadow," an idea introduced by Carl Jung, refers to aspects of ourselves that we may consciously or subconsciously dislike, repress, or bury (Jung, 1953). Providing a platform for the exploration of shadow aspects, such as lies, painful truths, and hidden or feared parts of oneself, without having to be verbal, written, diagnosed, or documented can be essential in working with these themes and parts.
- **Sensory grounding**: Using different artistic mediums and mixed media can be a powerful form of sensory grounding because the use of various tools, techniques, and materials may activate many physical or sensory sensations. By simultaneously engaging ones parts through cosplay, character, costume, role play, makeup work, etc. we can activate multiple sensory channels.

Personal Expressive Arts Exploration: Masking, Polarized Parts, and Internalized Biphobia and Bi Erasure

Featuring:

"I'm-not-queer-enough-if-I'm-not-the-perfect-rainbow" part

"Monotone palatable" part

"Yes, and" a core identity underneath (not really a part, more like a deep truth about myself)

Reflections on the Art

Art, for me, often becomes a way to explore the complexity of my identity and experiences. This expressive work becomes more than just representations. It becomes a conversation with my inner world, allowing me to process trauma through a non-verbal, visceral medium. By creating this work, I deepened my understanding of how internalized biphobia and bierasure has shaped my identity and my sense of belonging within the Queer community and in the world and expanded my compassion towards these aspects of myself.

When going inward to identify how I'd like to explore these issues, I sensed that I had two protective aspects of me that are often at odds. These polarized parts, the "I'm-not-queer-enough-if-I'm-not-the-perfect-rainbow" and the "monotone palatable" part, hold very different ideas, beliefs, experiences, and methods of protecting me and masking vulnerable aspects of my identity. The "I'm-not-queer-enough-if-I'm-not-the-perfect-rainbow" part holds complex experiences, beliefs, and fears around interacting in Queer spaces and not being "Queer enough". The "monotone palatable" part fears being punished or shunned for being too unique or open about my identities.

More About My Identities

Originally, I planned to solely focus on the stark contrast of the two conflicting parts. However, as I continued to work on this project, I felt a need from within to express the aspects of myself that are being masked. I also originally planned for this aspect of myself to be *only* bisexual pride colors, both to viscerally express my true self and also as a means of highlighting the right to display the bisexual flag colors and celebrating them. Though I realized throughout my process that this aspect of myself *also* holds the right to the standard rainbow as well as the bisexual pride colors, and that I shouldn't have to cast away the standard rainbow to express my true self. The bisexual pride colors are my true self, but the standard rainbow is also my true self. Underneath the exaggerated rainbow mask, which expresses the "I'm-not-queer-enough-if-I'm-not-the-perfect-rainbow" part, is a lush world where my identities flourish. Represented through vibrant color and wild and beautiful plant growth and an expansive nebula, my Queer identity feels expressed and seen. The "Yes, and" depiction embodies my truth through increased bisexual pride colors flowing harmoniously with the standard rainbow colors.

How We Got Here

I wrestle with the inner tension of not fully feeling accepted within the queer community. Being bisexual often means living with the fear that I'm "too straight" for queer spaces and "too Queer" for non-explicitly queer spaces. Additionally, bisexual identities are often oversexualized in both Queer and non-explicitly Queer spaces. This conflict intensifies when I encounter microaggressions or invalidation from both sides, like experiences of being told my type of identity is just a phase on the way to "picking a side" or that I'm privileged because I can "pass" as straight.

Exploring aspects of myself aids in a visceral yet safer and less direct way (through externalization) to connection to target memories. For example, the memory of [redacted][1] stunted my healing journey at the time, and it revealed the deep vulnerability I had in trusting

1 Upon checking in with my system about revealing personal queer experiences to the public, a part, which I'll call my "redactor part,"requested a chance to review the content before it is released. Portions flagged by my "redactor part" as too private may be blocked to the reader. These blocks have been included as a representation of honoring my systems boundaries related to sharing about my queer experience.

other Queer individuals, even mental health professionals, with my bisexuality. My "monotone palatable" part took this experience and filed it as "evidence" to double down on protecting me the way it sees fit.

I have many memories of my I'm-not-queer-enough-if-I'm-not-the-perfect-rainbow part being activated: essentially every memory of coming out as bisexual to Queer people who may not identify as bi or pan. This part feels like an imposter in Queer spaces, thus masking the bisexual pride colors with an exaggerated and very loud ROYGBIV (The colors of the rainbow: Red, Orange, Yellow, Green, Blue, Indigo, Violet).

This tension among my maskers and the aspects of myself being masked is present when I work as a therapist. As a clinician who sees many Queer clients, self-disclosure can be essential in building trust and a supportive environment. My internal conflicts create discomfort in the navigation of self-disclosure. I often question if I should be open about my bisexuality. My internalized biphobia worries me that my bisexuality isn't enough to have earned the right to empathize and empower others from the perspective of someone who is also a member of the queer community. "....am I... am I allowed to say I'm one of you?" However, at the same time, I know that my lived experience is valuable and necessary in my work and building comfort with confidently being myself can provide a model for my clients.

It appears that these parts could benefit from being better understood...

Conversation between Parts and Developing an Empowering Figure Resource

The use of expressive arts to facilitate dialogue with aspects of ourselves can be very useful in the healing process. Influenced by Gestalt principles, Jungian practices, and drama therapy, dialoguing serves many purposes in this work. Because expressive works come from our inner experiences, personifying them helps us connect with feelings and concerns that are hard to access through our typical thought processes (Mcniff, 2004).

After facilitating a dialogue between parts, I will work with my parts collaboratively to identify an empowering figure, based on the "protective figure" resource often used in EMDR preparation (Marich, 2022). The empowering figure can serve as a supportive, nurturing presence that validates one's identity and provides empowering support in times of peace as well as when experiencing difficulty related to one's identit(ies). An alternative to creating an empowering figure could be creating an empowering altar. This altar could include various elements which represent or embody empowering messages, emotions, figures, etc. related to your identit(ies). To take this practice further, the creative expression of an empowered version of oneself or one's system can be an element of the altar (Gutiérrez, 2022).

Suggested Reflection Questions

These questions may help facilitate a conversation between different parts engaged during the expressive practice. These questions can be used to explore qualities and concerns of parts that may be protective towards one's Queerness or hold wounding surrounding identities. These questions should be adapted to meet each individual's specific needs.

As a reminder, it may be helpful to provide the option to use expressive means such as color, shape, scent, taste, texture, imagery, energy, song, font, character, symbols, or metaphors.

1. Identify Your Parts: Which parts feel concerned or conflicted when exploring your Queer identit(ies)?

2. Ask each part these questions separately if possible.
   - What do you notice in or around your body or emotions when you notice these parts?
   - Are there any expressive qualities such as color, shape, scent, taste, texture, imagery, energy, song, font, character, symbols or metaphors that stick out to you?
   - What do these parts believe about your Queerness or Queer identities?

- What messages do they say to you about your identities or Queer experiences?

3. Create Dialogue:
   - Ask each part what it needs in order to feel seen or heard.
   - What does this part want from you?
   - What does it need to hear in order to feel more accepted?

4. Compassion: Explore how you can offer compassion to or nurture these parts. What would a compassionate or nurturing response look like for each part?

5. Empowerment
   - Ask your system and parts if they're open to shift to empowerment.
   - What does "empowerment" mean to each part?
   - Do you notice any responses (thoughts, emotions, body responses, etc.) when thinking about the idea of empowerment? Remember, you can use expressive routes here if you'd like. If your parts have different ideas of empowerment, make note of that.

6. Empowering figure
   - What form does it come in? It could be a person, a creature, a character, a version of you in an alternate universe or a future version of you, an image, or any other expressive representation that you connect to in this moment.
   - List the qualities or traits that make this figure empowering. These could include strength, compassion, resilience, wisdom, etc.
   - Are there any expressive qualities such as color, shape, scent, taste, texture, imagery, energy, song, font, character, symbols or metaphors that link to this figure?
   - Is there a message that goes with your empowering figure? One that it can say to you and your parts to empower you?

Here is an example of how I've worked with my parts using these questions:

1. Identify Your Parts		
Which parts feel concerned or conflicted when exploring your Queer identit(ies)?	I'm not queer enough if I'm not the perfect rainbow part	**Monotone palatable part**
What do you notice in or around your body or emotions when you notice these parts?	Fluttering in chest	Tension in shoulders
Are there any expressive qualities such as color, shape, scent, taste, texture, imagery, energy, song, font, character, symbols or metaphors that stick out to you?	Imagery: A tangled yarn ball of a bunch of different yarns in different colors and textures	Imagery: Black and white tv static
What do these parts believe about your queerness or Queer identit(ies)?	I'm not Queer enough because I'm "just" bisexual	It's best to just blend in, nod and smile, and hide it. Just. Act. Normal.
What messages do they say to you about your Queer identit(ies) or queer experiences?	You're not good enough and your Queer experiences aren't valid enough to be important.	If you are open about your bisexuality, it will annoy people or it will get you hurt or punished.
2. Create Dialogue		
Ask each part what it needs in order to feel seen or heard.	For me to be consistent in checking in with it since it might not be comfortable being honest at first.	To be able to share on its own time.

What does this part want from you?	To be nicer to myself.	To put less pressure on myself.
What does it need to hear in order to feel more accepted?	You are enough.	You're allowed to be yourself.
3. Compassion		
What would a compassionate or nurturing response look like for each part?	Allowing it to exist and hang out with me without trying to fix it.	Quiet, genuine acceptance.
4. Empowerment		
Ask your system and parts if they're open to shift toward the idea of empowerment. If so, continue forward	Yes	Yes
What does "empowerment" mean to each part?	Being accepted and seen as valid within the community.	Being allowed to find balance and express myself on my own terms.
Do you notice any responses (thoughts, emotions, body responses, etc.) when thinking about the idea of empowerment? Remember, you can use expressive routes here if you'd like.	I feel a little like jumping around in excitement.	A little tired because it has pushed itself to express itself a lot already.

5. Identify an Empowering Figure Resource	
What form does it come in? It could be a person, a creature, a character, a version of you in an alternate universe or a future version of you, an image, or any other expressive representation that you connect to in this moment.	It is a mystical and wise house cat.
List the qualities or traits that make this figure empowering. These could include strength, compassion, resilience, wisdom, etc.	Confident, doesn't care at all what people think, is reserved when wants to be reserved but energetic and playful when it wants.
Are there any expressive qualities such as color, shape, scent, taste, texture, imagery, energy, song, font, character, symbols or metaphors that link to this figure?	Its fur is long. It is emerald and purple in color. It has bright green eyes. It sits on a tall cat tree that is in the shape of an old, wise tree. Behind the tree is a glowing circular light.
Is there a message that goes with your empowering figure? One that it can say to you and your parts to empower you?	You are important and worthy just because you *are.*

Empowering Figure Expressive Arts

"Mischievious and mighty" by Sam Bergstein

Originally, I imagined my empowering figure as this wise, beautiful cat atop a glorious cat tree. The cat indeed is upon a pedestal, which all cats deserve (and believe they deserve). This work is my ode to my favorite thing to say to those who love cats and find strength in them: "*be as unapologetically yourself as your cat is.*" Throughout the process, I sensed that this cat had some bold and mischievous ways that it empowered and could support me. Thus, the empowerment kitty, doing as kitties do, is depicted as casually pushing cups and other items, representing oppressive forces, off of a surface and shattering them.

Potential EMDR Targets From This Work

Identifying Target Elements:
Several potential EMDR targets can emerge through this process. For example:

- **Theme:** Internalized Biphobia
- **Presenting Problem:** Anxiety around hiding aspects of my identity, fear around not hiding those aspects.
- **Core Beliefs/Negative Cognitions**: "I'm not safe when I am open about my identities," "I am not a true member of the Queer community because I'm *just* bisexual."
- **Memories**: The first time I remember hearing negative messages about bisexual people and began to feel fear and the need to hide my identity (the memory was made vague here per my redactor parts.)
- **Positive Cognition:** I am important and worthy just because I am.

When developing potential EMDR targets through parts work and expressive arts, it is essential to remember that the goal is not to target or eliminate specific parts, but to work with the experiences, responses, and beliefs that those parts may hold or provide insight on. Each part, even those who appear to create difficulty or conflict in our lives, do important jobs to protect us. We don't want to harm or undermine them by giving them the message that we want them to go away.

Exploring targets through the work we do with parts should also involve asking for explicit consent from the parts to explore targets and ultimately, to pick a target that they have helped uncover. An emphasis on consent, self-determination, empowerment, dignity, and collaboration with a lens of curiosity and non-judgement can create a setting conducive to compassionate and deep healing.

Challenges with the Integration of Expressive Arts into the Therapeutic Process

It may be difficult to access creativity when one is living in survival mode. Additionally, the societal pressures of productivity and perfectionism may make engaging in art-based activities difficult. If art-based expression is not accessible for any reason, there are still options to get started. Here are some gentle creative routes that may be helpful:

- Use of basic expression: Offer the option to use more basic expressive routes to describe the experience, part, emotion, somatic response, or belief using color, shape, scent, taste or texture. Basics toolbox: a toolbox such as a pre-made list of words or emojis, visuals of colors, shapes, textures or a basket of items with scents, taste, or textures to choose from can be helpful here as well.
- Use found images from the internet or magazines.
- Using AI: enter a prompt that describes the experience, part, emotion, somatic response, belief into an AI image generator or text generator if writing or a poem may resonate with the client.
- Focus on special interests of the client: Exploring if the use of existing interests as expressive means may be beneficial and may be more easily accessible. Does the client have specific music, video games, movies, etc. that they identify with? For example, can a song or an anime character represent a part?

Conclusions

Queering EMDR is about radically meeting our clients and their systems where they're at. As reflected in my creative expressions using art, internal dialogue and cooperative reflections surrounding my experiences with internalized biphobia and bierasure, it can be incredibly beneficial for Queer individuals and their parts to have opportunities to establish their own path of healing. By allowing the healing journey to naturally unfold, we can more openly create space for each unique individual, their protective parts, and their wounded parts to process in their own unique ways based on creativity, autonomy, empowerment, and consent.

Sam Bergstein (she/her), MA, MSW, LISW-S, REAT, lives and works in Columbus, Ohio, on occupied/stolen Myaamia/Miami, Kaskaskia, and Hopewell Cultural land. Sam focuses on the use of EMDR, IFS, and expressive arts therapy in her private practice, working with clients from diverse backgrounds and walks of life. Her passions include working with attachment wounding, dissociative systems, identity wounding and affirming care, Queer and LGBTQIA+ experiences, and individuals living with chronic health issues. She also enjoys supporting burgeoning EMDR therapists through consultation, serving as a practicum facilitator for EMDR training, and indulging in her hyperfixation of creating resources, guides, and worksheets for clinicians and clients. In her free time, she enjoys spending time with her friends, life partner, and five pets; making art and crafts; and tending to her dozens of tropical houseplants.

References

binaohan, b. (2014). *decolonizing trans/gender 101*. biyuti publishing.

Dana, D. (2021). *Anchored: How to Befriend Your Nervous System Using Polyvagal Theory*. Boulder: Sounds True.

Dana, D. (2024). *The science of feeling safe enough to fall in love with life*. Rhythm of Regulation. https://www.rhythmofregulation.com/polyvagal-theory

Goulding, R.A., Schwartz, R.C. (2021). *The Mozaic Mind: Empowering the Tormented Selves of Child Abuse Survivors*. Oak Park: Trailheads Publications.

Gutiérrez, N. Y. (2022). *The pain we carry: Healing from complex PTSD for people of color*. Oakland, CA: New Harbinger Publications.

Hinz, L. D. (2019). *Expressive therapies continuum: A framework for using art in therapy* (2nd ed.). New York: Routledge.

Jung, C. G. (1953). *Two essays on analytical psychology*. (Bollingen Series 20). Pantheon Books.

Marich, J. (2019). *Process not perfection: expressive arts solutions for trauma recovery*. Creative Mindfulness Media.

Marich, J. (2022). *Eye Movement Desensitization and Reprocessing (EMDR)*

Therapy: Training Course Part I & II. 10th edition. Warren, OH: The Institute for Creative Mindfulness.

Marich, J. (2023). *Dissociation made simple: A stigma-free guide to embracing your dissociative mind and navigating daily life.* Berkeley, CA: North Atlantic Books.

McKay, M., Wood, J. C., & Brantley, J. (2007). *The dialectical behavior therapy skills workbook: Practical DBT exercises for learning mindfulness, interpersonal effectiveness, emotional regulation, & distress tolerance.* Oakland, CA: New Harbinger Publications, Inc.

McNiff, S. (2004). *Art heals: How creativity cures the soul.* Boston, MA: Shambhala.

Schwartz, R. (2021). *No bad parts: Healing trauma and restoring wholeness with the internal family systems model.* Boulder, CO: Sounds True.

Shapiro, F. (2018). *Eye movement desensitization and reprocessing (EMDR) therapy: Basic principles, protocols, and procedures* (3rd ed.). New York: The Guilford Press.

Thom, K. C. (2023). *Falling back in love with being human: Letters to lost souls.* Dial Press Trade Paperback.

Chasing Normal

How I Learned to Stop Running Away From Myself and Embrace My Queerness: A Therapist's Journey

Daniel (Danielle) Godfrey, LCSW-R

I am pleased to have the opportunity to share my experiences as a queer-identified EMDR therapist. I will connect some critical periods in my life and their relevance to the sometimes arduous road to my development of a healthy, personal trans identity while living in contemporary American society. Throughout my life I have been impacted by micro and macro aggressions (and all that lies between!) related to my gender identity, intertwined with specific personal experiences which led to my formation of a personal queer identity in an often hostile social environment...and how EMDR helped me to heal.

A tragic life-changing event occurred about 15 years ago. I was a Clinical Director for a major non-profit mental health organization. This position was extremely stressful but still deeply gratifying despite deep budget cuts as funding for public mental health programming was drying up. As someone who was only marginally out, I was living as a stealth Male-to-Female (MTF) transgender person. In reality, I was living a double life.

We had just returned from being out of town for the birth of a grandchild. When we returned to our home I found my adult son dead from an overdose. He had just returned to live with us and was trying to overcome a series of bad life decisions. This event was horrifying, heartbreaking and traumatic. I still miss his biting sense of humor, magical gift with animals and bonds with people with whom he had faith in.

I was overwhelmed and reeling from this debilitating grief for many months after. I also experienced a recurrence of PTSD symptoms from traumatic events that had occurred in my childhood and youth. My PTSD symptoms consisted of intrusive thoughts and images which were happening several times each day. This was unnerving as I thought that the many years of talk therapy I had left these events behind in the personal rear view window of my life. My son's tragic death had reopened past wounds again. This traumatizing event eventually led me to EMDR. The ensuing healing process changed my life and helped me sustain a true recovery process as a survivor of abuse and a therapist. This benefited myself, and all those I love and work with. It fostered increased self acceptance and empowered me to embrace my queer self instead of running away from it.

In the Beginning

Looking back on my childhood and adolescence – I was raised conservative Catholic (pretty much the norm in the pre-Vatican II era) in a de facto segregated suburban community outside of New York City in the 1950's and 1960's. My parents were city transplants who joined the rapidly growing postwar middle class suburb of the time.

This was not the idyllic life described by some conservative pundits. I witnessed and experienced the excruciating impact of domestic violence, child abuse, religious/spiritual abuse, and alcoholism in an insular social environment. It covertly, and sometimes overtly, supported a wide spectrum of systemic and random oppressions that traumatized many, including myself. There was an absence of racial, ethnic and spiritual diversity with no place or tolerance for queer or gender diverse people. The word "queer" had not yet been reclaimed. At the time it was one of several damningly oppressive adjectives used to marginalize a group of people who didn't fit into the cis-hetero norms of the day.

I realized I was transgender before this word came into common use. I developed an awareness of my identity from an early age and very quickly learned I needed to suppress this part of myself. One has to be careful regarding assumptions about safety in a violent home within an intolerant society. I knew I was different and didn't know how I would fit in. I remember as a child seeing news stories in a New York tabloid about a drag ball in New York city being busted by the police. The participants, men beautiful in their Hollywood ball gowns, being dragged off to jail to the derision of jeering and leering spectators. I connected with the folks in the ballgowns. They were my people but this was a scary forbidden zone where active identification with this group of people would come with significant personal jeopardy.

This absence of cultural/familial support resulted in my internalization of my transphobia and homophobia in an era when being labeled "homosexual" resulted in becoming an outcast, sinner, or worse, a stigmatized "marginalized outsider," often relegated to jails and psychiatric institutions. I was living in fear of being discovered. Always realizing that self-acceptance would be the gateway to becoming an exile from any possibility of a "normal" life. Imagining such a discovery was terrifying to me.

My perceived need to suppress myself superseded all else. For most of my childhood and adolescence, I thought I was going to hell for who I was. My experiences in Catholic school were not helpful. I remember sitting in a religious studies class where you could get in serious trouble for not memorizing all of the answers to questions in the Baltimore Catechism. We had a particularly brutal priest teaching that class who incorporated threats of violence and humiliation into his lesson plans.

There existed a conundrum in being taught about God's love by an abusive predator. To me, that was the greatest mortal sin there could be. In class one day he spoke eloquently about the merciful love of God as the Good Shepherd. This was quite stirring and I started to believe that perhaps God loved me too and maybe I wasn't going to hell after all. I remember a female classmate asked this priest if this also included homosexual people. It seems clear to me now in retrospect that there was some personal connection for her to ask this question. His response was emotionally and spiritually brutal.

I thought this priest's head was going to blow up in front of us all! He turned several shades of crimson and purple and then released an enraged soliloquy about some sinners not worthy of God's love and deserving of eternal damnation. All in the class were silent and at least some in shock like me. Message received. Don't ever speak of such heresy again! And be careful what you bring to the confessional. Once again I learned not to trust. I included this as an example of how oppressive cognitions get reinforced by oppressive people representing oppressive institutions.

Entering adolescence with my significant trauma load, attachment wounding, and internalized oppressive cognitions was an almost constant reminder of my need for self-suppression, which led to many expressions of anger, self-sabotage, anxiety, multiple addictions, rebelliousness, and emotional isolation. I was without deep roots or emotional attachments, all of which endured until well into my twenties. After all, if I was going to hell for who I was, I might as well enjoy myself in my rebelliousness. I still feared myself, and ran from this by numbing myself in a myriad of ways.

An example I often reflect upon is the story behind the song "Lola" by the Kinks. Early on in their career the Kinks played in many underground clubs. They inhabited and played music in the same venues that many transgender people socialized in, although at the time they were referred to as transvestites or transsexuals. One of the band's entourage was smitten by a transgender woman who was a regular there which provides the basis for the story. The Kinks official video does justice to the story and is well worth the time to watch. I know in my emerging young adulthood, I became more aware of others like me who were struggling to find their place. Unfortunately so many, including myself, found comfort in places that put us at risk for addiction, violence and arrest. This was a painful stage which I have no desire to return to.

A Slow Journey to a Long and Painful Recovery

Gradually though I began a slow journey to a long and painful recovery, practicing my own form of harm reduction before self-help groups supported me in this process. Completing school, working in a variety of settings with survivors of institutionalization and child violence where I witnessed firsthand the impact of trauma before the PTSD diagnosis was applied to these groups of people. Motivated, I completed my MSW study with a strong interest in PTSD and recovery from trauma while working to figure myself out too.

Always being vigilant to not reveal my gender identity, I struggled with many of my own therapy experiences: some good, others awful, with varying effectiveness. Moving from direct clinical work to supervision then to administration, I always carried my trauma load and needed to suppress myself…until I experienced the tragedy of my son's death.

In my grief, I was overwhelmed with my own symptoms of PTSD which I could no longer deny. This led me to jump start my own recovery to resolve my childhood traumas through EMDR. Realizing that it was time to be honest with myself and others about my own identity. I came to understand that there was a big part of me that I couldn't and shouldn't shake. Recovery wasn't about having the willpower to resist myself but about self acceptance and celebration of finding healthy ways to express myself. In short, the willpower to fully accept myself.

From that point on I have had many experiences coming out as a person, therapist and advocate within the EMDR community. I plan to expand upon this in more detail and tie together my experience as an out queer identified EMDR therapist from both a personal and professional perspective.

Enter EMDR Therapy

One of the initial very gratifying events I experienced in my coming out process was to attend the 2019 EMDR International Association (EMDRIA) Conference as Danielle, a transgender woman. I had just attained EMDR certification as a therapist through EMDRIA, and I had completed a significant portion of my own EMDR therapy. I was fully committed to EMDR as a mode of healing. I joined EMDRIA and attended the conference.

I was very impressed when I was filling out my membership profile. The application was extensive and inclusive, which provided me the opportunity to describe myself as fully as the forms can allow. I was so used to squeezing my identity in a few narrow boxes as I have needed to do for other organizations. I felt refreshed and validated instead of frustrated by the process. Thank you EMDRIA!

This was a time of change as Francine Shapiro had passed away a brief time before the Conference and new leaders were emerging in the EMDR community. It was also an opportunity to reflect upon and honor her legacy. My experience at the conference was invigorating. I was received warmly by many of my colleagues and made a multitude of new acquaintances. These relationships were personally gratifying and felt sincere and honest. Coming out personally and professionally was freeing as I no longer felt I needed to conceal this part of me, rather, it was an opportunity to flourish in my self-expression.

I had another experience which countered this experience of "gender euphoria." Outside of the hotel there was a small demonstration against EMDRIA by a group who passed out literature protesting EMDRIA's stance on conversion therapy or one the more sanitized (deceptive) names for it. They asserted that "Unwanted Same Sex Attraction" was treatable as the result of childhood sexual abuse. This was their rationale for Sexual Orientation Change Efforts (SOCE). I handed the written materials back to the person who handed it to me. Quite frankly, I was proud that EMDRIA had taken a strong position against SOCE and I told him that. Months later I discovered how extensive this movement has been and in more places than I thought. I was appalled that a therapist could, and continue to, align themselves with methods which research had found were extremely harmful to the mental health of clients who were victimized by conversion therapy. I was very disappointed to learn that I could find more information on those who advocated for some form of conversion therapy with EMDR than I could find on those who utilized EMDR therapy as affirming care for transgender and queer identified clients. I am grateful that much has changed in these past few years and that I had some small part in this change.

Since then I have become an EMDRIA Approved Consultant and an EMDR Trainer for the Trauma Institute and Child Trauma Institute (TICTI). I have had an active role in training EMDR therapists and helping them to become Certified EMDR therapists. I also have had the opportunity to provide focused trainings and presentations on providing affirming EMDR therapy to queer and gender diverse clients at several conferences and trainings. I am proud to report that I have participated in several EMDRIA sponsored Diversity, Equity and Inclusion (DEI) panels, which based upon evaluations and feedback, have been extremely informative to therapists who participated and I'm sure their clients have benefited too!

As a trained Clinical Social Worker and EMDR therapist I have always been dedicated to the Principles of DEI. These are principles which are a major foundation of the code of ethics of my profession. Does "Singularity, Inequality and Exclusion" work or sound better, or is it just another strategy to justify privilege, oppression and intolerance? I will let you decide.

Perhaps the most fulfilling work for me is maintaining a small private practice since coming out. The majority of clients are gender diverse and queer-identified, mostly older adolescents and young adults in their twenties and thirties.

I follow evidence-based practice in my work and draw upon peer reviewed research and not the "junk science" which has become part of our current public discourse. I closely follow standards set by the World Professional Association of Transgender Health (WPATH) as embodied in their Standards of Care (SOC) for children, youth and adults. I also draw upon the work of Dr. Sand Chang, who has been providing affirming trauma work to gender diverse clients for decades. I follow their principle of practicing cultural humility, referenced by Dr. Chang as EMDR "Phase 0." The overarching approach that I take as a therapist is that each client is unique and different with differing motivations and expectations of their therapeutic process. As a therapist I am knowledgeable about gender diverse and queer people and respectful, open and receptive to their needs, ideas, histories and unique cultural experiences.

I make no presumptions about what clients are seeking from therapy and do not assume they are seeking therapy for issues related to their gender diversity. I also do not imply that there is any single path to their actualization of being gender diverse or queer. I support them and help them explore how they would like to proceed and live as a queer or gender diverse person if they choose to do so.

My experience has been that there is no one correct way to come out , not come out, or transition. Everyone has a right to their own process which is often on a continuum. As a therapist I support their right to make informed decisions about their care which is affirming and collaborative. Meanwhile, I work with them to prepare for trauma work if they wish to pursue this. Many of them are interested in pursuing EMDR or other forms of trauma therapy I provide which includes Progressive Counting and the Flash Technique.

Conclusion

As I engage clients in treatment and develop a plan of care, I am aware of certain commonalities and vulnerabilities. Peer reviewed research has revealed an increased risk of suicide, presence of discrimination, family estrangement, attachment wounding, and violence, negative experiences with previous medical providers and therapists with a higher rate of trauma and dissociative symptoms. Gender diverse people also experience a higher rate of neurodivergence and autistic spectrum disorders.

Being a therapist who practices cultural humility means that I consider these factors from a multicultural and intersectional perspective as a critical component of the assessment process and development of a plan of care which reduces risks and helps clients to develop the skills to resolve their trauma experiences through EMDR. This process often leads to a higher level of life satisfaction by following the EMDR 8 Phase model, individualized to the unique strengths and needs of each client.

I am honored to have the privilege to work with gender diverse and queer clients. I am also grateful to many others who have supported me, encouraged my work, provided feedback and inspiration since I was first trained in EMDR. Thank you all! I am humbled by your support and am grateful for the multitude of learning experiences you have provided to me.

Thank you!

Daniel (Danielle) Godfrey (she/her) is a proud transgender woman and practicing trauma therapist who works and resides in the occupied and unceded lands of the Haudenosaunee people (Buffalo, New York area, USA). She has assisted with and provided training through the Trauma Institute/ Child Trauma Institute (TICTI) and has participated in speaker panels and presentations for EMDRIA, the EMDR Canada Conference, and the EMDR UK Conference in collaboration with both the Trauma Institute and The Institute for Creative Mindfulness. She continues to advocate for the needs of LGBTQIA+ clients seeking psychotherapy and trauma services through EMDR. She is an EMDRIA-certified EMDR therapist, Consultant, and Trainer. She practiced Family Systems and Solution-Focused Therapy before practicing EMDR. She is also trained in Progressive Counting and the Flash technique. In her work she specializes in working with Gender Diverse, LGBTQIA+ other queer identified people who have been impacted by trauma, their families and allies. She is a strong advocate for therapist cultural humility in the provision of affirming care to all queer identified clients and has spoken out against the traumatization of queer people through the use of Sexual Orientation Change Efforts (SOCE) and other stigmatizing /non-affirming clinical practices.

References

Chang, S. (2017). EMDR therapy as affirmative care for transgender and gender nonconforming clients. In M. Nickerson (Ed.), Cultural competence and healing culturally based trauma with EMDR therapy (pp. 177-194). New York, NY: Springer Publishing.

Link to official version of "Lola" video (You Tube) bit.ly:bit.ly/45d5YEx

World Professional Association for Transgender Health. Standards of Care Version 8. WPATH. 1/6/23, from https://www.wpath.org/soc8 Link to official version of "Lola" video (YouTube)

Complicating Gender Binary Narratives

Using EMDR Therapy with Expansive Gender Identities

Michael Kuffel, LCPC

At the core of the transgender and gender expansive (TGE) experience is a deeply felt sense of one's gender identity. Gender identity is not determined by external factors such as sex assigned at birth, physical characteristics, or societal expectations, rather, by a subjective, intrinsic awareness of self. In understanding and addressing the complexities of gender identity, it is crucial to move beyond traditional binary narratives. This chapter will explore how integrating constructivism and queer theory into the framework of Eye Movement Desensitization and Reprocessing (EMDR) therapy and the Adaptive Information Processing (AIP) model can effectively validate TGE clients' subjective experiences and challenge societal structures that contribute to their distress. By complicating binary understandings of gender and adapting EMDR therapy accordingly, EMDR therapists can facilitate the adaptive reprocessing of oppressive and other negative experiences. This approach provides a comprehensive foundation for understanding the unique challenges faced by TGE clients by examining the specific intersections of social constructivism, queer theory, and the AIP model. By validating TGE clients' subjective lived experiences and challenging normative societal structures that contribute to pathogenic experiences, EMDR therapists can "complicate" binary narratives and adaptively reprocess negative experiences through EMDR therapy.

Complicating Binaries

Theoretical Orientation

The intersection of constructivism, queer theory, and the AIP model provides a comprehensive framework for understanding and addressing the unique challenges faced by TGE clients. This integrated approach acknowledges the subjective nature of gender identity, the societal context of oppression, and a mechanism for healing the resulting psychological distress and trauma.

Social Constructivism (Mahoney & Granvold, 2005) provides a foundational understanding that reality, including gender, is not objective but is actively co-constructed by persons through their experiences, interpretations, and environments. As a social theory, it maintains that truth is multiple, relational, and local. It assumes that meaning is constructed through language and social interaction and conceptualizes identity as ideological and culture-bound. In the context of gender identity, constructivism supports the understanding that a person's felt sense of their gender is a valid and personal construction (dickey & Puckett, 2023). Further, constructivism acknowledges that there will be multiple and at times conflicting perspectives on personal experiences (e.g., gender dysphoria) which can exist alongside one another (Cooper et al., 2020). This perspective is crucial in affirming the diverse ways in which TGE individuals understand and express their gender identities, moving away from rigid, binary understandings imposed by external authorities, including modernist approaches and theories of counseling. By valuing the individual's construction of their gender identity, this framework provides a necessary foundation for gender-affirming care.

Queer Theory (Tilsen, 2021) critically examines and complicates societal norms related to sex, gender, and sexuality, particularly transphobia and the supremacy of cisheteronormativity. Queer theory affirms that sex and gender are social constructs rather than fixed biological categories. It exposes the binary assumptions that underpin many societal structures and highlights how these norms marginalize and oppress those who do not conform to them (Ansara & Hegarty, 2014). Deconstruction (Hare-Mustin & Marecek, 1988) is the process that makes social constructs and their impacts more visible by seeking to de-center dominant ideas by asking questions about the assumptions embedded within. Further, it challenges social binaries and normativity, especially as it applies to cisnormativity (i.e., the assumption that all people are cisgender) and heteronormativity (i.e., the assumption that all people are heterosexual).

For example, the gender binary imposes and polices adherence to two "biological sexes" (i.e., that all people are either men or women). The gender binary dictates ideas about "normal" masculinity and femininity and assumes innate and universal differences between men and women (i.e., essentialism). Both cisgenderism and heterosexism are social constructs that promote the supremacy of these dominant narratives, relying upon and reinforcing stereotypes about gender and relationships. TGE clients may persistently experience barriers to well-being in contemporary society and are at disproportionate risk for psychological distress due to disaffirming environments and other external factors (Austin, 2016).

Minority stress theory, a key concept within constructivist and queer theory frameworks, posits that distress in marginalized groups is not solely caused by direct prejudice but also by the stress of navigating normative cultures (Lindley & Galupo, 2020; Puckett et al., 2022). This stress includes experiences of discrimination, stigma, microaggressions, social rejection, violence, and internalized transphobia, all of which can be significant sources of traumagenic stress for TGE clients (Austin, 2016). Constructivism, queer theory, and minority stress theory provide the social critical lens through which to understand these external, societal factors and how they contribute to unique traumagenic experiences (i.e., dynamics or processes that are trauma-inducing or related to the effects of trauma, particularly on the development or manifestation of mental health conditions).

Cisnormative Narratives about Gender Incongruence

Societal norms and stigma have a profound and multifaceted impact on the mental health and lived experiences of gender expansive clients. These negative influences contribute to significant psychological distress and create numerous barriers in their daily lives, including significant impacts on mental health. TGE people are more likely to experience mental health problems such as anxiety, depression, and posttraumatic stress compared to the general population. These higher rates are strongly linked to *gender minority stress* (Cardona et al., 2022), which encompasses the experiences of stigma and discrimination faced by TGE individuals related to their gender identity. This stress can be chronic and stem from interpersonal, institutional, and cultural contexts.

The DSM-5-TR definition of gender dysphoria (i.e., gender incongruence) focuses on the distress that may accompany the incongruence between one's experienced or expressed gender and one's assigned gender. This marked a shift from the DSM-IV, which used the term "Gender Identity Disorder" and was criticized for pathologizing gender identity itself. The DSM-5-TR aimed to be more specific, recognizing that it is the distress arising from the incongruence, rather than gender identity itself, that warrants a diagnosis when it causes clinically significant distress or impairment in social, occupational, or other important areas of functioning. Qualitative research (Cooper et al., 2020) on the lived experience of gender dysphoria in adults, as synthesized in a systematic review, offers valuable insights into how these diagnostic criteria align with TGE client's actual experiences. These social dimensions of distress, while deeply connected to the individual experience of gender incongruence, extend beyond the primary focus of the DSM-5-TR criteria, which tend to be more intra-individual. Gender minority stress theory provides a framework for understanding this socially driven distress, highlighting the impact of stigma and discrimination. Thus, we seek to expand the narrative about the distress related to gender identity to be inclusive of TGE individual's social context, as follows:

- *Distress due to gender and sex incongruence, exacerbated by social factors*. While gender dysphoria itself is defined as distress due to a discrepancy between one's assigned gender and gender identity, this distress is significantly compounded by societal responses.
- *Misgendering*. Being treated or labeled as a gender different from one's own gender identity is a frequent social stressor that is positively associated with psychological distress.

Participants in qualitative studies reported that an inability to "pass" or blend in would likely be associated with disappointment, sadness, and even suicidal ideation.

- *Mismatch between gender identity and societal expectations.* Dominant social narratives often assume that gender identity and sex-assigned-at-birth should align. This mismatch leads to internal and external conflict whose internal sense of self differs from these norms. Some studies found that participants felt they had been socialized to the incorrect gender, causing dissonance and distress.
- *Negative social consequences of gender identity.* TGE individuals often face social isolation due to a lack of support from friends, family, and community. This social isolation can lead to feelings of grief and loss.
- *Internal processing of rejection and transphobia.* The anticipation and experience of rejection due to one's transgender identity can lead to significant distress. This includes fear of rejection, sadness following rejection, hypervigilance for transphobia and a constant state of worry for personal safety, and internalized transphobia. Internalized transphobia involves the internalization of negative societal attitudes, leading to shame and self-hatred. Social messages portraying transgender individuals negatively can directly lead to self-hate, confusion, and shame.
- *Bullying, harassment, and violence.* TGE individuals face an elevated risk of physical and verbal harassment, hate crimes, and intimate partner violence due to nonconformity with the oppressive, socially constructed gender binary.
- *Discrimination in various settings.* Societal stigma translates into systemic discrimination in areas such as healthcare, employment, housing, and legal systems. Difficulty obtaining gender-appropriate identification can further exacerbate these challenges, blocking access to employment, housing, community, and other resources.

- *Barriers to gender-affirming care.* Despite the fact that gender-affirming care, including hormone therapy and surgeries, is an efficacious treatment for gender dysphoria, TGE individuals often encounter significant barriers in accessing this care due to financial and insurance issues, lack of service availability, gatekeeping, and bias within medical and mental health fields. Lack of medical provider awareness and education also contributes to these barriers.

Conversely, research (Puckett et al., 2022) and lived experience (McCullough et al., 2017) highlight the importance of affirmation and support in mitigating these negative impacts. For example, caregiver support is significantly correlated with higher quality of life and less mental health symptoms among transgender youth (Moody & Smith, 2013). Social connectedness, social support, and community advocacy also contribute to improved well-being (Nobili et al., 2018). Furthermore, gender-affirming healthcare can help to address concerns related to gender dysphoria and has been associated with better mental health outcomes (dickey & Puckett, 2023).

Unique Experiences Among Nonbinary Identities

Gender nonbinary people specifically experience minority stress in ways that share similarities with binary transgender individuals but also include unique challenges stemming from their identities existing outside the cisnormative gender binary (Shearer, 2019). Minority stress, as a framework, describes the excess stress experienced by marginalized groups due to stigma, prejudice, and discrimination. For nonbinary individuals, this stress manifests in several distinct ways.

Social Invalidation and Erasure

A primary source of minority stress for nonbinary individuals is the pervasive societal and often interpersonal invalidation of their gender identities (Bauer et al., 2009; Shearer, 2019). In cultures largely structured around binary understandings of gender, nonbinary identities are often rendered invisible or dismissed as not "real." One of the most pervasive forms of erasure experienced by nonbinary individuals is the lack of societal and institutional recognition of their gender identities (Richards et al., 2016; Austin, 2016). Many systems, from legal documents and identification forms to healthcare intake questionnaires, often provide only binary options for gender (Austin, 2016). This forces nonbinary individuals into categories that do not accurately reflect who they are, effectively making them invisible within these structures. This lack of representation in everyday life can send a powerful message that their identities are not valid or do not matter. Cisgenderism and sexism are reinforced, in part, by a lack of recognition of the diversity in how people identify their genders.

This systemic erasure is intertwined with the dominant societal assumption of cisnormativity. The very structure of society often operates on the unspoken assumption that everyone fits neatly into the binary categories of "man" or "woman," leaving no space for nonbinary identities. This forces nonbinary individuals to navigate their gender with a significant dearth of support due to a lack of accessible and accurate information and resources that could facilitate understanding and legitimization. While misgendering is a stressor for transgender clients in general, nonbinary people may face unique challenges related to pronouns and gendered language. Cisnormative pronouns (e.g., he/him, she/her) often do not fit their identities, and the consistent use of incorrect pronouns can lead to significant distress and feelings of being unseen or disrespected (Ansara & Hegarty, 2014).

Furthermore, they may face the added burden of constantly educating others about their pronouns and facing resistance or misunderstanding. Cisnormativity assumes nonbinary individuals are either "trying to be" male or female or are simply deemed "confused." This disregards their authentic gender identity and confines them within a binary with which they do not identify. Even within lesbian, gay, bisexual, and transgender (LGBTQ+) communities (Levitt et al., 2024), nonbinary persons can experience erasure or a lack of understanding if the focus remains primarily on binary identities (e.g., binary transitioning). They might feel their specific needs and experiences are not acknowledged or understood.

Unique Experiences of Gender Incongruence

Nonbinary persons may experience gender dysphoria differently than binary transgender persons (Arijs et al., 2023; Levitt et al., 2024). While they may feel distress related to their physical characteristics not aligning with their gender identity, their goals for affirmation may not involve fully transitioning to a binary gender presentation. Medical and social transition pathways are often geared towards binary outcomes (e.g., masculinization or feminization), which can create challenges for nonbinary clients who may wish to transition. Nonbinary clients seeking to affirm their gender may find limited options or have to navigate complex and less understood routes that align with their specific needs. Feelings of discomfort with their bodies or social roles might not be alleviated by binary-focused interventions, leading to ongoing stress related to their gender identity (Rosati et al., 2022).

They might experience internal conflict related to societal pressures to conform to cisnormative narratives, even as they know their true gender lies outside of it. Further, nonbinary individuals often face additional barriers in accessing healthcare due to a lack of understanding and education among medical and mental health professionals regarding nonbinary identities (Bindman et al., 2022). Many healthcare providers lack the knowledge and cultural humility to provide affirming care for nonbinary individuals. This can lead to misdiagnosis, inappropriate treatment recommendations, or disrespectful and invalidating interactions.

Intersectionality Within Nonbinary Identities

Nonbinary individuals encounter unique macro- and microaggressions that reinforce the gender binary and invalidate their existence (Shearer, 2019; Nadal et al., 2012). For nonbinary persons who also hold other marginalized identities (e.g., race, ethnicity, disability, socioeconomic status, etc.), these intersecting identities can compound their experience of minority stress (Wesp et al.,

2019; Kattari et al., 2017). They may face unique forms of discrimination that arise from the intersection of their nonbinary gender identity with these other identities, further increasing their psychological distress. For example, a nonbinary person of color may experience both transphobia and racism in ways that are distinct from either experience alone.

Internalized Cisgenderism and Rejection Sensitivity

Nonbinary individuals can internalize negative societal messages about their gender identities, leading to self-doubt, shame, and internalized cisgenderism (Shearer, 2019). The constant exposure to binary-centric norms and the lack of positive representation can fuel these negative, internalized beliefs. Furthermore, due to frequent experiences of invalidation and discrimination, nonbinary individuals may develop heightened expectations of rejection in social interactions, contributing to rejection sensitivity and increased anxiety.

Negative Impact of Systemic Erasure and Invalidation

Suicidality

TGE individuals face a multitude of unique risk factors that contribute to a higher prevalence of suicidal thoughts and attempts compared to cisgender individuals. It is crucial to reiterate the high prevalence of suicidality within the transgender community. Meta-analysis results show that approximately 48% of transgender individuals worldwide experience suicidal thoughts (Kohnepoushi et al., 2023). These statistics underscore the immense psychological burden carried by many TGE people. These factors extend beyond the general suicide risk factors found in the broader population and are often rooted in societal stigma, discrimination, and lack of affirmation. Experiences of rejection and invalidation are critical risk factors. This can manifest as rejection from family, spouses or children, families of origin, religious communities, and social communities. Encountering rejection or invalidation of their gender identity has been shown to lead to internalized stress processes and post-traumatic responses (Cardona et al., 2022). Furthermore, the expectation of rejection can be associated with fear and worry for personal safety, leading to hypervigilance (e.g., being easily startled, ready to react for safety, etc.) for transphobia. When TGE clients internalize negative societal messages and stereotypes (i.e., internalized transphobia), it severely impacts their self-worth, self-acceptance, and overall mental health, increasing the likelihood of suicidality. Some may even experience their own bodies as persecutory, leading to shame and self-hatred.

Importantly, many TGE clients who experience chronic, overwhelming minority stress (e.g. anxiety, depression, substance use, somatic/physical symptoms) come to expect and rely upon suicidal ideation as a form of psychological coping (Kohnepoushi et al., 2023; Moody & Smith, 2013). When an individual experiences persistent pain, rejection, and lack of control over their environment and identity, the thought of not having to endure this pain any longer can offer a sense of relief, even if the individual has no immediate intention or plan to act on these thoughts. For example, for TGE clients facing systemic discrimination, social rejection, and/or a lack of autonomy over their bodies, thoughts of suicide might provide a feeling of ultimate control over their own lives and destinies. In a society in which TGE clients may feel constantly acted upon and devalued, the ability to choose to end their suffering can feel empowering, even if this choice is never enacted. Further, chronic thoughts of not wanting to live can be an internal validation of the profound distress they are experiencing. It can be a way of acknowledging to oneself the severity of their suffering when external validation is lacking. Unfortunately, the function of chronic suicidality is often misunderstood and invalidated by loved ones and care providers, who inaccurately and dangerously mislabel it as "attention seeking." A chronic state of suicidality should be understood as symbolic representation of the client's intense pain and psychological distress and signifies a deep level of unmet needs.

Dissociation

TGE individuals can experience dissociation in various ways, often linked to the significant stressors they face related to gender minority stress. Dissociation, in general, refers to a "severing" (Marich, 2023) or disconnection from a person's thoughts, feelings, bodies, memories, or sense of identity. It can manifest in various domains, including sensory perception, memory, cognition, and emotion. Common dissociative symptoms include depersonalization (i.e., feeling out of body), derealization (i.e., feelings of unreality), analgesia (i.e., reduced pain sensitivity), gaps in awareness and memory, confusion, constricted attention, withdrawal, and detachment. For TGE clients, the experience of dissociation can be attributed to navigating chronic internal and external stressors and can be compounded by gender dysphoria, if applicable. Importantly, dissociation can be a response to acute traumatic experiences but also be a concurrent reaction to ongoing identity-related distress (Colizzi et al., 2015). Indeed, dissociation can be considered a normal, adaptive, and appropriate response to such internal and external stressors. As dissociation relates to gender identity, we can see dissociation as an inherent feature of gender dysphoria and not necessarily a trauma-related response (Sigurdsson & Cardeña, 2024).

Dissociation in TGE clients can manifest as disconnection from somatic experiences, emotional numbing, and a sense of detachment from their self-perceptions and identities. It can also involve body dysphoria as a specific dissociative experience. Social disconnection and hypervigilance, which are common experiences for TGE individuals facing societal stigma, are also listed as nuanced traumagenic experiences related to dissociation (Cooper et al., 2020). TGE individuals can experience dissociation as a multifaceted response to chronic minority stress, gender dysphoria, and often, a history of trauma. It can manifest as emotional detachment, altered perceptions of their body and reality, memory gaps, and a general sense of disconnection. Understanding dissociation in this population requires recognizing the unique stressors they face and the potential for dissociation to serve as an understandable survival mechanism in the context of persistent adversity.

Legal Anti-Trans Bias

The increase in anti-transgender laws over the past decade (Novotney, 2023), rising from 18 in 2015 to 516 in 2023, has corresponded with a steep decline in the mental health of transgender and nonbinary people. Center for Disease Control (CDC) data shows a doubling of depression diagnoses among transgender and nonbinary individuals between 2014 and 2022. An analysis of youth risk behavior surveys from 2017 to 2019 also revealed an increase in suicidality rates for transgender youth coinciding with more anti-transgender laws (Lee et al., 2024). Both research (Greytak, 2024) and lived experience (Tebbe et al., 2022) overwhelmingly demonstrate a significant and lasting negative impact of anti-transgender rhetoric and lawmaking on gender expansive individuals across multiple domains of their lives. These restrictive policies lead to increased anxiety, depression, and suicidality.

For example, the politicalization of TGE identities as an "issue of debate" and the direct impact of anti-transgender laws have a negative impact on the mental health of a vast majority (86%) of transgender and nonbinary youth. TGE adults also experience negative mental health impacts from anti-transgender laws. A national study (Greytak, 2024) found that 80% of transgender and nonbinary adults reported that gender-affirming care bans negatively affected their mental and physical well-being. Over three-quarters (79%) of transgender adults reported that recent anti-LGBTQ+ policies and related rhetoric harmed their mental health, with 58% stating it had a "very negative" impact (DuBois et al., 2023). Discussions about restrictive education laws, such as school sports bans, outing requirements, and book bans, similarly negatively affect their mental health, causing feelings of anger, stress, fear, sadness, and nervousness.

Anti-transgender laws are designed to restrict or prevent access to or support for transgender and nonbinary people, including restrictions on gender-affirming care (Greytak, 2024). Approximately 113,900 transgender youth in the U.S. have lost access to gender-affirming health care due to these laws since 2023. Anti-transgender laws and the surrounding rhetoric are instilling fear, reducing safety, and increasing violence against LGBTQ+ people and their allies. Eight in ten (79.1%) LGBTQ+ adults and nine in ten (94%) transgender and nonbinary adults report feeling less safe due to gender-affirming care bans. Following the passage of Florida's "Don't Say Gay or Trans" law, there was a 400% increase in anti-LGBTQ+ slurs on Twitter. Trend analysis of FBI crime data indicates an association between increases in anti-LGBTQ+ hate crimes and violence and increases in anti-LGBTQ+ policy. Correlational studies have found a link between the increase in anti-transgender legislation and an increase in homicides against transgender people. The rise in murders of transgender individuals from 2015 to 2022 outpaced the general increase in homicide rates. The constant exposure to negative rhetoric and discriminatory laws can exacerbate internalized transphobia among gender expansive individuals. Internalized transphobia, where individuals internalize negative societal attitudes, can lead to self-doubt, shame, and guilt.

Complicating Normativity within the EMDR Standard Protocol

Navigating the landscape of using EMDR therapy with TGE clients necessitates a critical examination and thoughtful adaptation of the EMDR Standard Protocol. While EMDR therapy, grounded in the Adaptive Information Processing (AIP) model, offers a powerful framework for reprocessing traumatic experiences, the standard protocol may require significant modifications to effectively address the complex interplay of minority stress, systemic oppression, and identity-specific challenges faced by TGE clients.

Adaptive Information Processing (AIP) Model

The Adaptive Information Processing (Shapiro & Laliotis, 2011; Shapiro, 2018) model is the theoretical framework to explain how traumatic or disturbing adverse life experiences that are not fully processed are stored in the brain and contribute to psychopathology. The AIP model (Hill, 2020) posits that the human brain has an innate capacity to process stressful information to an adaptive resolution, allowing for the integration of the experience. However, when traumatic or disturbing events occur, they can be encoded maladaptively or incompletely processed, preventing this natural integration. According to the AIP model, psychopathology arises from maladaptively linked and unprocessed information that has not been able to connect with more adaptive information. Earlier memories that are maladaptively associated with other maladaptive experiences can increase an individual's vulnerability to various forms of pathology, including anxiety, depression, PTSD, and physical symptoms of stress. These unprocessed experiences and memories can also interfere with the healthy development of an individual's sense of self-worth, safety, ability to assume appropriate responsibility, or sense of control and choices.

Frequent experiences of discrimination, stigma, and microaggressions from various sources can lead to feelings of isolation and internalized transphobia, potentially becoming traumatic. The elevated risk of physical and verbal harassment, hate crimes, anti-trans legislature, and other forms of violence represents chronic traumatic exposure. Limited access to affirming and competent healthcare, including gender-affirming treatments, can result in medical trauma and healthcare disparities. Family rejection and unsupportive family dynamics can be a profound source of emotional distress and trauma, impacting their sense of belonging and self-worth. Dealing with legal battles, name and gender marker changes, and navigating bureaucratic processes can also be stressful and potentially traumatic. Furthermore, intersecting marginalized identities can compound the stress and trauma experienced. The internalization of negative societal attitudes (e.g., internalized transphobia) leads to self-doubt, shame, and guilt. These varied negative experiences, underpinned by minority stress theory, can be understood within the AIP framework as events that overwhelm the person's natural processing capacity, leading to the maladaptive storage of these memories and associated distress.

The aim of EMDR Therapy within the AIP framework is to facilitate the resumption of the brain's natural information processing system, allowing for the effective reprocessing of traumatic events or adverse life experiences and associated maladaptive beliefs to an adaptive resolution (Hase et al., 2017). This reprocessing shifts all elements of a traumatic memory towards adaptive integration. Importantly, applying the AIP model effectively in EMDR therapy with TGE clients necessitates cultural humility, a gender affirmative approach, and an understanding of minority stress and intersectionality (Chang, 2022). By reprocessing these unique traumagenic experiences through the AIP lens, EMDR Therapy can help TGE clients heal from trauma, reduce stress, enhance resilience, improve self-worth, and embrace their affirmed gender identity.

The Role of the Therapeutic Relationship

The establishment of rapport and trust is a crucial element of the initial therapeutic relationship in EMDR therapy, which underlies every phase of the EMDR Standard Protocol (Hase & Brisch, 2022). Building rapport involves creating a safe and supportive environment where the client feels comfortable sharing their history and discussing potentially distressing experiences (Brayer, 2023). The therapist's ability to connect with the client is considered a key quality of a good EMDR therapist. For TGE clients, building and maintaining therapeutic rapport necessitates cultural humility, sensitivity, employing effective communication strategies, and demonstrating empathy for the client's struggles, especially when understanding the client's unique experiences of minority stress (Kuffel, 2022). Using gender-affirming language and demonstrating an understanding of their lived experiences are crucial for establishing trust. Maintaining a strong therapeutic relationship throughout all eight phases of EMDR therapy is vital.

The quality of the therapeutic relationship can impact the effectiveness of EMDR therapy as an anti-oppression model (Marich, 2012). Therapists working with clients from marginalized communities, including TGE clients, should assess their own biases and privileges and seek ongoing education in anti-racism (Archer,

2021) and anti-oppression (Levis & Siniego, 2017). The therapeutic relationship itself can be a tool for healing (Safran & Muran, 2003), allowing for rupture and repair, and the exploration of relational and attachment patterns that might generalize to other areas of the client's life. Non-affirming or incompetent care can lead to therapeutic rupture, exacerbate distress, and deter help-seeking. Therapists need to be mindful of power dynamics in the therapeutic relationship and create a judgment-free dialogue, especially when working with clients from different cultural backgrounds. The principle that therapy is a co-constructed relationship underscores the fundamental importance of a strong and collaborative connection between the therapist and the client in EMDR therapy.

Integrating EMDR Therapy with Gender Expansive Clients

Providing effective EMDR therapy to TGE clients requires a relationally-focused and culturally-responsive application of the EMDR standard protocol (Goodman, 2015; Chang, 2022). Gender-affirmative practice involves actively validating and supporting a client's gender identity, experiences, and expression without judgment or assumption. It moves beyond simply avoiding prejudice to proactively creating a therapeutic environment where clients feel seen, heard, understood, and respected. This stance is crucial because TGE individuals frequently encounter invalidation, pathologization, and discrimination within therapeutic settings (Lykens et al., 2018; McCullough et al., 2017). This section explores the imperative of complicating the normativity within the EMDR standard protocol (Shapiro, 2018), proposing affirmative and culturally humble adaptations across its eight phases to better meet the unique needs of this population and facilitate healing and resilience.

Phase 1. This initial phase involves gathering a comprehensive client history, identifying presenting problems and symptoms, and collaboratively developing a treatment plan. Specific traumatic memories or distressing experiences (i.e., targets) are identified for potential EMDR reprocessing. The therapist also assesses the client's internal and external resources and support systems. This phase establishes the foundation for therapy and determines readiness for trauma reprocessing.

Understanding both dysphoric and euphoric experiences provides a potentially more balanced perception of their gender identity development (Kuffel, 2022). Beyond standard history-taking, EMDR therapists explicitly inquire about the client's gender journey, including milestones, challenges, support received, and experiences of affirmation or lack thereof (Chang, 2022). We assess the impact of minority stress by asking about specific instances of discrimination, harassment, violence, rejection, and non-affirmation (Levis & Siniego, 2017). When exploring internalized transphobia, we approach with gentleness while asking about feelings of shame or discomfort related to their gender identity or societal messages they may have internalized. Identifying affirming relationships and community connections is vital for resource assessment.

Phase 2. In phase 2, the EMDR therapist teaches the client self-regulation and stress reduction techniques (e.g., safe/calm place imagery, containment skills, mindfulness, grounding exercises, etc.) to manage potential emotional disturbance during and between sessions. This phase ensures the client feels safe and equipped to engage in the reprocessing phases. The duration of the second phase varies depending on the client's trauma history and resourcing needs.

Building safety requires acknowledging the potential for and historical context of systemic harm and demonstrating trustworthiness through consistent affirmation and validation. Psychoeducation should normalize the client's reactions by linking them to the realities of minority stress and trauma. Resourcing strategies and techniques must be identity-affirming, drawing on positive gender-related experiences or internal strengths. Given the potential for dissociation linked to trauma and/or dysphoria, resourcing skills need careful selection and, often, modification. For example, techniques focusing heavily on body awareness might be counterproductive if body dysphoria is high. Grounding techniques focusing on the external environment may be preferable initially.

Phase 2 resourcing with TGE clients is significantly enhanced by developing resources specifically relevant to the client's gender identity and experiences (Chang, 2022). Resourcing strategies can be used to anchor positive feelings, images, beliefs, and sensations associated with the following: (1) gender euphoria (e.g., moments of joy, comfort, or alignment related to gender expression or identity affirmation); (2) internalized affirmed self (e.g., accessing and strengthening the felt sense of their true, affirmed gender identity, potentially conceptualized as a "future self" or core self resource); (3) affirming interpersonal connections (e.g., memories or images of supportive friends, family, partners, or community members who embrace and celebrate their identity); (4) community belonging (e.g., feelings of connection and belonging within the TGE or broader LGBTQ+ community); (5) resilience and strengths (e.g., identifying and embodying strengths developed through navigating adversity, such as courage, resilience, authenticity, and advocacy skills.)

Phase 3. For each identified target memory, the client identifies the worst part of the experience or memory. They identify a negative cognition (NC)—a negative self-belief associated with the memory (e.g., "I am powerless," "I am worthless")—and a desired positive cognition (PC)—an adaptive self-belief (e.g., "I am in control now," "I am worthy"). The client rates the validity of the PC using the Validity of Cognition (VOC) scale (1=completely false, 7=completely true) and the level of disturbance associated with the image and NC using the Subjective Units of Disturbance (SUD) scale (0=neutral, 10=highest disturbance). Associated emotions and body sensations are also identified.

Incorporating an anti-oppression lens (Archer, 2021; Levis & Siniego, 2017) in Phase 3 includes identifying NCs with sensitivity to how transphobia and discrimination become internalized (e.g., "Being trans makes me defective," "I don't deserve happiness," "It's dangerous to be myself"). PCs should be related counterparts to these, affirming the client's identity, worth, and right to exist authentically (e.g., "My identity is real and valid," "I am resilient and strong," "I deserve safety and joy"). Target selection necessitates care to avoid inadvertently focusing on distressing body parts if not the intended target. Specific events involving discrimination or violence may lead to shame or self-blame (e.g., NC: "I caused the attack by being visible"). Processing these events can help shift blame externally to perpetrators and societal prejudice, installing PCs like "The prejudice was wrong, not me," or "I did the best I could to survive".

Phase 4. This phase involves activating the target memory while initiating sets of dual-attention stimuli (DAS; e.g., bilateral stimulation such as eye-movements, tapping, etc.). After each set, the therapist asks the client to notice whatever is happening in that present moment (e.g., thoughts, feelings, images, sensations, etc.) without judgment. This process continues, allowing the client to make new connections and reprocess the memory, until the SUD rating associated with the target memory reduces significantly, ideally to 0 or 1. During the reprocessing phases (Phases 3-6), where the therapist aims to be largely non-directive to allow for the client's natural reprocessing, the therapist's presence, groundedness, and ability to contain intense experiences (e.g., abreactions) are crucial. The therapist needs to be attentive to signs of distress or dissociation and possess the clinical skills to manage these effectively, ensuring the client's safety. The therapist's ability to remain present and embodied in the face of strong emotions is essential for building the client's sense of safety.

Some clients may require titrated pacing and more frequent check-ins, particularly if dissociation or dysphoria emerges during reprocessing. When reprocessing oppression-related trauma, the use of interweaves can facilitate the shifting of focus towards the injustice of the experience and challenge any self-blame, thus distinguishing external prejudice from internal shame or fault. Feelings of anger, fear, or sadness related to experiencing transphobia are expected and should be validated. While EMDR typically focuses on specific events, the pervasive impact of a hostile sociopolitical climate can be a legitimate source of current distress or a trigger. The aim is not to change the external reality but to process the client's internal response to it. Thus, we target the feelings of powerlessness, fear, or hopelessness evoked by external events (e.g., anti-trans legislation) and desensitize their negative impact. It is vital to validate the reality of the external threat while empowering the client's internal capacity.

Phase 5. Once the experience's disturbance level is low (SUD=ecological 0), the focus of reprocessing shifts to strengthening the connection between the target memory and the desired adaptive belief (PC) identified in Phase 3. The client holds the memory and the PC together while DAS is applied, continuing until the PC feels fully true (VOC=7). This phase strengthens the adaptive beliefs related to the client's agency, resilience, access to support, and ability to choose their response (e.g., PC: "I have power in how I respond," "I can lean into my resources and support," "I am learning to cope and thrive"). The goal is not just belief-focused shifts, but embodied congruence. The PC should resonate with the client's core sense of their affirmed gender identity (e.g., "I am okay just as I am") and reinforce a sense of internal agency (e.g., "I have choices," "I can navigate challenges"). When reprocessing present triggers or recent oppressive experiences, it is helpful to remember that the PC should be realistic and adaptive and not necessarily "positive." For example, the belief of "I'm safe" may not be realistic to the client's lived experience of social oppression. Thus, a more adaptive belief of "I can find safe places/people" may be more appropriate. Similarly, we allow for the strengthening and integration of the adaptive belief to be flexible, fluid, and ever-evolving (e.g., "I'm learning that I'm a good person").

Phase 6. The client brings the original target memory and the strengthened PC to mind and mentally scans their body for any residual tension or uncomfortable physical sensations. If any disturbance remains, DAS is used to reprocess it until the body feels neutral or "clear." This phase requires the most caution regarding body dysphoria, thus it is helpful to offer explicit choice about engaging with the body scan. If the client opts in, the client's attention might be directed towards areas of the body that feel neutral or affirming, or simply noticing the felt sense of the PC without a detailed scan of the body. In general, we avoid interpretations that pathologize body dysphoria as solely trauma-related. We can acknowledge its distinct nature while reprocessing any linked traumatic residue.

Phase 7. At the end of every session, regardless of whether reprocessing is complete, the therapist ensures the client returns to a state of relative equilibrium. Resourcing techniques learned in Phase 2 may be used. In the presence of ongoing trauma or oppressive experiences, we remind clients that ongoing distress related to disaffirming environments is normal and to be expected. The client is reminded how to use their resourcing skills accordingly.

Phase 8. Each subsequent session begins with reevaluating the targets reprocessed in the previous session. The therapist checks the SUD level associated with the old target and the VOC of the installed PC to ensure therapeutic gains are maintained. This phase also involves assessing any new disturbances or targets that may have emerged and planning the current session's focus.

Adapting EMDR therapy through an affirmative, culturally humble lens holds significant promise for effectively addressing the complex tapestry of trauma, minority stress, and identity-related distress experienced by gender expansive clients. By integrating an understanding of TGE-specific stressors and resilience factors into each phase of the protocol, and by grounding the work in a foundation of safety and validation, EMDR therapists can facilitate profound healing and contribute to the well-being and liberation of their TGE clients.

The principles and adaptations outlined in this chapter offer a valuable roadmap for enhancing clinical practice, grounding interventions in affirmative psychological approaches, the AIP model, and the lived experience of those with whom we work. While we acknowledge the current paucity of rigorous empirical research specifically evaluating these EMDR adaptations for TGE populations, we also recognize the limitations of traditional empirical research in fully capturing the depths of the nuanced, lived experiences of diverse persons. Therefore, alongside pursuing empirical investigations, it is imperative to prioritize practice-based evidence by actively listening to our clients, valuing their narratives, and systematically incorporating their feedback to inform clinical modifications. Qualitative research is particularly valuable here, providing deep insights into how interventions work for real people, highlighting common barriers experienced by TGE clients in therapeutic settings (e.g., education burdening or missteps) and illuminating the specific factors that contribute to positive therapeutic experiences. For TGE clients navigating unique stressors and discrimination, adapting care based on their individual needs and perspectives is not merely a clinical preference but an essential component of ethical, effective, and trauma-focused practice, helping to counter historical systemic deficiencies and instances of erasure in mental healthcare. A comprehensive approach to evidence, combining rigorous empirical study with robust practice-based learning and client-centered adaptation, is necessary to truly advance the field and improve well-being for TGE clients receiving EMDR Therapy.

Ultimately, providing competent and ethical care to TGE clients requires an ongoing commitment to complicating binary narratives in EMDR therapy, including deconstruction, continuous learning, self-reflection, adherence to affirmative principles, and a willingness to adapt to meet the unique needs of this resilient community. By embracing these responsibilities, EMDR therapists can play a vital role in mitigating the impacts of trauma and oppression, fostering self-acceptance, and supporting the overall health and flourishing of transgender and nonbinary clients.

Michael Kuffel (they/them) is a genderqueer, bisexual, and neurodivergent EMDR trainer, consultant, and therapist at New Leaf Trauma Institute. With 11 years of clinical mental health experience, they integrate an intersectional, anti-oppression paradigm into their work. Michael is passionate about teaching EMDR therapy in an inclusive and compassionate way and guiding learners to become self-aware, excellent EMDR therapists.

References

Ansara, Y. G., & Hegarty, P. (2014). Methodologies of misgendering: Recommendations for reducing cisgenderism in psychological research. *Feminism&Psychology,24*(2),259–270.doi.org/10.1177/0959353514526217

Archer, D. (2021). An anti-racist EMDR approach. In *Anti-racist psychotherapy: Confronting systemic racism and healing racial trauma* (pp. 127–139). Each One Teach One Publications.

Arijs, Q., Burgwal, A., Van Wiele, J., & Motmans, J. (2023). The price to pay for being yourself: Experiences of microaggressions among non-binary and genderqueer (NBGQ) youth. *Healthcare, 11*(5), 742. doi.org/10.3390/healthcare11050742

Austin, A. (2016). "There I am:" A grounded theory study of young adults navigating a transgender or gender nonconforming identity within a context of oppression and invisibility. *Sex Roles, 75*(5–6), 215–230. doi.org/10.1007/s11199-016-0600-7

Bauer, G. R., Hammond, R., Travers, R., Kaay, M., Hohenadel, K. M., & Boyce, M. (2009). "I don't think this is theoretical; this is our lives": How erasure impacts health care for transgender people. *Journal of the Association of Nurses in AIDS Care, 20*(5), 348–361. doi.org/10.1016/j.jana.2009.07.004

Bindman, J., Ngo, A., Zamudio-Haas, S., & Sevelius, J. (2022). Health care experiences of patients with nonbinary gender identities. *Transgender Health, 7*(5), 423–429. doi.org/10.1089/trgh.2021.0029

Brayer, R. (2023). The therapeutic relationship in EMDR. In *The art and science of EMDR: Helping clinicians bridge the path from protocol to practice*. Eau Claire, WI: PESI Publishing.

Cardona, N. D., Madigan, R. J., & Sauer-Zavala, S. (2022). How minority stress becomes traumatic invalidation: An emotion-focused conceptualization of minority stress in sexual and gender minority people. *Clinical Psychology: Science and Practice, 29*(2), 185–195. doi.org/10.1037/cps0000054

Chang, S. C. (2022). EMDR therapy as affirmative care for transgender and nonbinary clients. In M. Nickerson (Ed.), *Cultural Competence and Healing Culturally Based Trauma With EMDR Therapy* (2nd ed.). Springer Publishing Company. doi.org/10.1891/9780826163424.0018

Colizzi, M., Costa, R., & Todarello, O. (2015). Dissociative symptoms in individuals with gender dysphoria: Is the elevated prevalence real? *Psychiatry Research, 226*(1), 173–180. doi.org/10.1016/j.psychres.2014.12.045

Cooper, K., Russell, A., Mandy, W., & Butler, C. (2020). The phenomenology of gender dysphoria in adults: A systematic review and meta-synthesis. *Clinical Psychology Review, 80*, 101875. doi.org/10.1016/j.cpr.2020.101875 dickey, l. m., & Singh, A. A. (2017). Social justice and advocacy for transgender and gender-diverse clients. *Psychiatric Clinics of North America, 40*(1), 1–13. doi.org/10.1016/j.psc.2016.10.009

dickey, l. m., & Puckett, J. A. (2023). *Affirmative counseling for transgender and gender diverse clients*. Newburyport, MA: Hogrefe.

DuBois, L. Z., Puckett, J. A., Price, S. F., Kuehn, K., Lash, B., Walker, T., Holt, N. R., Ralston, A. L., Huit, T. Z., Miles, M., Volk, S., Capannola, A., Tipton, C., Hope, D. A., Mocarski, R., & Juster, R.-P. (2023). *The impact of sociopolitical events on transgender people in the US*. Bulletin of Applied Transgender Studies 2 (1-2): 1-26. doi.org/10.57814/SDX3-7Y41

Goodman, R. D. (2015). A liberatory approach to trauma counseling: Decolonizing our trauma-informed practices. In R. D. Goodman & P. C. Gorski (Eds.), *Decolonizing "multicultural" counseling through social justice* (pp. 55–72). New York: Springer Publications. Available: http://link.springer.com/10.1007/978-1-4939-1283-4_5

Greytak, E. (Ed.). (2024, September 11). *The impacts of anti-transgender laws and policies: Evidence from empirical research*. American Civil Liberties Union. Available: www.aclu.org/publications/the-impacts-of-anti-transgender-laws-and-policies-evidence-from-empirical-research

Hare-Mustin, R. T., & Marecek, J. (1988). The meaning of difference: Gender theory, postmodernism, and psychology. *American Psychologist, 43*(6), 455–464. doi.org/10.1037/0003-066X.43.6.455

Hase, M., Balmaceda, U. M., Ostacoli, L., Liebermann, P., & Hofmann, A. (2017). The AIP model of EMDR therapy and pathogenic memories. *Frontiers in Psychology, 8*, 1578. doi.org/10.3389/fpsyg.2017.01578

Hase, M., & Brisch, K. H. (2022). The therapeutic relationship in EMDR therapy. *Frontiers in Psychology, 13*, 835470. doi.org/10.3389/fpsyg.2022.835470

Hill, M. D. (2020). Adaptive Information Processing Theory: Origins, principles, applications, and evidence. *Journal of Evidence-Based Social Work, 17*(3), 317–331. doi.org/10.1080/26408066.2020.1748155

Kattari, S. K., Walls, N. E., Whitfield, D. L., & Langenderfer Magruder, L. (2017). Racial and ethnic differences in experiences of discrimination in accessing social services among transgender/gender-nonconforming people. *Journal of Ethnic & Cultural Diversity in Social Work, 26*(3), 217–235. doi.org/10.1080/15313204.2016.1242102

Kohnepoushi, P., Nikouei, M., Cheraghi, M., Hasanabadi, P., Rahmani, H., Moradi, M., Moradi, G., Moradpour, F., & Moradi, Y. (2023). Prevalence of suicidal thoughts and attempts in the transgender population of the world: A systematic review and meta-analysis. *Annals of General Psychiatry, 22*(1), 28. doi.org/10.1186/s12991-023-00460-3

Kuffel, M. P. (2022, April 22). *Treating gender dysphoria with EMDR therapy.* Available: www.emdria.org/event/treating-gender-dysphoria-with-emdr-april-2022/

Lee, W. Y., Hobbs, J. N., Hobaica, S., DeChants, J. P., Price, M. N., & Nath, R. (2024). State-level anti-transgender laws increase past-year suicide attempts among transgender and non-binary young people in the USA. *Nature Human Behaviour*, *8*(11), 2096–2106. doi.org/10.1038/s41562-024-01979-5

Levitt, H. M., Kehoe, K. A., Day, L. C., Nadwodny, N., Chang, E., Rizo, J. L., Hand, A. B., Alfatafta, R., D'Ambrozio, G., Ruggeri, K., Swanson, S. E., Thompson, A., & Priest, A. (2024). Being not binary: Experiences and functions of gender and gender communities. *Sex Roles*, *90*(12), 1766–1786. doi.org/10.1007/s11199-024-01543-5

Levis, R. V., & Siniego, L. (2017). An integrative approach to EMDR therapy as an antioppression endeavor. In M. Nickerson (Ed.), *Cultural competence and healing culturally based trauma with EMDR therapy: Innovative strategies and protocols* (pp. 79–95). New York: Springer Publishing Company.

Lindley, L., & Galupo, M. P. (2020). Gender dysphoria and minority stress: Support for inclusion of gender dysphoria as a proximal stressor. *Psychology of Sexual Orientation and Gender Diversity*, *7*(3), 265–275. doi.org/10.1037/sgd0000439

Lykens, J. E., LeBlanc, A. J., & Bockting, W. O. (2018). Healthcare experiences among young adults who identify as genderqueer or nonbinary. *LGBT Health*, *5*(3), 191–196. doi.org/10.1089/lgbt.2017.0215

Mahoney, M. J., & Granvold, D. K. (2005). Constructivism and psychotherapy. *World Psychiatry*, *4*(2), 74–77.

Marich, J. (2012). What makes a good EMDR therapist? Exploratory findings from client-centered inquiry. *Journal of Humanistic Psychology*, *52*(4), 401–422. doi.org/10.1177/0022167811431960

Marich, J. (2023). *Dissociation made simple: A stigma-free guide to embracing your dissociative mind and navigating daily life.* Berkeley, CA: North Atlantic Books.

Moody, C., & Smith, N. G. (2013). Suicide protective factors among Trans adults. *Archives of Sexual Behavior*, *42*(5), 739–752. doi.org/10.1007/s10508-013-0099-8

Nadal, K. L., Skolnik, A., & Wong, Y. (2012). Interpersonal and systemic microaggressions toward transgender people: Implications for counseling. *Journal of LGBT Issues in Counseling*, *6*(1), 55–82. doi.org/10.1080/1553 8605.2012.648583

Nobili, A., Glazebrook, C., & Arcelus, J. (2018). Quality of life of treatment-seeking transgender adults: A systematic review and meta-analysis. *Reviews in Endocrine and Metabolic Disorders, 19*(3), 199–220. doi.org/10.1007/s11154-018-9459-y

Novotney, A. (2023). *'The young people feel it': A look at the mental health impact of transgender legislation.* Available: www.apa.org/topics/lgbtq/mental-health-anti-transgender-legislation

Puckett, J. A., Cleary, P., Rossman, K., Mustanski, B., & Newcomb, M. E. (2018). Barriers to gender-affirming care for transgender and gender nonconforming individuals. *Sexuality Research and Social Policy, 15*(1), 48–59. doi.org/10.1007/s13178-017-0295-8

Puckett, J. A., Huit, T. Z., Hope, D. A., Mocarski, R., Lash, B. R., Walker, T., Holt, N., Ralston, A., Miles, M., Capannola, A., Tipton, C., Juster, R.-P., & DuBois, L. Z. (2022). Transgender and gender-diverse people's experiences of minority stress, mental health, and resilience in relation to perceptions of sociopolitical contexts. *Transgender Health.* doi.org/10.1089/trgh.2022.0047

Richards, C., Bouman, W. P., Seal, L., Barker, M. J., Nieder, T. O., & T'Sjoen, G. (2016). Non-binary or genderqueer genders. *International Review of Psychiatry, 28*(1), 95–102. doi.org/10.3109/09540261.2015.1106446

Rosati, F., Lorusso, M. M., Pistella, J., Giovanardi, G., Di Giannantonio, B., Mirabella, M., Williams, R., Lingiardi, V., & Baiocco, R. (2022). Non-binary clients' experiences of psychotherapy: Uncomfortable and affirmative approaches. *International Journal of Environmental Research and Public Health, 19*(22), 15339. doi.org/10.3390/ijerph192215339

Safran, J. D., & Muran, J. C. (2003). *Negotiating the therapeutic alliance: A relational treatment guide.* New York: Guilford Press.

Shapiro, F., & Laliotis, D. (2011). EMDR and the adaptive information processing model: Integrative treatment and case conceptualization. *Clinical Social Work Journal, 39*(2), 191–200. doi.org/10.1007/s10615-010-0300-7

Shapiro, F. (2018). *Eye Movement Desensitization and Reprocessing (EMDR) Therapy,* (3rd ed.). *Basic Principles, Protocols, and Procedures* (3rd ed). New York: Guilford Publications.

Shearer, J. (2019). Enforcing the gender binary and its implications on nonbinary identities: An exploration of the linguistic and social erasure of nonbinary individuals in the United States. *Binghamton University Undergraduate Journal, 5*(1). doi.org/10.22191/BUUJ/5/1/7

Sigurdsson, E., & Cardeña, E. (2024). Dissociative experiences among transgender women: A phenomenological study. *Journal of Trauma & Dissociation, 25*(5), 561–581. doi.org/10.1080/15299732.2024.2372563

Tebbe, E. A., Simone, M., Wilson, E., & Hunsicker, M. (2022). A dangerous visibility: Moderating effects of antitrans legislative efforts on trans and gender-diverse mental health. *Psychology of Sexual Orientation and Gender Diversity*, *9*(3), 259–271. doi.org/10.1037/sgd0000481

Tilsen, J. B. (2021). *Queering your therapy practice: Queer theory, narrative therapy, and imagining new identities*. New York: Routledge.

Wesp, L. M., Malcoe, L. H., Elliott, A., & Poteat, T. (2019). Intersectionality research for transgender health justice: A theory-driven conceptual framework for structural analysis of transgender health inequities. *Transgender Health*, *4*(1), 287–296. doi.org/10.1089/trgh.2019.0039

The Pleasure Project

Lesbian Edition

Jenn Kennedy, PhD, LMFT

During graduate school for my masters in clinical psychology in 2014 and 2015, I failed to see my queerness reflected anywhere. As I read case studies and articles covering the various psychological theories, I noticed that basically none included same sex couples. Academically, we had one known queer instructor in our entire program, and I secured the only lesbian supervisor at my non-profit (or any other) training site. However, rarely did a case study arise in class that included same sex couples and our discussions were invariably through the heterosexual frame. I did not see myself reflected anywhere. By this point, I had been out for 23 years and considered my homosexuality just a singular part of my larger identity. However, I found the dearth of data on women as a whole and queer women, in particular, remarkable and disappointing. I felt like it was both a responsibility and an opportunity for me to show up and contribute to the literature.

Because the queer community is consistently neglected in research, our clinical guidance as therapists is limited. We can't do better if we don't know more. As I continued my education to pursue a doctorate degree in sexology, I chose to turn my attention, resources and voice to queer the community. Pairing my passions, my PhD dissertation was a systematic review of the literature—with a focus on best practices for clinicians doing sex therapy with lesbians.

So, while the lesbian identity may not be fixed or absolute, for the purpose of this writing, lesbian is defined as female-identified persons who self-identify as primarily same-sex attracted. My literature review included transgender lesbians, who "experience a parallel process toward self-socialization into girlhood and womanhood" (Tate & Pearson, 2016, p. 102).

As per Prunas (2019) as cited by Nimbi et al. (2020), "Sexology research [on the transgender community has] focused primarily on pharmacotherapy, surgical treatments, and mental health of this heterogeneous population," however, "few studies have attempted to understand transgender people's sexual needs, nor their desire to achieve a more satisfying sexual experience" (p. 164). Transgender lesbians' experiences negotiating intimate relationships have yet to be the focus of much research (Riggs et al., 2018; Goldberg, 2016).

I did not include bisexual data in this review, so the women discussed are primarily partnering sexually with females. As per Diamond and Alley (2018), "Exclusive lesbians differ in important ways from bisexually attracted women—showing less fluidity in their sexual attractions and patterns of arousal" (p. 1315). Additionally, lesbians engaging in sexual activity do not have considerations of pregnancy or birth control. Uncoupling female sexuality from reproduction allows for heightened prioritization of sexual pleasure (Diamond & Alley, 2018). Additionally, "[bisexual] women viewed equity in giving and receiving sexual pleasure as critical to sexual enjoyment in orgasm, and report expecting low equity during casual heterosexual encounters"—thus illuminating the value of viewing these populations separately (Diamond & Alley, 2018, p. 1317).

Bisexual women, who report higher sexual desire, tend to be more stable throughout their lifetime (Nimbi et al. 2020). Additionally, bisexual women show different response patterns to erotic stimuli than lesbian women, thus the value of considering them separately from lesbians in research (Nimbi et al. 2020).

While lesbians, by definition, are women, there are notable differences between straight and lesbian women. First, lesbian partners are both female, which potentially creates unique social and sexual dynamics, and also lesbians experience their sexuality in a society that defaults to heterosexual norms (Hardtke et al., 2010). That said, I consider research on women's socialization, sexual satisfaction and functioning as part of the body of relevant literature. In this writing, lesbian and woman are not used interchangeably. When data was available specifically about lesbians, it is stated as such. When the data was only about women, without being specific to lesbians, it will be referenced accordingly. I utilize the "she" pronouns for lesbians, however I acknowledge that not all lesbians exclusively use "her" as their identifying pronoun.

Literature Review Highlights

In order to do this work, I reviewed all studies about women's sexuality, queer psychotherapy, sex therapy with all populations, and anything we know about lesbians as a population. There was minimal research focused on women and almost none on lesbians. Women's sexuality is most affected by the following factors: body image, family of origin and culture, attachment history, trauma history, physical ability, age, relationship to self and to pleasure. These are familiar elements of any case conceptualization; however, they are particularly poignant when talking about sexuality with a woman. Her sex life cannot be considered in a vacuum, but rather, her age, attachment history, family and cultural impacts, trauma history, relationship to self and pleasure well as body image must all be factored in.

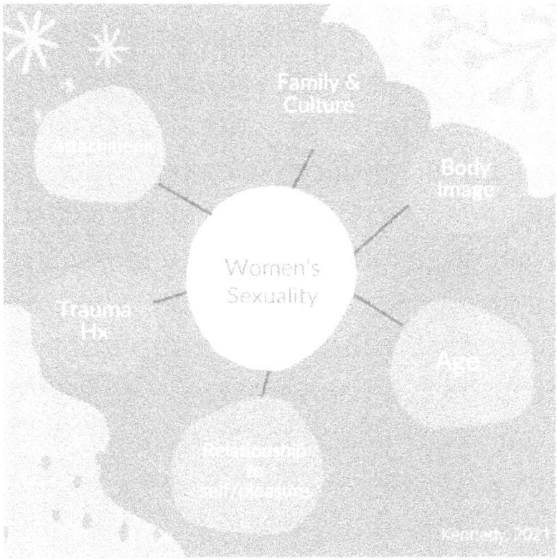

Figure 1: Women's Sexuality

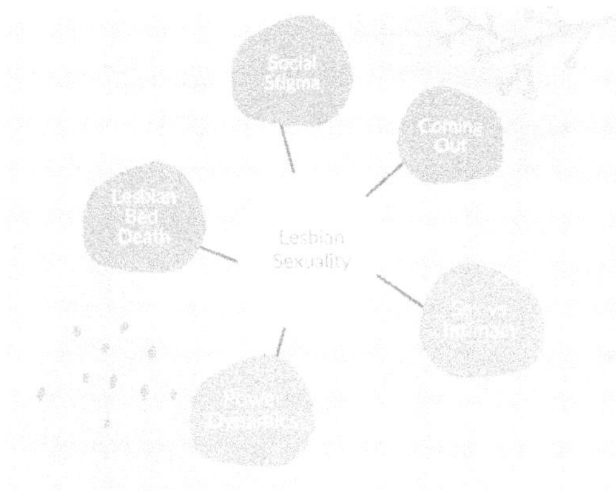

Figure 2: Literature Review Highlights

In addition to the issues that affect all women, lesbians (as a marginalized population) have additional stressors and considerations that impact their sexuality. These include the following:

Social Stigma

Lesbians face numerous unique societal and cultural challenges with the "combination of both homophobia – fear, dislike and prejudice against lesbian identities – as well as heterosexism, where society sees heterosexuality as the default, preferred or ""normal"" identity" (Wahlig & Long, 2017, p. 1683). Lesbian sexuality is both fetishized and dismissed as "not real sex." Partners of lesbians may be less celebrated, ignored, or altogether rejected by their partner's family (Wahlig & Long, 2017). While lesbian couples ranked highest for a tendency toward monogamy and levels of trust within a relationship (Gottman et al., 2019), we still tend to have particular challenges in other areas likely to impact their sex lives. This lack of support puts more pressure on the couple to provide necessary empathy, validation, companionship, and safety. Factors such as trauma (Gottman, 2019), "rejection, discrimination, concealment, and internalized heterosexism are "unique minority stressors faced by gays and lesbians--both at the individual and couples level" (Whitton et al., 2017, p. 879). *Strengthening Same-Sex Relationships Program, Female Version* (SSSR-F) is an example of a program designed to address these minority stressors. This program was the result of focus groups of same sex couples to understand unique needs when seeking relationship services. Post participant follow up indicated that the program ultimately offered effective, valuable tools for lesbian couples to decrease negative communication, increase relationship satisfaction and confidence (Whitton et al., 2017).

Coming Out

Coming out is a unique developmental milestone for Lesbian, Gay, Bisexual (LGB) individuals and far from being a singular event – more likely a long process. As per Johnson (2012, p. 519), "although coming-out issues may not be the focus of psychotherapy, clinicians should consider these unique phenomena during their initial assessment with LGB clients, just as one would likely assess for posttraumatic stress disorder in returning combat veterans."

As per Fassinger and Arseneau (2007), "Lesbians over the age of 55 are less likely to be out to their families of origin than are younger lesbians" (p. 62). These older lesbians likely came out in a historical context of pervasive stigma and discrimination, which may have them more isolated, less trusting and showing up for sex therapy with residual internalized homophobia. Vivienne Cass identifies six common stages of development in the homosexual identity formation: confusion; comparison; tolerance; acceptance; pride; synthesis (Brady & Busse, 1994). Clients may present for sex therapy at any of the above stages and therefore feel differently about their queer identity.

Sex vs. Intimacy

The research noted a pattern of lesbians prioritizing intimacy over sexuality. In a comparison by Masters and Johnson (1979), "heterosexual couples tended to be more performance oriented and preoccupied with orgasm attainment. This is reflected in the couples I see in my current sex therapy practice. Heterosexual couples are typically goal oriented and focused on finishing with orgasm, while the lesbian couples are oriented toward touch, exploration and mutual satisfaction. Lesbian couples took more time having sex and included whole body contact" (Iasenza, 2000, p. 61). Most lesbians tend to value intimacy above all--including sex.

A study by Scott and Rhodes (2014) highlights the importance of lesbian clients feeling their intimacy needs were understood by their clinician. Specifically, participants expressed that competence (in a therapist) included concerns that the helper understood external pressures experienced by the client, such as ostracism or rejection from family or society as well as "unique relationship dynamics within lesbian relationships (e.g., communication, intimacy)" (p. 346). A study by Cohen et al. (2008) considered the concerns and rewards of lesbian and gay sexual relationships. Benefits cited by study participants include emotional intimacy, companionship, physical intimacy, acceptance, safety and support, communication, more positive view of self, equality, and sexual compatibility (Cohen et al., 2008).

Power Dynamics/Roles

Role negotiation invariably arises with lesbian couples. Society has a heterosexist expectation of an active male and passive female, so when both partners are female, they must verbally or nonverbally assign roles and negotiate sexual initiation, relationship duties, and the power balance (Iasenza, 2002). Complementarity reflects how the couple's characteristics are different but interrelated (Winch, et al. as cited by De Jong & Reis, 2015). Each partner may be attracted to or aroused by different things, but it may be complementary to what their partner wants. An example commonly seen with lesbians is a butch/femme pairing. Sexually, it may play out as one partner likes giving and the other partner likes receiving oral sex. "Lesbian sex requires a greater degree of interaction, role differentiation, and coordination of behaviors and desire than most areas of a couples' life" (De Jong & Reis, 2015, p. 649). Clinicians cannot assume the roles or responsibilities held by lesbian couple clients—in or out of the bedroom. Rather, they need to inquire and stay open to a fluid, intricate system co-created by the clients. While lesbians value fairness and equality, they may also be drawn to partnerships with power differentials. That does not mean that either partner holds all power in all areas, but rather, they likely share power in various contexts. Clinicians are advised to stay curious and flexible to the mapping of the power dynamics organized by their clients. These relational dynamics are influenced by many factors, including age, financial status, gender expression, self-esteem, values, and sense of agency.

As per Clunis and Green (2000), "Questions arise about how [female] tendency toward others results in lesbians, as two women with this same female gender socialization, neglect their own personal needs to please or secure the relationship" (as cited by Hardte et al, 2010). This Author has seen a tendency by lesbian couples to be more deferential and accommodating toward one another's needs. That said, these couples also tend to be stronger at communication, and with the support of a therapist, willing to articulate their needs—sexual and otherwise. And while lesbian couples may come in for sex therapy, the literature has shown that, "lesbian study participants reported that "bed death" was perceived as purely sexual; it was distinct from lack of intimacy, which participants cited as non-negotiable" (Van Rosmalen-Nooijens et al., 2008). Therefore, the clinician should not assume that more frequent sex is always the goal with lesbian sex therapy. Sometimes their goal may be to increase closeness and build trust.

Lesbian Bed Death/Low Desire

A healthy debate continues about what Suzanne Iasenza (2002) calls "the Grandmommy of all lesbian sex myths: "Lesbian Bed Death," which describes a notorious drop off in sexual activity about two years into long-term lesbian relationships, which has become not only the subject of jokes by lesbian comics but a syndrome that a fair number of lesbian psychotherapy clients and their therapists believe actually exists" (p. 112). The Lesbian Bed Death phenomena is typically thought to occur after lesbians have been together for two years. However, Joy Whitman suggests that Lesbian Bed Death is "grounded in a heteronormative framework" and asserts that "lesbian sex needs to be explored and framed within the context of what is normal and regular for sex between women" (Dworkin & Pope, 2012, p. 242). Conflicting data exists about lesbian desire. For example, Breyer et al. (2010) found higher sexual desire among lesbian women as compared with heterosexual counterparts, while a Finnish study found women with homosexual experiences reported significantly lower levels of sexual desire and satisfaction (Burri et al., 2012).

The research reveals significant gaps in clinical and theoretical knowledge and practices around providing sex therapy treatment to lesbians. First and foremost, the studies that are available have not been statistically significant enough to offer data solid enough to create educational programming or create lesbian affirmative policy. The data about lesbian's sexuality is so sparse that, for example, the author could not identify even a basic population count for the number of lesbians living in the US. For the purpose of this dissertation, the author calculated a rough number in the following way: 2020 census data estimates there are 168,630,000 females (of all ages) in the United States. Based on the 2013 National Health Interview Survey (NHIS) data (collected in 2013 from 34,557 adults aged 18 and over), 1.5 percent of women identify as lesbian (Ward, 2014). The author then calculated that there are approximately 2,529,450 lesbians nationwide– a significant-enough sized population to warrant additional studies!

What Every Sex Therapist Should Know

There have been some attempts to address women's sexuality and specifically lesbian sexuality. In the table below, I provide a list of "knowledge deliverables"–things that comprehensively represent what every sex therapist should know. The right-hand column is a simple checklist indicating whether there is any literature at all covering that area.

The table shows at a glance where there is either limited knowledge on that topic, or simply no knowledge at all. Additionally, as clinicians working with queer women, we ideally should have awareness and understanding of the following: knowledge of queer history; knowledge of the social stigma attached to a queer identity; awareness of our own biases; awareness of clinician countertransference; awareness of privilege and oppression of minorities; understanding of the mechanics of sex between two women; signaling on the part of the clinician as to the comfort regarding the topic of sex in the clinical space.

Fortunately, the field of knowledge is growing, and we are starting to see more representation of queer women in research. In parallel to what we know from research, I'm continuing to form my own theories in the therapy realm with my clients. I see the field as wide open and ripe for contribution.

CURRENT LITERATURE on LESBIAN SEX THERAPY

Peer Reviewed Literature Available

Topics	Relevant Literature
Women's History	Yes
Female Sexual Development	Yes
Queer History	Some
Female Sexual Response	Some
Female Sexual Issues	Some
Wellness Through Lifespan	No
Transgender Considerations	No
Lesbian Relational Dynamics	No
Race & Culture	No

Riviera_Therapy
RivieraTherapy.com

Kennedy, 2021

Table 1: Current Literature on Lesbian Sex Therapy

Clinical Considerations

In addition to future research to aid clinicians working with lesbians, there are also clinical best practices that arose from this literature review. The following suggestions encapsulate topics that are pertinent to lesbians seeking sex therapy.

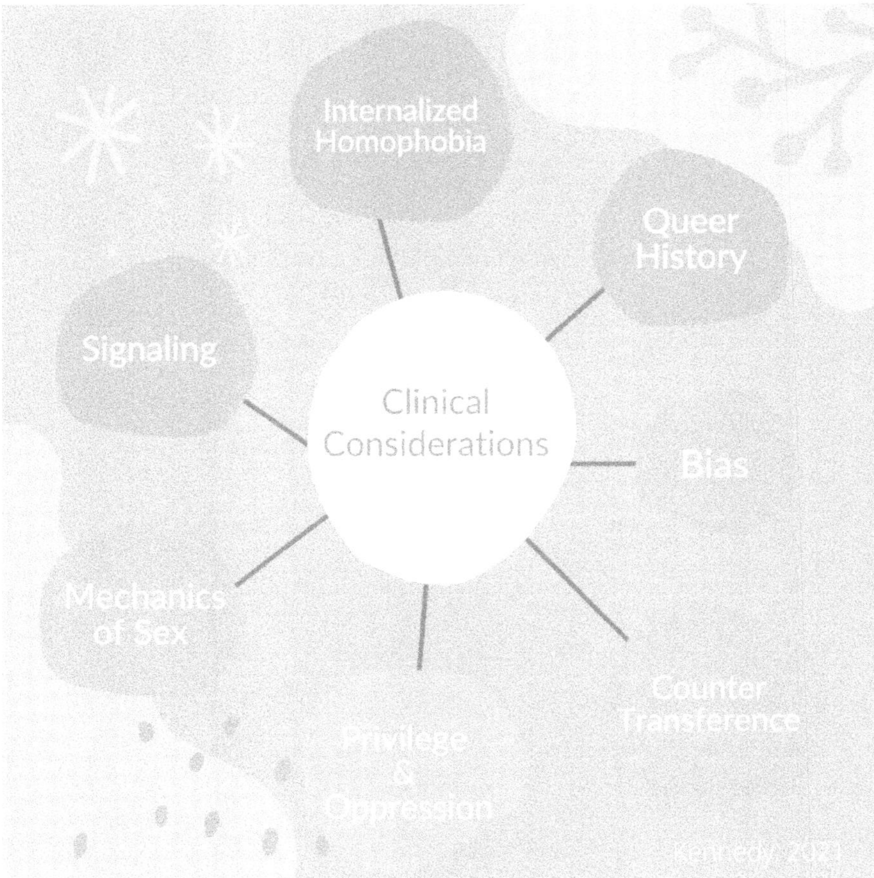

Figure 3: Clinical Considerations

Queer History

Clinicians working with lesbian clients should have familiarity with queer history to understand the context in which their client has formed a queer identity. This record would include the history of oppression, marginalization and even criminalization of LGBT people. Clinically, it would be imperative to know the history of the psychotherapy field pathologizing homosexuality until 1973. Shifting this label "...paved the way for decades of significant and dramatic improvements in the acceptance of queer couples and families..." (Stone Fish & Harvey, p. 1678). Additionally, familiarity with queer media and depictions of lesbian characters would be helpful to sex therapists serving lesbian clients. Examples include:

Film

- *Portrait of a Lady on Fire* (2019) - A beautifully shot period drama that explores a tender and passionate love story between two women in 18th-century France
- *The Handmaiden* (2016) - A psychological thriller based on Fingersmith by Sarah Waters, featuring an intense and empowering lesbian romance
- *Rafiki* (2018) - A groundbreaking Kenyan film about two young women who fall in love despite societal and legal challenges
- *Bound* (1996) - A neo-noir crime thriller with a strong, well-developed lesbian couple at its center, subverting many clichés
- *But I'm a Cheerleader* (1999) - A satirical comedy about conversion therapy that ultimately delivers a heartwarming love story
- *Imagine Me & You* (2005) - A lighthearted romantic comedy that challenges the idea of love at first sight in a same-sex relationship
- *The Half of It* (2020) - A coming-of-age film about a queer Chinese-American teen navigating her identity and feelings for another girl
- *Ammonite* (2020) - A historical romance about a fossil hunter and her growing affection for a young woman

TV Shows

- *Gentleman Jack* (2019-2022) - Based on the real-life diaries of Anne Lister, this show depicts a bold, confident lesbian woman in the 19th century

- *The L Word* (2004-2009, 2019-present) - One of the most influential series in lesbian representation, featuring diverse characters and relationships
- *Orange Is the New Black* (2013-2019) - Introduces multiple well-developed lesbian and bisexual characters, showing the complexity of their lives
- *One Day at a Time* (2017-2020) - Features a young Latina character, Elena, navigating her coming-out journey with humor and heart
- *Wynonna Earp* (2016-2021) - Features an iconic lesbian relationship (WayHaught) that is given depth, love, and a happy ending
- *Brooklyn Nine-Nine* (2013-2021) - Rosa Diaz, played by Stephanie Beatriz, is a strong, bisexual Latina detective whose relationships are treated with respect
- *Atypical* (2017-2021) - Features a sweet and realistic coming-out and love story between Casey and Izzie
- *She-Ra and the Princesses of Power* (2018-2020) - A beloved animated series with a beautifully developed lesbian romance at its heart

Bias

"Both client and clinician develop in a heterosexist culture that affects everyone, regardless of their sexual orientation...which is not necessarily mitigated by professional training" (Brown, 1988; Haldeman, 2002 as cited by Greene, 2007, p. 182). Clinicians would benefit from exploring their expectations, limitations, and hesitations regarding sex therapy with lesbians. This training is starting to be more available through certificate programs and psychology conferences offering LGBT tracks as well as graduate programs with courses specifically designed to highlight the needs and cultural considerations of the queer community. For example, Antioch University Los Angeles Masters in Clinical Psychology offers an emphasis in LGBT affirmative studies. Additionally, International Institute for Trauma and Addiction Professionals (IITAP) offer a Rainbow Advocacy and Educator RAE for their practitioners wanting to support LGBT clients.

Countertransference

Greene (2007) suggests that how the clinician feels about themselves in terms of gender and sexuality is likely to affect how they render services. Additionally, even lesbian therapists would need to be mindful of how they may project their own lived experience, stereotypes or myths onto the lesbian client. Clients may use different terminology or assume gender and sexual roles that are new or foreign to the clinician so consultation or additional training would be beneficial. Managing countertransference will be important for the clinician newly working with lesbian clients. Unfamiliar terms, sexual or relational dynamics may present in session and cause anxiety or self-doubt for the therapist. The clinician is beholden to seek consultation and perhaps do their own therapeutic work to effectively show up and support their lesbian clients. Brown warns that clinicians must not project their own fears or frustrations onto clients (1986).

As per Love and Farber (2017), "Clearly, the ways in which therapists approach the topic of sex can facilitate the conversation or shut it down. The therapist's open-minded, nonjudgmental, and affirmative stance toward addressing sexual topics can create an atmosphere of safety. Conversely, if the therapist avoids this material or handles it clumsily, clients may get the sense that this is an area that cannot be navigated safely or productively together. In turn, this experience may exacerbate clients' preexisting difficulties or shame with this material and/or lead to a fear that discussions of sex may jeopardize the therapeutic relationship" (p. 1490). Simply put, it takes courage to disclose, to be intimately recognized in the therapy space. But the felt risk of allowing oneself to be more fully known is especially heightened for clients who are struggling with fundamental aspects of their self-identity (Love & Farber, 2017, p. 1495).

Privilege and Oppression

Lesbians experience the oppression of sexism, which continues to stereotype and pressure women into a minority class with expected gender roles (Wahlig & Long, 2017). The therapist must "pay attention to hidden dynamics of privilege and oppression, as these may not be obvious presenting issues" (Addison & Coolhart, 2009, p. 67) and the therapist should not inadvertently repeat them in their patient-clinician dynamic. As per Whitman (2015), "Counselors who create a safe therapeutic relationship by examining their own biases and worldviews around sexuality for women and lesbian women and who can guide their clients in doing the same will have greater success exploring sensitive issues of sexuality" (p. 256). Therapists should be prepared to discuss racism, gender inequality, homophobia and other oppressions that frequently present in therapy with sexual minority populations, as these stressors can inhibit sex drive and intimacy (Addison & Coolhart, 2009).

Mechanics of Lesbian Sex

Given that sex therapy is sometimes about the physical mechanics of sex, in addition to the interpersonal dynamics, therapists should have a working understanding of how lesbians approach partnered and solo sex. This includes an understanding of toys, tribadism, anal and oral sex. Tribidism is a common form of sexual activity between women in which the external genitalia (vulva area) are rubbed together. Sometimes the colloquial term amongst lesbians is "scissororing" or "tribbing" and it allows for more direct clitoral stimulation. This can be achieved by rubbing the mons pubis directly together or one woman's vulva against the other woman's thigh or buttocks.

Clinicians should meet the client where they are in their sexual identity, which looks like letting the client determine the pacing of sessions and setting priorities for the sex therapy. The therapist would have knowledge of applicable resources (toy or vibrator recommendations, erotica, lesbian dating apps) to assist the sex therapy work.

In considering transgender lesbian sex, specific themes that have emerged include: the effects of cisgenderism, the effects of gender dysphoria and the medical aspects of transitioning and the impact on their sex lives (Riggs et al., 2018, p. 87). As per Riggs et al. (2018), transgender lesbians may feel either fetishized or delegitimized by their cisgender partner, which gets internalized by both partners and can impede real connection. As noted by Riggs et al. (2018), many but not all "transgender people experience dysphoria (typically dissatisfaction or discomfort with their bodies), which impacts willingness or capacity to enter into intimate relationships" (p.88). The transgender lesbian's sexual issues and thus clinical needs may mirror those of a cisgendered lesbian in certain ways and differ in other ways.

For example, both women may be receiving sex hormone treatment (HT), while the transgender lesbian may also have to contend with logistical and sexual ramifications of gender affirmation surgery (GAS), "which has effects on sexual drive, whereas it seems to be more linked to general body satisfaction, personal sexual identity recognition, and sexual pleasure" (Nikkelen & Kreukels, 2018, as cited by Nimbi et al., 2020, p. 169). Transgender women often experience a decrease in sensitivity and arousal after starting hormones, however they have shown to have longer lasting orgasms (Riggs et al, 2018). Goldberg (2016) cites mixed reports where estrogen has been shown to enhance libido and sexual response in some transgender women, while diminishing it in others and still others reporting an inverse relationship between sexual libido and response (p.1247). And while cisgender and transgender lesbians have nuances to their identity formation and interpersonal dynamics, body dysphoria and fear of fetishization are unique and relevant dimensions that should be considered when supporting all lesbians in sex therapy (Nimbi et al., 2020).

Signaling

Signaling is a series of messages – both directly and indirectly that a clinician is not only supportive and informed, but also skilled and prepared to meet a client's needs. This happens from the outset of services and continues throughout the professional relationship. Gay affirmative therapy includes messages from clinicians to clients that their feelings, sexuality, and relationships are normal, healthy expressions of their humanity. Gay affirming suggests the following clinical and administrative approaches with LGBT clients (Hinrichs & Donaldson, 2017, p. 951).

- *Welcoming environment*: positive, overt LGBT images and language on website, brochures and in waiting rooms; posted nondiscrimination policy; LGBT relevant publications and gender-neutral bathrooms.
- Intake forms and sessions: use language that does not assume sexual orientation, gender identity or relationship status; intake forms that allow write-ins for gender designations; regardless of presenting issues, staff should inquire about sexual orientation and gender identity (SOGI) as a default; asking open-ended questions regarding partnering, chosen family and pronoun use.
- *Treatment:* awareness about homophobia, heterosexism; validation surrounding fears—both with the therapist and with others; transparency about therapeutic goals – which may or may not focus on the client's lesbian identity.

As per Love and Farber (2017), talking about sexuality is not always easy—either for the therapist or the client. However, the therapist signaling that sex is both a safe and welcome topic helps clients come forward with their more sensitive material. Love and Farber (2017) suggest "therapists might inquire about clients' sexual attitudes more generally while normalizing the fact that talking about sex in therapy can seem challenging or even off limits at times. This can serve the function of bringing the topic of sex into the room, creating an acknowledgement that it is welcome and allowed in the therapy space while at the same time granting clients the autonomy to decide what is most important to cover in their treatment." (p. 1496-1497).

Internalized Homophobia

Sexuality is subtly influenced by infinite stimuli. Clients hear messages throughout their lives about desire, attraction, pleasure, intimacy, femininity, and commitment. These messages factor into their calculation about what they expect and deserve in a sexual relationship. Lesbian clients cannot be uncoupled from a society that has marginalized, objectified, eroticized, criticized, and fetishized lesbians as a culture and lesbian sex as an act. Thus, internalized homophobia is likely present in some form for most lesbian clients. As per Brown (1986), "When devising interventions in sex therapy with lesbian clients, therapists should be aware of internalized homophobia in the client's sexual concept, and then consciously avoid interventions that re-create the phenomenon in the course of the therapy itself "(p. 103). This can take the shape of assumptions about relational or sexual roles, frequency of sex or style of sexual activity.

Clinicians also signal support through inclusive intake forms, website imagery, waiting room materials, pronoun use and accurate knowledge of LGBTQ history and of female-female sexual acts. As per Long and Pietsch, "Women may be concerned about gender conceptualizations that tend to dichotomize sexual norms, such as the belief that initiating sex is a masculine role. When you compound this thought with possible internalized homophobia, lack of role models/road maps, and lack of support, one can see why some lesbian couples report a discrepancy in levels of sexual desire" (2004 as cited by Wahlig et al., 2017, p. 1685). "Looking at the mainstream MFT research, findings from a recent meta-analysis (Wood, et al., 2005) suggest that a full-treatment model is more effective than using isolated interventions from various models in the treatment for moderate marital distress" (as cited by Hardtke, et al., 2010, p. 314).

Sexual orientation labels are shifting, and fewer same sex attracted women are using the moniker "lesbian." However, more women are pursuing same sex relationships, so many of the dynamics and principles mentioned in this dissertation will have relevance. It is less important to know the exact label the client assumes at any given time and more important to know who and what they seek sexually and emotionally in their intimate relationships.

Summary

Removing stigmatizing diagnosis and laws have softened the public's perception toward LGBTQ persons. Decriminalizing queer sex and sexuality also allows for a less-guarded, more celebratory approach to healthy sexuality for lesbians. Unfortunately, we see how quickly the tides can turn with a new administration who is not only rolling back policies of inclusion, but also attempting to remove basic rights of bodily autonomy and equal marriage protection, thus reminding us of the fragility of the progress that has been made in the past few decades. The ramifications of long-standing institutionalized homophobia will echo the bedrooms of gays and lesbians for years to come. As a result, clinicians working with LGBTQ populations must be aware of the internal and external stressors that may be implicit or explicitly stated by the client.

Clinically, it may be important to parse the nature of reported dissatisfaction by lesbians, to clarify if one sexual act is dissatisfying or challenging versus all sexual expression. For example, a client may report avoidance of sex altogether or specific sexual acts for several reasons: feeling a lack confidence or skill; feeling repulsed or turned off by the behavior; feeling stressed or distracted; feeling guilty about the behavior from messages by her faith, culture, or family of origin. Clarification, by the clinician, about the context, frequency and nature of her presenting issues will assist the lesbian client in understanding and addressing her concerns.

EMDR has been an invaluable clinical tool. When working with couples with sexual issues, I regularly utilize EMDR to lower distress related to negative beliefs about a host of things, for example: body image, safety, needs attainment, worth, anxiety related to previous experiences or sexual initiation. I will sometimes work with partners separately or other times refer them to an individual therapist to get support before we proceed in the couples space. The desensitization achieved through EMDR removes roadblocks to connection and opens the client to new ways of thinking.

Considering a client's social location and how these various identities impact and affect other dimensions is critical for working with queer populations (Addison & Coolhart, 2015). In this role, the therapist is balancing her own identity as well as the client. Therapists must broach topics of gender, sexuality, race, class, and other aspects of culture with open ended questions and suspended ideas of outcomes (Addison & Coolhart, 2015). Sex therapy should examine and address the presenting issues through the lens of the client's complete identity. With the legalization of same sex marriage, many lesbian couples are choosing to pursue families in this traditional configuration. Media is becoming more LGBTQ inclusive and "out" role models are starting to take shape in politics, arts, professional sports, academics, literature, and the military. However, it is crucial that clinicians consider the cultural, familial, and psychological context of the client.

While there are more protections and perceived opportunities for lesbians, there may also continue to be barriers (real or perceived) regarding professional, relational, and sexual pursuit. The client should set the pace and name the psychological or literal obstacles to their clinical goals. The clinician's perception may not align with the client's, so it is worth asking the client about their outlook and perspective. Recent political shifts have increased the expression of concerns about protections and opportunities for women and queer clients in my practice.

While much of the clinical literature proposes that techniques effective in heterosexual relationships may be applied to LGBTQ populations, "an overview of relevant literature suggests that critical attention should be given to the generalizability of heterosexual healthcare models, and the unique needs of diverse populations" (Macdonald, 1998; Mayer et al., 2012; Spitalnick & McNair, 2005, as cited by Berry & Lezos, 2016, p. 2). Evans and Barker posit, "Research over the past decade has consistently confirmed that the majority of therapists are ill-equipped to work with lesbian, gay and bisexual clients, having had little training on the topic of sexuality, and often expressing a lack of knowledge about such clients" (2010, p. 375).

Lesbians have a unique history, culture and communication style. Sometimes they seek therapy about coming out, however oftentimes, their queerness is one aspect of their identity. However, having a clinician who sees the larger picture of their identity as a woman, in a relationship with women (even if she is single) matters in how she moves through the world. It influences her friendships, her finances, her decisions about parenting, retirement, her professional visibility, her outward appearance and many other aspects of her life.

The literature specific to couple therapy also habitually separates queer and multi-cultural issues. For example, "textbooks on couples therapy commonly approach the two topics in separate chapters, with no intersection between queer and non-White identities" (Addison & Coolhart, 2009 p. 55). "Using an intersectional lens to critique the assertion that these couples have been socialized the same around gender roles (Addison & Coolhart, 2009 as cited by Addison & Coolhart, 2015) caution clinicians that it is a mistake to assume that same-sex partners from different backgrounds will be operating from identical schemas (p. 441)."

Therapists working with lesbians of color must be acutely aware of the unique stressors that may exist between the couple or for the individual. Additionally, the therapist must see their own position and note how their bias and blind spots about how the client's ethnicity factors into their lesbian identity. It's incumbent upon the clinician to do this work separately to the client while also working in tandem with the client to understand their unique lived experience and how it informs the present clinical work. Thus, during a sexual history intake, the clinician must ask specific questions about early learning about lesbian sexuality as well as messages either partner may hold about their right to have a quality relationship where emotional and sexual intimacy are present (Brown, 1986, p. 103). Working with these internalized, negative messages will prove helpful to identify psychological barriers for the couple's sexual connection.

Suggestions for Change

There is a deficit of literature about sex therapy with lesbians. More research is needed in order to better inform clinical work. More research specifically focused on lesbian sexual identity, experience and preferences would offer useful and instructive information about how lesbians (and subsequently their needs in sex therapy) are distinct from gay and bisexual clients.

Additionally, we need researchers who are sensitive to the nuances of lesbian sexuality, asking about their unique needs and chief concerns in sex therapy. The above-mentioned theories and methodologies are only tangentially related to sex therapy. Except for Suzanne Iasenza's approach, none of these theories are designed specifically for sex therapy—let alone for lesbians with sex therapy needs. These theories aim to help more general therapeutic goals of individual clients: self-esteem, insight building and trauma reduction, and those of a couple, including communication, de-escalation of tension and negotiation of needs. While these skills are valuable and likely would contribute to the health of a lesbian and/or lesbian partnership, they do not holistically address the specific presenting issues of a lesbian seeking sex therapy. A more structured, repeatable, measurable approach would assist clinicians in replicating these tenets in the clinical space. Iasenza's approach would be worth operationalizing and replicating. The other theories and methods included in this dissertation offer best practice considerations (GAT, contextual theory, willingness model) and concrete interventions (Gottman, EFCT, SSSR-F and findings by Berry & Lezos) that would also be helpful in the larger conceptualization of serving this population.

The field of mental health needs data about how women who are attracted to women identify so we have an accurate sense of the population. We need to know more about the needs and issues that affect lesbians seeking sex therapy. We need more high-quality studies on lesbians to predict interventions and approaches that are statistically meaningful for lesbian clients. Clinically, we need to have significantly more data about transgender lesbian relationships, sexual preferences, and challenges as well as cultural considerations. We need to incorporate queer client considerations into the standard teaching curricula at the master's level that would include the items listed in this final table.

LEARNING OBJECTIVES *for* WOMEN'S SEX THERAPY

Clinical Training Focus Topics

Learning Objectives

Women's History

Queer History

Female Sexual Development

Female Sexual Response

Female Sex Therapy Presenting Issues

Wellness Through Lifespan

Transgender Considerations

Lesbian Relational Dynamics

Race & Culture

Riviera_Therapy
RivieraTherapy.com

Kennedy, 2021

Jenn Kennedy, PhD, LMFT (she/her) is a clinical sexologist and licensed marriage and family therapist based in Santa Barbara. She specializes in the areas of relationships, sex, addiction and LGBT. In 2019, she founded her clinical group practice, Riviera Therapy, and under this umbrella, she employs licensed therapists and supervises up-and-coming clinicians. In 2023, Dr. Jenn launched The Pleasure Project, which is dedicated to helping us all have a better sex life. Through this venture, she hosts a podcast called Pleasure Project: Sex & Relationships and offers small group intensives for women and couples. She recently launched a self-guided course and is coming out with a Pleasure Circle workbook in 2025. Dr. Jenn has been quoted in Redbook, Reader's Digest, Forbes Health, DailyOm, Shondaland, Parade, Allure, Yahoo!life and other publications. She is often tapped to discuss intimacy and sexuality for therapists and physicians.

References

Addison, S., & Coolhart, D. (2015). Expanding the therapy paradigm with queer couples: A relational intersectional lens. *Family Process, 54*(3), 435-453. doi:10.1111/famp.12171

Berry, M. D., & Lezos, A. N. (2017). Inclusive sex therapy practices: a qualitative study of the techniques sex therapists use when working with diverse sexual populations. *Sexual and Relationship Therapy, 32*(1), 2–21. https://doi.org/10.1080/14681994.2016.1193133

Brady, S., & Busse, W. (1994) The gay identity questionnaire:, *Journal of Homosexuality*, 26:4, 1-22.

Breyer, B. N., Smith, J. F., Eisenberg, M. L., Ando, K. A., Rowen, T. S., & Shindel, A. W. (2010). The impact of sexual orientation on sexuality and sexual practices in north american medical students. *The Journal of Sexual Medicine*, *7*(7), 2391–2400. https://doi.org/10.1111/j.1743-6109.2010.01794.x

Brown, L. S. (1986). Confronting internalized oppression in sex therapy with lesbians. *Journal of Homosexuality*, *12*(3-4), 99–107.

Burri, A., Rahman, Q, Santtila, P., Jern P., Spector T., & Sandnabba, K. (2012) The relationship between same- sex sexual experience, sexual distress, and female sexual dysfunction. *The Journal of Sexual Medicine*, 9(01), 198–206146

Clunis, D. M., & Green, G. D. (2000). *Lesbian couples: A guide to creating healthy relationships*. Toronto: Seal Press.

Cohen, J. N., Byers, E. S., & Walsh, L. P. (2008). Factors influencing the sexual relationships of lesbians and gay men. *International Journal of Sexual Health, 20*(3), 162–176.doi:10.1080/19317610802240105.

De Jong, D., & Reis, H. (2015) Sexual similarity, complementarity, accuracy, and overperception in same-sex couples. *Personal Relationships, 22, 647-665.*

Diamond, L. M., & Alley, J. (2018). Was it good for her? an alternative perspective on life history theory, female same-sex sexuality, and pleasure. *Archives of Sexual Behavior: The Official Publication of the International Academy of Sex Research, 48*(5), 1315–1320. https://doi.org/10.1007/s10508-018-1313-5149

Dworkin, S. H., & Pope, M. (Eds.). (2012). *Casebook for counseling lesbian, gay, bisexual, and transgender persons and their families*. American Counseling Association.

Evans, M., & Barker, M. (2010). How do you see me? Coming out in counselling. *British Journal of Guidance and Counselling, 38(4),* 375-391.

Fassinger, R. & Arseneau, J. (2007). "I'd rather get wet than be under that umbrella": differentiating the experiences and identities of lesbian, gay, bisexual, and transgender people. In K.J. Bieschke, R.M. Perez, K.A. DeBord (Eds.), *Handbook of counseling and psychotherapy with lesbian, gay, bisexual, and transgender clients* (2nd ed.). American Psychological Association. http://dx.doi.org/10.1037/11482-002

Goldberg, A. E. (Ed.). (2016). *The sage encyclopedia of lgbtq studies*. SAGE Publications.

Gottman, J., Gottman, J., Cole, C., & Preciado, M. (2019). Gay, lesbian, and heterosexual couples about to begin couples therapy: An online relationship assessment of 40,681 couples. *Journal of Marital and Family Therapy. 46*(2), 218-239. doi:10.1111/jmft.12395152

Greene, B. (2007) Delivering ethical psychological services to lesbian, gay and bisexual clients. In K.J.Bieschke, R.M. Perez, K.A. DeBord (Eds.), *Handbook of counseling and psychotherapy with lesbian, gay, bisexual, and transgender clients* (2nd ed.). American Psychological Association. http://dx.doi.org/10.1037/11482-002

Hardtke, K. K., Armstrong, M. S., & Johnson, S. (2010). Emotionally focused couple therapy: A full- treatment model well-suited to the specific needs of lesbian couples. *Journal of Couple and Relationship Therapy, 9*(4), 312–326. doi:10.1080/15332691.2010.515532.

Hinrichs, K.L.M, & Donaldson, W. (2017). Recommendations for use of affirmative psychotherapy with LGBT older adults. *Journal of Clinical Psychology: In Session, 73*(8), 945-953

Iasenza, S. (2000). Lesbian sexuality post-stonewall to post-modernism: Putting the "lesbian bed death" concept to bed. *Journal of Sex Education and Therapy, 25*(1), 59-69. doi:10.1080/01614576.2000.11074330

Iasenza, S. (2002). Beyond "lesbian bed death": The passion and play in lesbian relationships. *Journal of Lesbian Studies, 6*(1), 111-120, doi: 10.1300/J155v06n01_10

Johnson, S. (2012). Gay affirmative psychotherapy with lesbian, gay, and bisexual individuals: implications for contemporary psychotherapy research. *American Journal of Orthopsychiatry, 82*(4) 516-522.

Long, J. K., & Pietsch, U. (2004). How do therapists of same-sex couples "do it"? In S. Greene and D. Flemons (Eds.), Quickies: Brief approaches to sex therapy (pp. 171–188). Norton.

Love, M., & Farber, B. A. (2017). Let's not talk about sex. *Journal of Clinical Psychology, 73*(11), 1489–1498.

Macdonald, B.J. (1998). Issues in therapy with gay and lesbian couples. *Journal of Sex and Marital Therapy, 24(3),*165-90.

Masters, W. H., & Johnson, V. E. (1979). Homosexuality in perspective. Boston: Little, Brown.

Mayer, K.H., Bekker, L.-G., Stall, R., Grulich, A.E., Colfax, G., & Lama, J.R. (2012). Comprehensive clinical care for men who have sex with men: An integrated approach. *The Lancet,* 380, 378 387. doi:10.1016/S0140-6736(12)60835-6

Nikkelen S.W., & Kreukels, B.P. (2018) Sexual experiences in transgender people: the role of desire for gender-confirming interventions, psychological well-being, and body satisfaction. *Journal of Sex and Marital Therapy. 44*(4), 370–81. https://doi.org/10.1080/ 0092623X.2017.1405303.

Nimbi, F. M., Ciocca, G., Limoncin, E., Fontanesi, L., Uysal Ünal Batuhan, Flinchum, M., Tambelli, R., Jannini, E. A., & Simonelli, C. (2020). Sexual desire and fantasies in the lgbt community: a focus on bisexuals, transgender, and other shades of the rainbow. *Current Sexual Health Reports, 12*(3), 162–169. https://doi.org/10.1007/s11930-020-00262-8

Prunas A. (2019) The pathologization of trans-sexuality: historical roots and implications for sex counselling with transgender clients. *Sexologies. 28*(3), 54–60. https://doi.org/10.1016/j.sexol.2019.06.002.

Riggs, D. W., von Doussa, H., Power, J., & Dunk-West, Priscilla. (2018). In *Transgender people negotiating intimate relationships* (pp. 86–100). essay. https://doi.org/10.4324/9781315398785-6

Scott, S., & Rhoades, G. (2014). Relationship education for lesbian couples: Perceived barriers and content considerations. *Journal of Couple and Relationship Therapy, 13*(4), 339–364. doi:10.1080/15332691.2014.930704.

Spitalnick, J.S., & McNair, L.D. (2005). Couples therapy with gay and lesbian clients: An analysis of important clinical issues. *Journal of Sex and Marital Therapy, 31*(1), 43-56.

Stone Fish, L. S., Harvey, R., and Lebow, Jay. (2017). In *Lesbian couples* (pp. 1–6). essay. https://doi.org/10.1007/978-3-319-15877-8_487-1

Tate, C. C., & Pearson, M. D. (2016). Toward an inclusive model of lesbian identity development: outlining a common and nuanced model for cis and trans women. *Journal of Lesbian Studies, 20*(1), 97–115. https://doi.org/10.1080/10894160.2015.1076237165

Van Rosmalen-Nooijens, K.A., Vergeer C.M., & Lagro-Janssen, A.L. (2008). Bed death and other lesbian sexual problems unraveled: a qualitative study of the sexual health of lesbian women involved in a relationship. *Women and Health, 48*(3), 339–362. https://doi.org/10.1080/03630240802463343

Wahlig, J., Long, J., & Lebow, J. (2017). In *Lesbian couples in couple therapy* (pp. 1–8). essay. https://doi.org/10.1007/978-3-319-15877-8_498-1

Ward, B. W., & National Center for Health Statistics (U.S.). (2014). *Sexual orientation and health among U.S. adults: National health interview survey, 2013* (Ser. National health statistics reports, number 77). U.S. Department of Health and Human Services, Centers for Disease Control and Prevention, National Center for Health Statistics.

Whitman, J. S., & Dworkin, Sari H. (2015). Casebook for counseling. In *Sex and lesbian women* (pp. 241–257). essay, American Counseling Association: Alexandria, VA, USA. https://doi.org/10.1002/9781119221715.ch23

Whitton, S., Scott, S., Dyar, C., Weitbrecht, E., Hutsell, D., & Kuryluk, A. (2017). Piloting relationship education for female same-sex couples: Results of a small, randomized waitlist-control trial. *Journal of Family Psychology: Jfp : Journal of the Division of Family Psychology of the American Psychological Association (division 43), 31*(7),878-888.doi:10.1037/fam0000337

Winch, R. F., Ktsanes, T., & Ktsanes, V. (1954). The theory of complementary needs in mate- selection: An analytic and descriptive study. *American Sociological Review, 19*(3), 241–249. World Health Organization. (n.d.). *Sexual and reproductive health.* http://www.who.int/reproductivehealth/topics/sexual_health/sh_definitions/en

Wood, N. D., Crane; D. R., Schaalje, G. B., & Law, D. D. (2005). What works for whom: A meta-analytic review of marital and couples therapy in reference to marital distress. *The American Journal of Family Therapy*, 33, 273–287.

Mermaids, Trucks And The Kid In Between

Revisioning the Younger Self with Ego-State Therapy and EMDR

Dana Kamin MSW, RSW

When I look back, I see a pink and white jumper and a red and white dress. Little white tights with feet and patent leather shoes. Shiny white Mary Janes with little wee buckles, sized perfectly for my 5- and 7-year-old feet. A shy, quirky 1/2 smile for family and visitors.

Outside it was sunny. Beautiful spring and summer days. Perfect for celebrations. Not my celebrations, my older sister and my older brother's celebrations. Did they feel just as uncomfortable and weird in what they *had* to wear?!?

Smile for the camera! Everyone is smiling, proud, beaming. The photographer reminds me to smile too, look happy. "You look *so pretty*. Come on, give me a smile! Just *one* smile!"

My shy, lanky 5 year old's forced 1/2 smile, hung on our walls, literally, *for-ev-er*! At least that's how my 5-year old self saw it! Even worse, my 7-year old scowl, beautifully framed and hanging for the world to see, drew much attention over the years. You looked *so* pretty in pink! If *only* you had shown us your pretty smile!

Those pictures, a constant reminder of how pink jumpers and white tights can make you literally want to jump out of your skin.

Fast forward to the post-pink jumper era. Where, as a teen, I found a place to feel at home. The androgyny of the 80's! Crimped blue black hair, ripped jeans, narrow ties, safety pins. Make up for *everyone*! My rebellious teenage self, donned head to toe in a love/hate relationship with parental comments, "Why do you have to do your hair that way? Dress that way? That make up! Eishhhh!" The wall of family photos, "Such a shame, you were *soooo* pretty *back then*."

I never saw it that way. Little Pisces me, always felt like a fish out of water. Unless I was secretly doing kid-drag. *That* was different!

Dressing in my mom's sequined outfits and high heel sparkly shoes. My dad's suits, hats and ties. One moment, a disco queen in the making, the next, sophisticated, cultured, handsome and dashing!

Girls are supposed to like getting all dressed up in pretty dresses. Was I the only one who could see that the world got clothes *all wrong?* To little me, it was obvious. Pretty, 'girlie' clothes make everyone want to hide, don't they?

Today I understand what little me never could. That part that never understood why I didn't fit in. I've done a lot of healing work since then. Inner-child work *paired* with EMDR has led me to where I am today. I have learned to nurture that lost and confused part of me. The me that never understood, I really *did* fit in. It was the clothes, the perceptions, the expectations that were all wrong.

Retrospective work can be painful for LGBTQ+ folx, particularly for those who identify as Trans, Nonbinary, Genderfluid, or otherwise identify as outside gender binaries. Looking back on who we were in the past can be particularly painful, when the child we look back on doesn't represent who we may have been inside; and definitely does not resemble who we are today. Where *everything* may be different.

We know as practitioners, the healing power of EMDR, and the many benefits it can have. Processing traumatic memories, reducing the intensity and frequency of emotional triggers, flashbacks and trauma symptoms can be life changing. By reaching back to the most critical moments in one's life, EMDR transforms histories filled with shame, hurt, confusion and fear.

When we work with clients to go back in time, to their most traumatic experiences and memories, we often come upon younger parts of self in need of healing, attunement and care. As the EMDR International Association (EMDRIA, 2022) names, for those who identify as LGBTQ+, trauma such as the following, are quite common:

- Harassment, discrimination and othering at home, school and work
- Lack of access and safety in meeting health care needs
- Internalized fear, hurt and shame

- Family rejection
- Physical and sexual assault
- Other forms of marginalization and microaggressions

These experiences can have long lasting results, and are associated with depression, anxiety, PTSD, suicide and addictions in LGBTQ+ communities, and these circumstances can be very heightened for folx who identify as trans and gender diverse.

EMDR and Ego State Therapy

EMDR has so much to offer in our individual and collective healing. Processing trauma, reducing emotional distress, triggers and flashbacks are well documented benefits of EMDR. EMDR brings with it the possibility of healing deeply internalized hurt, shame, fear and pain, increasing resiliency, and self-acceptance, and shifting core beliefs from negative and destructive, to positive and long-lasting.

But what if we look back and don't recognize ourselves at all? What if looking back is too painful? Not just because of the things that happened to us – that alone is bad enough. What if we can't look back because nothing about ourselves then is what or who we, authentically, in essence, are?

Enter ego state therapy. Ego state therapy, developed from the psychodynamic psychotherapy tradition by John and Helen Watkins, sees one's psyche as made up of several distinct parts or egos. Each may have distinct identities and roles that the parts take on in the global make up of who we are. While to the external world, we generally present as one whole – me, myself and I are one. However, in reality, ego state therapy suggests that within each of us, is a number of "discreet ego states" that make up a "family of self" (Hartman & Zimberoff, 2003).

Our experiences lay the groundwork for the development of ego states. The more challenged our experiences are, the more intensive, maladaptive and protective these parts tend to be. Trauma may lead to hurt and scared parts stuck in a state akin to a frightened child. Other parts may take the role of protector trying to remain safe through controlling and protecting in whatever ways they can.

While these states and patterns of behavior likely made sense when we were younger, as we grow and enter adulthood, such ego states are often no longer beneficial. Protective parts that once helped us when we were young, today, can get us in trouble. Instead of being helpful, defensive, shutdown or hypervigilant, our otherwise protective parts can leave us with a myriad of challenges such as anxiety, depression, fear and isolation. These can distance us from the healing relationships we so often crave inside, and with others.

Ego State Therapy International (ESTI) identifies the following goals within ego state therapy:

- "To locate ego states harboring pain, trauma, anger, or frustration
- Facilitate expression, release, comfort, and empowerment. It is unresolved states that come out and make us feel out of control. They are our internal tender spots.
- To facilitate functional communication among ego states (the statement "I hate myself when I am like that" indicates two states lacking in proper communication and appreciation), and
- To help clients learn their ego states so that the states may be better used to the clients' benefit (e.g., allowing the client to, at one time, be open to enjoy emotional experiences and, at another time, be assertive to feel expressed when challenged)" (Emmerson, 2025).

Our goal in ego state therapy is to support our clients in their relationship to their ego states, and to move from maladaptive, conflictual, and dysfunctional ego states to more healthy states of being.

EMDR combined with ego state therapy, can have powerful therapeutic benefits. There are a number of places within the EMDR 8 Phase protocol where ego state therapy has been shown to be beneficial. Wade and Wade (2001) showed that ego state therapy integrated into the assessment and treatment phases of EMDR can help to uncover past experiences and associated ego states that may be at the heart of emotional reactions today, leading to positive effects that "promote:

(1) corrective developmental experiences
(2) resolution of grief and trauma
(3) acquisition of skills and abilities
(4) co-consciousness; and
(5) negotiation among ego states" (Wade & Wade, 2001, p. 233)

"The outcome is an integrated 'family of self' that has effectively overcome developmental crises, grief, and trauma, is aware of essential inner resources, and can consciously activate appropriate ego states" (Wade & Wade, 2001, p. 233).

When ego state therapy is used in conjunction with EMDR, as therapists and clients together, we can work to bring:

- **Differentiation** between the Adult Self (AS) and the traumatized part(s) of ourselves that live within us, that is, the parts that never understood why they felt wrong, different or bad.
- **Time Orientation** to move the hurt parts, increasingly toward the present. When triggered and scared, hurt parts of self may pull us out of the present and into the past. Time Orientation helps to safely help these parts *grow* into present day orientation and awareness. The tug-of-war between past and present can calm and become quiet.
- **Integration** of these parts into a more cohesive sense of wholeness and well-being today, within the healing of the Adult Self.

Revisioning inner child parts has helped me and many of the clients I have worked with to increase emotional well-being, inner-strength, authenticity, self-acceptance, self-awareness, self-compassion and self-love.

Combining EMDR and ego state therapy has the potential of shifting perceptions of self in relation to ourselves and others, whether it be family, partners and friends. I use this often in my work. JW expressed this idea well by saying: "I started to heal my inner child parts after my relationship ended. Realized I, well, my inner child, was seeking validation from my paternal figure, and that I was looking for and searching in the relationship I was in. Unpacking how that was intertwined with my gender identity helped!"

Many of the trans, nonbinary and gender diverse clients I have worked with, have referred to revisioning their inner child parts literally and figuratively, as *transformative* to their healing journey, their identity, and understanding who they are today.

JM states: "Something about the intentional acknowledgement of younger self as a boy" was very important to them.

ZW noted:

> "I used to struggle with coming out. My parts don't want to be an advocate, they just want to be safe and accepted. It's up to me to keep them safe. There is no way in hell I could have imagined that statement, that I would have said it with conviction, like it would have been in the realm of possibility. I wouldn't have even thought of it!"

In a systemic review of 10 studies from the US, Canada and Europe, examining the effects of the psychotherapist's statements on therapeutic alliance and patient outcomes, (Kadur, et al., 2019) the therapist's *exploration skills*, such as providing acceptance and reassurance, reflecting feelings, using open-ended questions, and restating responses in therapeutic ways, were highly correlated with symptom reduction and positive outcomes for clients.

Kadur, et al. (2019), further noted that in such cases, "significantly more frequent core analytic activities (clarifying, interpreting, addressing defences present in the session, and addressing intrapsychic conflicts) were applied by the therapist" (p. 172). These, along with the "warm hearted" (p. 172) and supportive nature of the clinicians, were noted to be factors in the positive outcomes for clients.

A decrease in depressive symptoms and increased stabilization were also highly correlated with bringing focus on how a client's history could be related to their current challenges. Initially, diving into a client's history, especially their direct familial and parental relationships, can bring with it a short-term increase in symptoms of trauma and dysregulation. However, psychoeducation, provided within the context of the therapeutic alliance, helped build client understanding, and safety within the process. Finally, having a safe and supportive setting in which to work, supports clients ability to "make changes and override self-protection mechanisms" (Kadur, et al., 2019).

EMDR therapists have a strong ability to create deep healing and lasting change. It is not uncommon for EMDR therapists to use ego state therapy on its own, or in combination with other *parts work* approaches, such as Internal Family Systems (IFS), to bring deep healing after a traumatic childhood.

To effectively and authentically support our trans, nonbinary, genderqueer, genderfluid or otherwise gender diverse clients, however, additional awareness, resources and connections may be needed. Hanville (2024), on a blog posted by the EMDR International Association, suggests that we must:

> Be mindful when resourcing or doing parts or inner child work. Ask the client if that works for them and if these parts or inner children have a gender, and honor that. TGD [Transgender and Gender Diverse] clients may have parts that identify as a variety of genders or have no gender.

My approach is similar, and still in development, bolstered by my own experiences and that of my clients. I'll start with myself. That awkward, scrawny little 5- and 7-year old. *She* remained inaccessible, ostracized, lost and longing. Alone, unrecognized, and frankly, unrecognizable for years. Long after growing out of the clothes and the expectations that never did fit her.

She was never a typical *she*. Little me loved dressing up. Sometimes like a boy, sometimes like a man, sometimes like a beautiful sequined diva. Today, I still do. All of those parts make up *me*, then and even now, at age 61. Today I have built a loving, kind, compassionate and healing relationship with all parts of me. The experience has been life changing.

A client similarly shared:

> I was not confused about my gender identity. I knew from the age of 4 years old. I naturally gravitated to stereotypical gendered female roles. All the signs were there from the beginning, the foundational years. I was told to assimilate into a boy role, male hobbies and interests were pushed onto me, to override my genuine interest in femininity. With the corrective behaviours I experienced related to gender, it took me until the age of 27 years old and the ending of a serious romantic relationship, to start transitioning and unpacking my inner-child experiences.

That client today, now well into her transition, reports her inner child today as "resilient, [with an] emphasis on freedom of expression, *and stubborn.*"

8 Phase Protocol

As we consider each phase of EMDR's 8-phase protocol, there is, no doubt, the possibility of incorporating ego state therapy with gender revisioning, throughout all 8 phases. The following 4 phases, in particular, provide a wealth of opportunities for revisioning parts in ways that can truly benefit and support the healing of queer, trans and nonbinary folx:

Phase 1 - History Taking, Treatment Planning and Case Conceptualization
Phase 2 – Preparation
Phase 3 – Assessment
Phase 4 – Desensitization

Each of these phases offers an opportunity to introduce the concept of using diverse approaches to connecting to younger parts of self. We can encourage asking and noticing, from a place of curiosity, what various parts might need, want, or feel. Creating safety by presenting an open and creative approach to thinking about oneself in the context of one's childhood can be a way to powerfully set up the experience for success.

Later, in Phases 5-8 (Installation, Body Scan, Closure and Reevaluation), additional opportunities present themselves to strengthen, reinforce and explore revisioned parts of self that may have developed in the earlier stages of processing.

Phase 1: History Taking, Treatment Planning and Case Conceptualization

In Phase 1, it is essential to ensure that a biopsychosocial history be gender affirming for gender-diverse queer, trans and nonbinary folx. Exploration can include bringing attention, not only to one's gender identity today, but also to their gender identity development.

I often use the EMDR Floatback technique to help clients access earlier memories connected to current distress. The Floatback method is a means of connecting current emotions, beliefs, and body sensations related to a present trigger to earlier time periods where one remembers feeling the same way. Floatbacks can be especially powerful for uncovering individual root experiences, and clusters of experiences related to identity, safety and belonging, many of which may have shaped current struggles for trans, nonbinary and gender diverse folx.

As part of gathering history while we float back, we might consider some or all of the following:

1. Were they exposed to binary beliefs, expectations and experiences of gender within their family of origin, schools or religious institutions?
2. Did they feel affirmed if they didn't quite fit the gender norms surrounding them at home, school and their community?
3. Did challenges with adhering to gender expectations and norms become a subject of criticism, rejection, ridicule, bullying or punishment?
4. Do pronouns 'assigned at birth' fit today?
5. Did the 'assigned' pronouns fit growing up?
6. Do various parts of self have different pronouns and names? If so, what might these be?

This final one is an interesting concept, one that may not have been considered yet by those we work with. Opening up the possibility to not only recognize different parts of self, but also to develop these identities, complete with names and pronouns that fit best for the healing of the individual, is a powerful way to validate, connect and integrate younger parts of self. This may, at first, be a new and validating concept for the individual. Many clients, throughout our work together, note that some parts may be male, some female, some neither, and some are both.

We delve into the spoken and unspoken expectations that parents, teachers, clergy and peers had about how boys and girls *should* act, dress, and feel. We look at how well gender expansive folx felt they measured up to these beliefs and expectations, that is, how well they "fit in" and/or could "play the game," as children and adolescents.

Policing of gender expression can profoundly affect the growing mind. Shame, fear, low self-esteem, internal conflict and confusion may result. As a part of our case conceptualization and treatment planning, I often ask, what does your young self look, sound and feel like today as you go back in time? What feels right for them to wear, do or play with today?

Many children are steered towards predetermined gender-based activities and toys. Finding out what we wanted to or liked to play with the most back then and what we would choose today, can be powerful. I played with my brother's Tonka trucks, not the dolls I was expected to like the most. With the exception of giving my Barbie's spiky haircuts and shaved heads (at a surprisingly young age) and letting them explore their immense interest in each other, (and *not* Ken!), my favourite activities were playing outside. Snakes, caterpillars, climbing trees, playing in the mud. Baseball, skateboards, toy cars, airplanes, and my brother's trucks.

I was lucky to have an older brother and parents that didn't limit my play. Many do not have this experience. Validating and revisioning today, the prohibited toys and games from the past can be a powerful way to build trust in the healing process for young, mistrustful parts. Barbie dolls, playing house, playing with Transformers or GI Joe, wearing makeup, dressing up, Mermaid and Superman outfits no longer have to be off limits where they once may have been. Creativity and imagination no longer have to be bound by societal *rules* and gendered expectations.

For some, revisioning hair length may be equally as important, especially where expectations around the length of girls' and boys' hair may be embedded within cultural norms. JM had long hair growing up, before getting a buzz cut near the end of high school. Bringing "intentionality to how I think about myself," has helped JM to look back and think, "That is a boy, who is me," with positivity rather than in a "dismissive" way.

AD similarly expressed, "There's a school photo of myself as a child that used to make me feel embarrassed and ashamed: I have long hair that I hold back with an uncomfortable pink headband and empty eyes that had lost hope of life ever getting better...I didn't really understand at first why Dana would encourage me to re-vision myself as a child. Things didn't click until I pictured shorter hair and fun clothes. Kid me stopped being a sad static school photo and came alive."

Treatment Planning in Phase 1 will lead us into target sequencing, where, as EMDR practitioners, we support those we work with to identify their worst memories, their earliest traumatic memories, and those that continue to create challenges in their current life. This may involve memories that span across their life, including recent events that continue to be distressing.

The memories in our target sequencing plan are at the heart of the maladaptive memory networks which have developed over the course of the client's life. When working with gender diverse and those identifying within the LGBTQ+ spectrum, target sequencing in Phase 1 must also honor the unique layering of trauma that has been experienced. Early memories of rejection, based within binary views of gender and sexuality, identity invalidation, and social isolation may be intertwined with more recent experiences of discrimination, misgendering, and oppression.

By approaching treatment planning through the affirming and intersectional lens described here, we create space for folx to not only process wounds from the past; also to reclaim a sense of internal connectedness, personal power and agency. With this help, people can strengthen identity and belonging in the present.

Phase 2: Preparation

In Phase 2, our focus is on building trust, establishing a Calm Place, and developing grounding strategies and internal resources for the processing ahead. As therapists, we are continuing to establish a relationship rooted in respect for pronouns, chosen names, and this is a perfect place to continue moving forward in connecting Adult Self and child parts.

As we work with clients to create their Calm Place, it's important to consider affirming clothes, names, rituals, and symbols of gender affirmation. The possibilities for Calm Place are vast, and for some, being in a space with symbols of acceptance, pride and community may resonate. This could be a Pride parade, a queer community centre, or an imagined place of peace, filled with love and acceptance.

For many, having a Calm Place that feels safe for Adult Self *and* child parts can be helpful. For others, parts of self may want a Safe Container or Calm Place that is all their own. Trauma hurts imagination and possibilities, and through Calm Place, the Container Exercise and other grounding strategies, we can promote healing.

Living with fear, shame, and confusion — in a world that doesn't understand you or your needs, and where hurt is real and ongoing — puts us in survival mode. Our brain and nervous system prioritizes keeping ourselves safe in whatever ways possible. Dreams are replaced with harsh realities, imagination with a sense of danger, and excitement with fear. Part of our work is to restore and heal imagination, and it is here that we may discover the potentiality of both internal and external resources.

- **External Resources:** As we look into a person's past and present, we may find gender diverse and allied external resources and role models that can represent safety and hope. Whether queer or trans elders who are paving the way for others through courage, advocacy and authenticity, or cisgender allies who bring solidarity and a belief that societal change is possible, such resources can be powerful. If none exist in the individual sphere, there are increasingly famous role models that may be an option.

- **Internal Resources:** There may be creative parts of self who may have found a way to imagine themselves beyond the binary, even if their play was in hiding – like my own creative love of dressing up as a man, as a hyper-femme woman or part man / part woman all at the same time. Finding enough confidence as a youth, young adult, or really, at any age, to say, even once, even just to themselves, "I think this (being gender diverse, nonbinary, or trans) *is* me," can be incredibly powerful. This alone can be a fantastic internal resource to support folx in the work to come.

Moments of gender euphoria or affirmation, as opposed to the experiences of gender dysphoria that many trans, nonbinary and gender diverse folx grow up with, may be useful to learn more about at this stage. Gender euphoria, as defined by The Trevor Project (2023), can be described as "satisfaction or joy caused when one's gendered experience aligns with their gender identity, rather than with the gender they were assigned at birth."

Experiences of gender euphoria or affirmation can be a powerful way of resourcing. In working with JM to strengthen his resources, he described there being only one time in his history, where he remembered experiencing truly positive affect – that was, when he was "mistaken for a dude."

Emphasizing a gender-affirming approach throughout Phase 2, can help increase positive affect, build imagination, confidence and trust for the healing work ahead. AD described it this way: "Once Kid AD knew I was there for them and I could be trusted to protect them, I could feel them relax: they became someone who liked to smile, play, run around, and was chatty!"

As we move into the Assessment and Desensitization phases, we are already supporting folx to gain and maintain the strength and ability to internally connect and dream as we enter into the phases of trauma processing ahead.

Phase 3: Assessment

In the Assessment Phase, the traumatic event to be targeted is selected from amongst those identified in Phase 1. The memory is elaborated on, with attention brought to the most challenging or worst aspects of the memory now, for the individual, as they look back on it, as well as the accompanying images, negative cognitions and emotions, the somatic experience present while discussing the target memory. A more positive cognition to be worked towards is also selected.

Each of these provides further opportunities to heal gender, sexuality and the intersectionality of oppression that many gender diverse folx experience.

1. **Identifying Target Memories:** Trauma-related memories of rejection, criticism, invalidation, bullying, and gender policing at home, school, and in the community may be relevant targets for processing. Spiritual, religious and medical trauma, can be common experiences to target amongst queer and trans populations. In fact, any memory that targets gender dysphoria, feelings of being misunderstood, socially isolated or unsafe can be appropriate for processing. These memories may not always appear "traumatic" by traditional standards but it is important to note the deep emotional wounds that these might cause, particularly when oppressive experiences of gender identity and sexual orientation intersect with abuse, violence and systemic oppression. In selecting a first EMDR target memory for processing, selecting a memory with a Subjective Unit of Disturbance (SUDS) rating that is in the midrange (6-8/10), may be advisable, when someone is new to EMDR. As comfort and familiarity with the EMDR process continues, your client may be more ready to move into processing their first or worst experiences, that is the memories locked within that elicit a SUDS rating of 8-10/10.

2. **Negative Cognitions (NC):** Trans and nonbinary clients may internalize harmful messages, in their experiences with family, peers, school, religious institutions, and these are often messages reinforced by society as a whole. Over time, repeated exposure to negative and invalidating messages can lead to deeply rooted and embedded negative core beliefs such as, "I am defective," "There is something wrong with me," "I am shameful," and "It's not OK to feel or show my emotions."

   Negative cognitions such as these can be seen as natural, yet maladaptive strategies that the brain has utilized to cope with the systemic and intersectional harm and trauma that has been experienced. Over time, and with repeated experiences of homophobia and transphobia, amongst a myriad of other 'isms' and traumatic experiences, such as abuse, domestic violence, separation, loss and abandonment, these experiences can become internalized into beliefs such as:

   - "I am not ok as I am."
   - "I am not worthy."
   - "I am unlovable."
   - "I am not in control."
   - "I am not safe."

3. **Positive Cognitions (PC):** Identifying the positive cognitions that can help guide us in our healing are an essential aspect of the Assessment and target development process. Working together to co-create positive cognitions can help, as ZW suggested, to "bring me to myself and the understanding of who I am, and why I have all of these parts and these conflicts" inside. Positive thoughts that are adaptive, healing and affirming of gender identity and sexuality may include:

   - "I am ok and healthy as I am."
   - "We are / I am worthy."
   - "We are lovable and beautiful inside and out."
   - "Today, I am in control."
   - "It's over, we are safe now."
   - "It's ok to take up space."

- "I am whole in my identity."
- "My truth is real and powerful."

Notice in some of these, I substituted "I" with "We." Positive cognitions that speak to the needs of a number of parts of self can have a profound impact on the healing of hurt, scared and traumatized parts. "We" or "you" can be substituted in almost any positive cognition, to encourage the strengthening of the Adult Self's ability to guide and support younger parts of self within the healing process.

For some folx, stepping into these and other positive cognitions will be an ongoing goal that will take time. Of course, the upcoming phase of Desensitization is necessary prior to installing the positive thought, however, waiting for this can feel like forever for someone who has been seeking relief from painful thoughts and feelings already for far too long.

I like to introduce early in my EMDR and ego state therapy work, the concept of *Emerging* or *Interim* Positive Thoughts, that can lead us on a path towards building trust and safety in the experiencing of positive thoughts and affirmations. Often the trauma brain focuses on the negative, and positive thoughts may, in and of themselves, evoke strong emotions of hurt, pain, disbelief, anger and fear. An emerging positive thought can create a bridge to begin experiencing positive thoughts in a safer way. I like to use such statements as:

"I am / we are learning..." (e.g., that we are safe today, that today we are valued)

"I am / we are beginning to believe..." (e.g., that we deserve to be happy, to care for ourselves, we can heal)

"I am / we are starting to see / notice..." (e.g., that today, we are lovable and beautiful inside and out)

4. **Emotions:** We may hide, change ourselves to fit in, or more often than not, rely on a combination of coping strategies to try and tamp down feelings of shame, fear, hurt, rage, grief, sadness and longing. Creating a space to name and begin explor-

ing these emotional truths as we explore negative emotions and build the EMDR target can be extremely hard, yet powerful. "Digging into the roots of the shame that I experienced in terms of gender identity was hard. It felt very emotionally charged (JW)."

5. **Body Scan:** For many who identify as trans, nonbinary or genderqueer, the body scan portion of the Assessment and target development phase may be complicated by a history of, and/or potential current experiences of gender dysphoria, trauma and or dissociation from parts or all of one's body. Noticing what is happening in the body, may be multi-layered, complex, and a work in progress. I often begin working from a more generalized point of view. I invite noticing a general sense of what's happening inside:

    - "Gently notice what, if anything, is happening within your body as a whole?"
    - "Let's check in and notice what's happening inside. Do you notice any tension, tightness in your muscles?"
    - "Has there been a shift in how you're holding yourself or sitting?"
    - "Some people notice tension in their back, shoulders, neck, jaw, abdomen. Some people notice their breathing changes. Are you noticing these or anything else?"
    - "Notice if anything feels different, lighter, heavier, or just neutral."

I try to stay away from terms that may be triggering due to gender dysphoria and/or trauma. In particular, I may ask about tightness or tension in the "core," or lungs, or if the person is noticing changes in breathing or heart rate, rather than drawing attention to a person's chest or chest wall. Using more ambiguous, non-invasive language can lessen the risk of gender dysphoria impacting the early stages of EMDR.

Phase 4: Desensitization

Phase 4, Desensitization, continues to present great opportunities to revision younger parts of self, which through earlier processes may likely be well established by this point. Whether the target itself is one that takes the client back into earlier ages and stages of development, or it is a more recent experience, the client may see themselves at younger ages and stages when processing a memory.

This may show up as emotions of grief, anger, hurt, loss and shame, and may be evident both emotionally and in somatic or body-based responses. During the desensitization phase, note any unique aspects of the child self that might be coming into view during processing. You might notice who, of the different parts, is present in a particular target or set.

Parts may have a wealth of information that can arise and be very helpful during processing. We can learn more about what the client experienced when young, as well as how parts of self continue to experience the accompanying thoughts, emotions and body sensations based on their earlier experiences and subsequent triggers. We can observe and learn about developmental lags and milestones that may have been missed or left incomplete due to trauma, and we can learn about who those younger parts were in the past.

AD described having, "realized they [younger self] were a person who wanted to talk to me, someone who was overwhelmed and needed care. It also made me realize how judgemental and unkind I'd been towards Kid [me]."

We may see where disruptions in the development of healthy self-concept and healthy attachment may have occurred. This is especially true when processing targets relating to caregivers, family members, teachers, friends, peers and other important people in the child's life, who may be intertwined with the client's experiences of denial, rejection, ridicule, punishment and other such pain.

Our own self-reflection and openness as therapists, can help us ensure we are attuned to clients' unique lived experiences, and any appearance of parts, while not letting our own implicit bias or assumptions, related to gender norms, values and roles, "get in the way" of client processing. We can show a true belief in the power of healing through parts work that is gender affirming, and "give permission" for parts exploration. As stated by ZW previously, there was, "no way in hell [or] realm of possibility" that they would have looked back and revisioned young parts prior to our work. However, ZW felt it was "the belief that I saw in you [Dana], in your conviction that opened the door for me to walk through." In ZW's own words, "it was the therapist's beliefs and conviction," that has opened up to the relationship ZW is building with their healing parts today.

As a practitioner, Cognitive Interweaves can be strategically used when processing stalls, seems stuck, or when a client needs additional support to move through the traumatic memory in adaptive and healing ways. Perhaps the young parts of self may feel safer with a cognitive interweave, where the Adult Self as they are today, directly steps into the memory to be there with and for the younger part(s) of self, giving support, encouragement and validation.

Pausing processing briefly, to learn and highlight *who* is present and *what* they may be feeling at the place they are in the memory, may elicit awareness of younger parts of self, even when processing a more recent memory. The Adult Self, as they are today, with the therapist's help, can guide and support younger parts of self through feeling frozen, panicked, alone or helpless.

If gender dysphoria is blocking processing, we can take the time needed to encourage the imagining and re-imagining of those parts in a way that can move processing forward. We might ask, "What, in this moment, if anything, do these parts want and need from us?"

"Go with that..."

As an example, perhaps the client will get an overwhelming sense from their internal parts, that they want to *feel* and *be* safe. We might ask:

- "What does this part look like as you see them in the memory?"
- "Do they *feel* safe with their hair, clothing or name as it is in the memory?"

- "Would they (or you) feel safer if something was different about these as we process the memory?"
- "Would they feel safer if they were more like you today, or how you aspire to be as you continue along your gender journey?"

Rather than being disconnected and abandoned strangers, the client is working towards integration, togetherness, and healing of fragmented parts of self. At this point, you will likely be able to use what is discovered as the cognitive interweave for the next set of BLS. You are, in essence, ready to say:

"Ok, go with that..."

Cognitive Interweaves are also very helpful to prepare for closure when the end of session is near and the target processing is incomplete. Where needed, the Adult Self or other resources, such as others further along in their journey of discovery related to gender or sexuality, can provide a sense of strength, comfort and safety. They might offer to be there with the younger parts of self, helping to validate and hold space, offer a break and to step out of the memory altogether, until the next EMDR session. They can encourage leaving the memory behind, and going somewhere safer and especially for younger parts, someplace fun!

In my experience, such cognitive interweaves can help, not only unblock processing and positively close a session; they can help a client move more rapidly through reprocessing of a memory. As we round off sessions, I encourage folx to continue *practicing* the revisioning and sharing of *togetherness* they experienced in session, to the extent that this is able to be tolerated.

Through desensitization, using cognitive interweaves as needed, and retaining the connection with parts, those we work with are strengthening healthy and adaptive beliefs and cognitions. Even before we have walked through each stage of the 8 Phase protocol, clients may already be experiencing positive changes in their internal relationships to self.

As JM noted earlier, seeing his "younger self as a boy" has been a tremendously important part of developing and strengthening "security and comfort in knowing myself."

Phases 5-8: Installation, Body Scan, Closure, Re-evaluation

It is here, in Phase 5 that the positive cognitions identified in the assessment phase will be installed and strengthened. This is a fantastic time to affirm and validate all that has been done to heal fragmented parts of self up to this point. Parts and the Adult Self can have their right to exist, experience healing and thrive as they are today, and see themselves into the future.

After Installation, Phase 6 Body Scan is used to ensure there is nothing further being held in the body related to the processed target. The client holds the target event in their mind, which at this point should feel more distant, blurry or vague, without the triggers that were previously associated with it. The client also holds the positive cognition in mind, while scanning their body from head to toe. Any lingering disturbance emerging from the body scan would then be reprocessed. As discussed previously, Body Scans can be triggering and bring up a history of trauma, abuse and gender dysphoria, both related to and beyond the subject of the target memory.

To lessen the likelihood of this happening the body scan may need to be adapted to ensure safety for the client. We may use more vague language for certain areas of the body, encouraging the building of safety and presence as we ask the client to go into and notice what is happening in their body, and build in reminders of the current date, year and safer location they are in today, to lessen the risks of flashbacks, triggers and dissociative symptoms.

The client can envision themselves in whatever ways feel safest as they work through the body scan with your gentle guidance. Sometimes I have clients have themselves and their child parts, as revisioned, take part in the body scan. At times, the body scan has brought up discomfort continuing to emerge from parts. In such a situation, I may spend time helping to reprocess somatic experiences of the memory still lingering for parts, before moving into the final phases.

In Phase 7, Closure, we may use the strengths the Adult Self has developed, and other role models who have overcome and shown strength against transphobia, homophobia, and other forms of oppression, to help strengthen the adaptive healing and positive cognitions identified in the EMDR processing.

Finally, as we move into the final phase of Evaluation, Phase 8, we can evaluate and continue to re-evaluate with the client whether there is increasing stability in relation to both targeted memories and parts. We may look at the next target memories to be processed, which may include past or present targets for processing, or new and additional targets arising as a result of this in-depth work.

Installing future templates and a future sense of self as a Resource may also be possibilities as a part of the Re-evaluation Phase. One can imagine a future version of self that is affirmed and thriving, both personally and within all areas of their life. The more this is practiced, the stronger the positive neural network, internal allies and resources will become.

JM described the importance of working towards having a "visual imagination," of himself in the future, even if he is currently having "difficulties imagining and speaking to future self, due to ambiguousness of future appearance [and] potential body changes," from hormone replacement therapy and gender-affirming surgeries.

In many ways, Phase 8 sets us up for what I like to think of, as EMDR's version of *rinse and repeat*—as we co-create the next target, we flow through this journey, alongside our client, back through Phases 3 to 8, each target bringing our clients closer to clarity, integration and healing.

Final Thoughts

I credit a great deal of my own trauma healing to EMDR, as well as inner-child work, which started for me even before ego state therapy was developed to the extent it is today. During the most intensive times of my trauma healing, my practitioners were working with the emerging evidence-based awareness of EMDR, combined with their own educated and informed gut wisdom. There wasn't a roadmap for this back then!

My trauma healing reaches back into the 1990's. I started with EMDR, and in those memories, I was still very much the little girl I was raised to be. Yet, some part of me was screaming inside – screaming to be heard, seen and understood. There was a strong protector part that was not okay with that, and younger, scared parts afraid to stand out in any way. Ego state therapy helped immensely with that. Today, young parts of me don't scream the same way anymore. They don't need to, and when there are triggers, I am able to hear, see, feel and connect to what young parts of me need. They, in essence, no longer need to scream, cry, or give up. I am there and we are one, even as we are many...

My inner-child parts and my adult parts reflect my own understanding of gender diversity. There are parts of me that still, to this day love to dress in drag – sometimes more masculine, sometimes hyper-feminine, mostly a combo of the two, and often at the same time. I have *she* parts, *they* parts and *he-curious* parts. They live within me, in peace and understanding. The *she* parts were the most hurt by my early history of childhood sexual abuse, and gender-based violence, and conversely, *most* empowered by my healing. EMDR and ego state therapy gave a place and space for all to be freer and freed.

Traditionally, trauma therapies were created to use frameworks that assume binary gender norms and cisnormativity. For trans, nonbinary, and gender expansive individuals, the trauma they have experienced, may be systemic, frequent and based in their identity, not only creating pain and isolation as a child, but also hitting at the core of who they are to this day. This pain may have been so intense, so limiting that for some folx, their true identities may be deeply buried, still to be discovered.

Healing that is imaginative and exploratory, identity-affirming and reparative is essential. This isn't a quick process, and in fact, can take years of undoing the hurt that has happened. ZW put it well in saying, how important it's been "to give myself permission and time to respect and honour wherever I'm at."

I offer this chapter as a roadmap that has the potential to heal and strengthen those of us that exist within the spectrum of gender diversity. A thoughtful and well laid-out plan such as this does not fully exist, certainly not one that reaches into the depths of healing that so many trans, nonbinary and gender diverse folx might need and want. When thought of this way, EMDR, though potentially still helpful, risks, at minimum, falling short and at its worst becoming inaccessible to a client.

AD, as an example noted:

> "If we tried to use [EMDR and ego state therapy] without a 2SLGBTQ-affirming approach, I'm 100 percent certain it would have backfired. Giving Kid [me] creative control over how they looked was foundational for me to understand Kid [me] as a person who is deserving of independence, liberation, autonomy, and emotional safety. If we did parts work without acknowledging my transness and queerness, I likely would have defaulted to seeing my younger self with great discomfort...[and] would feel like I was betraying my adult self's choice to live authentically."

There is a long way to go to make EMDR safe for gender diverse individuals. Having said this, using ego state therapy or other parts work approaches, such as Internal Family Systems (IFS), have enormous potential to support true integration and healing of painful childhood experiences for trans, nonbinary and gender diverse individuals.

As therapists, introducing the exploration of gender identity throughout the trauma healing process, can help build awareness, possibilities and safety. Imagine the difference for those of us who lie outside the gender binary, between being locked inside a painful, critical self, and emerging into a world of true and unapologetic healing. A world where, as described by ZW, we can be "encouraging self love, self acceptance, being authentic..., [and] inclusive" of all of our parts.

Re-visioning inner-child parts using EMDR, in combination with Ego-State Therapy, can be a deeply transformative act—especially for gender diverse, nonbinary, and trans clients whose early experiences were often filtered through experiences of shame, invisibility, and assimilation.

While it might take time for once inhibited and frightened parts to emerge, creating space for the discovery and blossoming of parts who may not yet know how they identify, reminds the client and their parts that they don't need to have it all figured out. "That's ok," ZW reflected. "They can figure that out, [and] decide for themselves, as opposed to being told who and what they are," like so many of us were in the past.

While the past may still echo like "an emotional undercurrent that [ebbs] into all... relationships" (AD), now, there is space where choice, self-compassion, confidence, and control can truly emerge. This is the space where one's true authentic *and* unapologetic self can come out, and where incredible healing becomes possible.

Author's Note

Thanks to the four current clients that agreed to be interviewed for this book chapter. All appear with pseudonym initials to protect their privacy. My deep gratitude to AD, JM, JW and ZW for their genuine interest in supporting this book chapter and willingness to contribute the intensity of their experiences to help us *all* in our growth and learning.

Dana Kamin (they/she) is a Registered Social Worker with more than 20 years experience working with adolescents, youth, adults and families. Kamin works extensively with queer, trans, non-binary and LGBTQ populations, and those with chronic pain, PTSD/C-PTSD, OCD, hoarding and other physical/mental health challenges. Kamin is a queer, adoptive parent within a transracial family, and lives with chronic pain, and both personal and professional insights into trauma recovery. These intersecting identities have made Kamin a passionate advocate for living life with determination, strength and resiliency despite the challenges we've faced in the past.

References

EMDRIA. (June 9, 2022). EMDR Therapy with LGBTQ Populations. https://www.emdria.org/blog/emdr-therapy-with-lgbtq-populations/

Emmerson, G. (2025) What is Ego State Therapy? Ego State Therapy International (ESTI). https://www.egostateinternational.com/ego-state-therapy.php.

Hanville, C. (August 9, 2024). Gender-Affirming EMDR Therapy. https://www.emdria.org/blog/gender-affirming-emdr-therapy/

Hartman, D. & Zimberoff, D. (2003). *Ego states in heart-centered therapies.* Journal of Heart-Centered Therapies, Vol. 6, No. 1, pp. 47-92.

Kadur, J., Lüdemann, J, Andreas, S. (2019). Effects of the therapist's statements on the patient's outcome and the therapeutic alliance: A systematic review. *Clinical Psychology & Psychotherapy, 27*(2): pp. 168–178.

The Trevor Project (Nov 2023). Affirming Actions and Gender Euphoria Among Transgender and Nonbinary Young People. Available: https://www.thetrevorproject.org/research-briefs/affirming-actions-and-gender-euphoria-among-transgender-and-nonbinary-young-people/

Wade, T. C., & Wade, D. K. (2001). Integrative Psychotherapy: Combining Ego-State Therapy, Clinical Hypnosis, and Eye Movement Desensitization and Reprocessing (EMDR) in a Psychosocial Developmental Context. *American Journal of Clinical Hypnosis*, *43*(3–4), 233–245. https://doi.org/10.1080/00029157.2001.10404279

There is Nothing Wrong With Me

Reflections of a Cambodian-American Therapist on the EMDR Experience

Somaly Nou, LCSW

For a long time, I thought there was something wrong with me. Why do I keep engaging in reactive, unhelpful behaviors? The question would often float in my head even though I was familiar with the root cause. For a large period of my early adulthood I was unable to be alone. I would overwork, socialize constantly and use substances to avoid my own anxiety and self-loathing. At the time I was aware of this behavior and could even tell you the underlying reasons for these maladaptive choices but I was unable to stop. These questions of "Why can't I stop? What's wrong with me?" stemmed from a decade of therapy as well as my lifelong fascination with the human condition. Even as a kid I was sensitive to subtleties that other children around me would not notice such as when adults were trying to placate me or when my peers would say one thing but mean another.

I had always been aware of how I was different and how my lived experience had shaped my present psychology but something was missing from my healing. No matter how much self-awareness I possessed, I felt stuck in my actions and triggers. I could not understand why there was a ceiling towards enacting the change I wanted.

In 2020, during the height of the COVID pandemic, there was a rise of Asian Pacific Islander (API) hate crimes. This was another layer to the suffering that so many people were already feeling. I was devastated to see elderly members of my own community being harmed and attacked. At the time, I was a therapist working primarily with Queer and Trans BIPOC people and was offered an opportunity to be trained in EMDR in an all API therapy cohort to help those affected by the violence.

I felt this was a great opportunity to expand my clinical skills and dive into a more holistic approach to healing. Little did I know that the training would not only help me clinically but fundamentally change the way I looked at my own trauma, the relationship I had with my body, how I related to my outer world and my perception of reality.

My first EMDR session was done virtually through the Institute for Creative Mindfulness as part of a practice session to train upcoming API therapists. We were each placed with a practice partner and entered Zoom breakout rooms to begin the sessions. First, my demo partner directed me to my chosen target traumatic memory. This is a memory pertaining to my "negative" core belief of, "There's something wrong with me." For me, this core belief was in relation to my complex post-traumatic stress disorder (CPTSD) from my experience of poverty, migration from Cambodia and punitive parents (as they lived with their own unprocessed trauma of war and genocide). Initially, as the bilateral process began and my eyes began moving to the therapist's fingers, I did not feel much, though the active eye movements kept my attention focused and the therapist would occasionally check in with "what are you noticing?" each minute.

It felt very meta as I noticed my thoughts first coming online. Usually when we have a thought, we actively engage with it. You might develop a feeling from your thoughts or you might continue to a new thought as you manipulate these ideas and beliefs. You might think "I'm a bad person" which causes you to feel guilt, which might then make you think of all the different times and ways you've hurt other people in the past. This is an example of you engaging with your thoughts and repeating the cycle of your continuous mental framework. During this first EMDR session, after some time, this framework became interrupted. It felt like time had slowed down and I was able to witness the way my mind worked without having the immediate opportunity to verbally express myself. This was a change from regular therapy where my mind would lead the conversation.

The pauses in bilateral movements allowed me not to jump to my automatic pattern of intellectualizing. I was forced to stay in the present with what was coming to the surface. Beyond the thoughts came images, uncomfortable sensations and deep buried emotions. This was able to happen because EMDR had interrupted my learned "adaptive" pattern of over-intellectualizing. This allowed the scared, vulnerable parts of myself to come forward. I was finally able to feel the pain and grief but not in a way that felt retraumatizing or *too much*. My brain was engaged with the movement and the therapist's voice and presence and this titrated the experience to an intensity where I could touch and release my trauma.

EMDR was what was needed for my nervous system to feel contained enough to release the traumatic energy and stuck belief of "There's something wrong with me."

After my reprocessing session with my therapist, I remembered feeling like I'd opened a portal in my body that left me exhausted, sad, and scared... also optimistic. I remember ordering Thai food and indulging in the noodles after a long day of learning and lending my nervous system to my therapist. As I ate my *Pad See Ew* I remember wondering how so much had happened with very little verbal processing. How I was able to emote and cry in front of my practice partner, a complete stranger, when at that time I couldn't even cry in front of my close friends or partners? The next day I woke up with a lot of curiosity, awe and also some worry. This all felt so unfamiliar, I was scared as to what I'd discover along the way. Healing often isn't fun, but I trusted in the process and in myself to do EMDR again the following week.

EMDR taught me that for the majority of my life, I had lived outside of my body. Frankly, I was constantly in a functional freeze. "Functional freeze" meant that I was able to move through life and perform my duties but I was not fully present and was often detached yet I appeared "normal." Before I found EMDR my life appeared full and healthy, I had a strong community of friends, a job I loved and was engaging in fun and nourishing activities during my spare time. But underneath, I noticed that I wasn't fully present within the world around me. I could not fully connect to the sensations of my body and when I did go a bit deeper, there was fear, but from what? I did not know at the time and thus, it was more optimal to be in freeze than to engage with the terror within my nervous system.

Of course, this was not sustainable and was the reason I was in a constant cycle of reactive, maladaptive behaviors, because anything else would make me confront my unsettling internal world.

It wasn't until I sat through EMDR that I was able to confront the sensations that were underneath the freeze.

After completing my EMDR training what I found most interesting about the process was the absence of relying solely on the cognitive mind.

In traditional talk therapy, there is an intellectual part of yourself that is in control, the part that rationalizes and deep dives into the context five different ways to try to understand it from multiple perspectives and experiences. On one hand, I appreciate my intellectual self because it creates meaning and develops nuances in situations and relationships in my life. On the other hand, it blocks me from being present with the discomfort and intolerable feelings that are coupled with my experience. Defenses can be so sneaky! Not being in touch with my sensations or emotions hindered my healing capacity.

The thing is, I am often unaware that there's a block. I have been a verbal processor my whole life. I am chatty and social and intrigued by the human condition. In the past I had always thought this was how I moved through and processed the world. But this was a form of masking so that I could feel protected and in control. However, with EMDR there was no longer a lifeline to my masking to save me from what was happening inside my nervous system.

Language can be both powerful and can be a block, especially in the west. Here in the west we prioritize the cognitive mind and what can be expressed through words. There's so much that our bodies want to say and sometimes words can't quite capture it all. English was not my first language. In my native language, Khmer, there are concepts and expressions that do not translate to the

English language, or if they do, they do not capture the full essence or meaning. This can feel both frustrating and interesting when I try to describe to English speakers what I am trying to say.

EMDR was a powerful experience for me because it allowed me to go into my memories at different times, connecting to different developmental stages, including languages. In traditional talk therapy, there might be more time focused on converting my experience or thoughts in Khmer to English so my therapist can understand. But in EMDR, my thoughts can just emerge freely in their original form. This allowed my system to take in these thoughts and have them relayed to my various channels of processing.

This experience took me back to my time in elementary school. I migrated to America from Cambodia at the age of five and was thrown into kindergarten without knowing a word of English. It was a challenging time as I was removed from my family and culture. I remember being a five year old and often being angry because I could not advocate for myself or express my needs through the English language. This resulted in punitive measures from teachers due to misunderstanding. During EMDR, it was liberating to notice my body do what it's meant to do—release and heal—without having to rely on finding the "right" words to make sense of my experience or even my worry that my therapist wouldn't understand. EMDR is a powerful tool in allowing my body to speak and release whatever is stored, often without words but through images, movements, and emoting.

Somaly Nou (she/her), LCSW holds a bachelor's degree in Psychology from the University of Florida and a Master of Social Work from The City University of New York (CUNY) at Hunter College. She owns a small private therapy practice in NYC where she works with LGBTQ+ and BIPOC folks who have experienced cPTSD. Somaly utilizes body based modalities such as Somatic Experiencing and EMDR to help clients go beyond their thoughts to address the root in their nervous system. When she's not working or yapping with her friends about the human condition she enjoys laying in the sun, biking, theater and art, a glass of wine and force cuddling her cat, Moonlight.

An Interview with Sauce and Roshni

Sauce and Roshni

The following interview took place in April 2025.

Roshni: So, I know we're here to talk about your experience with EMDR. And before we get into that, can you tell me a little bit about yourself?

Sauce: Sure. Yes. My friends call me Sauce. I'm 47. I identify as Black, queer, and non-binary. I'm a foster adoptive parent to a really cool eight-year-old. I'm originally from Chicago and I currently live in the Bay Area in Oakland. I work as a therapist in community mental health. I spent a bunch of my time being a social worker before getting my therapy license. I also provide trainings in the community about SOGIE (Sexual Orientation, Gender Identity, and Expression) and I train new foster parents.

Roshni: Awesome. What do you like to do for fun?

Sauce: I like to do a lot of things for fun. I am really into gardening since the pandemic. I am a reality TV junkie. I'm currently watching *90 Day Fiancé*. I love *Survivor*. My newest favorite show is *Traders*, I don't know if you've seen it, but there's multiple versions and it's a murder mystery show. I got really into that. I am obsessed with French bulldogs. I have one who is two and a half. His name is Shortbread. I'm grateful since getting a dog, I spend a lot more time outside. We are at the parks and enjoying the redwoods that are all around the Bay Area. Redwoods are one of my favorite things about the Bay.

What else? I bake. I love playing and learning new board and video games.

I'm also really into watching sports these days. I used to play softball. I don't anymore. I got really into March Madness. I just got season tickets for the Valkyries. I'm really excited about the Bay's new women's NBA team.

Roshni: Awesome. Thank you. Okay, so prior to EMDR, had you participated in mental health services?

Sauce: I did, yes. My mom passed away when I was 20. I was old enough to be considered an adult, but I didn't really feel like an adult emotionally. So, to get support with that I had a handful of different therapists while I was in college and then a few after. When I moved to the Bay when I was 25, I found a therapist within the first week of living here. I just sort of picked someone. Knowing what I know now, I may have picked someone different. It's kind of a long story but at that time I didn't know that my dad's family is Black. I was raised as a white person. My whole family knew that I was Black, but no one ever really talked about it.

I've had the same therapist for almost, I don't know, 20 years now. But if I knew then what I know now, I probably would have picked a Black therapist or a POC therapist. Just because there's so much stuff that has gone into my identity development, which was kind of curbed and shifted at that time. I was maybe 27 when my family told me that I am Black. Even though everybody I knew was telling me I was Black or I had to be something, I had to be Puerto Rican, I had to be Dominican, I had to be something. I could not be White. And I remember arguing with so many people about it. So yes, I did participate in talk therapy and I'm still participating.

Roshni: Awesome. Thank you. And had you heard anything, or did you know anything about EMDR before you got started?

Sauce: I had heard about it through my own training becoming a therapist. I knew it was a modality. It felt new so it wasn't really a topic covered. It wasn't something that I really put much thought into. I think that I kind of knew it had something to do with your eyes following the light back and forth. But other than that, I really didn't understand much about it at all.

Roshni: So, what made you choose EMDR as a modality?

Sauce: There was a lot going on. My therapist was going on maternity leave and I was ending a relationship. I knew I was going to need support and I had gotten a recommendation from a friend who had said it was helpful to them. And so, I was like, well, I might as well try it. I got a referral. I did have to pay out of pocket, but I just was willing to try anything at that time. I just wanted to have support while my therapist was out. And also, not go over the rails with my relationship ending at that time.

Roshni: What did you hope to get from doing EMDR?

Sauce: I really wanted to work on the grief of losing my mom. Like I said, I was 20 when she passed away. The years preceding her death, I was a rotten teenager and kind of angry. Not very nice to her at all. At 30 or so I was watching my friends that I went to high school and college with and their relationship with their parents. I was just so sad that I didn't get to have that adult relationship with her. I didn't get to share with my mom how much I appreciated all the things, right? I think as you get older and you have to pay your own insurance and you have to decide what healthcare option from whatever job you have, like all those things, all those times that I wanted to call my mom I just couldn't. And I think I couldn't get past the feeling of just feeling abandoned that she left me at such a really hard time in my life. I was grumpy about it. You know, I was in my 30s and I just was trying to be in relationships, but I just felt like the patterns kept repeating. I would get close and then I would panic. And, kind of bail, not bail like physically, but like emotionally bail on the people I was trying to be in relationships with.

And so even though I was trained as a therapist, I didn't understand EMDR. I was like, maybe this will help.

Roshni: So, did you get what you were looking for by getting EMDR?

Sauce: I think so. Yeah. The person that I found was a person of color and there was something just warm and friendly about her. She had her private practice out of her home. There was something really warm about that and it was exactly what I needed at the right time.

There was a way that she made me feel seen and heard. I can only relate it to this. I remember when I was thinking about who I needed as a therapist whether I wanted to see a man or a woman. I was like, I want to see a woman because I won't ever have to explain what it's like to have cramps.

There was something about being in front of a person of color, a woman of color that I just didn't have to explain a lot of things. I didn't have to explain how racism is terrible and how homophobia is so real and all those kinds of things.

I don't remember much about the process itself. I remember I was holding buzzers and they would go back and forth. I remember her asking me questions and closing my eyes. The only prompt I remember is because I was playing softball at that time, I kept getting hit by the ball, I'm a pitcher. I just was scared to play anymore because it felt like every time I'd get hit by the ball, it would leave these huge bruises. And I remember her taking that feeling back to me not feeling protected as a young person. I remember her just having me repeat: "I can protect myself. I can keep myself safe." That had a lot of impact and I still use it when I get scared. Sometimes I'm able to remember if I just say that, it moves me from the initial – oh I'm scared -- kind of thing. I think the biggest shift for me was I was able to move from feeling abandoned by my mom to noticing how my mom is around me all the time.

So, I have different things that I associate with her. Every time I see a butterfly, I will say, "Oh, hey, mom." Or anytime I hear something unusual like birds chirping at night. I remember the first time I heard birds chirping at night and I had text this therapist that I was seeing for EMDR and she said, "Yeah, that's your mom." And I'm like, oh, okay, cool, cool, cool.

Anytime I see the type of car that she drove or an Illinois license plate. Anything that reminds me of her. It could be The Olympics, you know. I know she enjoyed the Olympics. We watched them together. Anytime there's a mention of the Olympics, it really is like, oh, she's with me. That's so cool and I really like it. It feels like I have many more guardian angels or there's someone around me protecting me all the time rather than just feeling like, oh, it's another birthday and I'm sad that my mom isn't around to celebrate with me.

I went to EMDR for about six weeks while my therapist was out on maternity leave. And then I went back when she was on maternity leave again. I've been back for a couple of boosters in between like when I was fostering children. I fostered four and adopted one. And any other time where relationships have ended or I'm having a hard time. I remember I had to put one of my dogs down because they were old and weren't doing well. So I went for a booster.

Roshni: Would you recommend EMDR to others? And if so, why?

Sauce: I've recommended EMDR to at least two people that I'm close to. They were going through breakups and needed support. And I was like, hey, this worked for me. I don't know if it'll work for you. This person was influential in my life and I'm forever grateful. So yes, absolutely, I would.

Roshni: What would you want to say now? To pre-EMDR Sauce that you think might be helpful. Were you nervous going in? Do you remember thinking back to that moment? As all this was coming together, do you remember, were you nervous? Did you have any concerns at that time?

Sauce: That's a good question. I was nervous. I think what I would say is that you can trust that people have your best interests. I think what I was worried about then, and I'm even worried about now sometimes; it's like there's some kind of judgment. First, this is my job, I'm a therapist. So, in some way it feels like I'm maybe not well enough to do my job. Or that my story is so out there, and I don't know that there's just going to be some judgment around how far I am getting through my own trauma. Why am I not better at relationships or why can't I seem to get my fiscal story together? You know, things like that. I think I was hesitant of telling another person all the things that you just leave in a dark corner. There's like shame and fear of judgment around it.

So, I would say just get the help that you need because, you'll feel so much better after because I really did. I mean, it was really a push in the right direction for me to participate in EMDR.

Roshni: Do you think any of that was your mom's influence? You know, I want to believe so.

Sauce: I would say as I've gotten older, I'm watching my peers manage aging parents. There's just so much around that. The emotional toll of it, in addition to the career shifts people have had to make during the pandemic. There's a lot going on. And I feel like, I don't know if it was EMDR related, but I do know that there was a shift for me.

Even though I felt abandoned at the time and it's a shitty situation. I wouldn't wish it on anyone, but I think that I'm grateful that my mom's death was kind of a ticket to freedom. I was able to move from the Midwest all the way across the country by myself. It kind of felt like... what I would have described at the time as the American dream. As a young person assigned female at birth, I didn't have anybody pressuring me to get married. I didn't have a lot of the pressure that many of my friends had. I think that's exactly what my mom would have wanted for me, freedom. All the things that she felt burdened by. I don't think that I was a burden to her, but I think working, the bills, caring for her own mother being the oldest child in her sibling group of four. I didn't have any of that. I was an only child and I got to just go. My mom set up a new car as a gift for me for graduating college.

I drove my Chevy Impala across the country and landed here in The Bay. I know she loved water and boats and things. That's just something that I get to see on a regular basis. My office right now is across the street from the Embarcadero. So, I walk out and I see boats every single day.

So, in a lot of ways, yeah. All the things that I do, all of the ways that I've not gotten by or how I've gotten in trouble in my life have been influenced by her. I've been a little bit of a troublemaker since the start. In some ways, good trouble, in some ways, not good trouble.

I do think that she's a big influence in my healing. My career path of helping others too. I think that that's something that my mom would be proud of. I know she is proud of me.

Roshni: Definitely. And it sounds like she's with you all the time, like you said just the boats. That's so beautiful. I love that. There's something very majestic about just being near the water and feeling that energy. Especially when there's so much going on and there's a lot for us to learn from nature about healing. Constantly, yeah.

Sauce: Agreed.

Roshni: What would you want someone to know? If they are going into or even thinking about trying out EMDR? Based on some of the things that you were concerned about and then being on the other side of that and knowing how it's impacted you? Is there anything that you would want someone to know?

Sauce: Yeah, I think the first thing that comes to mind is that healing is a lifelong journey. It's not just, take a class and then you know everything.

Like the way they used to teach cultural competency, right? There's no way we can be competent in any, not even our own cultures. Whatever cultures we identify with, we don't know everything about them. And I think that it feels very similar to me in terms of how EMDR has influenced my outlook, my healing, my own therapy. I remember when my therapist came back, I was like, you have to do this. This is amazing. This was influential in my story. And she went and she got trained.

So, it was something that had an influence on me and influenced others. And I think that's another testament of the experience. Right now, my therapist is on medical leave and you know I'm considering going back. Because I want to... just continue. There's always something.

Parenting is also something that changes and shifts me. Every time my child experiences something, I'm like oh that tap dances on that trauma nerve! Or where the government is and working in community mental health. The fears around funding and your information being out there.

I'm moving in the direction, even though I don't want to call myself an elder in the LGBTQ+ community. There's a way that I must do the process of healing. I think my message is whatever you want to get out of it right now may be totally different than what you need to get out of it in five years or 10 years.

I'm hoping that that would reduce the pressure of feeling like I must be better. I must feel better. I must get this done. Sometimes it's just the seed that gets planted, and you have to wait for the tree to grow.

Roshni: It's beautiful. Thank you. Let's see. I had another one. Is there anything else you'd like to share about your experience?

Sauce: I would just say that I went in to really get a handle on my grief and loss. And grief and loss are something that keeps happening right? So, as I said before, I fostered four babies. Three of those babies I had to care for pour my heart and soul and energy and every ounce of sleep that I didn't get into. And then I had to hand them to complete strangers.

People ask all the time, "how did you do that?" Or would say I could never do that! I know it's not for the faint of heart. It's absolutely changed my worldview. My child is my world. She's made me a better person. And I think that because I had a foundation from EMDR about grief and loss these babies are around. They're all around me. I have a plant in my yard that represents each of them so they literally are around me, all the time.

I think similarly about relationships that have come and gone. You know, some people are still around, some people are not still around.

But I think that, as I'm aging I'm watching as my friends lose their parents. And I just feel like the experience of just getting a handle on what it is to grieve and how to process it is so important. This country is just not good at grief. We just have a weird way of saying goodbye. And I don't think a lot of time has been spent really building up that muscle of what it's like to lose folks that are really important to us. We are encouraged just to kind of move on. You get encouraged to just get up and get back out there. You'll be okay kind of stuff. And it's like, no, I need to figure out what's happening for me. I really need to slow down and just sit in it.

So, I think... That is one thing.

And I think EMDR pushed me into that journey. Maybe that was my mom too. I never really wanted to birth a child but I always imagined that I would just take care of a child who needed me. And I didn't quite have a full picture of that of how that would look. As I got older and people were taking care of their nephews and people were doing that. I landed in social work. I was working with kids in child welfare. It seemed like that was the place to go, but I don't know that I would have been able to do it. I'm hesitant to say as well as I did if I didn't have the experience of EMDR. I would say at least for grief and loss, I'm sure that EMDR is beneficial for other things. I'm in a similar place now like back when I started, I haven't spent a ton of energy thinking about EMDR or learning more about it or how it works or any of that. I just sort of trusted the process, trusted that the therapist that I went to was going to hold me and care for me in that way.

And... yeah so, I hope to go back to be on this lifelong healing journey.

Roshni: Thank you. A couple more questions. What is the thing that surprised you most about EMDR? If anything.

Sauce: Hmm. I think what surprised me the most was that I sort of imagined it as just like watching lights go back and forth. I didn't know anything about the buzzers. After the buzzer story I kind of went on field trips with my therapist. She's like, we're going to go around the block and you're going to use EMDR anytime you're moving your body, if you're walking, if you're riding a bike, whatever, it's doing the same thing. I didn't really know that it could be applied outside of a traditional in-office therapy session. And I don't even know if that's like a widely recognized way of doing things necessarily, but it really worked for me. I needed that.

I needed to be able to know that if I'm feeling rattled in some kind of way, I can take a walk and I can repeat the things that were sort of brought to my attention at that time. I feel protected. I am safe. I can do this. I am loved. All those kinds of messages. I can walk around the block and I'm not saying them the whole time, but it just feels like being able to move my body, being able to apply the concept outside of the therapy room was really important to me.

Roshni: And yes, that is a widely accepted thing so bilateral stimulation or sometimes it's called bilateral dual attention stimulus.

Sauce: Awesome.

Roshni: It is very natural to what our brain does and what our body does a lot. So, it's really just activating one side of the brain and then the other and we're doing it all the time, walking, running, swimming, even singing causes a natural bilateral rhythm in your brain. So that one always blows me away. I think one of the really amazing things about EMDR is that it's ancient Indigenous medicine, right? This is drumming. This is dancing. This is how people have healed for centuries. So being able to harness that and utilize it to be able to assist people in their healing process is really cool. I think that that is not stressed enough, the Indigenous roots of it.

And I think it's really important that we do that. I understand why Francine Shapiro may not have done that in the 80s or 90s because she possibly wouldn't have been taken that seriously, especially as a woman in psychology. I know the mindfulness element and some of the roots of this was not acknowledged and still is not acknowledged by many, unfortunately. It's important that we highlight that this is what our brain does to heal. It knows how to do it. And that's the thing about EMDR,when we learn it, it's a big thing to learn because you're going there with someone with their trauma, and so I was nervous learning it. Everyone I teach is nervous about going in and providing this for their client. They want to be the best therapist and not trigger people. And I always remind them, this is what our body already knows, so, it's very hard to mess up once we understand the mechanism of how to provide it, yeah.

And one more question I had. Let's see if I can remember it.

Maybe it was more of a statement, but just having known you through graduate school and you came in very much having the experience on the ground, working with foster care, working with young people with the system. I've always seen you as somebody who's really grounded and on the ground doing the work, you are very much in it, doing it, having the ethics necessary, being able to show up. And you've got to push the line to get something done and take care of a young person. You've always just been that really stand-up amazing person and I think that if I can say this, I don't know if you identify with this word with the word or the concept of angels but it sounds to me like you have a lot of angels surrounding you, especially your mom. I see you as that angel for so many people. You've really been there to help folks in their hardest times and I know just being your friend and knowing what great hugs you give that your heart is all in this. It is very much an honor to know you and I'm so glad that you got the healing support you needed. I hope that continues in whatever way you're needing it.

So, thank you, Sauce. Thanks for being you.

Sauce: Awesome. Big hugs. Thank you.

Roshni: Yeah, right back at you.

Sauce: Thank you, I appreciate it. You never know what you're going to need, on a Friday when the world's falling apart. It's complicated. And I still appreciate it. I will take that with me for the next as many days as I need it. I will just be like Roshni said.

Roshni: Sometimes we forget we are the angels showing up.

Sauce: Awesome. Thank you. I so appreciate it.

Roshni: Yeah, I'm glad you're doing this project. It's giving us an excuse to reconnect. It's been really nice.

Sauce: I would like to dedicate my healing journey first to my mom and now to my daughter. Thank you both for encouraging me to be the best person I could ever be. Although you have never met, may your experience of me bring you two together some day. Thank you, mom, for being all around me in your life and now your death. Alearia, never forget I will always love you and I will forever be with you. Just look for me, I will be around.

A. Saucier (Sauce) (they/them) is a Black, Non-Binary, Queer radical resource parent and therapist, residing in the Bay Area. They have been in the field of Social Work/Behavioral Health for over 25 years, and have served in many capacities - consultant, moderator, speaker, and trainer - in a variety of settings and on topics they are directly engaged with and deeply committed to. Over the years, Sauce has provided services at a handful of community based organizations, presently holding a position within Alameda County Behavioral Health Care Services, where they also serve as the co-chair for the ACBH PRIDE Committee. Sauce also serves as an Alameda County Resource Parent Trainer/Professional Expert with Chabot Community College.

Too Many Pathways, Not Enough Light To Grow

Mishma Kumar-Jonson, AMHSW

In something like our ancestors we grew,
all bent limbs and
far too much backbone to show up straight in this world,
far too many –
neural pathways to walk - typically - I would not indulge in being an encyclopedia but when he says
“There was no such thing as a queer or non-binary, ADHD or autism back in the day,”
I paint him the Sistine chapel, but not the ceiling,
no,
I paint the dictionary definition of joy back then
on his back for four years painting the sky,
tell me,
who else
if not, a hyper fixated guy could hold up their arm and paint the gods with such precision,
that is still
the best option of getting out of small talk I have *ever* been given.

I hum him 16 BC monks, chanting and kneeing for hours
beads of stim rolling down their arms,
walking around their quiet towers,
eating the same meals daily
sticking to their robes and routines tighter than the chokehold of their brotherhood. Tell me
if that sounds typical-y straight to you.

I take him to grandma’s house, where there was always a vice grip of a squeeze to put you back in your body

where her time was intricate geometry patterns being knitted into sleeves where rocking was the essential component of any after evening meal. Where every utensil had a place,
and every place had a bag of memories
to be sorted
but kept in eye view just in case
we have all been duped by object permanence.
-
We ride the train together,
watching as grandpa keeps time down to the minute
knowing every component of every train,
every tick and every name of every engine,
building his own mind through the tunnels and the gates of the models in his basement, his workshop of tinkering
on that one thing he can't get his mind not thinking.
-
You see,
we have always existed,
we have always been here.
It's just taken us a while to recognise that the definitions weren't exactly clear I could ask you to take a moment to put down the apathy, the sneer But the inertia of double empathy is pretty loud and pretty clear, But either way,
and because you might not see it,
and just as an FYI,
I thought you should know,
that a whole lot of us have in fact always been neuroqueer.

Mish Kumar-Johnson (they/them), a plural system that is non-binary, queer, disabled, neurodivergent and a social worker of colour on land that always was and always will be Aboriginal Land, is an EMDR consultant and Practitioner. Mish is the Chair of The Iceberg Foundation and principal practitioner at Niram EMDR where they bring an anti-oppressive and anti-colonial lens to their practice with the LGBTIQAP+ and Neurodivergent communities across so called Australia.

Acknowledgments

First and foremost I want to thank Jamie Marich for making this project possible and for all of your hard work! Jamie, you have always believed in me and encouraged me and you went with me on this ride when I had this Queer idea, thank you! Love you, my friend.

I cannot express the depth of my gratitude for each of the authors, artists and poets who have gone on this journey of Queering EMDR. Each of you have made this project possible by bearing your soul here in these pages. Thank you for Queering the crap outta stuff with me! So much love and respect to you all!

To my family, thank you for all of your support and love! My dearest Angel Mother, all that I am and all that I will be is because you believed in me and you worked hard to learn how to love me the way I needed, thank you. Saajan, thank you for being you, your deep compassion and sweet heart fills up my bucket so I can move that line forward. Lots of love, dearies!

Stephen Dansiger, you have been my Pardner through a lot but you are family now and I don't know where I would be without you guiding me, Thank you for EMDRing me, Stevie D!

Finally, I wish to thank the folks who worked tirelessly behind the scenes to bring this project to life. First, our brilliant cover artist, Irene Rodriguez, who worked with feedback from all of our contributors to create vibrant visual imagery for our book. To graphic designer Chris Berge, who patiently worked with our edits and production requests. And to the Institute for Creative Mindfulness/Creative Mindfulness Media home office team for taking care of the necessary business that is required to bring a book's vision to fruition: Garrett LaValley (web and marketing design), Alicia Hann (contributor relations and business), Katie Dougherty Zuercher (general assistance and text formatting), and Jasmine Shafley (social media and marketing).

Advocacy Resources

Abbey of the Arts: www.abbeyofthearts.com

Advocates For Trans Equality: https://transequality.org/

American Civil Liberties Union: https://www.aclu.org/

Believe Out Loud: https://www.believeoutloud.com/

Christian Closet: 100% Virtual LGBTQ Mental and Spiritual Health Services: www.thechristiancloset.com

Church Clarity: Database of Verified LGBTQ-Affirming Churches:

www.churchclarity.org

Eastern PA Trans Equity Project: https://www.patransequity.org/

Gay Lesbian Alliance Against Defamation: https://glaad.org/

GLAAD Transgender Resources: https://glaad.org/transgender/resources/

Genderbread Person: https://www.brainbowfire.com/blogandvideos/maries-genderbread-person

Human Rights Campaign: https://www.hrc.org/

IMAAN: The UK's Leading LGBTQ Muslim Charity: https://imaanlondon.wordpress.com

Intersex Definitions- interarACT: Advocates for Intersex Youth: https://interactadvocates.org/intersex-definitions/

It's Pronounced Metrosexual: https://www.itspronouncedmetrosexual.com/

Kaleidoscope Youth Center (Ohio): https://www.kycohio.org/

Keshet: For LGBTQ Equality in Jewish Life: www.keshetonline.org

Light After Loss (For Survivors of Suicide) LGBT+ Affirming: https://lightafterlossstark.org

National Association of Lesbian, Gay, Bisexual, Transgender Addiction Professionals and Their Allies: https://nalgap.org/

National Black Trans Advocacy Coalition: https://blacktrans.org/

Pennsylvania Youth Congress: https://payouthcongress.org/

Progressive Christianity: https://progressivechristianity.org

Q Christian Fellowship: https://www.qchristian.org/

Reclamation Collective: www.reclamationcollective.com

Southern Poverty Law Center: https://www.splcenter.org/

Supporting Trans and Gender Expansive Children: https://www.hrc.org/resources/supporting-trans-non-binary-gender-expansive-children

The Trevor Project: https://www.thetrevorproject.org/

Trans Lifeline Glossary of Terms and Definition : https://translifeline.org/resource_category/glossary/ -- donation site

Trans Lifeline Resource Library: https://translifeline.org/resources

Trans Women of Color Collective: https://twocc.org/

The Williams Institute: https://williamsinstitute.law.ucla.edu/

World Professional Association for Transgender Health: https://wpath.org/

You Might Be Intersex If: https://www.brainbowfire.com/blogandvideos/you-might-be-intersex-if

1946 [Documentary]: www.1946themovie.com

988 Suicide & Crisis Lifeline: www.988lifeline.org

Canadian Resources

Action Canada for Sexual Health and Rights: https://www.actioncanadashr.org/ (Gender Galaxy Available Here)

Egale Canada: https://egale.ca/

It Gets Better Canada - supporting LGBTQ+ youth across Canada: https://itgetsbettercanada.org/

Rainbow Health Ontario: https://www.rainbowhealthontario.ca:

Trans Health Knowledge base: https://www.rainbowhealthontario.ca/lgbt2sq-health/trans-health-knowledge-base/

Resource Library: https://www.rainbowhealthontario.ca/lgbt2sq-health/resource-library/

Transcare BC: https://www.transcarebc.ca/

International Resources

ILGA World - the International Lesbian, Gay, Bisexual, Trans and Intersex Association: https://ilga.org/

It Gets Better Global Project - supporting LGBTQ+ youth globally through storytelling and other life-affirming support: https://itgetsbetter.org/global/

Interviews

Pastor Mark Sandlin, "Clobbering 'Biblical' Gay Bashing" (June 2016): bit.ly/462SWZa

Jamie Interviews Pastor Mark Sandlin (June, 2021): bit.ly/46jqBOb

Jenn Kennedy

Rev. Karla Fleshman

Jamie Marich

horizon greene

Dr. Lanza

Cash Waller

Lisa Hayes

Steven Halady

Sauce

Carmine Abigail

Mariena Joy

Dana Kamin

Tawanna Woolfolk

Danielle Godfrey

Roshni Chabra

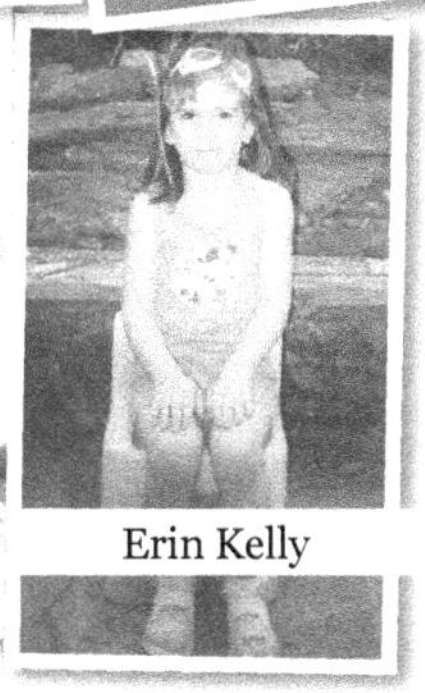
Erin Kelly

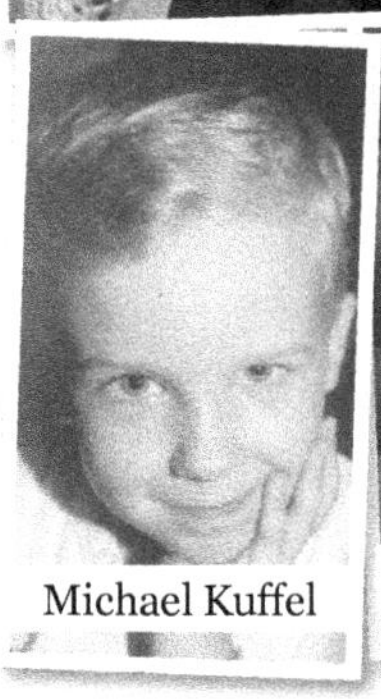
Michael Kuffel

Sam Bergstein

Queerbook

Index

A

B

C

D

F

G

J

K

L

M

N

O

P

Q

R

U

V

W

Y

www.ingramcontent.com/pod-product-compliance
Ingram Content Group UK Ltd.
Pitfield, Milton Keynes, MK11 3LW, UK
UKHW020202290926
15471UKWH00005B/1014

9 798218 660758